WHATEVER
BECAME
OF . . . ?

WHATEVER BECAME OF...?

by
RICHARD LAMPARSKI

Introduction by
CLEVELAND AMORY

CROWN PUBLISHERS, INC., NEW YORK

Acknowledgments

The author would like to express thanks to the following people who helped in the preparation of this book: Eric Benson, William K. Everson, Bob B. Frederick, Robert Ginsberg, Peter Hanson, Don Koll, Dick Lynch, Alfred Monaco, John Robbins, Romano Tozzi, and John Virzi.

The photographs contained in this book are from the author's own collection, were kindly supplied by the personalities themselves, and are part of the collections of: Peter Hanson, John Robbins, John Virzi, and Francis Young.

This book of nostalgia is dedicated to the best remembered and most greatly missed lady in my life, my maternal grandmother: Ellen Downey, 1867–1945.

CONTENTS

In Alphabetical Order

INTRODUCTION

by Cleveland Amory

The word "celebrity" is far older than we are inclined to think it is. Once upon a time, it is true, a person might have been said to *have* "celebrity," or fame, but it would have been as meaningless to say "a celebrity" as it would, nowadays, to say "a fame."

But that was a very long time ago—in fact, America's first generally recognized celebrity was John Jacob Astor I. Indeed, as far back as 1836, the *American Quarterly Review,* speaking of Mr. Astor, said, "From an obscure stranger he has made himself one of the 'celebrities' of the country."

In those days, however, the word was still used with quotation marks. But, as far back as mid-century, in 1856, we find no less "a celebrity" than Emerson himself using the word, and without quotation marks, in *English Traits.*

One thing is certain. Although fame itself was once defined by Nicolas Chamfort, the great French wit, as "the advantage of being known to those who do not know us," the fact is that some celebrities at least—as this book amply demonstrates —are remarkably enduring, if not always endearing, people.

In this book, for example, you will find the answers to dozens of your questions about "whatever happened to"—and, more often than not, you will be amazed to find that even if the celebrity no longer has M. Chamfort's "advantage," he or she has substituted for this advantage something that, for them, may well be, in the long run, far more advantageous.

There are, of course, all kinds of celebrities. The star of a TV series this year may well be, in another year, a "has-been," two years from now a "was," and three years from now not known at all. "The world," the English critic John Collins said, "like an accomplished hostess, pays most attention to those whom it will soon forget."

Mr. Collins' words, translated to modern show business terms, become the textbook story:

(1) Who is Hugh O'Brian?
(2) Get me Hugh O'Brian.
(3) Get me a Hugh O'Brian type.
(4) Get me a young Hugh O'Brian.
(5) Who is Hugh O'Brian?

Just how ridiculous the whole question of fame can be was illustrated when a columnist in World War II took a poll to find the "world's favorite personality."

8

The Pope (Pius XII) finished behind Bing Crosby and Frank Sinatra. Others, in order, were Eisenhower, Father Flanagan, MacArthur, Walter Winchell, Sister Kenny, and Bob Hope. Joseph Stalin finished fifteenth.

Once more, translated to modern show business terms, the story becomes that of Kim Novak arriving in Paris and being driven by a chauffeur who proudly informed her that he'd had many other celebrities in his cab. "I have driven Gloria Swanson," said he, "and Cary Grant and President Coty. I have even driven *your President.*"

"What!" exclaimed Miss Novak delightedly. "Harry Cohn!"

But this is one type of celebrity only. There is a second type—as again this book so amply proves—whose names will ring a bell as long as they live, even if we don't know what they are now doing, or even where they are.

And then, too, there is a third and final kind of celebrity—the celebrity who, literally, never dies.

In this book you will find all three kinds. And, among these three kinds, the author had a wide field to choose from. He has chosen not only wisely but interestingly—and perhaps most important of all—entertainingly.

December 27, 1926, his heavy-weight crown only three months old, taken from Dempsey.

GENE TUNNEY

The retelling of World Heavyweight Champ Gene Tunney's story reads like pulp fiction from pre-World War I. He is a Horatio Alger character, a Rover Boy, and Jack Armstrong, all rolled into one. His real name is James Joseph Tunney.

Born in 1897 in Lower Manhattan of Irish-Catholic parents, Gene learned to fight just to exist in his neighborhood. His remarkable good looks made it necessary to fight a little better and far more often than most of the kids. Gene worked for a steamship company for a while before entering the United States Marine Corps during World War I, and in 1919 he won the Light-Heavyweight Championship of the A.E.F. in Paris. Upon his discharge he continued boxing.

After ending Georges Carpentier's career by knocking him out in 1924 he became a leading contender for Jack Dempsey's crown.

As much as the press and public disliked Dempsey, Tunney made him liked by comparison. Dempsey had been called a draft-dodger and a shirker. Tunney, because of his refusal to allow the newspapers to exploit his personal life and by admitting that he read poetry and Shakespeare, was the press's whipping boy. Veteran sports writers such as Westbrook Pegler and Paul Gallico now admit that they sat up nights thinking of angles for articles on the contender to humiliate and infuriate him. He didn't sound or act like any boxer they had known, and they disliked him for it. Years later Gallico said of him, "Tunney was never a natural fighter, born to the sport. On the contrary, he was synthetic, and he acquired the mechanics of his trade through long, bitter hours of practice, trial and error. Pegler and myself took an almost perverse joy in hounding this character. When we should have been cheering him to the echo for the perfection of his profession, we

10

hated him instead for working his deceitful arts upon that hero image of ourselves, caveman Dempsey."

The first encounter between Tunney and Dempsey took place on September 23, 1926, at the Sesquicentennial Stadium in Philadelphia. The odds were 4 to 1 on the Champion. Over 120,000 fans paid $1,895,733 to see an upset, after 10 rounds.

Their second meeting still holds the record for the largest gate in the history of boxing—$2,658,600. It was held in Soldiers Field, Chicago, one year and four days after the first match. Tunney was ahead on points until the seventh round. Then all at once Dempsey let loose and Gene was down for the first time in his life. The challenger failed to go to a neutral corner giving Tunney those vital extra seconds to recover, to get back on his feet after the famous "long count." After ten rounds Tunney remained World's Heavyweight Champion.

The next year Tunney fought Tom Heeney, and after winning by a TKO retired from the ring undefeated.

On October 3, 1928, he married Mary Josephine Lauder, a millionaire's daughter he had fallen in love with and vowed to win. They are the parents of three boys and a girl. In 1964 their oldest boy, John, was elected to the House of Representatives from the State of California.

During World War II Gene served as Director of Athletics and Physical Fitness for the United States Navy. He is the author of two books: *A Man Must Fight* (1932) and *Arms for the Living* (1941).

Gene Tunney made several million dollars in the ring, and after he quit he put it to work for him. He is a director of such companies as the Schick Safety Razor Company, Independent Bank of Commerce, Quaker City Life Insurance, Technicolor, and Eversharp, Inc., as well as others. Gene commutes to his New York office from his Stamford, Connecticut, home daily.

Seen recently enjoying a joke with his old friend, Jack Dempsey. *Paul Cordes—Gallery of Modern Art*

During a 1931 broadcast.

FATHER CHARLES E. COUGHLIN

Father Coughlin made his first radio broadcast in 1926. He confined himself to remarks on morality and Christian virtue. By the early thirties he had become a listening habit to over 30,000,000 Americans on Sunday afternoons, and had turned with passion and eloquence to politics at a time when this country was in the midst of its worst depression.

In 1931, the Columbia Broadcasting System attempted to censor an attack by Coughlin on the Versailles Treaty. Immediately following, the network received 1,250,000 letters of protest against its interference.

At the time of the London Conference on economics in 1933, 85 members of congress petitioned F.D.R. to send the Catholic priest as an official advisor.

In 1934, according to a national poll, Charles E. Coughlin was the second most powerful and popular man in the United States. He was topped only by the President, Coughlin's archfoe, Franklin D. Roosevelt.

In 1935, 20,000 Coughlinites packed Madison Square Garden in New York to hear the priest deliver one of his bitterest attacks on the New Deal. In one of his speeches he referred to President Roosevelt as "the great liar and betrayer." His Bishop, who had up until that time backed him fully, made him apologize to the chief executive. The same year Coughlin referred to Roosevelt as the "Scab President."

In the 1936 elections Coughlin joined forces with Gerald L. K. Smith, and the late Dr. Francis Townsend (father of the Townsend Plan) to form the Union Party. Their candidate, the late Congressman William Lempke, received 900,000 votes. It was during this campaign that Coughlin began to couple his denunciations of President Roosevelt with attacks upon Jewish "bankers." As a result, the Catholic Laymen's League condemned him for "cowardly Jew-baiting and shameless use of the cloth to insult the President."

The National Union for Social Justice with its 8,500,000 members and the *Social Justice* magazine, both under Coughlin's control, continued right up until Pearl Harbor, when the publication was banned by the federal government, and the organization dissolved.

Social Justice was banned from the mails as a result of charges by the Attorney General in April, 1942, as "a systematic and unscrupulous attack upon the war effort." Coughlin condemned the Government's action as the work of "the Jews, Communists and New Dealers."

At the peak of his popularity Father Coughlin's broadcasts, which were heard at 4:00 P.M. E.S.T., were carried over 47 radio stations. Although he was refused a renewal of contract with CBS, independent stations throughout the country formed another network of sorts, and his weekly addresses to the nation continued as usual. His mail reached as high as 1,000,000 letters and cards a week and he retained 4 secretaries and 106 clerks.

Father Coughlin's voice was silenced on the air by his Ecclesiastical superiors in 1940. He continued, however, to speak out on political issues from the pulpit of the Shrine of the Little Flower in Royal Oak, Michigan.

In 1965 parishioners had complained to the Detroit Chancellory office that the Royal Oak pastor had been indoctrinating their children over the public-address system in the parish school. He retired in June of 1966 at the time of his fiftieth anniversary as a priest.

In one of the few interviews the "Radio Priest," as he was called in his heyday, has granted since 1940 he conceded that the transition from a world figure to that of a parish priest had been "a trying one." He allowed that he was for Senator Goldwater in the '64 elections. He had recently been paid a visit from the wife of his old friend, Joseph P. Kennedy.

Father Coughlin lives a short distance from his million-dollar church built by contributions during his days on radio.

In retirement. *Detroit News*

As far back as 1924, Sally was shedding her clothes in *The Dressmaker from Paris.*

SALLY RAND

While still a teenager in the early twenties Sally Rand, who became one of America's most famous strippers, was doing acrobatic dancing at carnivals around the country. She even spent one full season with the Ringling Brothers Circus. It was her agility that got her into pictures playing rough-and-tumble scenes. Throughout the silent era she appeared in many films, the most important of which was the C. B. de Mille classic of 1927 in which she played the handmaiden to the star, Jacqueline Logan, who portrayed Mary Magdalene. The picture was *King of Kings.* Some of Sally's other efforts were *The Dressmaker From Paris* (1924) with Leatrice Joy, *Manbait* (1926) which starred Marie Prevost, *Getting Gertie's Garter (*1927) with Franklin Pangborn in the cast, and *The Fighting Eagle* (1928) with Rod La Rocque.

The girl from Hickory County, Missouri, never achieved stardom in Hollywood. By the time the Depression hit she was stranded in Chicago after a play she was in folded. She took a job dancing in a speakeasy. Trying to save money on costumes she got the idea of using fans. A year later she was doing the same dance in the same club at the same salary—$75.00 a week. When the Chicago World's Fair of 1932–33 was announced Sally tried to land a job at the "Streets of Paris" concession but with no luck.

On the eve of the opening of the Fair, there was a preview for the press and aristocracy of Chicago. Sally invested a week's salary in a white horse and a trailer to transport her to the fairgrounds where, to the amazement of everyone, she did a Lady Godiva act. The next day she was on every front page of every paper in the city. The "Streets of Paris" took her on and the customers poured through the gates to see her, to such an extent that many credit Sally and her fans for the success of the Century of Progress (as the Fair was called) at a time when money was very tight.

After Chicago, Sally toured the United States until 1936, stopping only long enough to appear with George Raft in the 1934 film *Bolero*. Her appearance at the San Diego World's Fair of 1936 set gate records, and in 1939 she repeated the feat at the San Francisco Exposition.

Over the next twenty years she has continued to be a major attraction in burlesque and nightclubs, and still works steadily. When Lyndon Johnson was nominated for the Presidency in 1964 in Atlantic City, Sally Rand was playing the famous Boardwalk. Her act is exactly the same. She still uses Debussy's "Clair de Lune," a Chopin waltz, Ravel, and Brahms for her music. The costume has also remained unchanged—ostrich plumes and not a stitch of clothing. In 1965 when Ann Corio became ill, Sally replaced her as emcee for the successful Broadway revue *This Was Burlesque*.

Not long ago, Sally made a minor stir in Chicago. She was on a television panel program with the columnist Irv Kupicent, and the book *Harlow* was being discussed. Someone mentioned that in the book, which Sally had not yet read, it was stated that Jean Harlow's husband, Paul Bern, had been impotent and that that was probably the reason he had committed suicide. To a rather startled panel and public Miss Rand announced that the author should have checked his facts as they were completely inaccurate. Bern, Sally said, was one of the finest men she had ever known and he was a superb lover as well. No one was more surprised than the author, Irving Shulman, who was a member of the panel that day.

Sally, who admits to being born in 1904, has no intention of putting away her fans. Although her act has grossed several million dollars since she broke out of the South Side Chicago speakeasy and therefore doesn't need the money, she looks forward to her work, the traveling, and to meeting people. In Glendora, California, where she lives with her mother and teenage son, Sally owns a number of pieces of real estate, is a rancher, cultivates citrus orchards, raises chickens, rabbits, and ponies. She has been married several times but is now single. "I lost my last husband," she says jokingly, "lost him to a young girl"—Sally's measurements are 36-24-37.

Still fluttering her fans today.

ALGER HISS

In August of 1948 Whittaker Chambers, a writer and editor and former member of the United States Communist party, told the House Un-American Activities Committee that Alger Hiss had committed treason against the United States of America. Thus began one of the most puzzling and complicated cases in this country's history.

Although Hiss had not been well known to the general public before his name began appearing in the headlines in 1948, he was a prominent figure in and around the federal government, and had been, since he was made law clerk to Justice Oliver Wendell Holmes in 1929 at the suggestion of Felix Frankfurter. He had been also one of the "bright young men" around F.D.R., and was present at the Dumbarton Oaks talks and at Roosevelt's meeting with Churchill and Stalin at Yalta.

Hiss was born in Baltimore in 1904 and attended Harvard Law School. He had acted as counsel to the Nye Committee during its investigations of the munitions industry in 1934 and 1935. In 1936 he was made an assistant to Francis B. Sayre, Assistant Secretary of State. He specialized in Far Eastern Affairs, and eventually became Director of that office in the State Department. At the first meeting of the United Nations in San Francisco he was named as temporary Secretary General.

There were accusations, denials, counteraccusations, and endless hearings. Chambers and Hiss stood face to face, and repeated what is undoubtedly the most conflicting testimony any congressional committee, and perhaps any court, has ever heard. Chambers said that Hiss had been his closest friend while they were Communists. Hiss said that he was not and never had been a Communist and that he did not know Whittaker Chambers. The only thing that was certain was that one of them was the coolest, most calculating liar on record. Further to confuse the press and public, both men seemed on the surface and by their records to be quite well balanced and intelligent, and during their testimony appeared straightforward and sincere.

It was high drama but no play or movie ever had such a bizarre plot. A few of the props which were to become world famous were the Woodstock typewriter #230,099, a 1929 Ford which Hiss thrice denied owning, and the most incredible of all—the "pumpkin papers," State Department documents on microfilm that Chambers turned up on his farm hidden in a hollowed-out pumpkin. Among the cast of characters was a young California Congressman full of questions for the witnesses and statements for the press, Richard M. Nixon.

Hiss was indicted on a count of perjury. His first trial in June, 1949, ended in a hung jury. A second jury convicted him in November, 1949, and he served 44 months at the federal prison in Lewisburg, Pennsylvania.

While in prison, in 1952, Hiss was denied a motion for a new trial. After his release, August 25, 1954, he worked as office manager for a small New York firm. He and his wife separated, and are still living apart. His son Tony attended Harvard on a scholarship and is now on the staff of a top national magazine.

In May, 1957, Hiss's book *In the Court of Public Opinion* was published, one of the most eagerly awaited books in years. It was disappointing in every way, including sales, being little more than a legal brief of the trials. Even his strongest supporters had to admit that it offered no new evidence. Hiss's answer to the criticism was that it was not written for money.

The entire affair has been compared with the Dreyfus case in France, but Hiss has refused to be treated as a *cause célèbre*. One writer referred to him as: "rather than a martyr—the man is the non-hero of his own case."

When Hiss discusses the case it is with a peculiar detachment. He has stated that since he knows he is innocent of the charges he is convinced that he will eventually be cleared. When asked about the evidence presented by the prosecution he refers you to his book. When queried about new evidence of his innocence he says it must wait to be presented at the new trial his lawyers still hope to get. (Chambers died several years ago.)

He stopped granting interviews after his book came out and explains in a gentlemanly fashion that he is now a private citizen and as such will not permit his privacy to be invaded. The last time he appeared on radio or television was shortly after Richard Nixon was defeated in his race for the California governorship in 1962. His comments on the former Vice-President's career and character, solicited by a newsman, drew objections from many groups and individuals including Dwight D. Eisenhower.

Alger Hiss since 1960 has been an office supply salesman for a stationery company in New York City. He looks very much like the same tall gaunt figure that dominated the news so much in the late forties. There is no trace of bitterness, and the slightly arrogant manner he displayed on the witness stand is gone. He is, in fact, charming and unusually polite.

In 1948, at the time Whittaker Chambers made his accusations, Hiss was serving as President of the Carnegie Endowment for International Peace. *Culver Pictures*

A theatre and symphony patron (*right*), frequently recognized. *UPI*

Probably the most popular man in pre-Hitler Germany, World Heavyweight Champion, 1930. *Ring Magazine*

MAX SCHMELING

The only German to become the World's Heavyweight Champion was born in Brandenburg in 1905. He began boxing in 1924 and developed a reputation for having a deadly punch and an amazing ability to withstand punishment. Before coming to America in 1928, he was also known for two disqualifications for fouling, a lost decision to Jack Taylor, and losing to the Englishman Gypsy Daniels.

The first thing sportswriters noticed about Max was his facial resemblance to Jack Dempsey, but they soon discovered that he had more than looks to qualify him for main events. In 1929 he KO'd Joe Monte in the eighth round and flattened Johnny Risko, something even Gene Tunney was unable to do, although he beat Risko.

When Tunney retired in 1928 the title was up for grabs, and there were few around of championship stock. One was Spaniard Paulino Uzcudun until Schmeling beat him, thereby becoming one of the top contenders. He was sidetracked for the time being, however, when England's Heavyweight Champion Phil Scott got first crack at leading contender, Jack Sharkey, in 1930. (Although Sharkey won the match he made a poor showing).

When Sharkey and Schmeling finally entered the ring on July 12, 1930, in New York City the odds were on the German. The winner of the match was to receive the title that had gone begging since Tunney had called it quits. The gate was $749,935, a hefty gross even in good times, and this was one of the worst years of the Depression. For the first three rounds Sharkey was ahead on points, although Max was aggressive and obviously in good form. Then in the fourth round Sharkey let go with a wild wandering punch that landed on Schmeling's stomach and sent him to the canvas. Though probably unintentional, the blow was a foul one, and by virtue of its illegality Max Schmeling was crowned the new Champion.

After a visit home to Germany—where Adolf Hitler cited him as a perfect example of the Aryan superman—Max was matched in July, 1931, against Young Stribling in Cleveland, who lasted until the middle of the 15th round when the fight was stopped by the referee and declared a victory for Schmeling on a TKO. Most of the experts had picked the challenger.

In June, 1932, a startled crowd in New York City heard Jack Sharkey proclaimed the new Champion after 15 rounds, during which, according to just about everyone's scorecard, Max had outpointed him. It was a bitterly disputed decision and a sour chapter in the annals of boxing.

In September, 1932, Schmeling knocked out former Middleweight Champion Mickey Walker. In June the following year Max Baer did as much for Schmeling by stopping him in the tenth round.

When Schmeling met Joe Louis in June, 1936, the press referred to Max as "the condemned man." So heavy were the odds on the young Negro that it cut the gate a quarter of a million dollars below expectations. Some 42,000 spectators sat dumbfounded as the German KO'd the Brown Bomber in one of the sport's biggest upsets. Contrary to what everyone had expected—it seemed perfectly reasonable—Max was not given a chance at the title, which, since 1935, was held by Braddock. Also, anti-German feelings were running high in the United States, and at his advanced age Braddock seemed a setup for just about anyone.

In 1938, a year after he had taken the title from Jim Braddock, Joe Louis and Schmeling were rematched. Max's attempt to regain the title resulted in a humiliating defeat for him when the Champion knocked him out in two minutes and four seconds in the first round.

Schmeling returned to Germany where he continued to box until he was drafted into the army. He was reported killed in 1941 while a member of Hitler's paratroopers invading Crete. It turned out that it was only a leg injury and not even a bad enough one to keep him from teaching boxing in his homeland for a while after the war ended. A few years ago his fortunes took a turn for the better when he was named an executive of the Coca-Cola bottling works at Essen, Germany, a position he still holds.

Former heavyweight champion of Germany, Albert Westphal, listens to some advice from an elder statesman of boxing. *Wide World*

Miss America of 1919 is presented with a golden apple, the symbol of her title. She is surrounded by prominent artists of the day: (*left to right*) Harrison Fischer, Penshyn Stanlaws, James Montgomery Flagg, and, kneeling, Howard Chandler Christy.

MISS AMERICA OF 1919

Though an unofficial event (nor was there a contest in 1920), the first Miss America was chosen by a group of the most distinguished artists in the country at the Chu Chin Chow Ball, held in the Hotel des Artistes on Central Park West in New York. The date was February 1, 1919. All the contestants (who included movie and Ziegfeld beauties Hazel Dawn, recently retired from a New York ad agency, Mary Eaton, and Mary Hay) wore costumes.

It was all so casual in those days that the title went to a girl who couldn't really have been "Miss" anything. She was at the time a married woman and a mother of two. Her husband was Tod Robbins, a Riviera playboy, and author of *Freaks* and *The Unholy Three*. Miss America's photograph, taken a month after she won the award, was the first ever to be transmitted from New York to Chicago by a revolutionary process called "wirephoto" which had then just been perfected. It appeared in newspapers and magazines more because of her beauty than title, since the country was not yet used to the pageant as an annual event.

Shortly after being chosen, Edith Hyde (the name she gave reporters at the time—actually it was her maiden name) divorced her writer-husband.

Offers poured in from vaudeville, movies, and the stage. One, who was quite persistent in his attempts to get the young lady in one of his shows, was Florenz Ziegfeld, at a time when he was at the height of his fame and power. In those days, however, going on the stage for a well-bred girl was frowned upon. Edith told the producers that because of her family name and her children she couldn't possibly consider a theatrical career.

20

The real reason, and one she will admit readily to today, is that she had developed a taste for the very thing that had just become illegal in the U.S. —liquor. Very little else mattered.

Along with great beauty, Edith had been gifted with clairvoyance. She began at first just for fun to give friends readings with a deck of cards. The cards were used more as a prop than a guide. Edith had an uncanny ability to predict the future and advise merely by sensing the person's "aura." Her accuracy became quite well known among café society. Her services were in such demand that just to discourage so many people from asking for readings she set a fee. Those who had been embarrassed to ask her when she charged nothing now called at once.

During the twenties Edith worked at her readings in various night clubs around Manhattan. She developed a huge clientele of free-spending celebrities and wealthy people who came back over and over again. The table that she occupied was never far from the bar.

It has now been twenty years since Edith Hyde Robbins Macartney has had a drink. She was by her own admission "a complete alcoholic for years." With the help of friends she regained her sobriety, and she claims to have been able to stay sober by helping others who have had a problem with alcohol.

The first Miss America lives near Sutton Place in Manhattan only a block away from her first son, who is a songwriter. Her second boy is an executive with an advertising agency.

When Edith stopped drinking she left night clubs. She now works at the Gypsy Tea Room on Broadway in New York. She is there every day working under the name of "Pandora." Many of her old clients, some of Broadway and Hollywood's biggest names, still consult her regularly.

"Pandora" today.

CHARLES A. LINDBERGH

The greatest hero of them all was born in Detroit, Michigan, in 1902. He was brought up in Nebraska, where he became an Air Mail pilot, stunt flier, and barnstormer during days when aviation was still at a primitive stage.

On May 20, 1927, Lindbergh took off in a plane he named "The Spirit of St. Louis," bound for Paris. No one had made it before, and few gave this young man much of a chance to make the 3,600-mile journey nonstop. Then news came across the wires that he had landed at Le Bourget Airport after 33½ hours in the air. From that moment on it was like all the celebrations ever known or heard of happening at once. Not just in Paris or the United States but all over the world in every town and city bells rang, whistles sounded, and people were near hysteria. What they said couldn't be done and shouldn't be attempted had been done by a slim young American.

Charles Lindbergh seemed everything one could ask for in a hero. He was tall, blond, and handsome. He came from a good middle-class home, and perhaps what made him loved and cheered more than anything else was that he seemed embarrassed and a little frightened by it all.

After the crowned heads of Europe had a brief glimpse of him, a cruiser sent by President Coolidge brought him back home to a welcome never before nor since accorded anyone. There were receptions and parades in 100 cities. He refused offers totaling over 7½ million dollars and gave to a museum gifts he received worth over 2 million dollars.

In 1929 he married Anne Morrow, the daughter of the United States Ambassador to Mexico, and three years later the most admired man in the world was subjected to the vilest crime on earth. His son, Charles, Jr., was kidnapped and later found dead. In a sensational trial, Bruno Richard Hauptmann was convicted of the crime and subsequently electrocuted, but the Lindberghs were still plagued with threats against the lives of their other children. In 1935 he took his family to live in England.

During a trip to Germany in 1938, Lindbergh was decorated with the Service Cross of the German Eagle by the No. 2 Nazi, Hermann Göring. It has been alleged that Lindbergh had not been warned that this was going to happen and did not understand the speech Field Marshal Göring made preceding the presentation Lindbergh was severely criticized for accepting. Nonetheless, upon his return to the United States in the late thirties, the celebrated flier began to make isolationist speeches for the America First Committee. When President Roosevelt criticized him on April 25, 1941, for his isolationist stance, Lindbergh resigned his commission.

Several months later, in a speech he made at a nationally broadcast America First Committee rally in Des Moines, Iowa, Lindbergh charged that, "The three most important groups who have been pressing this country toward war are the British, the Jews and the Roosevelt administration. . . ." He stated that ". . . their [the Jews'] greatest danger to this country lies in their large ownership and influence in our motion pictures, our press, our radio and our government. . . ."

Lindbergh was condemned for attempting to inject anti-Semitism into the issues of the day. The New York *Herald Tribune* said that in doing so Lindbergh had "sinned against the American spirit." The New York *Journal American* (a Hearst paper) said that "the raising of a racial issue by Lindbergh was the most unfortunate happening in the United States since the present tense international situation developed."

Although never officially a member of any of the Armed Forces during the Second World War, Lindbergh flew many dangerous missions in the South Pacific and received the Congressional Medal of Honor after V-J. Day.

Both the kidnapping and the treatment by the press and public for his antiwar sentiments left the Lone Eagle a man determined to avoid publicity. He grants no interviews of any kind and makes very few public appearances. When Lindbergh finally got around to writing his story *The Spirit of St. Louis* in 1954 it won the Pulitzer Prize and was a best seller; the movie made from it in 1957 starring Jimmy Stewart was a financial failure.

Lindbergh lives in Darien, Connecticut, with his wife, three sons, and two daughters. Although it is never publicized, he is a consultant and a director of Pan-American Airways, and makes trips around the world for them as often as several times a month. He keeps a small house in Switzerland which he and his wife use for their writing. Lindbergh is an enthusiastic skin diver and skier, and he has never smoked nor tasted alcohol in his life. He has long ago reaccepted his old commission in the Air Force and is now a Brigadier General. He was among the group who selected the site for the Air Force Academy, and was a member of the committee that advised the go-ahead of the Atlas missile project.

His mail in 1927 ran to nearly 4 million pieces. It contained over $100,000 just in return postage. He now receives nearly 1,000 cards and letters a week, none of which he opens. Like all his papers, and much of his memorabilia, they go into a large vault at Yale University.

Perhaps the first man on the moon will be acclaimed as Charles Augustus Lindbergh was—it is to be hoped that fate will be kinder to him than it was to "Lucky Lindy."

In 1927 beside his famous monoplane, now hanging from the ceiling of the Smithsonian Institution in Washington, D.C., and (*right*) today a director of Pan-American.

The Presidental
candidate in 1936.

ALFRED M. LANDON

During the campaign of 1936 President Roosevelt made a remark about Landon's symbol, the sunflower. He said it was only good for parrot food. That is about as personal as the race ever got. One New Deal historian wrote that when Landon and F.D.R. met in the middle of the campaign they got on so well one observer said he was surprised one of them didn't withdraw from the race.

Although he was a comparative unknown when the powerful Senator Borah threw his support to the Kansas Governor, he came up as the winner on the first ballot at the G.O.P. Convention. His running mate was the late Frank Knox, who was later to serve in F.D.R.'s cabinet. Landon fought a vigorous campaign, and criticized every point of the New Deal program with the exception of its farm relief.

It is assumed that Alf Landon felt he could win, but—whether because of the Democrats or in spite of them—the economy was beginning to rally and the voters did not want to chance a change in direction.

Not even Barry Goldwater's defeat in 1964 was as decisive as the Roosevelt landslide that buried Landon. He lost every state but Maine and Vermont with a popular vote of 27,751,597 to 16,679,583. In the electoral college the incumbent candidate received 523 with 8 going to the G.O.P. One of the most personally satisfying aspects of the tally to President Roosevelt was that it was the first and only time he ever carried his home district in New York.

In spite of the lopsided results of the elections, as late as October bets were being made in New York with Landon getting even odds. The newspapers were for the most part supporting him and *The Literary Digest,* a leading magazine of the day, announced the results of its poll—he would most certainly be our next President.

At the time it seemed that Landon had a good chance to unseat F.D.R. James A. Farley, Roosevelt's campaign manager and one of the smartest political observers of any year, did not take Alfred Mossman Landon lightly.

Not only would the Democratic ticket have the Union party (Coughlin, Smith, and Townsend) to contend with, but Al Smith's Jeffersonian Democrats were sitting this one out after Smith "took a walk" at the Democratic Convention.

The final figures showed that many crossed party lines in 1936. The one conversion of note that Alf Landon accomplished was to be an important one four years later when Wendell L. Willkie admitted that although he had been a registered Democrat until then, he had voted for the Republican ticket that year. Although Landon left public office in 1937, at the 1940 convention he was Kansas' favorite son candidate, and after holding out for several roll calls gave Willkie his support, becoming one of the candidate's most effective stumpers in the Midwest during the campaign.

Since 1937 Alf Landon has become a prominent figure in Kansas business. He is at last President—president of the radio stations he owns in Dodge City, Liberal, and Topeka, Kansas. He lives in Topeka where part of his time is taken up by the several oil, gas, and real-estate properties he owns.

Much to the surprise of the audience at a S.A.N.E. rally, he appeared on the speakers' platform alongside Mrs. Eleanor Roosevelt and he supported Lyndon B. Johnson in the 1964 elections.

A prominent businessman today.
Topeka Capital Journal

In the early 1940's.

ROCKWELL KENT

Rockwell Kent, born in Tarrytown, New York, in 1882, has become one of the best known, most versatile, and most controversial artists this country has ever produced.

Over his long career he has worked in watercolor, pen and ink, lithography, wood block, and oil—all with equal skill. Kent combines the classic in form with the romantic in feeling, and is represented in various media in the permanent collections of both the Metropolitan Museum of Art, and the Whitney Museum in New York City, the Gallery of Fine Arts in Columbus, Ohio, the Brooklyn Museum, New York, the Art Institute of Chicago, the Pushkin Museum of Moscow, and the Hermitage in Leningrad. He is one of the highest paid illustrators in commercial art, some of his work being the design of corporative advertisements seen in magazines.

Kent studied at Columbia University, and was the pupil of Kenneth Hayes Miller, Abbott H. Thayer, Robert Henri, and William Chase, prominent names in American art at the beginning of the twentieth century. Although he made his debut as an artist in 1910, he did not become well known until his first book *Wilderness, a Journal of Quiet Adventure in Alaska* was published in 1920. He followed this success with another travel book in 1924, *Voyaging,* which was set in Tierra del Fuego. His later books on wanderings were *N by E* (1930) about Greenland, and *Salamina* (1935), named for his Eskimo housekeeper in Alaska. He also wrote *Rockwellkentiana* (1933), a book about his pictures with reprints of criticisms of them.

Although artistically conservative, Rockwell Kent has been known as the "stormy petrel of the art world" for his liberal politics. He has written irate letters over the years to just about every conservative journal in the country; at the time of the execution of Sacco and Vanzetti in 1927, he sent a blistering letter of resignation to the Worcester Museum in Massachusetts, and he was passionately devoted to the cause of the Loyalist government in Spain during the Civil War.

In 1938 he incorporated an inflammatory message in an obscure Eskimo dialect into a mural on the wall of the United States post office in Washington, D.C. The painting pictured a United States mailman delivering mail to Puerto Ricans. A letter read: "To the People of Puerto Rico, our friends! Go ahead. Let us change chiefs. That alone can make us free." After a loud uproar from political quarters it was finally removed.

He has lectured extensively and is the author of two very well received autobiographies, *This Is My Own* (1940) and *It's Me, O Lord* (1955).

Kent has been the subject for congressional investigations on several occasions. Joseph McCarthy, the Wisconsin senator, was one of those who accused the artist of fellow-traveling. In 1953 Kent's name figured in the congressional inquiry over alleged Communist writers in the State Department libraries overseas. Although he has stated publicly that he does not believe in a form of Russian communism for the United States, he took the Fifth Amendment when asked under oath whether or not he was or ever had been a member of the Communist party. He still denies party membership.

Before Americans were permitted by their government to travel behind the Iron Curtain, Kent defied the ban and attended a number of Communist-sponsored rallies in Eastern Europe. When he returned to the United States the State Department voided his passport. In 1958, after nearly eight years of litigation in federal courts, the Supreme Court granted Kent another passport, stating that he was entitled to the document in spite of his associations. He testified at the time that he was "only working for peace" and knew "very little about the Communist party." Upon hearing the decision Kent said, "I am one American who does not like having his corns stepped on . . . be yourself, be yourself as an artist, be yourself as a man."

His illustrations for Voltaire's *Candide* (1928), Wilder's *Bridge of San Luis Rey* (1929), Chaucer's *Canterbury Tales* (1930), Shakespearean plays, Melville's *Moby Dick* (1931) and an edition of *Beowulf* have kept these editions in print throughout the years.

Kent has remained very busy with art commissions for nearly a half century, and though he has been less productive and less vocal in recent years, he still does occasional illustrations, and holds very strong opinions on current events. He lives quietly in Ausable Forks, New York.

At home recently in Ausable Forks.

In 1925, United States Amateur Champ.

BOBBY JONES

Golf's immortal, Robert Tyre Jones, Jr., was born on St. Patrick's Day in Atlanta, Georgia, in 1902. At the age of seven he was practicing his swing; at twelve he posted a notice on the bulletin board in his father's club, "Out in 36, back in 24," thereby tying the amateur record for the course.

Though even while in school Bobby was copping titles such as the Southern Amateur Golf Championship of 1917, 1920, and 1922, throughout his teenage years he lost tournament after tournament and was becoming better known for his fits of temper than for his mettle. In 1922, however, he tied for second place with Gene Sarazen in the Open at Skokie, and from then on his tantrums subsided and his fame spread. That same year he was graduated as a mechanical engineer from the Georgia Institute of Technology, and two years later received a B.S. from Harvard.

There were an estimated 250,000 golfers in this country in 1915. By 1925 there were five million. The rise can be attributed to the prosperity of the twenties and the additional leisure time—and to the admiration the public had developed for Bobby Jones. Paul Gallico said of him, "He was the finest golfer and competitor ever produced in the United States or anywhere else, the King himself of the Golden People."

A typical example of his sense of fair play is when in the 1925 United States Open Championship, Bobby called a penalty stroke on himself which seemed so severe that he was called before the officials and asked if he had actually taken his stance. After some discussion and much amazement on the part of the crowd—and cynical sportswriters—the penalty was allowed to

28

stand. It inspired one newspaperman to call him "the best sportsman, the greatest gentleman, and the champion of champions." Ten years after retirement Jones was still being lauded by those who knew him during his days of competition. In 1940 Grantland Rice wrote: "There is no more chance that golf will give the world another Jones than there is that literature will produce another Shakespeare."

From 1923 through 1929 Jones took slightly more than a trophy a year: He won the United States Open Championship in 1923, 1926, and 1929; the United States Amateur Championship in 1924, 1925, 1927, and 1928; the British Open in 1926 and 1927.

In 1930, after confiding only to his father what his goal was that year ("I felt myself reluctant to admit that I considered myself capable of such an accomplishment"), he won the grand slam of golf by taking the British Open, with a score of 291; the British Amateur; the United States Open Championship at Interlachen, with a 287; and the United States Amateur Championship at Merion Country Club in Ardmore, Pennsylvania.

When he came back to this country—halfway on his way to the grand slam—he was met by Grover Whelan, who took him from his liner onto a tug that brought him to the Battery to be greeted by Mayor Jimmy Walker. Jones was seated in the Mayor's car, and the two proceeded to drive northward on the isle of Manhattan for a ticker tape parade that still ranks as one of the city's biggest and most enthusiastic.

Jones retired from competition after his 1930 triumph but was a familiar face on the links until 1948, when he was first stricken with a spinal ailment which has grown increasingly worse over the years until he is now confined to a wheel chair.

Bobby is the father of two girls and a boy, is a member of the Georgia Bar Association, until recently practicing out of his father's Atlanta office, is a Vice President of the A. G. Spaulding Company and a board member and founder of the Augusta National Golf Club, one of Dwight Eisenhower's favorite haunts.

He has written several books including *Golf Is My Game,* and has just contributed a foreword to a large illustrated book on the history of the game.

A corporation vice-president today. *U.S. Golf Association*

ALEXANDER KERENSKY

Had events gone just a bit more favorably for him, Alexander Kerensky might today be a major Russian political figure, and the world divided much differently from the way it now is. Kerensky was born in Simbirsk, Russia, in 1881, the son of a minor nobleman. After studying law he gained a reputation for his frequent and skillful defense of socialists who were constantly being arrested by the police of Russia's last Czar, Nicolas II.

After the Socialist Revolution party was outlawed he was elected in 1912 as a Labor party member of the fourth State Duma. Although rather young at the time, he achieved respect and fame as an orator and mediator.

After the Revolution of 1917 Kerensky was named to the post of Minister of Justice in the first Provisional Government, and was simultaneously one of the Vice-Presidents of the Petrograd (Leningrad) Soviet. After the resignation of the Liberal party ministers he became Minister of War on May 5, 1917, and prepared the renewal of offensive action on the front against Germany and Austria-Hungary. In his speeches and pronouncements he attempted to rally the Russian people to continue a war of which they had long before wearied.

On July 17, 1917, he ordered Cossack troops to Petrograd in order to smash the first attempt of the Bolsheviks to seize power. At the same time he was responsible for freeing some of the top Bolshevik leaders, one of whom was Leon Trotsky, who had been arrested after another unsuccessful uprising.

After the reorganization of the Provisional Government Kerensky became Prime Minister of Russia on July 25, 1917. The following September he and General Kornilov, supreme commander of the Russian armed forces, clashed when the General wanted to make the government into something close to a dictatorship. During this quarrel Kerensky ordered the arming of the factory workers of Petrograd, who in a few months' time were to turn against him and his government. After futile attempts to maintain his government in power he proclaimed Russia a republic. The order was challenged as unconstitutional.

On November 6, 1917, the second Bolshevik revolt broke out. Kerensky fled the capital, ostensibly to bring loyal troops to the defense of Petrograd. The move failed, and he left Russia for the last time.

In early 1918 Kerensky turned up in London, and joined the campaign against the new Soviet government, but his policies and acts during his tenure of office made no friends for him among the White Russians who were the strongest group advocating the liberation of their homeland.

Until the Germans invaded France in 1940 Kerensky lived and worked in Paris. He was the editor of a Socialist Revolutionary newspaper *Dni*. Some of the books he wrote during that period were *Prelude to Bolshevism* in 1919 and *Catastrophe* in 1927.

Kerensky has been living in the United States since 1940. Although he has always been a bitter critic of Stalin and his policies, when the Nazis invaded Russia in 1940 he pleaded with the United States Government for aid and with the American people for private contributions for Russian Relief.

In 1965 an account of his life as head of the Russian government was published in the United States. While he granted some interviews to publicize the book, *Russia and History's Turning Point,* it was with the understanding that all questions were to be submitted to him beforehand. Most critics complained that the book historians had long awaited contained no answers to the key questions that had gone unanswered for so long.

Kerensky is still defensive about the accusations made over the years by White Russians as well as objective observers that his government, because of its vacillation and indecision, was directly responsible for the success of Lenin.

Since he has been in this country Kerensky has contributed an occasional article to national magazines on the changes in Russian foreign and domestic policies, and lectured at various universities. Until recently he was with the Library for the Study of War and Revolution in Palo Alto, California, a foundation set up by Herbert C. Hoover, former United States President. Kerensky is currently conducting classes on Russian history at Stanford University in California.

At his office at the Socialist Revolutionary newspaper, Paris, 1918. *John P. Gilligan*

At his home recently, Berkeley, California.

MARTIN DIES

Martin Dies was born in Colorado, Texas, in 1901. His father, Martin Dies, Sr., who served in Congress for ten years, had been an outspoken opponent of America's entry into World War I.

By the time Congressman Dies was nineteen years old he was practicing law in Texas; at thirty the Democrat was elected to the House of Representatives. At the time he was considered to be a protégé of Texan John Nance Garner. Throughout President Roosevelt's first term in office Dies supported most of the New Deal legislation. By 1936, however, it was clear that Martin Dies was a political maverick.

Once Dies began to differ with the party leadership his flair for making headlines became obvious. One of his well-publicized ideas concerned the high unemployment rate at the height of the Depression. The Texas Congressman suggested that the federal government make more jobs available to native-born Americans by deporting the six million aliens living in the United States at the time. In 1936 Dies lashed out against the unions during the bitter General Motors sit-down strikes. In 1937 he followed the lead of Vice-President Garner in his opposition to F.D.R.'s plan to pack the Supreme Court.

Communist and Fascist groups in the United States had been investigated with fanfare by other politicians but Dies went about it with an expertise and sense of publicity that was not to be equaled until the advent of Joseph McCarthy. In May, 1938, the House Un-American Activities Committee was created by Congress with an appropriation of $25,000 with Dies as chairman. So strongly did he dominate its workings and its headlines that it was referred to as the Dies Committee. From its very inception the Committee was criticized by liberals, leftists, and members of Congress from both parties. In spite of the attacks on its tactics and the dearth of genuine subversion it exposed, the Committee had its budget increased to $100,000 by 1939.

A few of the things that came under its scrutiny were the W.P.A. Federal Theatre and Writers' Project, the National Labor Relations Board, the Department of Labor, the Workers' Alliance, and the American Youth Congress.

One of the criticisms leveled at the Committee was that it seemed obsessed with communism while paying too little attention to the organizations that were admittedly Fascist and Nazi in the United States prior to Pearl Harbor. Dies ignored the denouncements of civil libertarians and unions such as the C.I.O. who claimed that his investigations infringed on the rights of Americans. One of his statements is characteristic of his intentions and philosophy: "America is a free country and I would defend with my life the rights of its citizens, but when they take the oath of allegiance and seek to undermine our government I say what amendment in our Constitution protects these spies and agents of foreign governments?"

In 1940 he wrote a book called *Trojan Horse in America* which outlined the plan, according to Dies, of foreign powers to infiltrate and take over the United States Government. When it was pointed out to him that the country already had a number of investigative branches that were perhaps much better equipped to protect us than his Committee, Dies stated that the F.B.I. was ineffectual in comparison to the results achieved by his Committee.

In 1945 he decided against running for reelection, and returned to Texas and the practice of law. In 1953 he was reelected to Congress and served until 1959, thereafter retiring from politics and returning to Texas.

Since leaving the House, Dies has been writing for a number of right wing journals, and in 1963 wrote another version of his Committee's work entitled *The Martin Dies Story*. Dies continues to practice law in Lufkin, Texas, and spends some time hunting and shooting pool. When asked for a comment on the current political scene the former Congressman replied, "I think we have scraped the bottom of the barrel."

In 1938 at the height of his fame and power, and (*right*) today in Lufkin, Texas.

Mowan Studio

33

In 1935 she played the title role in the film *She*. RKO

HELEN GAHAGAN DOUGLAS

Few personalities have had as varied a public life as this lady, becoming a success in politics long before entertainers were being taken seriously by the voting public. She began life as the daughter of a wealthy conservative Republican family and became a staunch New Dealer. On Broadway and in Europe she starred both as a singer and an actress. Some of her legitimate stage work was *Manhattan* (1922), her first, *Trelawney of the Wells* (1926), *Tonight or Never* (1930), and *The Cat and the Fiddle* (1932).

Although she appeared in only one film, the 1935 production of *She*, it became a science-fiction classic and had to be withdrawn from release so that it would not compete with a recent remake.

When she moved to Los Angeles in the thirties Helen became interested in social work. In 1939 she was involved with the New Deal as part of an advisory group for the Works Progress Administration and the National Youth Administration.

Her political career as an elected official started in 1945 when she began serving as Congresswoman from a working-class district in Los Angeles. She was the "Democrats' answer to Clare Boothe Luce" in the House of Representatives in the 79th to 81st Congresses. Much to the distress of the press there was no battle of the beauties while they served in the House together. Even when Mrs. Douglas was named to the Best Dressed Women list, an honor Mrs. Luce had enjoyed many times, no cattiness developed. Recently Mrs. Douglas remarked, "I didn't feel at all competitive. She was always better dressed than I was." The two ladies had a mutual respect for each other which has lasted through the years.

In 1950 Mrs. Douglas ran for the Senate of the United States from California on the Democratic ticket against a young Congressman fresh from triumph in the Alger Hiss inquiry. The contest is still remembered as one of the dirtiest ever waged in that state because of her opponent's insinuations and tactics. The winner by a wide margin was the future Vice-President Richard M. Nixon.

About her feelings concerning Mr. Nixon now that so many years have passed, she said: "I really feel sorry for him. The election was at the time of the Korean War. The Democrats were on the defensive. I really think he probably would have won anyway."

Helen Gahagan Douglas lives in a large apartment overlooking the Hudson River in New York City with her husband, Melvyn Douglas, whom she married in 1932. They are proud grandparents. She is still popular as a lecturer on humanitarian causes and a fund raiser for the Democratic party. Although she doesn't rule out a return to the theatre she seems much more interested in assisting local candidates. Her last Broadway appearances were *First Lady* (1952) and *Family Reunion* (1954).

For all the time that has passed since she entered public life Helen feels that her ideas have changed very little: "I'm afraid that you can still put me down as a liberal. I can see, however, that there is often more than one answer to a problem—not always but often. And I am constantly surprised to find how really conservative the so-called liberals are that I meet. And the conservatives, I'm pleased to find, they are often not nearly so Right as I've been led to believe."

Mrs. Douglas is
now a grandmother.

Her comeback film in 1932, *A Woman Commands*, is memorable only for the song she introduced in it, "Paradise."
RKO

POLA NEGRI

The famous silent picture star was born Appolonia Chalupec in Poland. She was well established in Europe through her films *Gypsy Blood* and *Passion* when she came to Hollywood in 1921 with her director, the talented Ernst Lubitsch.

Paramount Pictures, the studio that brought her to this country and spent a fortune to promote her, gave her such vehicles as *The Last Payment* (1922), *The Red Peacock* (1922), and *Hotel Imperial* (1927). Pola was the first to complain that her American-made pictures were inferior. Quick to second her were the critics and public.

Although Paramount was never quite able to put her across, she made many pictures for them. By the late twenties the star who was once thought to be a threat to Gloria Swanson was so unpopular with the exhibitors that some refused to feature her name in their advertising.

Pola Negri's life in her films and in her personal world were hard to distinguish. It was a toss-up which was the more dramatic. On the screen she was the Vamp who led her prey into danger and sin. And yet she too suffered for her deeds. In *Men* (1924) the advertising copy read: "the woman who pays and makes men pay." When Valentino died suddenly in New York in 1926 she left a movie in the middle of production, rushed across the country, and threw herself on his casket. When Gloria Swanson married a Marquis, Pola countered by wedding a prince. She had been married to a Polish count before that.

In spite of a disappointing career in this country Pola Negri is one of the handful of silent stars whose names are known to young people today. It is a great tribute to her as a personality because, unlike many silent stars, her films are seldom shown at art houses or film festivals. She had great beauty, enormous glamour, and a sense of publicity second to none.

After her dismal failure in Hollywood talkies she went back to Europe where she worked mostly in Germany during the thirties in films and cabarets. The recordings that she made during that period in her deep Slavic accent are still for sale in Germany rerecorded from the old 78's onto LP's.

Even in the twilight of her career before the Second World War Pola Negri was able to manage a headline now and then. Somehow the press learned that no less a personage than Adolf Hitler was enamored with her. When questioned she replied, "Why not? All of the men in my life have been important men. Take Valentino, for instance."

Pola returned to this country just before the fall of France in 1940, penniless, her career over. Thanks to the generosity of a close friend, with whom she lived quietly since retiring and who has recently died, she is financially secure with a beautiful home in San Antonio, Texas, and a trust fund.

Today Pola spends most of her time writing her autobiography. *Walt Disney Productions*

JOHN L. LEWIS

The labor leader whose power was for a time second only to that of the President of the United States was born in Iowa in 1880. His parents had come to this country from Wales, and his father was for a time on a blacklist put out by the mine operators after he had protested working conditions in the pits.

John Llewellyn attended school for only seven years before he, too, became a coal miner. In 1906 he was named a delegate of the United Mine Workers, and traveled around the country talking with the miners, and observing the deplorable conditions that existed.

In 1918 he became Vice-President, and two years later was President. From the very beginning it was obvious to the mine operators that they were not dealing with any ordinary labor agitator. During negotiations they were amazed by his huge vocabulary and dramatic manner. John L. also set to work consolidating his power within the union.

It was during the New Deal that Lewis' power and fury really were felt in the nation. He supported F.D.R.'s first two terms with funds from the union's treasury, and his own oratorical skills. The Vice-President, a conservative, was another matter. He called John Nance Garner, "a labor-baiting, poker-playing, whiskey-drinking, evil old man."

In 1935 he split with the A. F. of L. and formed the C.I.O. Lewis had wanted to organize unskilled labor, and the A. F. of L. was interested only in trade unionists. Under Lewis' leadership the C.I.O. organized with enormous success, notably in Detroit, where the sit-down strikes brought scab workers that in turn brought violence, ending in state troopers being called in.

In 1938 Lewis and F.D.R. broke while Lewis was scrapping with the steel industry. He had expected the President's help and instead received the famous curse, "a plague on both your houses."

Seldom have two adversaries been more perfectly matched than Lewis and Roosevelt, both colorful, both powerful, and each a master at insult and mockery. In attempting to keep F.D.R. from becoming President again Lewis made his biggest mistake. When it became obvious that Roosevelt was going to run for a third term Lewis backed the G.O.P. candidate Wendell L. Willkie, and promised to resign if the Republican candidate was not elected. He quit as President of the C.I.O. in 1940 and to this day his union has remained aloof from the subsequent A.F.L.-C.I.O. merger.

He pulled his miners out of the pits during the Second World War, probably making him the most unpopular man in the nation. Several times the government took over the mines, and once a federal judge assessed him and his union a combined $2,130,000 in fines for ignoring a court order to return to work.

While many former miners accuse John L. of a "sellout" during the last years of his reign, most observers feel that his agreement to allow automation in the mines was the only sensible thing he could do. Oil, gas, and atomic power had begun to replace "King Coal" in many industries, and Lewis knew it. While the membership dropped from a peak 6,000,000 in 1945 to 4,300,000 in 1960, the wages of those miners who retained their jobs were still among the nation's highest.

When he announced his retirement in 1959 the mineowners presented him with an eighteenth-century set of Shakespeare in 15 volumes as a tribute to their most worthy opponent in the bitterest and hardest fought battles in American labor history. After his retirement Lewis was made President Emeritus of the United Mine Workers. In 1963 he retired as Chairman of the National Coal Policy Conference.

Whatever one thinks of Lewis' methods, manners, or motivations, his record speaks for itself. When he came to head the union in 1920 the average pay scale was $6.00 per day. When he retired it had risen to $24.25 daily. Members of his union are covered by some of the lushest sickness-accident and pension and welfare agreements in any industry in the nation. In 1920 they didn't receive so much as sick pay or vacations. Even his severest critics will concede that Lewis, more than any other man, brought about federal legislation making safety measures mandatory.

To just about everyone's surprise Lewis is truly retired in the sense that he does not meddle in union affairs and will not comment on strikes, contracts, or conditions in the coal or any other industry. He drives in from his Alexandria, Virginia, home every morning and busies himself with matters concerning the U.M.W.'s pension and welfare fund in the union's offices in Washington. His wife died in 1942. His son is a Washington, D. C., doctor; his daughter died a few years ago.

During a radio speech in 1936, and (right) in retirement today.

CBS   UPI

"RED" GRANGE

The only football player known to people who had never seen a game—nor cared to—was born in 1903, the son of the Chief of Police of Wheaton, Illinois. Playing for the local high school, he averaged five touchdowns a game. Although he had been offered scholarships from a score of colleges because of his record, when "Red" registered at the University of Illinois he was hesitant to join the team during his freshman year for fear of not being good enough. He was a genuine amateur athlete, and delivered ice in his hometown during summer vacations to earn spending money. He weighed around 170 pounds, and was 5 feet 11 inches. In an era of great heroes he became a living legend, later being elected to the Football Hall of Fame.

His real name was Harold Grange, but friends and fans referred to him as "Red" because of his shock of flaming red hair. The press had its own name for him: the "Galloping Ghost." He was the Touchdown King the way Babe Ruth was the Home-Run King. And like the Babe, Red had the kind of personality the sportswriters and public love to idolize. The greater his victory the more embarrassedly he seemed to discuss it, always going to great pains to mention the names of those who helped him during a game.

Notre Dame at the time had the Four Horsemen, but that was a group, and the twenties was a time of the individual in America. Until the advent of Red, college football was little more than a social event—boys and girls got to wear their coonskin coats, and the weather was an excuse to carry a hip flask full of bootleg booze. But now there was someone out on that field that people either loved or hated. The latter category was made up of all of those who did not root for the University of Illinois. The star system had come to football.

Sportswriters even today can't make up their minds which his best game was, a case of an embarrassment of riches. An idea of his playing can be gathered from the record of what for Grange was his worst year: In 1925 he went scoreless in four games out of seven. He gained 1,213 yards running and accounted for 119 yards by 15 passes.

Soon after graduation, in 1926 he played a series of exhibition games and was paid the colossal fee of $300,000 to star in a silent film called *One Minute to Play*. In 1927 he was signed by the now nonexistent New York Yankees, and after a year with them went with the Chicago Bears. Pro football was looked upon before Grange's time as something slightly more respectable than ladies' wrestling matches, and wasn't very popular until he played it. The average attendance for a pro game at the Polo Grounds in New York had been about 18,000. On December 6, 1925, a total of 73,651 spectators came out to see the New York Giants throttled 19–7 by Red and the Chicago Bears.

Although he played even better football during his pro years, Grange is

40

best remembered for when he wore the Illinois blue jersey with his orange 77 on the back, since retired on the Illinois campus. When in the 1964–65 season Jim Grabowski broke Red's old record by ripping off 239 yards from scrimmage against the 212 yards that Grange had compiled during a legendary performance against Michigan, Arthur Daley of *The New York Times* wrote: "Bully for Grabowski. He put on a fine show last Saturday and is fully entitled to take bows. But whenever he encounters 'Red' Grange henceforth, he still should tip his hat." Paul Gallico called him "The Artful Dodger of the Century," and columnists linked him romantically with a string of beauties including Bebe Daniels and Clara Bow.

Grange had a few critics. One occasioned a classic remark—paraphrased many times since—when the Michigan campus newspaper placed Red on its second rather than first All-American list, he stated loftily: "All Grange can do is run." "And all *Galli-Curci* can do is sing," cracked Illinois coach Bob Zuppke. Galli-Curci was the great coloratura. After he retired from pro football in 1934 Red went into a job as sales manager for a bottling company, and then managed a nightclub in Hollywood for a while. In the late thirties he went into the insurance business as an agent. After a serious heart attack in the early 1950's, Red began to take things easy in the insurance business. After recuperating for a few seasons he did a television commentary of the Bears' games.

He had made a fortune during his pro years and invested it profitably. The last few years he has spent in semiretirement in his home in the Indian Lakes Estates of Florida. During the 1966–67 football season Falstaff Beer engaged him to do some commercials for them in the Midwestern markets.

UPI

NBC

In 1927, during his one season with the New York Yankees, and today (*right*).

De Mirjian

LIBBY HOLMAN

Her fans will tell you that no one ever sang the blues better than she. She introduced such standards as "Body and Soul," "Can't We Be Friends," and "Moanin' Low." That Libby had the right to sing the blues, no one would deny.

She was born Elizabeth Holzman in Cincinnati, Ohio, and first came to New York to get her law degree at Columbia University. Instead she made her Broadway debut in *Garrick Gaieties* in 1926.

Libby Holman was one of the brightest stars on Broadway, appearing in *The Little Show* (1929) and *Three's a Crowd* (1930), in which she introduced the song "Something to Remember You By," sung to a young man she selected from the band—Fred MacMurray, wearing a sailor suit, with his back to the audience. Then in 1932 her husband, Zachary Smith Reynolds, heir to a tobacco fortune estimated at $30,000,000, was killed. "Skipper" Reynolds, as he was called by his family and friends, was shot to death.

At first the coroner reported the death to be a suicide, but after Reynolds' tutor told the sheriff about Skipper's mood at the time he was supposed to have killed himself, the case was reopened, with the coroner holding an inquest.

Libby was indicted for murder in the first degree, which later was reduced to second degree. Throughout the entire affair Miss Holman conducted herself beautifully—she had been a law student before going on the stage, and her father, who was also her lawyer, was one of the most prominent attorneys in Ohio.

After a letter from the Reynolds family to the authorities asking that the case be dropped, Libby Holman was freed. No one was ever brought to trial, and to this day the shooting remains unsolved. During the years following the tragedy in 1932 Libby was very frugal with her public appearances. Her last Broadway show was *You'll Never Know* in 1938, with costar Rex O'Malley (now living in Manhattan not far from Miss Holman's town house in the East Sixties.) Also in the cast was Lupe Velez.

After leaving Broadway, Libby played summer stock in *Burlesque* (1939), *The Greeks Had a Word for It* (1940), *My Sister Eileen* (1941), and *Over 21* (1945).

In 1941 Libby married Ralph Holmes, an airman in the R.A.F., son of the stage actor, Taylor Holmes, and brother of actor Phillips Holmes. Phillips was killed during the war flying for the Canadian Air Force. After Ralph and Libby separated he died from an overdose of sleeping pills in 1945. After that she went into seclusion, except for sporadic singing engagements.

Libby's only child by Reynolds, a boy born two months after charges were dropped against her in the death of his father, was killed while climbing a mountain in California in 1950.

It was her meeting with her old accompanist, Gerald Cook, that induced her to begin performing again after a long hiatus though in 1958 she appeared in *Yerma*, a play about a wife who kills her husband. In 1966 she cut an album of her standards for a small record company. "Moanin' Low," "Can't We Be Friends?" and "Body and Soul" were on one side with a selection of folk songs on the other. These are the numbers she does with Cook when the spirit moves her in her one-woman show, "Blues, Ballads, and Sin Songs," which she has played in New York for limited runs and in little theatres up and down the East Coast as well as on television once, in Eindhoven, Holland, during a tour of Europe with her one-woman show.

Unfortunately, none of the magic that Broadway audiences saw during her heyday was ever captured for the screen. Miss Holman dismisses her fans' laments by saying that it was simply not the medium for her. The spell she created then is still, however, evident in her old 78's.

Miss Holman's official residence is shared with her husband, artist Louis Shanker, in a house she calls "Tree Tops" in Stamford, Connecticut.

With Rex O'Malley (*left*) and Clifton Webb in the Broadway show *You Never Know* (1938), and today.

AMOS 'N' ANDY

The popularity of *Amos 'n' Andy* has no counterpart in television, movies, or the stage. Their tenure on radio was the longest, their salaries were the highest, and their impact on life in the United States from the late twenties through the forties was the greatest. Throughout their careers they were the undisputed Kings of Radio.

The original names of the couple were "Sam 'n' Henry," one of the many blackface acts playing the vaudeville circuits from the time they met in 1919 until they went on station WGN in Chicago in 1925. The program was only mildly successful at first, but began to pick up listeners as they started to add some of their famous characters. In 1926 they moved to station WMAQ, also in Chicago, and changed their names to "Amos 'n' Andy." On August 19, 1929, the National Broadcasting Company put them on from coast to coast. Their appeal was immediate and seemingly universal—they were popular on Park Avenue as well as in Harlem. They were referred to in speeches on the floor of the United States Senate, and "Silent Cal" Coolidge spoke out long enough to advise his staff that he was not to be disturbed while the show was on the air.

Amos, the working member of the team, was played by Freeman F. Gosden. He was supposed to run the Fresh Air Taxicab Company, consisting of one old car. His wife was Ruby, and they had a little girl, Arbadella. Andy, who had no job or business, was portrayed by Charles Correll. In spite of his lack of ambition he maintained an office and a secretary, Miss Blue.

Sponsored by the Pepsodent Tooth Paste Company, Amos 'n' Andy were heard Monday through Friday from 7:00 P.M. to 7:15 P.M. E.S.T. in every state in the Union, plus Canada. In some sections of the country theatre marquees announced that the feature film ended before 7 P.M. and did not begin again until after 7:15. Department stores that stayed open late some evenings broadcasted the shows on every floor, lest the patrons stay home for fear of missing an episode. When Andy was about to marry Madame Queen (which he never did) and when she brought a breach of promise suit against him, streets were deserted while America listened to "Brother Crawford," "Lightnin'," and "The Kingfish" testify.

Much of the show's activity centered around the Hall of the Mystic Knights of the Sea, the lodge to which all male members of the cast belonged. There was Lawyer Calhoon who conferred with his clients in the alley behind the jail, and Needle Nose Fletcher, and Sapphire Stevens, the Kingfish's wife. There were expressions which became a part of the American idiom: "Buzz me, Miss Blue," "Check and double-check," "I'se regusted!" and their famous lament, "Ow wah! Ow wah!" A foreigner walking down a typical American street during those years could hear the show's theme, "The Perfect Song," coming from every window on the block as though it had been piped in by government order.

In 1948 Gosden and Correll sold *Amos 'n' Andy* to CBS lock, stock and barrel, giving them an enormous tax break through capital gains and they continued to do the shows as employees of the network.

There was, however, a segment of the country that never found the characters amusing. After the war the rumblings of discontent among civil rights organizations protesting the stereotypes of Negroes the show created became more and more vocal. In the fifties the format was changed to permit guest stars, and the racial humor was toned down considerably. They were now on only once a week for 30 minutes in a program they called *The Amos 'n' Andy Music Hall,* and when Negro actors played the parts on the TV series (with Gosden and Correll keeping a hand in behind the scenes) it was hoped the complaints would cease, but if anything, the pressure grew.

Gosden and Correll discontinued the radio shows in 1958, and in 1965 CBS announced that the television series was being withdrawn from circulation, although the network denied the reason was protests from Negro organizations.

How the pair feels about being canceled after so many years of tremendous popularity can only be guessed at. They still maintain offices in Beverly Hills, but there are no announcements of future shows. When queried about their plans and opinions their answer is that they are still under contract to the Columbia Broadcasting System, and can make no further comment. The network's legal department refuses to confirm or deny that a contract exists, and the program department simply says that no program is scheduled for them in the foreseeable future.

Gosden and Correll are still the closest of friends, and play a lot of golf together in Palm Springs and on courses around Los Angeles. They were both married in 1927. Correll is an avid movie fan, and has flown his own plane for years. Gosden and he both enjoy fishing. In fact, the only time they ever missed a show was once in the thirties when they got so engrossed with a big catch they forgot the time, disappointing more Americans than ever voted for a Presidential candidate.

Amos (*left*) 'n' Andy in a scene from their movie *The Big Broadcast of 1936.*

(*From left to right*) Charles Correll (Andy), announcer Bill Hay, and Freeman F. Gosden (Amos) on a visit to the CBS studios in Hollywood. *CBS*

Testifying before a Senate committee in 1941 against Lend-Lease, and (below) today. *Wide World*

GERALD L. K. SMITH

When "Kingfish" Huey Long was assassinated in 1935, the man who took his place was a former Disciple of Christ minister who in 1933 had left his pulpit to become the Louisiana Senator's right-hand man. Gerald L. K. Smith delivered the eulogy at Long's funeral, and has continued over the years to carry on the Long tradition of fiery oratory and controversy.

Smith threw his "Share-the-Wealth" strength in with Father Coughlin and Dr. Townsend in 1936 to form the Union Party in an attempt to split the Democratic vote and thereby defeat Franklin D. Roosevelt in the Presidential election of that year. Smith still blames F.D.R. for many, if not most, of the ills of America and the world.

He was a strong and articulate opponent of Lend-Lease, and continued after his friend, Father Coughlin, was silenced to call for isolationism up to just before the attack on Pearl Harbor. His speeches were peppered with such phrases as "Let's keep America American," "America first" and "They want us to water the dry sticks of the earth with American blood and gold."

Until he moved his headquarters in the late forties from Detroit, Michigan, to Los Angeles he operated under the banner of the Committee of One Million.

Smith's major stock-in-trade for decades has consisted of raucous hate-mongering. Crude invective against the Jews, Negroes and other minority groups has made up much of his propaganda line.

In 1944 Smith ran for President on the America First party ticket, and again in 1956 he made the race under the banner of the Christian National-ist Crusade. In 1952 he ran General Douglas MacArthur with no official nod from the General in a write-in campaign. The General was one of Smith's heroes along with Senator Joseph McCarthy and Henry Ford, Sr. When in 1956 Smith tried to associate himself with the Vice Presidential candidacy of Richard Nixon, his bid was met with a vigorous rebuff. "There is no place in the Republican Party," stated Mr. Nixon, "for the race-baiting merchandisers of hate like Gerald L. K. Smith."

Although Gerald L. K. Smith is as active as he ever was, unless one subscribes to *The Cross and the Flag,* the official organ of the Christian Nationalist Crusade, little is known of his statements and plans. Among his claims in this monthly magazine, which has a circulation of 40,000, is that it is a "big lie" or "pure fiction" that the Nazis murdered six million Jews in World War II.

Far from having mellowed with the years, his editorials warn America of emigration by national and ethnic groups of lower mental and physical capacities than those which Smith feels founded and developed the United States. He has supported Barry Goldwater for the Presidency, called for the impeachment of Chief Justice Earl Warren, and for the withdrawal of this country from the United Nations.

Throughout his public life Smith has been encouraged by his wife Elna, who often appears with him on the speaker's platform. It was in her name that in 1966 he constructed a huge concrete statue of Christ atop a 1,500-foot Ozark mountain in Eureka, Arkansas. Called Christ of the Ozarks, its height of 65 feet is over twice the size of the famous Christ of the Andes, and is built, says Smith, "to stand for 2,000 or 3,000 years."

Smith divides his time between Los Angeles and Tulsa, Oklahoma, maintaining homes and offices in each. His title is the National Director of the Christian Nationalist Crusade, which he describes as being "more or less the right-wing godfather and godmother to some 1,700 right-wing groups."

Summarizing its appraisal of Smith in 1948 in a report entitled "Subversive Activities of Hate Groups," the Americanism Commission, Department of Illinois of the American Legion, stated that "Gerald L. K. Smith is probably the most vicious of the rabble-rousing and sensational hate-mongers operating today."

Chase Photo, Ltd.

Mr. and Mrs. John Barrymore, 1939.

ELAINE BARRIE BARRYMORE

The Barrie-Barrymore affair has been rivaled only by the Liz Taylor-Richard Burton liaison of recent years. Miss Barrie and Barrymore, however, carried on for a much longer time, and had the Great Depression for the drab backdrop to their colorful capers.

It all began when Elaine Jacobs, a teenage student at Hunter College in New York City, left her home with her mother one day to see the greatest matinee idol of his day, John Barrymore, in the film, *Svengali*. She never really returned. From that day on Elaine called herself Elaine Barrie. It was that name that she signed to a note she sent to Barrymore who was undergoing one of his periodic alcohol cures in a hospital. The "interview" he granted was a long one, and was followed by another every day after that until he was discharged and moved into the Jacobs' family apartment on West End Avenue.

Barrymore's divorce from his second wife, actress Dolores Costello, was not yet final. Elaine was thirty years younger than he and still a minor. The press went wild. With Mrs. Jacobs in tow they were seen at nightclubs, theatres, and parties all around New York until he fled to Hollywood. Elaine was quick to follow and the tabloids reported every ridiculous detail. "Ariel and Caliban" was what the headlines dubbed them, and they pushed the New Deal right off the front pages.

In 1935 the Associated Press named Elaine Barrie and Republican Presidential Candidate Alf Landon as the two people who had made that year

48

most interesting. She was to make news for the next six years with their marriage and many separations until they were divorced shortly before his death in 1942.

The little girl who made up her mind to meet and marry John Barrymore succeeded in doing both. In the process she made a brief appearance in one of his films, costarred with him on Broadway, and acted with him in a number of radio dramas. By the time it ended, her mother, who had been with them most of the time, was divorced, Elaine's acting career was ruined, and Barrymore had become nearly as well known for his protégée as he had been for his profile.

Says Ariel about the Great Lover: "He made me unashamed of the natural. He made me glory in my sensuality. My head still whirls from the memories."

Barrymore's other wives were the writer Michael Strange, now deceased, and the beautiful Dolores Costello, who is living on a ranch in Fallbrook, California.

Although her mother and father were remarried, Elaine has remained Mrs. Barrymore. Over the years she has been involved in a number of endeavors. In the forties she took courses at a school for writers in California, but waited until 1964 to write her book, *All My Sins Remembered*. From 1950 until 1952 she was a customers' girl at a New York brokerage house.

In 1952 her father died, and Elaine and her mother went to Haiti for a week's vacation. They stayed nine years, and developed a very successful business of exporting straw baskets and handbags which are sold in such stores as Nieman-Marcus and Saks Fifth Avenue under the trade name of Elaine Barrymore Originals. Because of the political climate in Haiti they returned to New York in 1963.

In 1966 Elaine was engaged as a Special Consultant to the Alliance for Progress as a result of her firsthand knowledge of several South American nations.

That same year the Barrymore operation was moved to Trinidad, where mother and daughter now reside.

Now a businesswoman.

A young high school teacher in 1925, and (*below*) a geologist now, living quietly with his wife and two sons. *Culver Pictures*

JOHN T. SCOPES

When the General Assembly of the State of Tennessee passed a law forbidding the teaching of Darwin's theory of evolution in the public schools, John T. Scopes was a twenty-four-year-old mathematics teacher in the little town of Dayton. He was a soft-spoken young man who coached the football team and generally kept to himself. That was in the spring of 1925.

Shortly after the bill became law Scopes met with three lawyers in Robinson's Drugstore, and over a few bottles of soda pop decided to become the key figure in one of the world's most famous trials. It was a matter of conviction on the part of the freckled young man, for he shied away from publicity, and even during the heat of the controversy managed to keep in the background as much as possible.

A few days after he made up his mind to test the law in the courts, Scopes deliberately read to his students a portion of Hunter's *Civic Biology* which stated that man has descended from a lower form of mammal. He was indicted, and a trial was set for July, 1925.

By the time the proceedings got under way Dayton had been swollen to nearly three times its normal size of 1,500. It was a sleepy little country town nestled in the foothills of the Cumberland Mountains. From all over the world there came reporters, sightseers, souvenir hawkers, telegraph operators, and some of the finest legal minds in America. It was to be immortalized in history books, plays, motion pictures, and newspapers as the setting for the "Monkey Trial," or as some referred to it, the "Trial of the Century."

Scopes was prosecuted by three-time Democratic Presidential candidate, William Jennings Bryan, who had also been a United States Secretary of State and one of this country's most colorful orators. He was defended by Clarence Darrow, the most famous criminal lawyer in America, fresh from his triumph in the Loeb-Leopold case in Chicago. Assisting Darrow were Arthur Garfield Hays and Dudley Field Malone, highly respected attorneys in their own rights. But even with such a team on the defense the deck was stacked against Scopes. Dayton was what H. L. Mencken, who covered the trial with great glee for the *Baltimore Sun,* called "the buckle on the Bible Belt."

The heat was so great that Judge John T. Raulston moved the trial out onto the shaded lawn, which lowered the temperature somewhat but did not affect the heated insults a bit. Bryan announced that he had come to "defend the word of God against the greatest atheist and agnostic in the world today." He meant Darrow, who in turn called the aging "Great Commoner" to the stand as a witness for the defense, humiliating him by making his religious beliefs seem ludicrous.

Theoretically Bryan won. Scopes was found guilty and fined $100, which the *Baltimore Sun* offered to pay. But the press had laughed at Bryan, and even the crowd in the courtroom had become disappointed as he floundered foolishly on the witness stand under Darrow's barrage of cutting questions. In less than a week the "Defender of the Word," as he liked to be called, died of an apoplectic stroke.

Darrow announced that his client would not pay the fine, and that the case would be appealed. The higher court found that the judge had erred in setting the sentence rather than permitting the jury to do so.

In the years that followed Scopes avoided the limelight like a plague. He left Dayton the day the trial ended, and the only time reporters had a real opportunity with him was in 1943 when he turned up in Kentucky and announced that he would run for the United States Congress on the Socialist party ticket. But he would discuss only the campaign issues. He was defeated as expected. He did not return to Dayton again until 1960, when the town that had scorned him as an "infidel" thirty-five years before feted him on the occasion of the world premiere of the film, *Inherit the Wind*—adapted from the successful Broadway stage play dramatizing the trial. (Scopes was played by actor Dick York and, like all the real characters in the picture, was given a fictitious name.)

Once the world's most famous schoolteacher, John T. Scopes now lives and works quietly in Shreveport, Louisiana, as an executive for an oil and gas company, taking time out to write his memoirs. He says it has been a long time since he has received one of those letters asking him if he believes that his grandmother was an ape. When asked if he would do it all over again, he replied that perhaps someone should because that same law is still on the books of Tennessee.

Wide World

In 1936, a ranking Republican Congressman, and powerful adversary of Roosevelt foreign policy.

HAMILTON FISH

Had he done nothing from 1920 to 1945 in the House of Representatives
but show up for roll calls, Hamilton Fish would be immortal because of
the 1940 speech made by President Roosevelt which ended with the famous
words, "Martin, Barton, and Fish."

After leaving Harvard in 1910 he went to France as an officer with the
famous 369th Infantry where he and his men (all of them Negroes, with
the exception of the officers) fought in the Battle of Champagne. At the end
of World War I Fish was a Major, he had been decorated with the *croix de
guerre,* and his outfit had one of the finest fighting records in the United
States forces. It was at this time that he entered politics.

Even as a freshman, Congressman Fish took the lead. He proposed legislation for the establishment of the Tomb of the Unknown Soldier, and
during the twenties, when the Negro Civil Rights bandwagon was offering
"immediate seating," Fish introduced countless bills to guarantee equality
for the men who fought alongside him so valiantly during the war. Far
from being the conservative he was later thought to be, he fought for prison
reform, and recommended that the three who figured prominently in the
Teapot Dome Scandal, Fall, Doheney, and Sinclair—all millionaires—be
sent to prison. One of the founders of the American Legion, Fish defended
the veterans' bonus at a time when many on his side of the aisle were firmly
set against it.

In 1930 he formed the Fish Committee, which was the precursor of the
Dies Committee, but his attempts to unearth Communists were unsuccessful. He continued, however, as one of the first well-known politicians to
make communism an issue, and in 1931 asked that the Communist party in
the United States be outlawed. His first big break with Roosevelt came in
1933 when the new President recognized the Soviet Union. He did support
many of the New Deal economic measures because he felt they were necessary under the circumstances of the Depression. But he was vehemently opposed to America's interference in European politics.

By the late thirties, when World War II seemed a probability, Fish
through seniority had become the ranking Republican on the House Rules

Committee and the Foreign Affairs Committee, two of the most powerful groups in the federal government. By this time Fish was making speeches for groups such as America First and the Liberty League, warning the American people that the powers Roosevelt was asking for were those of a war President. He fought the President on the floor and in the cloakroom of the House on such measures as lend-lease and the draft, and campaigned vigorously against the repeal of the arms embargo. The powerful National Committee to Keep America Out of Foreign Wars, an isolationist movement that got under way in 1939, was a Fish brainchild.

When Pearl Harbor was attacked, one of the first voices heard was that of Hamilton Fish in support of President Roosevelt.

When Fish ran each time for office it was from the district that included F.D.R.'s ancestral home, Hyde Park. Try as he did to unseat Fish, the congressman returned to office each year until the district was gerrymandered in 1945. Confronted with a new electorate, he was at last retired by the voters. Since 1945 Fish has been active in speaking before various patriotic groups, campaigning for candidates of his political persuasion, and as President General of the Order of Lafayette (an organization of such eminent citizens as Admiral Chester Nimitz, General Omar Bradley, former Postmaster General James A. Farley, and former French Ambassador Hervé Alphand).

Since the death of Mrs. Fish several years ago he has lived in a midtown New York City hotel near the Harvard Club, of which he is a member. He can now laugh about his heated disputes with F.D.R. but has lost none of his old vigor when defending his old stands. About Roosevelt, he says: "He had great personal charm. An excellent public speaker, but he was a small man. Small in his outlook and petty in his anger. He lied us into that war. It was a low and despicable thing to do. What he wanted was power."

About the famous speech which had the nation howling, Fish remarks: "I was very pleased, actually. Those other two—Barton and Martin—two fine men. I considered myself in good company. Of course, it was funny. Roosevelt knew just how to time it so it would be funny. What historians neglect to mention is that he didn't write the speech. He didn't write any of his speeches."

At the Harvard Club in New York City recently. *John P. Gilligan*

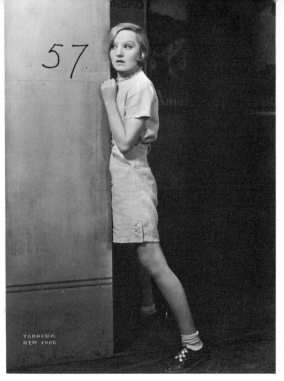

In her 1935 stage debut in the United States, starring in *Escape Me Never. Vandamm*

ELISABETH BERGNER

The famous actress, who had her training at the equally famous Vienna Conservatory, made her first success in 1921 opposite one of the most renowned actors of the time, Alexander Moissi, as Ophelia to his Hamlet.

Almost immediately Elisabeth Bergner was one of the biggest stars in Germany and her native Austria. The legendary Max Reinhardt guided her in a number of Shakespearean plays in the twenties, and she was also to be seen in *A Doll's House* and *Miss Julie*.

Her husband, Dr. Paul Czinner, directed her in a number of silent films beginning in 1924. In *Nju* and *Violinist of Florence* she costarred with the late Conrad Veidt. The latter film as well as *Donna Juanna* were released through U.F.A., the MGM of Germany, and produced by her own firm known as the Elisabeth Bergner Poetic Film Company.

With her triumph in *St. Joan* on stage in 1924 the Bergner reputation was sufficient to warrant a tour of Holland, Sweden, and Denmark. In 1926 she essayed the title role in a popular play of the time, *The Last of Mrs. Cheyney*. For the 1930–31 seasons in Germany and Austria she appeared under Reinhardt's auspices in Eugene O'Neill's *Strange Interlude*. During 1932 she made the films *Der Traumende* and *Ariane* in Paris.

The hit of West End's season in 1933 was Elisabeth Bergner in *Escape Me Never*. She played an enchanting and gallant gamine named Gemma Jones. The bobbed blond hair and shorts she wore in the play in England and on Broadway (1935) and in the film set fashion trends.

Another style set by Elisabeth Bergner was the bare midriff, which she introduced in her 1937 movie *Dreaming Lips.*

After Hitler came to power in Germany and Austria all of the star's appearances were either in England or America. The films she made in England were well received in the United States. But those big, brown, pleading eyes were in all too few motion pictures. Even in a poor one such as *Catherine the Great* (1934) her performance was outstanding. Her leading man in *As You Like It* (1937) was the promising young actor Laurence Olivier, and in *Stolen Life* (1939) her leading man was Michael Redgrave. In 1943 Bergner was once again charming Broadway audiences in the chiller *The Two Mrs. Carrolls.* She toured Australia in it in 1950.

In England and on the Continent, the Viennese actress has through the years appeared in such plays as *The Boy David,* playing the title role (this was Sir James Barrie's last play), Terence Rattigan's *The Deep Blue Sea* in which she toured Germany and Austria in 1954, and *Long Day's Journey into Night* at the 1959 Berlin Festival. On another tour abroad during the late fifties she did *Dear Liar,* the dramatization of the George Bernard Shaw-Mrs. Patrick Campbell correspondence.

She did not appear in this country again until she accepted the mother role in *First Love,* a play for the 1961–62 season from the book by Romain Gary. Unfortunately while the company was in out-of-town tryouts Miss Bergner and director Alfred Lunt agreed that the "difficulties" were too great. She withdrew and was replaced.

The lady, whom Alexander Woollcott praised as "probably the ablest actress in the world today," makes her home in London. She and Dr. Czinner have been married over forty years.

Miss Bergner now lives quietly in London.

CHRISTINE JORGENSEN

On more than one occasion the Presidential election campaigns of 1952 were bumped from the front pages of United States newspapers with revelations concerning a former G.I. named George Jorgensen, Jr., who had gone to Denmark and had been changed into a woman.

Born in New York City in 1926, Jorgensen, who was an only child, had felt an overwhelming desire through school, the Army, and various jobs, to look, act, sound, and dress feminine. While groping in every direction toward some answer to the obsession that alienated him from every group, he came across a book entitled *The Male Hormone*. Shortly after reading it he sailed in 1950 for Denmark on the pretext of making a color travel film on the country.

During 1950, 1951, and early 1952 Danish doctors performed a series of operations, and treated George with hormones. In June of 1952 he wrote to his parents in the Bronx informing them of the fact that he would be coming back to America shortly—as Miss Christine Jorgensen. Mr. and Mrs. Jorgensen, who had always been aware of how deeply troubled their boy was, took it quite well. Several months later the story broke all over the world. What seemed a welcome, if somewhat bizarre, answer to a great problem changed into a nightmare as their home was turned into a circus by newspaper reporters and the plain curious.

Christine arrived back in this country and stated that, contrary to reports, she was not going to star in a Hollywood movie. She said her career was behind the camera, not in front of it: "I am a photographer, not an actress." Miss Jorgensen insisted that she did not want any publicity. She insisted on it during newspaper and magazine interviews, on TV and radio shows, and in her life story which was published in a national magazine.

The former soldier who turned lady for a lifetime took an apartment in Manhattan's Gramercy Park area, and was seen at openings and parties around town for several years. The travel films were somehow forgotten and she was seriously considered by a Hollywood producer for the title role in the remake of *She,* but nothing came of it. After interest in her bizarre story waned she submitted to one of Mike Wallace's grueling personal TV interrogations. A small company put out an LP record album of an interview with her. Although in sales it fell somewhat short of the Top 40, it is today something of a classic in recorded bad taste, and a much-sought-after collector's item among discophiles.

Miss Jorgensen has twice taken out a marriage license but has yet to marry because she "simply wasn't in love." She feels that many women over thirty-five make the mistake of marrying just because they are embarrassed to be single at that age. Although she thinks she may never marry, she does not rule out the possibility. To the question of whether or not marriage for Christine is legally possible she points out that the United States State Department in 1952 changed her passport, thus making her gender legally female.

As her name began to appear less and less in the columns, and comics found new personalities to joke about, Christine began to do summer stock and nightclubs. She has played Madame Rosepetal in *Oh Dad, Poor Dad, Mamma's Hung You in the Closet and I'm Feelin' So Sad, Tom Jones,* and the title role in *Mary, Mary* on the strawhat circuit during 1963, 1964, and 1965. In 1966 she took her nightclub act, in which she sings a little, tells jokes, and answers questions from the audience, to Hawaii.

Between engagements Miss Jorgensen is kept busy answering letters that still pour in from around the world, written by young men and women who are unhappy with their gender. Although she maintains she has never had the slightest regret about changing her sex, the advice she gives them is to seek psychiatric and medical help before undergoing surgery. According to Christine, sex changes are not at all uncommon in the United States. She claims that one took place recently in the hospital of a United States prison and another on a United States naval base.

She says that she has many friends who are homosexuals, but that she was never one herself in the usual sense of the word. In fact, she maintains that she really doesn't understand the problem in others.

Her parents moved to Massapequa, Long Island, in 1953, and when her father died a number of months ago Christine began living with her surviving parent. When told about this recently, the writer Dorothy Parker quipped, "And what sex, may I ask, is the mother?"

Among her plans for the future is her long-awaited autobiography, which she is working on now. Those who expect to find it full of glimpses into her sex life and transvestite humor will be greatly disappointed. Miss Christine Jorgensen thinks of herself as a lady in every sense of the word, and takes the whole thing very seriously.

George before leaving for Denmark, 1949 (*left*).

Now Christine, portraying Madam Rosepetal in *Oh Dad, Poor Dad, Momma's Hung You in the Closet and I'm Feelin' So Sad.*

Counsel to millions on *The Goodwill Hour,* at the height of his popularity, 1939.

JOHN J. ANTHONY

The little man who gave advice to tens of thousands during his career was for a time so successful that his radio shows were carried by two networks at the same time.

His famous phrases, "No names, please." and "What is your problem, Madam?" became known to all. John J. Anthony was a household word. "Tell it to the Marines" was replaced by "Tell it to Mr. Anthony."

Mr. Anthony, or "Mr. Agony" as many called him, got the idea for his radio program in jail. He had been given a three-month sentence for failing to pay alimony to his first wife for the support of their two sons. After that he served another shorter sentence, and twice was cited for contempt of court—all because he didn't believe in alimony.

In those days he went under his real name, Lester Kroll. He went to jail in New York City as a cab driver. He emerged as the head of an organization he created and called "The Alimony League," a movement he was later to use in lobbying against many of the archaic marriage and divorce laws on the state's books.

He began his broadcasts on April 10, 1930. The show would open with his announcer, the distinguished actor Roland Winters, saying: "You have a friend and adviser in John J. Anthony. And thousands are happier and more successful today *because* of John J. Anthony!"

Mr. Anthony never permitted his guests to mention names (only initials were used), religion, or to give too many details. If at all possible, the suggestion of sex crept into the conversation. Though never blatant, if there was a way to titillate the audience without offense it was done.

Although a great many who listened to him during his more than twenty-five years on network radio did not take him seriously, he claims a good deal of the credit for making premarital blood tests mandatory in many states, and the establishment of the three-day waiting period between the granting of a license and the marriage ceremony. John J. Anthony's peak of popularity was at a time in this country when a great many Americans were hungry and depressed. The sorrows interviewees poured out to the little man on the radio, perhaps made them forget their own problems. Whatever the reasons for people listening and people confessing, he has never had a single complaint from anyone he advised.

Mr. Anthony, author of a book, *Marriage and Family Problems,* which sold over 400,000 copies, is now living in Los Angeles. After his network shows were cancelled in the mid-fifties he had for a time a local radio program and TV show. Now all of his time is spent as a Commissioner of Human Relations for the County of Los Angeles. To this day he is in touch with people who came to him seeking his advice many years ago.

When asked about his own family life he said, "I have been married to the same woman now for over thirty years. I think I must be in a rut."

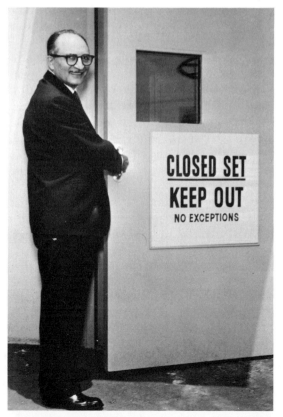

Entering a sound stage for his appearance in the recent movie *Divorce, American Style,* with Debbie Reynolds and Dick Van Dyke.

Circa 1935.

CHARLES ATLAS

Body-builder Angelo Siciliano migrated in 1904 along with his family to Brooklyn from the farm in Acri, Italy, where he was born. Angelo was a weak, sickly boy, listless and unhappy. One night, when he was fifteen years old, while returning home he was attacked and beaten severely by a bigger boy. It must have hurt an awful lot because he has never forgotten it—nor has the public.

The 97-pound teenager brooded over the incident, and then after being impressed with a statue of Hercules set about exercising at the local gymnasiums. The more he lifted weights the more tired he got. While visiting the zoo one day Angelo, impressed with the lion's muscles, wondered how it could be so powerful with no room to exercise in that small cage. While staring at the animal, it got up and stretched. Seeing the beast pit one muscle against the other gave the boy the idea for what was to change his life and the lives of many others around the world. It was the basis for the system he called "Dynamic Tension."

Employing the principles he worked out on himself, he won a national contest in 1922, conducted by Bernarr Macfadden, to name the "World's Most Perfectly Developed Man." When he again won the following year, MacFadden in disgust retired the title.

Someone remarked how much he looked like the statue of Atlas that stood on the site of a local bank. It flattered the young man, who at the time was working as a $5-a-week strong man and janitor for a Coney Island sideshow. He decided to change his name to Charles Atlas.

In the early 1920's a friend got him a job as a life model. Within a short time he was in demand and earning $100 a week allowing people to admire and to draw his body. But if they liked it so much, why not show them how

60

such a physique can be theirs—for profit? In 1929 he began a correspondence course which had only mild success until a young man from an advertising firm, Charles P. Roman, gave him some ideas for promotion.

In 1942 Atlas publicized his system by pulling six cars chained together for a full mile while the public and the press looked on in awe. Another time he towed a 72½-ton railroad car 112 feet along the tracks with a rope. His imaginative advertising ran in comic books, Sunday supplements, and just about every type of magazine that a man was likely to pick up. It was presented in a series of simple drawings any male could understand and identify with. The situation is set on a beach. A puny man's girl is taken away from him, and sand is kicked in his face by a bully. If that puny guy were you, the easy thing to do was to send for the free illustrated booklet which encouraged you to sign up. Around the world, millions did.

Atlas takes his body building method seriously and with good reason— it works. Most of the principles of the "new" isometrics are based on exercises that Atlas pioneered thirty years ago. He is most proud of some of his famous pupils, Fred Allen, Max Baer, and Mahatma Gandhi.

Charles Roman, who gave Atlas the idea for promoting himself and his system, still runs the mail-order business. The ads are very much the same, and the symbolism is as always a photograph of Charles Atlas in the classic Atlas pose with the globe resting on his back.

Atlas gave up his gymnasium in New York several years ago. He visits his offices in London, and when traveling within the United States flies in a twin-engine plane piloted by Charles Roman.

When he is in town the paunchy businessmen at the New York Athletic Club stare in wonderment at the physique of the man in his sixties working out in the gym.

Some years ago Charles Atlas moved near an abandoned Coast Guard lookout station on Point Lookout, Long Island. Here he spends most of his time. He has made his house a most unusual one, furnishing it with furniture he built himself from the driftwood that floats up on the shore.

Mrs. Atlas, to whom he was married for forty years, died in 1965, leaving a son and a daughter.

Today, a little gray and a different bathing suit.

At the peak of his popularity, 1943. From the smile on his face it is a safe guess that there was good news that night. *Mutual Network*

GABRIEL HEATTER

During the Second World War, despite his "Voice of Doom" delivery, his famous "Ah, yes, there's *good* news tonight" lightened the worries of many who had boys in the service.

In 1909 when William Randolph Hearst, the late publisher, was running for the office of Mayor in New York, he hired a teenager from the Lower East Side named Gabriel Heatter to precede him at rallies as a boy orator, a fad at the time among evangelists and politicians. Hearst lost the election, but the young man worked for his paper, the *American,* and several others as a messenger and cub reporter until he made the grade as a full reporter. By the end of the First World War he had done well enough in the newspaper business to become the representative in Paris for several American papers.

By 1930, back in New York, his debates on Socialism with Norman Thomas, which were published in *The Nation,* had made him a name among his colleagues. The press if not the public was aware of Heatter.

Gabriel Heatter was propelled into national prominence when in 1936 he reported over the radio the electrocution of Bruno Richard Hauptmann, the kidnapper of the Lindbergh baby. Something went wrong with the apparatus that circulated the electricity into the electric chair in New Jersey's death house. Caught with no script, no preparation, and no warning, Heatter did an amazing 53-minute ad lib giving listeners across the nation the background of the crime, the trial, and the last-minute legal maneuvers. His colorful descriptions of the prison, death chamber, and atmosphere that prevailed that night held audiences spellbound until the execution was finally able to proceed.

This was at a time when radio was really beginning to come into its own as a news medium. The press considered it a bastard form of reporting and treated it with contempt when they mentioned it at all. The Heatter-Hauptmann scoop did not help make friends between the two media, nor did it endear him personally to the newspapers.

The events in Europe as the raging of Hitler sounded across the Atlantic made the public all the more anxious to get their news right away. Heatter, along with the many other reporters in radio news, emerged as a personal contact between Americans and history as it was being made. Heatter's extremely personal delivery made him seem like a family friend—one whose word was to be trusted, counted on, and waited for eagerly each day.

His salary was for a while as high as $3,500 weekly. His Monday through Friday 15-minute newscasts around the dinner hour were carried by a 450-station hookup over the Mutual Network. Although his folksy approach made him the brunt of many jokes during those years, his popularity was every bit as great as that of his contemporaries, Lowell Thomas and Graham McNamee. For special events such as political conventions and famous trials he was Mutual's man-on-the-spot. During his network days he also did remote broadcasts from a coal mine, the roof of a skyscraper, and an airplane in flight. Heatter's distinctive voice was also familiar to newsreel audiences during the late thirties and forties as he narrated the events of the day.

Gabriel Heatter at seventy years old gave up his network program when he moved to Miami Beach in 1960. For a while he kept busy with broadcasts heard in Florida over WIOD. Of late, however, his health is the cause for giving up broadcasting, and he is concentrating all of his efforts on getting well. Gabriel lives with his wife, Sadie, in Miami Beach. He lists his hobbies as "fishing, reading, and martinis."

On a new station, WIOD, these days in Miami Beach, Florida.

He was "Black Lightning" when he reached the 1936 Olympic Games in Berlin. *UPI*

JESSE OWENS

The man who is generally regarded as being the greatest Negro athlete of all time was born on an Alabama tenant farm in 1913. One of seven children, Jesse moved with his family to Cleveland when he was quite young. His real name is James Cleveland Owens, and after he took to calling himself "J.C." his schoolmates and family soon made it "Jesse."

In junior high school he established a new record by making the 100-yard dash in 10 seconds flat. At the 1933 National Interscholastic Championships at the University of Chicago everyone sat up and took notice when he made the 100 yards in 9.4 seconds, the 200 yards in 20.7 seconds, and a broad jump of 24 feet $9\frac{5}{8}$ inches.

During his freshman year at Ohio State University he worked as a gas station attendant until a Negro member of the Ohio Legislature had him put on as a page in the House of Representatives in the State's capitol.

He began earning names such as "Brown Bombshell" and "Buckeye Bullet" when in 1935 he broke three world records and tied for a fourth at the National Collegiate track and field Championships held at the University of Michigan. In what *The New York Times* has described as "the greatest day in the history of track" he made a 100-yard dash in 9.4 seconds, a 220-yard dash in 20.3 seconds, a 220-yard low hurdle in 22.6 seconds, and a broad jump of 25 feet 9 inches. He did it all on May 25, 1935.

"Owens was so matchless in sheer grace and speed," wrote Arthur Daley of the *Times* after observing the Negro at the 1936 Olympic Games, "that his like may never be seen again." Propaganda Minister Joseph Paul Goebbels, however, referred to him as "black American auxiliary." As though in defiance of Hitler's remarks before the games, about Aryan superiority, Owens established new world records: the 100-metre run ($10\frac{3}{10}$ seconds), the 200-metre run ($20\frac{7}{10}$ seconds), and the broad jump (25 feet $9\frac{27}{32}$ inches). He came away with four gold medals and the friendship of Lutz Long, the German athlete who finished second. Ignoring Hitler's remarks about the Negro race, Lutz walked across the field with his arm around Owens' shoulder in full view of the Führer.

In 1936 Owens received an A.B. degree from Ohio State and announced that he was going to become a performer, whereupon he joined Bill "Bojangles" Robinson in a tap dancing act. That same year he supported Alf Landon for the Presidency and bought his parents an 11-room house in Cleveland.

From 1937 to 1939 he appeared around the country with his own swing band, served as an official of the WPA, and won a sprint against a race horse in Havana. At the end of 1939 several of the businesses he owned had failed and he declared bankruptcy.

From 1940 to 1942 he was with the Office of Civilian Defense in Philadelphia. Then he was in charge of Negro personnel during the war at the Ford Motor Car Company in Detroit. After the war he sold sporting goods, and was part owner of an all-Negro baseball team. In 1950 a national poll of sportswriters named him "the world's top track performer since 1900." Jim Thorpe came in second. In 1955 he made a tour of India for the State Department, which was considered an enormous success. He also appeared in European capitals as an emcee during the Harlem Globetrotter exhibitions put on by the famous Negro basketball team.

Owens is not rich today, and says he has no desire to be so again. He is the proprietor of a public relations firm that specializes in promoting Negro products, and he is heard over a Chicago radio station as a disc jockey. He lives comfortably with his wife, to whom he has been married since 1931. They have three daughters. The athlete, who was the first American to jump over 20 feet, is a member of the Illinois Youth Commission, and has stated that it is his belief that if children of any race, any economic class, are keenly interested in sports they won't have the time or energy for delinquency.

In 1966 Owens paid a $3,000 fine to the Federal Government for evading $68,166 in income tax. He said he felt the court had been very fair, considering the offense carries with it a maximum of four years in prison and a $40,000 fine.

Army football coach Paul Dietzel gets an autograph at a recent convention of the NCAA in Chicago. *UPI*

In a publicity picture
for NBC Radio in 1935.

JESSICA DRAGONETTE

There is no popular singer either in television or movies today who could be compared with Jessica Dragonette. At her peak she was singing to 66,000,000 Americans weekly. She commanded a loyalty from her fans equal to that of the late Jeanette MacDonald. When she left NBC in the late thirties after a disagreement with her sponsors over the format of her programs, her admirers threatened to boycott not only the product but radio itself until she returned. She was quickly snapped up by the rival network, CBS.

Jessica was born in India and brought to this country at an early age. She was still a little girl when she was orphaned and put in the care of nuns at a convent. As the Angel Voice in the New York stage play *The Miracle* she attracted the enthusiastic praise of the great Russian opera singer Boris Chaliapin.

Truly a broadcasting pioneer, Miss Dragonette appeared on one of the first telecasts in history, February 5, 1928, which was designed to evaluate the new medium. She was among the array of stars heard on the first broadcast from the new NBC studios when they opened in Radio City on November 11, 1932. She has appeared on radio for Palmolive Soap, Pet Milk, Ford Motor Company, Cities Service, and others.

No radio star did more for the war effort during the forties than Jessica Dragonette. Her countless appearances at War Bond rallies and tours of bases and camps entertaining troops brought her the United States Treasury Silver Medal and Wings from both the Army and Navy. She holds the rank of honorary colonel in the United States Air Force.

Jessica's one appearance in a motion picture, *The Big Broadcast of 1936*, was a segment made at the Paramount Studios in New York.

Her career on the concert stage was extremely successful—150,000 people turned out to hear her in Chicago's Grant Park; and in Minneapolis, in spite of a blizzard and taxi strike, she drew 15,000 at one performance; at the Potomac Water Gate in Washington, D.C., an overflow crowd of 18,000 heard her; at New York's Lewisohn Stadium, she appeared with the Philharmonic Symphony Orchestra before an audience of 22,000.

Jessica wrote her autobiography in 1952, *Faith Is a Song*, in which she explained in great detail the misunderstanding between her and the National Broadcasting Company. Until its publication the details had been one of the most widely speculated-about events in radio.

Because of her refusal throughout her career to allow her personal life to be publicized she became known in the columns as "The Garbo of Radio." Coincidentally, she has maintained a long friendship with the mysterious Greta Garbo, who lives close by in Manhattan.

In 1952, for her promotion of Spanish music, the Spanish Ambassador to the United States presented her with the medal of the Knot of the Order of Isabella the Catholic. A devout Roman Catholic all her life, Miss Dragonette was invested as Lady of Grand Cross of the Equestrian Order of the Holy Sepulchre of Jerusalem and awarded the Pro Pontifice et Ecclesia Cross from the Vatican.

She is the wife of Nicolas Turner, a New York businessman. They live on Manhattan's East 57th Street just a few doors from two of her contemporaries, Lanny Ross and Lucy Monroe. Jessica's friends are as varied as was her repertoire. A few of the most prominent guests who attend her parties are: former President Harry Truman, William Buckley, Jr., Jack Benny, Lily Pons, and Bishop Fulton J. Sheen.

Although Jessica tells interviewers that she has never given up her singing career, her concerts are certainly unknown to her many fans who still have vivid memories of the lady who was at one time known as "The Jenny Lind of the Air."

As she looks today.

At the microphone for his call, with Russ Morgan, in a 1941 broadcast. *CBS Radio*

JOHNNY

Johnny Roventini, the world's most famous midget, was born of Italian immigrant parents who, like his brothers and sisters, are of normal size. The exact year, according to Johnny, is a "midgetary secret."

Johnny was working as a page boy in the Hotel New Yorker during the Depression when the President of Philip Morris and the advertising man, Milton Biow, sent him on a fool's errand through the hotel's lobby calling for a man named Philip Morris. No one took that call, but the Philip Morris Company took Johnny and made him into one of the world's few living trademarks.

Johnny's perfect B-flat "Call for Philip Morris" backed by Ferde Grofé's "Grand Canyon Suite" (the popular "On the Trail" portion) was first heard on radio on April 17, 1933. The program featured baritone Ronny Weeks. The opening to each Philip Morris program was "Johnny presents . . . ," as when Johnny presented "Great Moments from Great Plays," "The Philip Morris Frolics," and one of the great dramatic shows from radio's golden days, "The Philip Morris Playhouse." Throughout the years in magazines, newspapers, cigarette cartons, and on TV and radio Johnny became the most recognized and valuable advertising gimmick in the country.

By his own conservative estimate, he has shaken the hands of close to a million people during his years for Philip Morris.

During World War II Johnny volunteered for both the Navy and the Coast Guard, but was repeatedly rejected because of his size. He even invited the commander of one recruiting district aboard the EVA-R, his cruiser, to demonstrate his facility as a sailor.

Johnny's radio career, the medium he still misses, was during the era of the big bands. A few with whom he appeared are: Ray Bloch, Harry James, Johnny Green, Jerry Gray, Russ Morgan, and Leo Reisman.

Some of the radio and television programs on which Johnny appeared are: *Life With Lucy, This Is Your Life, The Rudy Vallee Show, Candid Microphone* (forerunner of *Candid Camera*), *The Philip Morris Playhouse, Break the Bank, Crime Doctor,* Walter Kiernan's *One Man's Opinion, The Kate Smith Show, It Pays to Be Ignorant,* and *Casey, Crime Photographer.*

Over the years he has done a great deal of traveling for his sponsor. Wherever he goes he is invariably asked to give his call, which he has learned to deliver in Spanish, French, German, Swedish, Italian, and Chinese.

Although the Philip Morris Company ceased using both Johnny's picture and presence in their advertising and promotions during the early fifties, he is still under lifetime contract to them, and appears around the country at company sales meetings, conventions, and parties.

Johnny has never married and lives in Brooklyn with his sister in a house full of furniture and clothes scaled down to suit his 50-inch height. Since signing with the cigarette company Johnny has grown over an inch, a common occurrence among adult midgets. His employers still carry a huge insurance policy on his life, and pay the salary of his brother who acts as chauffeur and bodyguard. The famous midget drives about in a Sunbeam Alpine, plays lots of golf, and pilots his own 26-foot cruiser in Sheepshead Bay, Brooklyn.

Although he never appears in public without his little bellboy's uniform, Johnny has been caught off duty smoking a brand of cigarettes other than Philip Morris—his close friends will tell you he favors Marlboro (a Philip Morris product).

In a recent visit to his sponsor's office on Park Avenue. *Edward Oleksak*

In 1943, weighing in on opening day at Belmont Park. *UPI*

EDDIE ARCARO

Horse racing's richest, most famous jockey was born in Cincinnati, Ohio, in 1916. He left school after the ninth grade and has been racing horses ever since.

The expression "riding a winner" can be reversed to describe the career of Eddie Arcaro—more often than not it was a case of a horse being ridden by a winner. His incredible skill on the track with horses not ordinarily expected to come into the money decreased the track odds on whatever animal he rode.

His ability and luck began to show at seventeen, when he won on a gelding named No More at Washington Park in Chicago in 1935, and two years later in his first Kentucky Derby he came in fourth on the Calumet Farms horse Nellie Flag.

Although Arcaro has been six times a top money winner of the year, he was never counted among those jockeys with the most victories because he was always discriminating about what he rode and where rather than with how many. A glance at his record indicates his good judgment:

KENTUCKY DERBY (Churchill Downs)

Year	Horse	Purse
1938	Lawrin	$47,050
1941	Whirlaway	61,275
1945	Hoop, Jr.	64,850
1948	Citation	83,400
1952	Hill Gail	96,300

BELMONT STAKES (Belmont Park)

Year	Horse	Purse
1941	Whirlaway	39,770
1942	Shut Out	44,520
1945	Pavot	52,675
1948	Citation	77,700
1952	One Count	82,400
1955	Nashua	83,700

PREAKNESS STAKES (Pimlico)

1941	Whirlaway	49,365
1948	Citation	91,870
1950	Hill Prince	56,110
1951	Bold	83,100
1955	Nashua	67,550
1957	Bold Ruler	65,250

Arcaro, Johnny Longden, and Sir Gordon Richards are the only three jockeys ever to ride over 4,000 winners. He is twice winner of racing's Triple Crown (Kentucky Derby, Preakness, and the Belmont Stakes), in 1941 on Whirlaway and in 1948 on Citation. In 1955, on Nashua, he lost to Swaps by a length and a half in the Kentucky Derby, but in a special match race later for $100,000 he won by six and a half lengths.

Arcaro has ridden and won for stakes well over $23,000,000 during his career, which ended in 1961 with his retirement. In most cases his share was a flat 10 percent.

Although the lack of a formal education is apparent in his poor grammar, Eddie must have been very good in the arithmetic class. He is a multimillionaire from his track earnings and his shrewd business sense with investments. With the exception of stock market and oil speculation his money has been kept in and around racing, which he dearly loves. He has a share in a saddlery business which sells equipment to racing people all over the country, and spends most of his time at the Manhattan offices of his Livestock and Casualty Insurance Company, which provides coverage for every possible facet of the racing business. A top winner of stakes for 11 years, he is the author of *I Ride to Win*.

Arcaro lives in Garden City, Long Island, with his wife and two children, not far from another great jockey of yesteryear, Earl Sande, who resides in Munsey Park, Long Island. (Another legend of the racetrack, Ted Atkinson, is a State Steward at Arlington Park in Illinois.) When Eddie is not attending most of the major races around the country, he fits in some golf.

Now a businessman. *Millie Cole*

In 1926 she had youth, integrity, and the kind of pluck that America loves in its idols.

GERTRUDE EDERLE

The first woman to swim the English Channel was the daughter of a German emigrant who ran a delicatessen on Amsterdam Avenue in Manhattan. When Trudy, as she usually is called, first became interested in swimming her father told her that if she did well he would give her permission to bob her hair.

Miss Ederle was a product of the famed Women's Swimming Association, which has produced such champions as Eleanor Holm (an interior decorator now in Miami Beach, Florida) and Esther Williams (living in retirement in Los Angeles). She joined the club when she was thirteen years old—five years before conquering the Channel—and set about to break and establish more amateur records than any woman in the world.

Her first attempt at the Channel was financed by the W.S.A. in 1925. It was a valiant try, but she finally admitted defeat.

When she returned to Cap Gris Nez in France for her next attempt it was with a contract from both the New York *Daily News* and Chicago *Tribune,* paying her expenses, a modest salary, and bonus in exchange for exclusive rights to her personal story, plus the jump on every other newspaper in the country.

Among the party aboard the boat alongside Gertrude on August 6, 1926, were Westbrook Pegler and his wife, Julie Harpman, Westbrook "ghosting" the swimmer's account of her experience for the *Tribune.*

By the twelfth hour the sea had become so troubled by unfavorable winds that her trainer, Thomas Burgess, shouted to her, "Gertie, you must come out!" The exhausted girl lifted her head from the choppy waters and asked, "What for?"

Only five men had been able to swim it before. The best time had been 16 hours, 33 minutes by the Argentinian, Enrique Tiraboschi. Gertrude walked up the beach at Dover, England, after 14 hours and 31 minutes. The first person to greet her was an English immigration officer who asked the bleary-eyed, waterlogged teenager for her passport.

Instead of immediately returning to this country she visited her grandmother in Germany's Black Forest, for nearly three weeks. By the time she came back another woman, Mrs. Mille Gade Corson, had swum the Channel, although it took her an hour longer.

In addition to a few endorsements and an appearance in a Bebe Daniels movie, *Swim, Girl, Swim* (1927), Gertrude toured vaudeville in a swimming act for two years.

To understand why Miss Ederle was the idol she was at the time it is necessary to remember that the period was the Roaring Twenties. Everything was exaggerated. She was the first and the fastest, but she was also simple, unassuming, loyal, and very likable. Add to this the reports in the United States press that both England and France had been against her effort, hoping that one of their countrywomen might do it first, and you have the ingredients that turned New York City into a madhouse when Grover Whalen and Jimmy Walker escorted her during a ticker tape parade not to be equaled until Lindbergh came back in 1927.

Captain Patterson, publisher of the *Daily News,* gave her a red Buick Roadster as an added bonus. Most of the money she received was turned over to the Women's Swimming Association, which had given her the chance in the first place.

She was engaged once but has never married. After a nervous breakdown in the early thirties she suffered from an accident in 1933 which put her in a cast for over four years. In 1939 she made a comeback at the New York World's Fair when she appeared in Billy Rose's Aquacade.

In retrospect, Gertrude Ederle seems an even more exceptional personality than she was thought during the time of the parades and banquets. She had to give up the athlete's cherished amateur standing in order even to attempt what she did. Although with the proper management she could have been very rich, she has never uttered a word of bitterness about her financial circumstances. Her head was so buffeted about by the large waves that day in 1926 that her hearing was permanently impaired. Instead of asking for sympathy she has employed empathy by spending a great deal of time over the years teaching deaf youngsters to swim.

Trudy shuns publicity. She shares a house in Flushing, Queens, with an old friend.

Conducting one of her Saturday morning swimming classes at the Women's Swimming Association in Manhattan. *Wide World*

The Astaires appearing together on Broadway in *Apple Blossoms*, 1919.

ADELE ASTAIRE

The famous dancer was born Adele Austerlitz in 1899 in Omaha, Nebraska. Her father was a brewer, and her mother was determined to see that her daughter—and son Fred—would become stars in the theatre. At the age of three Adele was enrolled in a dancing school in Omaha, and when she was eight both brother and sister were brought by their mother to New York, where they studied with Ned Wayburn and at the Metropolitan Ballet School.

From 1906 until 1916 Fred and Adele toured the United States with the Orpheum and Keith vaudeville circuits. When not booked for an engagement they attended school in Weehawken, New Jersey.

The Astaires made their Broadway debut in the show *Over the Top* in 1917, and took it on tour. *The Passing Show of 1918* was their first big success, and they played in it both on Broadway and on the road. Their co-stars were Charles Ruggles, the late Frank Fay, and Nita Naldi. After that their names were on Broadway marquees every season.

John Charles Thomas the singer was with them in *Apple Blossoms* (1919), Adele playing Molly, and again in *Love Letter* (1921) when Adele played the role of Aline Moray.

In 1922 Fred and Adele sang and danced in two shows, *For Goodness Sake* and *Bunch and Judy*. The former became the vehicle for their London debut in 1923, although the title was changed in England to *Stop Flirting*. They became instant favorites in Britain.

In 1924 the team did George Gershwin's *Lady Be Good* with an assist from the late Cliff Edwards. It was an enormous hit in New York as well as in London, where they played in it in 1926.

In 1930 they were seen in *Smiles*. The next season, 1931, was to include the last musical the Astaires ever did together and the last Broadway ever saw of Adele. The show was *The Bandwagon*, and despite a Depression year it did well at the box office.

One of their most successful shows was another one which Gershwin wrote especially for them, *Funny Face* which they did on Broadway in 1927 and in London in 1928. Adele made up her mind that when she left show business it would be after a solid hit. She met Lord Charles Cavendish and promised to marry him, provided *The Bandwagon* was equally successful in London. (It was a smash, they were married in 1932.)

Unlike a lot of actresses, Adele meant it when she said good-bye to the boards. Composers, producers, and her brother begged her on various occasions to do just one more but she has never relented. When Fred tried working with another partner, Claire Luce (who is now teaching theatre in New York), one critic wrote that he seemed to sense him looking off into the wings, wondering when Adele would enter.

Each of Adele's three children by Lord Charles died shortly after birth. After her husband's death in 1944 she moved back to New York where she met and married a Wall Street investment broker, Kingman Douglass.

Mrs. Douglass divides her time among her homes in Middleburg, Virginia; on Manhattan's East 57th Street; and on the lush beaches of Jamaica. She is very social, very rich, and very uncommunicative to interviewers.

Accepting an award given to them by *Dance Magazine* recently. *Dance Magazine*

In 1934, at the height of her fame.

RUBY KEELER

The musical star, born in Nova Scotia and moving to New York at age three with her family, went into show business as a dancer in speakeasies during the Roaring Twenties because it was the only profession that permitted high school girls to work nights. The money she received came in very handy at home where her mother had a houseful of children to care for.

She was in the chorus at Texas Guinan's El Fey Club when she caught the eye of a man who was at that time the biggest name on Broadway, Al Jolson. She became Mrs. Jolson in 1928. Jolson helped place Ruby in the Great Ziegfeld's *Show Girl* (1929). Every night she would do a tap dance onstage while Jolson strolled down the aisle of the theatre to a front row seat singing the song "Liza." Jolson received no billing and no money. It was the one and only time he ever worked for Flo Ziegfeld.

Jolson and Ruby were married in New York, and came to Hollywood in the early thirties when nearly all of the films being made were taking advantage of the new sound systems by adding songs.

Ruby was an unknown to movie audiences when Warner Brothers took a chance on her by giving her the lead in the 1933 film *42nd Street*. It was one of the most successful pictures that studio ever made and is today considered the classic musical of the 1930's. Her costar was a young man not much better known than Ruby, Dick Powell. Ruby and Dick costarred in a series of singing and dancing films such as *Dames* (1934), and *Shipmates Forever* (1935). Also in 1935 she and Al Jolson appeared together in a picture about backstage life called *Go Into Your Dance*.

76

Altogether Ruby Keeler made nine films, her last, *Sweetheart of the Campus* (1941), before she retired in 1941. She and Al Jolson had been divorced a year before she gave up movies, remaining in California, and was not heard from until *The Jolson Story* appeared. Ruby was awarded custody of their adopted son, Al, Jr.

When Columbia Pictures decided to make *The Jolson Story* (1947) they offered her a goodly sum of money for the use of her name. She refused to grant permission, and when the picture was made Mrs. Jolson, played by Evelyn Keyes, was given a fictitious name. (Evelyn is married to Artie Shaw.)

In 1966 when tributes to Busby Berkeley, her former director, were held in nine cities throughout South and North America and Europe, Ruby toured and appeared with her old friend. As the director's works were screened she stood in the back of one of the theatres and shook her head. "It's really amazing. I couldn't act. I had that terrible singing voice, and now I can see I wasn't the greatest tap dancer in the world, either."

All of what Miss Keeler said may be true, but she had a quality during those bleak Depression years that people could identify with. Her parts, those of a kid trying to get a break on Broadway, were so close to her own story that it didn't matter how she read the lines because she felt them, and the audiences were rooting for her to make good.

For more than twenty years Ruby Keeler has been the wife of John Lowe, a prominent Southern California land developer. They live with their four teenage children near the Pacific Ocean in Newport Beach, California. (Two of their neighbors are Cass Daley and Evelyn Ankers.) She is well known as one of the best lady golfers in those parts.

At a recent public appearance with her former director, Busby Berkeley. *Paul Cordes—Gallery of Modern Art*

In 1938, the year of his "grand slam."

DONALD BUDGE

Donald Budge at eighteen years of age won his native state's (California's) Junior Championship in 1933 and made the Davis Cup team two years later. By 1937 the boy whose older brother had to coax him away from football onto the tennis courts played 12 championship matches and won every one of them: his Davis Cup matches against Germany, Japan, Australia, and England (doubles with Gene Mako), plus the United States, Australian, and Wimbledon singles.

His 1937 game against Germany's champion, Baron von Cramm, is still talked about among tennis buffs as one of the most incredible exhibits of the game ever staged. The match was also the occasion for an international incident in the world of sports. The loser was imprisoned by Hitler's government upon his return on a morals charge which many thought was nothing more than punishment by the Nazi government. Had Von Cramm won that year the coveted Davis Cup would have gone to Germany for the first time in history. As a protest Budge refused an invitation to play in Germany the following year.

Of all Budge's many awards the one he prizes most is the James E. Sullivan Memorial Trophy for the Most Outstanding Amateur Athlete of 1937.

In 1938 he created a record that has never been equaled. He won the Australian, French, Wimbledon, and United States (Forest Hills) singles championships, which in the world of tennis is a "grand slam."

His partner for the mixed doubles at Wimbledon in the games of 1937 and 1938 was Alice Marble, now secretary to a doctor in Tarzana, California.

A story widely circulated and never denied concerns Budge during his first trip to Wimbledon. It is the custom of the Queen to arrive a bit late for the games. Queen Elizabeth, wife of George VI, was regally tardy, and Budge and his opponent had their game interrupted by her entrance. It is the custom for the players to wait until Her Majesty is seated, bowing toward the Royal box before resuming their game. Don, instead, lifted his racket in a salute and yelled, "Hi, Queen!"

Donald's first professional match was held in Madison Square Garden on January 3, 1939, and 16,000 fans filled the auditorium. Thereafter he toured the country for a number of years as the top draw in his field.

Through the years Donald has been involved in a number of business ventures. From 1941 until 1965 he was a partner with Sidney Wood in the Budge-Wood laundries in the Bronx. He now divides his year in thirds: in the summer he is in charge at the Chatham Hall School, one of the oldest and finest boys' schools in Virginia; in the fall and spring he commutes between the Racquet Club in Montego Bay, Jamaica, and the Peach Tree Bath and Tennis Club in Atlanta, Georgia. The remaining months he reserves for a vacation to be taken wherever he pleases.

Budge has remained active in his game, and his two books *On Tennis* and *How Lawn Tennis Is Played* are still basic for any serious participant.

In a recent visit to New York.
Bachrach

Fifteen-year-old Beverly, shortly after Errol Flynn's death in 1959.

BEVERLY AADLAND

Who could ever forget that real-life Lolita, Beverly Aadland.

She was a fifteen-year-old dancer when the late Errol Flynn met her. Together they made a dreadful movie called *Cuban Rebel Girl,* a lot of vulgar headlines, and according to Beverly, beautiful love. Her mother, the late Flo Aadland, told about it in the opening passage of her book *The Big Love:* "I want the world to know that my baby was a virgin when she met Errol Flynn."

For all the jokes about her at the time and since, Beverly must have had something. She was far from being a great beauty. In fact she is more attractive now than at the time of her fame. Yet Flynn, who never lacked for female companionship, and Beverly remained together until his death in 1959.

In 1960, after a series of unfortunate incidents in the Aadland household, Beverly, still a minor, was taken away from her mother by court order, and custody was given to the wife of a Pasadena, California, minister. At first Beverly did not take to the comparatively quiet atmosphere, but by the time she left the family at eighteen years of age they had become and still are close friends. In 1964, when she was nearly killed in an automobile wreck, her former guardian was the first to lend a helping hand. In 1965, when Mrs. Aadland died, it was the minister's wife that Beverly leaned on.

During the early sixties Beverly finally evaded the press which had dogged her every footstep. She left Southern California, where she was born and raised, and married and divorced a young architect with practically no fanfare.

In 1966 a New York daily reported Miss Aadland to be a stripper on the burlesque circuit. A simple phone call to her agent would have disclosed that Beverly was at that very moment playing a club date in the Midwest. She is and has been a singer in supper clubs for several years, playing such smart bistros as The Living Room in Manhattan.

Beverly has lost a lot of the defensiveness that she displayed at the height of her notoriety. She is quite courteous to interviewers, and answers questions about Flynn willingly. In reply to a query about the difference in their ages she replied recently, "At the time I was all over the front pages I really believed there was something very unusual about it. After he was gone and I got a good look at life up close I wonder what all the excitement was about. Younger girls and older men fall in love every day. Nobody says anything about it, and it certainly doesn't get into the papers—unless one of the two parties happens to be a movie star. One of these days somebody in a city room of a newspaper is going to get wind of a woman who happens to like a younger fellow, and two more people are going to be crucified."

Miss Aadland admits to several suicide attempts and periods of horrible depression when she was at the zenith of her fame, but seems to have come through it all with more than a usual amount of self-confidence for a girl in her early twenties.

Asked about her ambitions she says, "I think I'd like to own my own club. I like to entertain, and get along pretty well with the general public."

For over two years Beverly has been living in Springfield, Massachusetts. Why? She likes the town, and the newspapers are friendly. Before they print something they check it out with her for accuracy. But for an unmarried girl to settle in a comparatively small town seems unlikely. "What's swinging there? What do you do?" old friends ask her. "I learned to cook and I love it. Besides, at my house Springfield does swing," is Beverly's reply.

Now a chanteuse, she has blossomed into a beautiful woman.

In 1922 at a time when she was one of the reigning queens of the silent screen.

BLANCHE SWEET

Blanche Sweet was the name given, quite aptly, to a beautiful child born in 1895. "B. Sweet," as she signs her checks, was to become one of the earliest and greatest of silent stars.

Miss Sweet was a protégée of the great director D. W. Griffith, and was with him from 1909 on at the Biograph Studios on Manhattan's 14th Street. Until 1913 when she starred in the four-reeler *Judith of Bethulia* she appeared in shorter photoplays such as *Smile of a Child* (1911) and *Eternal Mother* (1912). Mae Marsh and the Gish sisters, always thought of as very early players in silents, had only small roles in *Judith of Bethulia* in support of Miss Sweet.

Her screen image was less delicate than those of most of her contemporaries. In a number of her early pictures such as *Goddess of Sagebrush Gulch, Fighting Blood,* and *The Last Drop of Water* she was the Pioneer Woman. When all the others had dropped by the wayside, Blanche was still whipping the oxen. Her most famous film of this type was *The Lonedale Operator* (1911).

In 1922 she married Marshall "Mickey" Neilan, director of such milestones as *Rebecca of Sunnybrook Farm* (1917) with Mary Pickford and *Tess of the D'Ubervilles* (1923), one of Miss Sweet's best remembered efforts. She and Neilan were divorced in 1929.

Her competition in *In the Palace of the King* (1923) was the original "It" girl, Aileen Pringle, now living in retirement in Manhattan. She costarred with Neil Hamilton (now playing the Chief of Police on TV's *Bat Man* series) in *Diplomacy* (1926). Ben Lyon was her leading man in *Bluebeard's Seven Wives* (1926).

Blanche Sweet made only three talkies, all in 1930. In *Woman Racket,* which Jean Harlow's husband Paul Bern directed, she not only spoke on the screen but sang as well. *Show Girl in Hollywood* gave her another chance to sing, but neither picture clicked with the fans. Her last appearance in movies was a minor role in Rex Beach's *The Silver Horde.*

After her failure in talkies Blanche became a vaudeville entertainer and achieved considerable success. She toured the United States in the early thirties with an act called *Sweet and Lovely.* For both the Fanchon Marco and Orpheum circuits she was a good draw with songs, comedy skits, and a scene from one of her most popular silents, *Anna Christie.*

Her last husband was Raymond Hackett, whom she met on the Metro-Goldwyn-Mayer lot several years before they were both offered parts in the road company of the play *The Party's Over* in 1935. She admits that the main reason she took the part was to get to know the handsome young man better. In 1936 they were married and lived together until he died in California in 1963. Throughout the thirties the husband and wife team did road shows of plays which had been hits on Broadway. Hackett, who had the advantage of stage experience, was of great help to cinema-oriented Blanche.

She and Hackett had been living quietly in retirement in Los Angeles for over twenty years. Upon his passing she moved back to the East where she was born and got her start in pictures.

Blanche Sweet lives in an apartment on Lexington Avenue within walking distance of where the famous Biograph Studios once stood. NBC Television recently did a documentary on those days, and Blanche appeared as the narrator. She would like to work a bit, but only if she really feels the part suits her. She has refused many offers for her autobiography, which she maintains she will never write.

In a recent television appearance.
NBC

Both in and out of character in 1941. "Lum" (Chester Lauck) on left and "Abner" (Norris Goff) on right.

LUM 'N' ABNER

In 1930 a bank clerk by the name of Chester Lauck quit his job and joined up with his lifelong friend, Norris Goff, who in turn left his job in the wholesale grocery business, to form a comedy team for a radio station in Hot Springs, Arkansas. Their original idea was to do a black-face act, but the director convinced them that since the success of "Amos 'n' Andy" there had been too many imitators. On April 26, 1931, the characters "Lum 'n' Abner" were born. In the twenty-three years that followed on radio there was not a single letter of complaint.

Their success at playing two small-town bachelor hicks was immediate. Within months they were signed by NBC. The show became so popular that it was broadcast over NBC's Red and Blue networks simultaneously. Their first sponsor was Quaker Oats, followed over the years by the Ford Motor Company, Horlick's Malted Milk, and Frigidaire.

"Lum" was played by Chester Lauck and "Abner" by Norris Goff, but they also played many of the other colorful bumpkin characters they used on the show. They made the mythical town of Pine Ridge, Arkansas, so famous that a little town in that state went to the trouble of getting an act of Congress to change its name to capitalize on the publicity.

Chester and Norris were born and raised in Mena, Arkansas, and knew their country people well. Rather than being annoyed by the ribbing given them by the pair, it was shown that the biggest audiences the shows had were in rural areas, where there are still "Jot 'em Down" general stores in many small towns. They got the name for their establishment after running a national contest in the thirties.

"Lum 'n' Abner" had more than a leisurely pace and folksy humor. In a 1948 review *Variety* said of the team who did their own scripts: "Some of the cracks would have done credit to the writing stables of higher-rated comics." Although the programs never had high ratings, the sponsors were kept happy with the sales results from the low-keyed and well-integrated commercials. The comics' mail averaged 15,000 letters a week and went as high as 23,000.

Some of the performers who were regulars on the series were Zasu Pitts, Andy Devine, and a character actor who wasn't as well known then by the name of Cliff Arquette, "Charlie Weaver."

In 1939 they began making movies, such as *Dreaming Out Loud* (1940), *Bashful Bachelors* (1942), and *Two Weeks to Live* (1943). As an example of their popularity, *Bashful Bachelors* cost $165,000 to produce and grossed $675,000 in one year on domestic release alone. Throughout their career in movies they had to wear heavy makeup which required two and a half hours of preparation each morning before they came on the set. Says Abner, "We have grown into our parts."

In 1954, just about the time that most of radio's big names were making the switch to television, Norris "Abner" Goff was told that he had to have an operation because of a cancer. Abner had wanted to retire anyway, and this was a perfect time to do so. Although the operation was a success, and he has been in good health since then, he has been reported dead by the press four times. He is visited several times a year by his friend and former partner at his home right on the green at the Indian Wells Golf Club in Palm Desert, California.

When Abner called it quits Lum decided to go into the oil business. He is the Executive Assistant to the Chairman of the Board of the Continental Oil Company in Houston, Texas, and is on the road a good deal of the time doing public relations work for the firm. His handshaking and after-dinner speaking have taken him over one and a half million miles since going into the business.

To queries about missing show business Lum says, "I feel like I'm still in it with the traveling and applause. And then, radio has changed so much there seems to be no place for shows like ours. Abner said when we went off the air that he was 'awful fer behind in my sittin',' and that's the business he's in right now—sittin' and lots of it. He never really enjoyed it the way I did, anyway, so I guess things worked out pretty well for both of us."

"Lum" Chester Lauck today.

LARRY PARKS

The Al Jolson impersonator, whose real name is Samuel Klausman, was born in Olathe, Kansas, in 1914. After receiving a B.S. from the University of Illinois he came to New York City where he ushered at Carnegie Hall and was a guide at Radio City.

Larry worked in stock companies in the mid-thirties and finally got a role in the 1937 Broadway production of *Golden Boy*. After several more years of stock and small parts he turned up in Hollywood in 1941.

Few actors worked more than Parks in the early forties, and it would be hard to find anyone who made worse films. A few of the clinkers Columbia Pictures put him in during that period are: *Mystery Ship* (1941) with Lola Lane (owner of a real estate business in Pacific Palisades, California), *Honolulu Lu* (1941), *You Belong to Me* (1941) a Barbara Stanwyck-Henry Fonda starrer, *Sing for Your Supper* (1941), *Blondie Goes to College* (1942) with Arthur Lake (married to the niece of Marion Davies and living in a huge home in Santa Monica, California), *Hello, Annapolis* (1942) which starred Tom Brown (who turns up from time to time on TV and lives in Sherman Oaks, California), *You Were Never Lovelier* (1942) a Rita Hayworth and Fred Astaire picture, *Boogie Man Will Get You* (1942), *Black Parachute* (1944), *Sergeant Mike* (1944), *Racket Man* (1944) with Tom Neal (serving a manslaughter sentence in a California prison for the death of his wife), and *Counter-Attack* (1945). In some years he made as many as a dozen pictures.

Then in 1946 something happened to Parks that usually happens only in the plot of a picture. Columbia gave him the role of Al Jolson in *The Jolson Story*. The songs were dubbed by Jolson himself, but the rest was all Larry Parks. He had survived a score of B pictures to become overnight one of the hottest leading men in the business. The Academy of Motion Pictures Arts and Sciences nominated him for the Best Actor of the Year. The film created box office records that still hold in some cities.

Columbia quickly put him into *Down to Earth* (1947) with Rita Hayworth and *The Swordsman* (1948). Metro-Goldwyn-Mayer wanted to borrow him for a picture with Elizabeth Taylor, but had to wait until he completed the sequel, *Jolson Sings Again* (1950).

In 1951 the House Un-American Activities Committee descended upon Hollywood. The very first witness called before that body was Larry Parks. Before he could even be asked the big question, the actor volunteered the information that he had been a member of the Communist party in the early forties and pointed out that he had left the party some years before. "The only loyalty I know is to America," he said in an emotional examination. After begging the Committee not to make him name names of fellow Hollywoodites the hearings were closed to the public. After his testimony in closed session a spokesman for H.U.A.C. said that Parks had "come through in fine style." The word around town was that he had given at least a dozen names of film personalities.

While the uproar over the affair continued, other stars, Lucille Ball, for one, paraded before the Committee and admitted party membership in the past. It was Parks, however, who made the headlines, and Columbia looked frantically for a loophole in his contract, which was canceled shortly thereafter. M-G-M released *Love Is Better Than Ever* (1951) which starred him with Elizabeth Taylor, but with little enthusiasm. John Wayne, one of filmdom's strongest supporters of H.U.A.C., asked that Hollywood forgive Larry his mistake and remember that he had been man enough to tell the truth.

Larry Parks was never blacklisted as were some 300 others, such as Alvah Bessie (recently living in San Francisco and working as a lighting director at a nightclub) or Karen Morley (residing in Los Angeles and still without work). He was more of an embarrassment to the industry—he couldn't be a *cause célèbre* because he had cooperated, and the right wing wasn't altogether happy with him, either.

Larry appeared on TV in plays in 1953, 1956, and 1958 and played on Broadway for a short time in 1957 with his wife in *The Bells Are Ringing*. Of the play, *Variety* said he was "more skillful as both singer and hoofer" than Sydney Chaplin, for whom he was substituting. He did two Broadway shows, one in 1960 and one in 1963, but both flopped. He was in John Huston's *Freud* (1962) in a prominent role, but the film was not a commercial success. His last engagement was a road tour of the play *Any Wednesday* in 1965.

Parks has been married to Betty Garrett, also of stage and films, since 1944. They live in the Nichols Canyon section of Hollywood with their two sons.

The Jolson Story, one of the hottest properties in movies, and in *Freud* (*right*), a rare appearance. *Universal Pictures*

A Universal Pictures contract player in 1937.

ELLA LOGAN

When she was three years old Ella Logan, the girl who introduced "How Are Things in Gloccamorra?" in the show *Finian's Rainbow,* walked onto the stage of the Grand Theatre in Paisley, Scotland, and made her debut singing "A Perfect Day." Ella (her real name is Ella Allan, born in 1913 in Scotland) stopped that show and has been stopping others ever since.

After a series of music hall tours in Great Britain, Ella came to London in 1928 in the show *Darling, I Love You,* and in 1931 and 1932 she appeared in vaudeville in Holland and Germany.

It was in 1934 that she made her Broadway debut, appearing in *Calling All Stars* with Judy Canova and Gertrude Niesen and two years later made her first motion picture, *Flying Hostess.* The following year she made *Woman Chases Man* with Miriam Hopkins and Joel McCrea, *Top of the Town* with the future California Senator George Murphy, and *52nd Street* with Kenny Baker, now retired in Solvang, a Danish community in California, and in 1938 was in the all-star *Goldwyn Follies.* One of her costars was the beautiful Vera Zorina who is married to the head of Columbia Records, Goddard Lieberson.

Ella returned to New York and musical comedy in the *George White Scandals of 1939,* the last of producer White's famous shows, and in its cast were Ben Blue and Ann Miller.

Throughout the late thirties and into the forties Miss Logan was a popular guest vocalist on some of the top radio shows of the day. In 1940 she was one of the featured performers in the summer replacement program for the *Eddie Cantor Show* on CBS. With her were Igor Gorin and Jacques Renard and his orchestra.

In 1941, she was with the late Carmen Miranda in the Olsen and Johnson show *Son o' Fun* and in 1942 in *Show Time* with Jack Haley, the De Marcos, George Jessel, and Kitty Carlisle.

In 1944, 1945, and 1946 Ella toured Africa, Italy, and other parts of Europe, entertaining Allied troops. When she returned to the United States in 1947 it was to play in what proved to be the highlight of her career, the part of Sharon McLonergan in the smash hit *Finian's Rainbow*. The show ran for over 500 performances, and introduced such standards as "Old Devil Moon," "Look to the Rainbow," "When I'm Not Near the Girl I Love," and, of course, the song that has been associated with Ella ever since, "How Are Things in Gloccamorra?" For reasons she has never adequately explained, Ella Logan has not been seen on Broadway since.

In 1956 Ella divorced Fred Finklehoff, writer and producer of plays—with a personal fortune of several million—after four years of marriage.

Since leaving Broadway Ella has appeared in the title role of a show called *Maggie* on the strawhat circuit, and at such nightclubs as the Monsignor, Piccadilly, and Ambassadors in London as well as Ciro's and Scheherezade in Paris. She has also done an occasional television show for Ed Sullivan and Jack Paar.

Recently Miss Logan accepted a part in the musical *Kelly*, produced by David Susskind. The show received a great deal of fanfare, costing its backers just short of $750,000. The day after it opened in New York the critic for *The New York Times* began his review by congratulating Ella Logan for having the good sense to step out of this production before it reached Broadway. It closed after one performance.

Ella Logan maintains a house in Mandeville Canyon in Los Angeles and an apartment in New York City.

In a New York restaurant recently.
John Virzi

In 1925.

CHESTER CONKLIN

One of the silent screen's all-time great funnymen, Chester was born in Oskaloosa, Iowa, on January 11, 1886. Before becoming a clown with the Barnum Circus he traveled the country for a while as part of a stock company.

Chester found his way into pictures in 1913 and appeared in most of the Chaplin one-reelers made in 1914. Two classics from that period are: *Face on the Bar Room Floor* and *Between Showers*.

In 1915 he became a Keystone Cop, with such beauties as Gloria Swanson, Mable Normand, and Marie Prevost as foils for his nonsense, and continued working for Mack Sennett for four years.

Although he worked steadily through the twenties and into the thirties, Conklin's days of glory ended when he left Sennett, though he did appear in such silents as *Greed* (1923) the Erich von Stroheim masterpiece, *A Woman of the World* (1925) with Pola Negri, *Sybil* (1926) with Constance Talmadge, and *Rubber Heels* (1927) with Ed Wynn.

Conklin, who made as much as $3,500 a week at the peak of his career, lost everything in the stock market crash of 1929. In 1933 Chester and Minnie V. Conklin, his wife of 19 years, were divorced.

His sound films include: *The Virginian* (1929), *Swing High* (1930) with Helen Twelvetrees (who committed suicide in 1958), *Her Majesty Love* (1931) with Marilyn Miller and W. C. Fields, *Call of the Prairie* (1936) with William Boyd, *Hollywood Boulevard* (1936) in which he played himself, *Modern Times* (1936) with his old friend Charlie Chaplin, *Every Day's a Holiday* (1938) which starred Mae West, *Cinema Circus* (1939) a two-reeler for MGM with Lee Tracy, *Hollywood Cavalcade* (1939) with Don Ameche (now a resident of Phoenix, Arizona), *The Great Dictator* (1940) another Charlie Chaplin feature, *Hail the Conquering Hero* (1944) with Ella Raines (now Mrs. Robin Olds of Washington, D.C.), *Goodnight, Sweetheart* (1944) with Ruth Terry (now Mrs. Gilmour of North Hollywood, California), *Sunday Dinner for a Soldier* (1944) with the late John Hodiak, *Knickerbocker Holiday* (1944) with Nelson Eddy, *The Perils of Pauline* (1947), *The Beautiful Blonde from Bashful Bend* (1949), and *Jiggs and Maggie in Jackpot Jitters* (1949).

In 1954 newspapers throughout the country carried a sad feature article datelined Los Angeles. Chester Conklin, who had found acting jobs in movies hard to come by, was playing Santa Claus at J. W. Robinson's Department Store. The aging comic took the notoriety very well and told the reporters that he liked acting and kids, and that with this job he had lots of both. He did, however, appear in *Li'l Abner* in 1960.

In 1961 Chester checked into the Motion Picture Country Hospital with every intention of staying for the remainder of his life. He was not feeling well and was a little depressed over his lack of activity during the past years. The Hollywood community was advised accordingly by the trade press, confirming that one of the truly great comedians of their industry had retired.

Then in 1965 filmdom learned that the seventy-nine-year-old veteran was marrying June Gunther, whom he met in the hospital, and that the newlyweds would be moving to their own home in Van Nuys, California.

The Conklins live in a cottage complete with rose garden, which Chester tends faithfully. He says that he feels fine again and to prove it turned up in a small role recently in the Henry Fonda-Joanne Woodward starrer *A Big Hand for the Little Lady*.

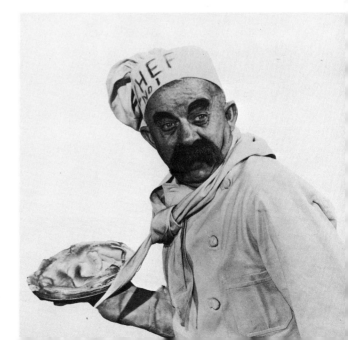

A recent shot—not much change over nearly a half century.

Beside *Lizzy* in 1938.

DOUGLAS "WRONG WAY" CORRIGAN

The Atlantic Ocean had been crossed many times between Lindbergh's flight in 1927 and Corrigan's in 1938. All kinds of men in all kinds of planes had made the trip, but never—before or since—"by mistake."

Corrigan was a thirty-one-year-old mechanic who had been working at the Northrop Corporation aircraft works in Inglewood, California. Six years before he had bought a 1929 Curtis-Robin monoplane at an auction for $900. In 1937 he applied for permission to make a solo flight across the Atlantic, but after inspecting his plane the Bureau of Air Commerce had turned him down, advising him that they disapproved of suicide. The ship had no safety devices, no radio, and no beam finders. He had loaded it with so many extra gas tanks to carry the 320 gallons of gas and 16 gallons of oil, that he had to look out the side windows in order to see in front of him.

In mid-July, 1938, Douglas Corrigan flew from Los Angeles to Floyd Bennett Field in New York in 27 hours, but the feat went unnoticed in the wake of Howard Hughes's three-day trip around the world, which climaxed at the same time.

At dawn the next morning Corrigan advised the field's manager, Kenneth Behr, that he was going to fly back home. The ship was so heavy with fuel that it went 3,200 feet on the runway before taking off.

After 23 hours and 13 minutes he put "Lizzy," as he called the plane, down at Baldonnel Airport in Dublin. The date was July 17, 1938. "I've just flown from New York," said Corrigan to the startled airport officials. "My God, not in that thing!" someone cried. Then when he was told where he was, the pilot uttered the words that were to make him overnight a household word around the world: "I flew the wrong way."

92

Corrigan claimed his compass had got stuck and that he really had meant to fly to California. The story was so ridiculous and his delivery so barefaced it endeared him to his generation. He was like a throwback to the past decade, when foolishness was expected. But this was 1938, a grim Depression year. The more he told his story the more incredible it became. Altogether he had spent $100.15—$100 for gas, 10¢ for chocolate bars, and a 5¢ deposit on the bottle he took along, filled with drinking water. In London the United States Ambassador, Joseph P. Kennedy, congratulated him, America welcomed him home with a ticker tape parade down Fifth Avenue, and the press gave him the nickname "Wrong Way."

Corrigan made over $85,000 from endorsements and barnstorming appearances, and the 1939 movie based on his adventure, *The Flying Irishman* (in which he played himself). Thereafter he worked as a commercial pilot, and during World War II was in the Ferry Command, the civilian arm of the military flying aircraft for delivery abroad.

In 1946 he made an unsuccessful bid for the California Senate seat. After that he settled down with his wife and three sons in an orange grove in Santa Ana, California. His wife, Elizabeth, died in 1966.

In spite of his brazen act, Corrigan was always rather shy. Although he has lived in Santa Ana for about twenty years, the local paper has yet to be granted an interview with its only local celebrity. Letters requesting photographs and autographs go unanswered, and his neighbors agree that he keeps pretty much to himself.

In the middle of the orchard is an old barn, where he keeps "Lizzy." He hasn't decided whether to donate it to a museum or leave it to his children. The famous leather jacket he wore on the flight also is still in his possession.

Only recently someone asked him point blank if he really meant to fly back to Los Angeles, and he answered, "Sure. Well, at least I've told that story so many times that I believe it myself now."

Making certain the pilot is headed in the right direction during a recent flight to New York City. *Trans World Airlines*

HUBERT F. JULIAN: The "Black Eagle"

The world's most famous Negro aviator and soldier of fortune was born to a prosperous Trinidad plantation owner in 1897. His parents sent him to school in England, but when World War I broke out in Europe he was removed to Canada where he stayed until entering the United States in 1918.

Hubert Fauntleroy Julian came to the United States in order to patent his invention, a contraption bearing a crude resemblance to both a helicopter and a parachute. Although he was granted a patent, the machine never was put to practical use. He maintains that it is the basis for a device used to bring astronauts to earth after orbiting, and that it also inspired the helicopter.

While trying to promote his invention, and himself, he learned to fly an airplane. In 1922 during the Long Island Air Show, Julian became the first Negro to parachute from a plane over New York City. He readily admits that his chief motivation for attempting this seemingly senseless and dangerous stunt was to make himself known. Two years later, when even a transcontinental flight was a major feat, he announced his intention to fly from New York to Africa. His plane crashed into Flushing Bay, but Julian accomplished his objective—his daring, ridiculous flight had made him world famous. The press dubbed him the "Black Eagle of Harlem."

Through the rest of the 1920's, Julian lived in Harlem and continued to earn money and notoriety by stunt flying. In Harlem, he became friends with the black nationalist Marcus Garvey.

In 1930 he flew in an air show as part of the entertainment to celebrate the coronation of the new Emperor of Ethiopia, Haile Selassie. Julian's plane crashed. In 1932 he became a $100-a-day personal pilot to the religious leader, Father Divine, during that prophet's American barnstorming tour of what he called his "heavens."

Julian is probably best known for his Ethiopian Period—sometime after his introduction at the coronation air show, Emperor Haile Selassie gave him the rank of Colonel, and made him Military Governor of Ethiopia during the 1939 invasion by Mussolini.

In 1940 he came to his earlier employer's aid. During a trial in which Father Divine was being sued by one of his "angels" for the return of her $6,500, Colonel Julian marched into the courtroom and dramatically announced that he would personally settle the claim. When others came forth with similar demands, he withdrew the offer.

When in 1940 the Russians attacked Finland, Julian flew a fighter plane and with the rank of Captain led a squadron in the Finnish Air Force. During the Battle of Britain he challenged Field Marshal Hermann Goering to an air duel with Messerschmitts over the English Channel. The Germans replied to Julian's invitation to their Luftwaffe head by suggesting that the

Negro paint a black baboon on the side of his plane so that he could be readily identified.

During World War II he served for a short time in the Army Air Corps, thus becoming a citizen, but because he was considered too old for combat the Pentagon released him for the duration for a job with the Ford Motor Company's Willow Run aircraft plant near Detroit. After the war he served for a time as the head of Ethiopian Airlines.

During the 1948 elections Julian worked hard in Negro districts for Harry Truman, and was later sent to Germany to investigate reports of discontent among Negro troops during the Berlin airlift by the President's military aide, Major General Harry Vaughan.

In 1951 he and his wife purchased a duplex in the Bronx only a few minutes from Yankee Stadium, and Julian took out a license as a registered arms dealer, taking time out to dabble in gold purchases for foreign countries as well. In 1962 he was arrested and held for four months in Elisabethville, Katanga, charged by United Nations forces in the Congo with attempting to smuggle arms to his old friend, Moise Tshombe.

During the Watts riots of 1965 the Black Eagle arrived in London to announce that he was so ashamed of the behavior of some Negroes in the United States that he and his family were moving to England. He claims that it was only through the persuasion of "very important people in Washington" that he decided against giving up residence in the United States. On the subject of civil rights and the call for "Black Power" Julian says, "I am interested in Black Power, but through black productivity—not violence or defiance of authority."

Although he claims that he has grown too old for the high adventure he used to thrive on, the Colonel has lost none of his flamboyance. When he is not on a business trip to Bombay or Port-au-Prince he can be seen driving around the Bronx in a gold-fitted Rolls Royce, wearing custom-made English clothes, and with a monocle dangling from a black silk ribbon.

In 1934, making money and headlines flying for Ethiopia, and (*right*) disembarking at London on one of his frequent transatlantic business trips. *UPI*

MAGDA LUPESCU

Here was a story that asked the question: Can a little Jewish girl from the simple town of Hertza, Bessarabia, grow up to become the mistress to the King of Rumania, the most powerful woman in Eastern Europe, and a Princess? The answer is a resounding Yes.

Elena Wolff was born in 1896. Her father Latinized the family name shortly afterward to Lupescu. The press arbitrarily dubbed her "Magda" after her affair with Crown Prince Carol became known. At court in Bucharest she was referred to contemptuously as "the Lupescu." To her lover and friends she was always "Duduia." Elena has been called a few other names along the way, but none a lady would ever answer to.

For a brief time during World War I she was the wife of an artillery officer by the name of Tampaneau. They were divorced shortly after the Armistice. Exactly when and how she and Carol met is not certain. Most sources think it was in 1923. All agree that neither Carol nor his country was ever the same again after he came under her influence. He had a morganatic marriage to Zizi Lambrino, the daughter of a Rumanian general. After producing a son, Mircea (married to an American heiress and living in England), the marriage was annulled by his father, King Ferdinand, and Carol was wed to Princess Helen of Greece. Two years later, because of his relationship with Lupescu, he was exiled and his four-year-old son Michael assumed the throne upon the death of Ferdinand. Carol and Lupescu went off to live on the Riviera. Helen divorced him in 1928.

Carol returned to Rumania and the throne in 1930 without the Lupescu. She was, however, not far behind, and with her arrival the country's most colorful decade began. (Because of the "she-wolf," another one of her titles, Carol was never actually crowned.) During a family squabble Dowager Queen Marie was shot in the side, but those who knew Lupescu couldn't believe that she was that poor a shot.

One of the most powerful forces in Rumania was the fascist organization known as the Iron Guard. At the top of its list of those it considered enemies of the state was the Lupescu. That the King had a mistress was immoral. That this woman all but ruled Rumania was disagreeable. But that she was Jewish was too much. There were numerous plots and counter-plots. A Prime Minister was assassinated, and for fear that he would be next Carol did not attend the funeral. Lupescu persuaded the King to ally with France rather than Germany, which made her even more unpopular. In 1938 Carol proclaimed himself Dictator, but no one paid much attention. By 1940 things had become so dangerous for them as the war spread in Europe, that he abdicated.

For nearly a decade they moved about from Spain to Mexico, from Cuba to Brazil, until the Lupescu in 1949 became "gravely ill." It was her last wish that she die as an honest woman and, incidentally, a princess. The ceremony brought miraculous results. In no time she was up and about

96

giving everyone orders, as usual. Cynics said that she had nothing more than a minor fever, but if so it would have been the only minor thing she ever had in her life.

After Carol died in Portugal in 1952, to the amazement of most royalists, she was received by the German branch of the Royal House of Hohenzollern, thus making her title of Princess official. It was suggested at the time that the Hohenzollerns had in mind the many, many millions that Carol had taken with him when he left Rumania. It must have been a great disappointment to them to learn that Lupescu had a reputation for many things, but generosity was not among them.

Queen Helen lives in regal splendor in Italy. Her only son, Michael, who didn't get a single leu from his father, lives in Switzerland where he is engaged in international banking. Zizi Lambrino is dead.

Since Carol's death, the Lupescu has lived in seclusion in a palatial villa called Mar y Sol in Estoril, Portugal. She leaves her house, which overlooks the Mediterranean, from time to time for short trips to Paris and Switzerland. Exiled Rumanians in New York and Paris hear nothing from her, and very little of her. She used to keep a monkey and a parrot, but both are rumored as deceased. The only visitor she has that the international colony in Estoril knows of is her cousin who is married to a Portuguese Marquis. To while away the hours she plays cards, for companionship she has the former Marshal of the Royal Palace, a man called Urdareanu, and for comfort there is all that lovely money.

King Carol II and Lupescu in Paris, 1929. *Kermit Kelly*

Princess Elena now, accompanied by Prince Andrew of Yugoslavia, on a visit to the tomb of King Carol. *Wide World*

With Robert Woolsey (*left*) in a scene from their 1936 movie *Silly Billies.*

BERT WHEELER

As long ago as 1914 Bert Wheeler was a comedy headliner. At that time he was with his first wife, Betty, in vaudeville. They made as much as $1,500 a week, which was top money in those days when every bill in every theatre had at least one comedy act on it.

The Great Ziegfeld made no secret of his lack of interest in and appreciation for comedy. Since his shows always had a strong element of it, he was forced to hire the funny men and women by reputation alone. That Bert Wheeler worked for the producer twice is his proudest boast: "You could never get the stage to rehearse. He'd be using it to drape those gorgeous dames. You could rehearse in the alley for all he cared. But when you worked for Mr. Ziegfeld you had made it. That was the tops."

Wheeler's first show for Ziegfeld was the *Follies of 1923.* During the New York engagement Fanny Brice also starred in it, but she had another commitment and did not take it on the road. Before the show left she asked her good friend Wheeler to visit her husband, Nick Arnstein, who was doing time in Leavenworth Prison, when the show got to Kansas. When he went to the penitentiary Bert took with him the former Heavyweight Champion of the World, James J. Corbett, who was in the Follies that year doing a song and dance. When word got out that the great fighter was in the prison an actual riot ensued among the prisoners who wanted to see him. Wheeler and Corbett had to be taken from the grounds under heavy guard while the convicts were kept at bay with fire hoses.

In the 1920's Wheeler was one of the biggest names in show business. He worked at all of the top vaudeville houses in the country, and was countless times the name on the top of the bill at the Palace in New York.

To movie fans, Bert Wheeler is always a name associated with another— the team of Wheeler and Woolsey made over 30 movies during the thirties. They worked together for the first time in Ziegfeld's smash musical, *Rio Rita,* in 1927. The two comedians were the only members of the original cast taken to Hollywood for the motion picture version. The show that has become a standard for light opera companies over the years had its premiere in the Ziegfeld Theatre, which the producer had recently purchased and named for himself. It ran for over two and one-half years and boasted, along with other big names of the day, the Paul Whiteman Orchestra. (Whiteman lives with his wife, the former film star Margaret Livingston, in New Hope, Pennsylvania.)

Wheeler and Woolsey were the first comedy team to emerge as stars from sound films. All through the thirties they continued to turn out money-making comedies for RKO. Two of their best remembered were *Girl Crazy* (1932), the original movie version which Judy Garland and Mickey Rooney remade years later, and *So This Is Africa* (1933) a typical Wheeler and Woolsey piece of wackiness. One of the talents that was unleashed in several of their features was the amazing child comedienne, Mitzi Green, who is today married to movie director Joe Pevney.

Wheeler made a couple of movies after his partner died in 1938, but he was no longer comfortable in Hollywood without Woolsey. One was a colossal flop called *Las Vegas Nights* (1941) with Tommy Dorsey and his orchestra. Wheeler sang a song in it called "Dolores" while Dorsey's vocalist sat by. That singer was a young man from Hoboken, New Jersey, named Frank Sinatra.

The two trademarks of Wheeler and Woolsey pictures were Robert Woolsey's ever-present cigar and a cute little blonde by the name of Dorothy Lee, who after an unsuccessful marriage to Hollywood gossip columnist Jimmie Fidler, settled down in Chicago.

One of the best remembered stars of yesterday and best loved men in show business, Bert Wheeler is an honorary lifetime member of both the Friars and the Lambs clubs. Two of his fellow Lambs with whom Bert often spends an afternoon playing cards are the former actor-director-playwright Elliott Nugent and the character actor from stage and screen Bernard Nedell. He lives at the Lambs in New York City. Over the years he has done an occasional stint in summer stock, nightclub engagement, or guest shot on radio and television shows. Far from being retired he admits he is a bigger ham today than when he started. He has a new partner in Tommy Dillon, a young man who has worked with the veteran in Las Vegas and Manhattan's Latin Quarter in recent years.

Bert is an even bigger ham today.

July 29, 1920,
Heavyweight Champion of Europe.

GEORGES CARPENTIER

Anyone meeting Georges Carpentier before the First World War would have guessed that he would be a success in whatever field he chose. He had looks, bearing, intelligence, and charm. He would certainly go far in the arts. He did, indeed, but the art was boxing. Georges mastered it, and in 1913 at the age of nineteen became the Heavyweight Champion of Europe by knocking out British fighter Bombardier Billy Wells in the first round.

Fame did not change Carpentier's style. In the ring it was the French pugilistic style called *savate*. Out of the ring it was sufficiently suave for him to knock about Paris with Colette, Chevalier, the Aga Khan, and Mistinguett.

Georges fought well in the war also and was awarded the *croix de guerre* and the *médaille militaire*. When it was over he retained his title by knocking out another Englishman, Joe Beckett, in only 74 seconds. One of the first to shake his hand afterward was the Prince of Wales, now the Duke of Windsor. The year was 1919.

The Dempsey-Carpentier bout was held on July 1, 1921, at Boyles' Thirty Acres in Jersey City, New Jersey. The match was promoted by the late Tex Rickard, who promised to pay both fighters a half million dollars each. The fees were considered so enormous that Rickard's backers withdrew. The promoter combined a genuine love of sports with an unfailing sense of the theatrical. He reasoned that Jack Dempsey would be a huge draw because he was very unpopular with the public and press at that time. The fighter had beaten charges of draft evasion in court, and he was not a sympathetic figure in the eyes of most people. (It is Rickard who is credited with making boxing a sport attended by women as well as men. Until then it was strictly a man's game.) Carpentier was cast as the good guy. He looked nothing like a prizefighter—he was handsome, and French to boot. The ladies would love him.

100

The match was called "The Fight of the Century." Americans were already familiar with Dempsey, and Ring Lardner introduced them to Carpentier: "He registers the most frightening agony in the ring. The only thing I have seen to match this phase of his art was John Barrymore's reaction to amputation as Captain Ahab in *Moby Dick.*"

Frenchmen held high hopes for their Georges to return to France with the title. Planes were to fly over Paris dropping red flares if he won and white if he lost. H. L. Mencken gave an objective account of what happened: "Carpentier decayed like an autumn leaf in Vallambrosia. Gently and pathetically he fluttered down." It was a KO by Dempsey in the fourth round. But even defeat did not seem to mar his image. Lloyd George when he received the news spoke for France as well as England when he cabled Carpentier, "I admire you more than ever."

Rickard's gamble paid off. The gate was $1,789,238, the third largest in the history of boxing.

Carpentier held the World's Light Heavyweight Championship from 1920 until 1922, when he lost it to the Senegalese "Battling Siki," and gave up boxing completely after Gene Tunney defeated him in 1924 by a KO in the first round.

One of his most ardent fans was George Bernard Shaw who called him "the greatest boxer in the world."

During the late twenties and into the thirties Carpentier was an attraction on the music-hall stages of England and the Continent and in films. In 1930 he appeared in the early talkie-musical for Warner Brothers *Show of Shows.* Also in the cast were silent stars Viola Dana (now married to a golf pro and living in Santa Monica) and her sister Shirley Mason (living in West Los Angeles).

In 1935 Georges, who never felt comfortable as a performer, became a Parisian restaurateur. He is the proprietor of the restaurant in the Hôtel de Paris on the Right Bank, which has become a mecca for tourists looking for the finest in French cuisine and a glimpse of one of the Golden People of Sports.

Jack Dempsey takes a right from Carpentier while Tommy Loughran, Light Heavyweight Champion 1927–29, referees. The occasion was a recent showing of George Bellows fight drawings and paintings at the Gallery of Modern Art in New York City—*Paul Cordes— Gallery of Modern Art*

Under contract to
Twentieth Century-Fox, 1940.

ANNABELLA

The blonde film beauty of the thirties was born Suzanne Georgette Carpentier in 1910. She dropped all three of her names in favor of one, after reading Edgar Allan Poe's "Annabel Lee."

Annabella began working in motion pictures in 1930 when the distinguished director René Clair chose her for his film *Le Million* because, he said, she bore a striking resemblance to the silent star Bessie Love. Another of her pictures made in her native France was *Un Soir de Rafle* (1931).

In 1934 she was brought to Hollywood to costar in *Caravan* with Charles Boyer and Loretta Young, but her debut in American films was something less than sensational. She returned to Europe where she made movies in Hungary, Germany, and Austria, and by the late thirties Annabella was one of the most sought-after leading ladies in continental film making. By the time she caught the attention of United States moguls again her career was firmly established abroad.

The picture that brought Annabella to Hollywood in a blaze of publicity and enthusiasm was the first color film ever made in England, *The Wings of the Morning* (1937) which costarred Henry Fonda. Also featured was the Irish tenor John McCormack. The color process was glorious and Annabella was very appealing as the girl who masqueraded throughout much of the film as a boy. She was put under contract to Twentieth Century-Fox.

Some of her American films are: *Under the Red Robe* (1937) with Conrad Veidt, *Dinner at the Ritz* (1937) opposite Paul Lukas, *The Baroness and the Butler* (1938) which costarred William Powell, *Suez* (1938), in which she played opposite Tyrone Power. Her bathing scene in that picture was very daring for the time, and the studio made much of it in their publicity for the big-budget picture. What developed between Annabella and Power, however, proved to be much better box office than planned. When the actor was sent to Rio de Janiero on a public appearance tour his costar followed.

102

After a whirlwind courtship they were married in 1939 in the garden of Charles Boyer's home. Don Ameche was the best man, and Mrs. Boyer the maid of honor. During that year Annabella appeared in *Bridal Suite* with Robert Young.

In 1941 the couple appeared together on the strawhat circuit in *Liliom*. Power adopted her daughter by a previous marriage; she is now married to actor Oskar Werner.

The following year Annabella headed the Chicago company of Noel Coward's hit play *Blithe Spirit,* and in 1944 played on Broadway in *Jacobowsky and the Colonel.*

Brooks Atkinson in 1946 wrote in *The New York Times* of her performance in *No Exit:* "As the homosexual, Annabella is giving a bold and calculated performance that packs one corner of Hell with horror." The Jean-Paul Sartre play was directed by John Huston, and costarred Claude Dauphin. Thereafter she made *13 Rue Madeleine* (1947) with James Cagney.

Annabella had been given the complete Hollywood treatment. She endorsed Schaefer beer and attributed her complexion to Lux toilet soap, but unlike so many of the exotic beauties the film capital imported, the French star emerged with her distinct personality intact. Although none of her pictures were of exceptional quality, the lady was and could never be confused with any other actress in appearance or manner.

The Powers were divorced in 1948 with Annabella reportedly receiving a cash settlement, plus a yearly alimony of $70,000. The actor, who was her fourth and last husband, died of a heart attack in 1958.

In a recent interview Annabella lamented that she was forced to give up the American citizenship she took out in 1942 when she returned to France a number of years ago to take care of her aging mother. Although she still visits this country and says that in her heart she will always be an American, most of her time is spent on her farm, where she pastures a flock of sheep on her 26 acres, in the Pyrenees Mountains of France—not far from the château of silent star Eleanor Boardman.

Presenting the Best Actor Award to Gregory Peck for his performance in *To Kill a Mockingbird* during one of her visits. *Academy of Motion Picture Arts and Sciences*

In 1939.

PATSY KELLY

Patsy Kelly never received star billing or had her picture on the cover of *Photoplay,* but she has more fans than many of the big stars of her era.

The comedienne began her career on Broadway where she appeared in 1931 in *The Wonder Bar* opposite Al Jolson.

Hollywood cast her in a series of memorable comedies paired with Thelma Todd, the blonde counterpart to Miss Kelly. These two-reelers made for Metro-Goldwyn-Mayer are considered by authorities on screen comedy as among the finest the sound era produced. (They have not yet been released to television.) In 1935 Thelma Todd died of carbon monoxide poisoning under most peculiar circumstances. The case has never been solved.

The studio then put Patsy with Lyda Roberti in a series of comedy shorts, but that association was also ended when Lyda died in 1938.

In 1934 Patsy played Jean Harlow's best friend in *The Girl From Missouri.* The next year she made three of her best features: *Every Night at Eight* starring Alice Faye and Frances Langford (who divides her time between Florida and Chicago as the wife of the boat manufacturer, Ralph Evinrude), which was the film that introduced the song "I'm in the Mood for Love"; *Thanks a Million* in which she supported Dick Powell and Ann Dvorak (now living in Honolulu, Hawaii, with her husband, Nicholas Wade, the president of a chemical firm); and *Page Miss Glory,* appearing with Marion Davies.

Some of Miss Kelly's other credits are: *Sing, Baby, Sing* (1937), which was a spoof of the Elaine Barrie-John Barrymore antics; *Wake Up and Live* in which Patsy played the girl Friday of the star, Walter Winchell; and

Road Show in 1941 with the beautiful Carole Landis who committed suicide seven years later. The same year she had a supporting role in the RKO film *Playmates* in which John Barrymore received second billing to the popular orchestra leader of the day, Kay Kyser (he's still married to singer Georgia Carroll and lives in a small town in North Carolina where he is a practitioner of Christian Science). Another in the cast was Ish Kabibble (until recently a salesman for Ginny Simms's real estate development corporation. In 1966 he moved to Seattle, Washington, and another real estate job under his real name of Merwyn A. Bogue). In 1942 she appeared in *Sing Your Worries Away* with Bert Lahr.

None of her pictures could really be considered important, but in each Patsy's performance stands out as the highlight of the picture. Many times when some of her movies are shown on television after some thirty years, TV magazines and newspapers will recommend an otherwise dated film with the comment: "worth watching for the Patsy Kelly scenes." Her only peer was the late Joan Davis.

For reasons which have never really been made clear Patsy Kelly faded from pictures thereafter. In 1955 she toured the country with her old friend Tallulah Bankhead in a farce called *Dear Charles*. Patsy was onstage no more than 15 minutes, but at the final curtain she got as much applause as the star. It was more than just sentimentality on the part of the audience. Patsy took the small part and went wild with it. She was still a very funny lady.

Miss Kelly lives in Hollywood. She has never married. In 1960 she had a part in *The Crowded Sky,* and in 1966 she distinguished *The Ghost in the Invisible Bikini* by her appearance in it.

Today, still clowning. *American-International Pictures*

JAMES J. BRADDOCK

"The Cinderella Man," as he was called when he became World's Heavy-weight Champion, was born in New York's Hell's Kitchen in 1905. At six-teen he left his job as a printer's devil in favor of fighting for prizes and working as a sparring partner in local gyms for the professionals.

During 1926, his first year as a professional, Jim was undefeated in 16 fights, 11 of them won by knockouts. He beat some of the best boys around at the time: Phil Weisberger and Carmine Caggiano, both flattened, and Lew Barba, beaten on points; and in 1927 he took eight decisions and knocked out three men, Stanley Simmons, George La Rocca, and Johnny Alberts.

The next year he was matched with Pete Latzo, the ex-World Welter-weight Champion, in Newark. Against the odds Braddock not only whipped Latzo, who had been on his way to a comeback until that night, but broke his jaw along the way. Again that year, Braddock scored an upset when he defeated Tuffy Griffith in Madison Square Garden.

After losing a decision to Leo Lomski and KOing Jimmy Slattery, Jim was put up against one of the shrewdest and hardest hitting fighters in ring history, Tommy Loughran (see recent photo in Carpentier segment). In the Yankee Stadium on July 18, 1929, Braddock was made to look like a kid with his first pair of gloves. After that bitter lesson, Braddock lost to Yale Okun, Leo Lomski, Maxey Rosenbloom, and John Henry Lewis, among others, although during the same period, 1930–32, he knocked out Jake Warren and Phil Mercurio, and won a decision against Dynamite Jackson. It was far from being the record of an impending champion.

In 1933 he was losing as many as he was winning until on September 25 he cracked both hands in a bout with Abe Feldman. He couldn't fight, it was the middle of the Depression, and by this time he had a wife and three children to support. He was forced to work on the docks again in Hoboken, but even that wasn't steady enough to keep the Braddocks in food and clothing. In desperation James J. Braddock entered his name on the New Jersey relief rolls.

In 1934 the promoters of the Primo Carnera-Max Baer match were look-ing around for someone to fight the promising Corn Griffin in the semifinal bout preceding the main event. Although Braddock was considered retired, someone thought that the money he'd get for the beating he was sure to take would be of interest to him. It was. On June 14, 1934, the crowd that had come to see Baer and Carnera battle it out first watched Braddock hit the canvas in the first round, only to come back in the second frame with a right that KO'd Griffin to the amazement of all in the Long Island Bowl that night.

Again Braddock was supposed to be a scapegoat when he was set to fight John Henry Lewis on November 16, 1934. The opponent was younger, faster, and had the psychological advantage of having beaten Jim once before. But after ten blistering rounds, during which Braddock looked better than ever, he was given the decision.

He next met Art Lasky on March 22, 1935. Lasky was taller, had a greater reach, was 15 pounds heavier, and was favored by the experts and gamblers to win. From the first round straight through to the fifteenth Jim confounded all present by outsmarting and outpunching Lasky all the way.

The two leading contenders to fight Champion Max Baer were Max Schmeling and Jim Braddock. It was proposed that Schmeling fight Jim first, but Schmeling refused, thereby giving Braddock a crack at the title.

The twenty-nine-year-old Braddock, who only a year before had been accepting welfare from the country to keep his family alive, outmaneuvered Baer to win in a 15-round decision that left the boxing world in a state of shock. That was on June 13, 1935. For the next two years he toured the country making vaudeville appearances, radio program guest shots, and giving exhibition bouts.

Schmeling was still a top contender, and he demanded a chance at the crown. Braddock, who knew he was past his prime, decided to take on instead a young Negro, Joe Louis, figuring that since he was going to lose anyway it would hurt less to have the title remain in the United States.

Over 45,000 fans paid $715,470 to see the Champion make a good showing in the first round, only to be outpointed by Louis until knocked cold in the eighth round. It all happened in Comiskey Park in Chicago on June 22, 1937.

Instead of retiring as he announced at first, Jim came back seven months later to win, again against the predictions of nearly every sportswriter in the country, against a younger opponent, Tommy Farr. It was Braddock's last official fight.

During World War II Braddock was a Captain in the Army Transportation Corps. Thereafter, until 1956, he conducted a business in North Bergen, New Jersey, dealing in marine equipment. He is still a member of Local 825 of the Operating Engineers Union, which handles all the shipping into New Jersey ports. His two boys and one daughter all married and moved from their home in North Bergen.

In 1935, World Heavyweight Champion. *Ring Magazine*

From left to right: Joe Louis and James J. Braddock with the new title holder, Cassius Clay. *UPI*

In 1930, after making the transition from silents to talkies.

LILA LEE

The silent screen star, whose real name was Augusta Appel, was born in New York City in 1901. One night when Lila was seven years old the famous producer David Belasco found her crying backstage in a theatre in Rochester, New York, because the Society for the Prevention of Cruelty to Children would not allow her to perform due to her age. He offered her his diamond watch to play with, and when she continued to cry he added his diamond stickpin and ring. Still she cried. Finally Belasco told her that when she was sixteen years old he would make her a star. Before she reached sixteen, however, after touring the country with the famous Gus Edwards' *School Days* vaudeville act, Lila was signed to a contract with Famous Players-Lasky Company which was soon to become known as Paramount Pictures. While with the vaudeville troupe she was called "Cuddles."

Her first major film, *The Cruise of the Make-Believe* (1918), was a smash. The next year Lila was in the Gloria Swanson starrer *Male and Female*, with Cecil B. de Mille as director. This was the cinema version of the classic *The Admirable Crichton* (a title some movie executive thought too toney). Other silent pictures include: *Blood and Sand* (1922) with the late Nita Naldi and Rudolph Valentino, *The Dictator* (1922) opposite Wallace Reid, *Broken Hearts* (1926), *New Klondike* (1926), *One Increasing Purpose* (1927), *Million Dollar Mystery* (1927), *You Can't Beat the Law* (1928), *Just Married* (1928), and *Black Butterflies* (1928).

Although Lila never enjoyed the same popularity in talkies, she worked right up until the late thirties in pictures such as: *The Show of Shows* (1929) with many stars of the silent period including Alice White (who resides in a house a block away from the Hollywood Bowl), *The Unholy Three* (1930) with Lon Chaney in his first and only talkie, *The Gorilla* (1930) with Walter Pidgeon, *Misbehaving Ladies* (1931) opposite Ben Lyon, *War Correspondent* (1932) in which her leading man was Jack Holt, father of Tim Holt, sales manager at a radio station in Oklahoma, *Night of June 13th*

(1932), *Face in the Sky* (1933) opposite Spencer Tracy, *The Ex-Mrs. Bradford* (1935) costarring with William Powell (who is semi-retired in Palm Springs, California), *The People's Enemy* (1935), and *Two Wise Maids* (1937) in which two of the screen's best remembered funnywomen appeared, Allison Skipworth and Polly Moran.

In the forties Miss Lee appeared in *Blind Alley* (1940) on Broadway and on the road, in *Claudia* (1941), and headed the Chicago company of *Kiss and Tell* (1943). Miss Lee had suffered three serious attacks of TB. The first in 1930 and then again in 1944 and 1946, thereafter living quietly and completely inactive.

In 1957 Ralph Edwards feted Lila on his *This Is Your Life* television program on NBC. A few of those who appeared on the show were Monte Blue; her ex-husband, James Kirkwood, who was also a silent film star; and her son James Kirkwood, Jr., who is a novelist, playwright, and actor. Unlike many of the stars who had paraded before the Edwards cameras, Lila was not there to plug a picture or a book. She had no idea she was to be the subject of the program, and was well deserving of the tributes paid to her.

In 1960 her son published a book which was both very funny and very sad about the life of a little boy whose mother is a beautiful screen actress. It was called *There Must Be a Pony*. Unfortunately, the stage production starring Myrna Loy was not as successful as the book, and never played in New York.

In 1964 Lila moved from New York City to Key West, Florida, and lives near her contemporaries Olga Petrova, who is in Clearwater, and Dorothy Dalton, who has a home in Lantana. Lila has not quite retired, having just done a television pilot in Florida.

Miss Lee came to New York recently for the opening of her son's play, *U.T.B.U.*, starring Tony Randall. The letters stand for Unhealthy to Be Unpleasant. Although the majority of reviews were favorable the production came at the time of a newspaper strike and lasted only a few weeks.

In retirement in Florida. *Poray Studio, Key West, Florida*

In a 1933 M-G-M publicity still.

JOHNNY WEISSMULLER

Until Johnny Weissmuller, who was to make a career out of playing Tarzan, came along, swimming was one of the most ignored sports in America. It was considered more an exercise than a competitive sport. "Big Johnny," as he was called, gave it glamour and excitement. He was six feet, three inches in height, and looked about as much like an Adonis as one could imagine. He had the kind of smile that city editors slap on the front pages rather than burying in the sports section. And to endear him further, he had an easygoing charm and sense of humor that won him friends among the press, the public, and even those who lost to him in competitions.

From 1921 until he turned professional in 1929 he won every free-style race he entered, an accomplishment never equaled or approached to this day. Under the sponsorship of the Illinois Athletic Club he swam on two Olympic teams and won five Gold Medals. In each of the five races he broke a world's record.

Of the 38 men's swimming records approved by the A.A.U. in 1922, 11 of them were Weissmuller's. He held the outdoor titles for the 100- and 400-yard races in 1922, 1923, and 1925 through 1928. In 1925 and 1927 he took the half-mile splash as well. In the Olympic races, in 1924 he won the 100-meter in 59 seconds and the 400-meter in 5 minutes 4.2 seconds, and in 1928 in Amsterdam he won the 100-meter in 58.6 seconds.

After appearing in a number of short sport films, he was spotted by scouts to make movies. In 1932 he made his first screen appearance in the role of Tarzan in *Tarzan, the Ape Man*. He made over a dozen feature films playing the Edgar Rice Burroughs character in such pictures as *Tarzan Escapes* (1936), *Tarzan's Desert Mystery* (1943), and *Tarzan and the Mermaids* (1948) with a number of leading ladies. One of the questions most frequently asked of the swimmer today is the whereabouts of the actor who played "Boy," Johnny Sheffield. (He lives with his wife and two sons in Santa Monica, California).

He made two feature films as another jungle hero, Jungle Jim: *Jungle Jim* (1949) and *Jungle Jim in the Forbidden Land* (1952). In 1958 his Jungle Jim series was a popular television show which was syndicated throughout the country. His only appearance in a movie other than as Jungle Jim or Tarzan was *Swamp Fire* in 1946.

Johnny, who was born in 1904, seldom misses a day's swim. He performed all of the stunts in his Tarzan films himself as well as one in which he rode a rhinoceros, a feat no animal handler or stunt man in Hollywood would undertake. At over sixty years of age he weighs 220 pounds and looks near forty.

Weissmuller has been married five times. His most famous wife was Lupe Velez, the Mexican actress, whose quarrels with Johnny made headlines. There were Camille Louier, Bobbe Arnst, a dancer, and Beryl Scott, a society girl. His last marriage was to the golf champion, Allene Gates.

Johnny's sense of humor has not always met with universal acceptance. Once during an Olympic swimming race in which he was not competing he and some of his teammates staged a comedy routine in the pool that had the judges in a rage and the audience in hysterics. A few years ago in Coral Gables, Florida, he failed to amuse the local authorities when he turned in a false fire alarm.

Since his movie days he has been vice-president of the Johnny Weissmuller Swimming Pool Company, with headquarters in Chicago. Johnny commutes between the Windy City and his home in Fort Lauderdale, Florida.

Looking very tan and healthy in a recent photo. *John Virzi*

Sonja in 1940.

SONJA HENIE

The world's most famous ice skater was born in Oslo, Norway, in 1913. She began to skate when she was only seven years old and at eleven became the Figure Skating Champion of Norway. At thirteen she placed second in the World's Championships, and the next year, 1927, she won the title which she held for ten consecutive years.

Some of the records she set during her years as an amateur have yet to be equaled or broken. At the Winter Olympics held in St. Moritz, Switzerland, in 1928 Sonja won the Women's Figure Skating competition with 350.3 points. She repeated her victory at Lake Placid in 1932 with 328.94 points. She turned professional after taking the contest again in 1936 with 424.5 points in Garmisch-Partenkirchen, Germany.

Her first motion picture, *One in a Million* was released in 1937. The same year she made *Thin Ice* with Tyrone Power. Sonja Henie's films had musical numbers, handsome leading men, and her skating. They were very successful.

Her film credits include: *My Lucky Star* (1938) with Richard Greene, *Happy Landing* (1938), *Second Fiddle* (1939) opposite Rudy Vallee, *Everything Happens at Night* (1939) with Ray Milland, *Sun Valley Serenade* (1941) which was her best, costarring John Payne, *Iceland* (1942), *Wintertime* (1943) with Jack Oakie, and *It's a Pleasure* (1945). Her last movie was the remake of the 1934 Fay Wray (living in retirement in her home on Tigertail Road in West Los Angeles) starrer, *The Countess of Monte Cristo* (1948).

Even while making films Sonja found time to tour the United States and abroad with her ice revue. It was, in fact, the enormous financial success of the Henie ice shows that started the trend of frappé entertainment both in theatres and in arenas. The two biggest and oldest are Ice Follies and Ice Capades. Both shows have always been lavishly produced and have fared very well at the box office, but neither had Sonja Henie, nor anyone else of a comparable drawing power. Arthur Wirtz, who produced many of Sonja's shows, presented Barbara Ann Scott (married to an executive of the Merchandise Mart and proprietress of a beauty salon in the suburbs of Chicago) in his ice shows, and John H. Harris' Ice Capades featured his wife Donna Atwood (divorced from Harris and living with her three children in Los Angeles), but neither lady had the star quality possessed by the Norwegian skater. While both were excellent skaters and considerably younger than Miss Henie, they could never match her showmanship. Follies and Capades spent fortunes on acts and costumes that Sonja would never have permitted. However slow the rest of her show might have been, when the star skated onto the ice it would all but melt with that famous dazzling smile.

A typical year during her active period, 1942, saw her company gross $240,000 during an engagement at Madison Square Garden and over one million dollars on tour in addition to her movie money.

Much of the success of the famous Center Theatre in Rockefeller Center is attributed to Sonja Henie, whose shows there were very popular before it was turned into a TV studio. She played also at the now demolished Roxy Theatre, as well as Madison Square Garden and just about every arena in America. She has skated before crowned heads at Command Performances, on the "Ed Sullivan Show," and in 1956 on her own TV spectacular.

Sonja has been married three times. Her first husband was millionaire Dan Topping, her second was millionaire Winthrop Gardiner, Jr., and her present spouse is millionaire shipping magnate Nils Onstad, whom she married in 1956.

The Sonja Henie art collection is one of the most valuable accumulations of modern paintings in private hands. It includes Klees, Rouaults, Braques, Bonnards, and Matisses. When they were brought from Oslo, where they are kept, several years ago for a showing in Los Angeles, Sonja donated the proceeds of over $100,000 to the Heart Fund.

Miss Henie says that since her marriage she is no longer interested in touring and that "the ice seems so much colder these days." She does skate during her frequent stays in Switzerland and when she is living in her home in Norway. The Onstads divide their time between their native country and their big colonial house in Bel Air, California. Sonja, who is a national heroine in Norway, has received the Order of St. Olaf from the King.

Arriving at a recent Los Angeles première.

July, 1951, Heavyweight Champion of the World. *Wide World*

"JERSEY JOE" WALCOTT

The man who was to become the oldest prize fighter ever to hold the World's Heavyweight Championship and one of the most admired men in the ring was born in Merchantville, New Jersey, in 1914. His real name is Arnold Raymond Cream. He changed it when he turned professional in 1936 in honor of a famous welterweight from the early part of this century who was greatly admired by Walcott's father.

"Jersey Joe" grew up in a neighborhood where fighting was something every boy had to learn in order to survive. His parents had twelve children, and when his father died Joe, who was only fourteen, had to go to work to support the family. He sold newspapers, delivered groceries, and labored in a soup factory. Marrying at eighteen, he and his wife lived for eighteen months on a $9.50 home relief check when he couldn't find work. When he did manage to get another job it was as a hod carrier on a construction project, and finally as a longshoreman, to which he attributes his massive build and remarkable endurance.

For his first paid ring encounter he was given $7.50, winning the fight. Thereafter, when Joe fought regularly for money his record wasn't one of a future champion—he lost 15 of his 64 early fights because "hunger was a guest in my house,"though in 1936, while acting as a sparring partner for Joe Louis at the Champion's New Jersey training camp, he floored the great heavyweight in the first round.

On his way up the ladder Walcott beat some of the leading contenders around during the late thirties and forties. A few of those he either KO'd or beat by decisions were: Johnny Allen, Al Blake, Tommy Gomez, Jimmy Bivins, Lee Oma, Joe Maxim, and Elmer Ray. (Two of Walcott's matches before he had a shot at Louis' title were promoted by another New Jersey-ite, Frank Sinatra.)

When he finally met Louis officially in 1947 no one thought of him as a serious challenger until shortly after the first bell. To the amazement of everyone there the Champion hit the canvas twice in the first round, and was nearly knocked out in the seventh. Out of the 47 sportswriters who were present, 30 felt that the decision in favor of Louis was a raw one. Not since the famous Tunney "long count" has there been a more controversial outcome in a championship fight.

The Louis-Walcott rematch was held in Yankee Stadium on July 25, 1948. A record 42,667 people paid $841,739 to see the Champ KO Walcott in the eleventh round.

On June 22, 1949, Jersey Joe tried again for the Crown when he fought the new champ, Ezzard Charles (now a wholesale wine salesman in Chicago), but lost in a fifteen-round decision.

When he met Charles again in Pittsburgh on July 18, 1951, Walcott was thirty-seven years old. He had been beaten three times before in tries for the title, once by Charles. Then, during the seventh round, against all odds, Jersey Joe Walcott KO'd the Champion in front of 25,000,000 surprised TV viewers. When he was asked how he felt, the new Heavyweight Champion said, "I've worked twenty-one years for this night. I read my Bible before I fight. I prayed between every round. I asked God to help me."

Jersey Joe's only successful defense of his title was against Ezzard Charles in Philadelphia when he outpointed the former champion on June 5, 1952.

Four months later Rocky Marciano knocked Walcott out in the thirteenth round in Philadelphia. The gate was $504,645. Although he held the title for a short time, Joe's clean fighting in the ring and his gentlemanly behavior out of it earned him the admiration of the public and the respect of the professionals. In one of the world's most unsavory businesses Jersey Joe Walcott emerged as a winner at his sport while remaining faithful to his deep religious principles.

Since 1953 Walcott has worked with the Juvenile Division of the Camden, New Jersey, Police Department, and in 1965 was appointed Assistant Director of Public Safety. Always a family man, Joe seldom leaves Camden, where he lives with his wife and six children in a ten-room house, though he still finds time to spar with the local kids and teach Sunday school at the Methodist church in his hometown of Merchantville.

From left to right: Former Champs Jersey Joe Walcott, Joe Louis, and James J. Braddock with the new title holder, Cassius Clay. *UPI*

Starring in *Carmen, Jr.* in 1922 at the tender age of three.

BABY PEGGY

Baby Peggy's career began when she was only twenty months old. Her first efforts on the silent screen were two-reelers. Starting in 1920, she turned out over 150 of them. Peggy made feature-length films as well. Perhaps the best remembered of them is *Captain January* (1923), remade by Shirley Temple in 1936.

An indication of the popularity of the child star is evidenced in a 1923 advertisement placed in a trade paper by her studio, Universal Pictures. Of the four columns the studio bought, three of them were devoted to Baby Peggy's latest picture, *The Darling of New York*. Universal's classic *The Hunchback of Notre Dame* received one paragraph at the bottom of the advertisement. The headline as well as the photograph that accompanied the advertisement were about and of Baby Peggy.

All through the twenties Peggy toured the country as a vaudeville entertainer. Her act was so popular that years after she had retired an injunction was taken out by Peggy's parents to stop another child from performing under her name at the Chicago World's Fair of 1932. The impersonator was one of many.

In the mid-thirties Peggy emerged from her retirement on a Wyoming ranch to try a comeback in talkies as an ingenue. She gave up after a few small roles, and was little more than a curiosity in Hollywood during the sound era.

For a while Peggy was married to Gordon Ayres, who used to play Freckles in the silent version of *Our Gang* comedies. They were divorced at the end of World War II. (Ayres is now manager of the local Arthur Murray Dance Studio in Riverside, California. He ran unsuccessfully for Mayor in 1965.)

Peggy's real name was Peggy Montgomery. After divorcing Gordon she changed her Christian name to Diana. It was at this time that she was converted to the Roman Catholic faith. She is now known as Diana Serra Cary. The middle name is for the Spanish priest, Father Junipero Serra, who brought Christianity to Mexico and California. The surname of Cary was supplied by her present husband, artist Robert Cary, whom she married in 1954.

In 1957 the Carys moved from California to Cuernavaca, Mexico, where their son Mark was born in 1960. In 1966 the family moved to Spain where they now live, although their wish is eventually to settle in nearby Majorca.

Under the name of Diana Serra Cary the former star has published articles in *Esquire, Catholic Digest,* and *The Saturday Evening Post.* She is currently finishing her book on what she recalls from her years in motion pictures and vaudeville. Instead of the usual autobiography which recounts stories about famous silent stars who were her contemporaries, Peggy is concentrating mainly on the unknowns who made her era so outstanding. It will be a tribute to the cameramen, executives, character actors, and technicians who made ordinary men and women into idols of their time.

Another of Peggy's projects is the canonization of her patron, Father Serra. In the current campaign to elevate the Spaniard to sainthood, Peggy is in charge of public relations.

Of the past, Baby Peggy says, "As a child I enjoyed picture work, but not as an adult. I suffered emotionally from the stresses and strains of growing up in the limelight, but I have long since passed through the period of crisis. And I bypassed it not through the usual route of alcohol, love affairs, and self-pity. My religion has been the decisive factor in my happiness today, just as psychoanalysis has helped other child stars.

"Occasionally, even here people find out that I was once a child star. But the name confuses them, and they say, 'So this is whatever happened to Baby Jane!'"

With baby Mark in Cuernavaca recently.

Ursula Bernath

Heavyweight Champion
of the World, 1933.

PRIMO CARNERA

The Italian giant who became the Heavyweight Champion of the World was born in a town outside Venice in 1907. He left home at fourteen and traveled to France where he worked as a carpenter's apprentice and as a strong man in a circus. The veteran French heavyweight, Paul Journée, noticed Carnera's 6-foot 5¾-inch frame moving a piece of furniture with ease one day in the street, and got the idea of training him for the ring.

During 1928 and 1929 he ran up a rather impressive record fighting all over the Continent. In December, 1929, American promoters brought Carnera to the United States in a blaze of publicity that would have done credit to Barnum. He was taken all over the country and matched with opponents who were either aging or hopelessly outreached by the mammoth boxer. While the sportsmanship of this period in his career is questionable, the showmanship was superb.

On October 12, 1931, Jack Sharkey defeated him in Ebbets Field. But Primo turned right around and beat King Levinsky in Chicago, and then knocked out Argentine giant Vittorio Campolo, proving he had something more than size.

The first half of 1932 saw an impressive list of wins for Carnera all over Europe with the exception of his surprise defeat by ring veteran Larry Gains. He returned in July for another barnstorming tour, in which he defeated everyone put in front of him with the exception of Stanley Poreda. In most cases, however, he was meeting a man who had been carefully chosen to make the big boy look very good.

Then on February 10, 1933, he fought Ernie Schaaf in Madison Square Garden. Schaaf's performance was worse than anyone thought him capable of, and a blow that felled him in the 13th round did not seem to be a hard one. When Schaaf went down the crowd yelled "fake," and the sportswriters echoed the chant the next day in the papers. Three days later, the entire boxing world, and in particular those who had accused the Italian of a "fix," was shocked when Schaaf died of the results of that punch.

On June 29, 1933, Carnera took the Heavyweight title away from Jack

Sharkey by a knockout, and followed up his victory by whipping Paulino Uzcundun in Rome and then aging Tommy Loughran in Miami. Also in 1933 he made a movie called *The Prizefighter and the Lady* which had in the cast Max Baer, Jack Dempsey, Myrna Loy, and Walter Huston.

The Champion was favored when he stepped into the ring with Max Baer the night of June 14, 1934. Over 52,000 fans paid $428,370 to see one of the most exciting fights in ring history, with Baer flooring Carnera ten different times before the referee finally stopped the fight in the 11th round. He outweighed Baer by over 50 pounds and actually won several rounds, but Baer was the superior boxer.

Carnera remained a factor in boxing for a full year after losing the title. He KO'd Ray Impellitiere in early 1935, but Joe Louis ended his hopes for a comeback when the Brown Bomber flattened him in the 6th round on June 25, 1935. He returned to Europe in 1936 after losing a few more fights, only to find that he fared no better on the Continent. By 1937 his name had vanished from the news completely.

In 1939 he was in Yugoslavia on a public appearance tour, when he met his future wife, Pina, then a postmistress. The ex-Champion eked out a living by appearing at the openings of stores and movies in Southern Europe. During the War he fought in the Italian underground until he was captured and interned. He was released by Allied forces after Italy surrendered in 1944.

He then returned to this country as a wrestler. He did well enough at his second chance in the ring to buy a mansion in Italy, some forest land, a farm, and several houses, which he rents. In 1956 Humphrey Bogart starred in *The Harder They Fall,* a thinly veiled account of the career of Primo Carnera. It was Bogart's last film, and featured Mike Lane in the role of the giant prizefighter.

Although Primo isn't bitter, he does regret allowing people to take advantage of him when he was boxing. After that career was over he had no money—even after making as much as $122,000 in a single match. He is sorry also that he continued boxing after Louis beat him. Although he stopped wrestling several years ago, he has managed to keep his weight to just about what it was when he was Champion, 265 pounds. In addition to his holdings abroad, he prospers today as the proprietor of an Italian delicatessen and liquor store in Glendale, California. The Carneras have a married daughter and a son who is studying medicine.

The ex-Champion and Mrs. Carnera with their daughter Jean Marie and her husband Philip Alderson. *UPI*

GERALD P. NYE

The highly controversial Senator has been called many things during his tenure in office from anti-Semite to dangerous appeaser, from reactionary to liberal. Domestically he could accurately be described as an old-fashioned agrarian rebel and internationally as a consistent isolationist.

Gerald Prentice Nye was born in Hortonville, Wisconsin, in 1892. He was, until appointed to a Senate vacancy in 1928, a crusading editor of a North Dakota newspaper which backed Robert La Follette's presidential bid in 1924. After being appointed by the Governor of North Dakota, Nye had to wait a full month while the Senate debated whether or not a governor had this power. After being backed by the powerful Senators, Norris and Borah, Nye was confirmed by a majority of two votes and took his seat. His appearance was described at the time as "an Old Oaken Bucket haircut and bulbous yellow shoes."

Several months later Nye ran in the regular election and won a full term. He chaired what was until then an obscure committee, the Public Lands Committee. Shortly after Nye took it over, his investigation into the financial dealings of Harry F. Sinclair and Andrew Mellon proved very embarrassing to both millionaires, and shook the structure of the Republican National Committee. The exposure for the first time gave him headlines he did not have to write, and from then on his career figured prominently in the news of the day.

Nye was a fighter from the very beginning of his political career. He fought for farm relief and against the World Court. He fought President Coolidge over North Dakota patronage, and won. The Baltimore *Sun* called him "Gerald, the Giant Killer."

In the Democratic landslide of 1932, Republican Nye was reelected by a ratio of 3 to 1. The new President, F.D.R., was a liberal, and since Nye hadn't liked Hoover or Coolidge many observers expected the Senator to fall into the fold of the New Deal. Instead Nye called the blue eagle symbol of the National Recovery Act "a bird of prey on the masses." When Hugh Johnson in 1933 invited him to join the board of the National Recovery Administration he declined.

In 1934 Nye carried on one of the most highly publicized investigations of the decade when he examined the munitions industry in this country, and created a sensation in the press which proved to be an embarrassment to J. P. Morgan. The general consensus about the effects among liberals was that they revealed the arms industry as a menace to world peace.

In 1935 the North Dakota Senator drafted the neutrality law forbidding arms shipments to belligerent nations, and in 1939 helped defeat F.D.R.'s attempts to remove the embargo. In 1940 Nye was seated on the Senate Foreign Relations Committee, affording him a perfect opportunity to fight the President tooth and nail on foreign policy.

The image of Nye during his public years is blurred by the seemingly inconsistent statements he made as well as the stands he took—in 1939 the German-American Bund cheered his name because he had called England "the greatest aggressor in modern times," whose "impending doom ought not to alarm us." Yet, that same year, he endorsed the controversial film *Confessions of a Nazi Spy* saying that propaganda from Hitler was just as dangerous as that from England. In early 1941 he lashed out against anti-Nazi films noting that they were made by an industry that was controlled mostly by foreigners and Jews. He confirmed the statement of Colonel Charles Lindbergh that people of the Jewish faith were leaders in the movement toward war, and encouraged Lindy to run for Congress. Nye opposed aid to the Soviet Union in 1940 stating that the country was ruled by "thieves, human butchers, and murderers of religion." He opposed the draft, lend-lease, the Great Lakes-St. Lawrence River development.

An accomplished speaker, Nye addressed such diverse movements as America First and the American League Against War and Fascism and on December 7, 1941, delivered an anti-war speech before 2,000 American Firsters. When he was told that Japan had bombed Pearl Harbor he said, "just what Britain planned for us. We have been maneuvered into this by the President [F.D.R.]." The next day he voted in the Senate to declare war.

Nye was defeated for reelection in 1945 and assumed the position of president of Record Engineering, Inc., in Washington, D.C. In 1959 he became Special Assistant for Elderly Housing in the Federal Housing Administration, resigning in 1963 for an appointment to the professional staff of the Senate Committee on Aging. He retired from government services in 1966, with a party given him by Senate Minority Leader, Everett Dirksen.

Nye lives with his wife in Chevy Chase, Maryland, and maintains an office in Washington, D.C., as a "consultant agent." He ardently supported Senator Goldwater in 1964 and approves of Medicare so long as it is economically feasible. The former Senator is very concerned over the fiscal policies of the present administration: "The frightening degree of inflation which has destroyed the values the old folks had laid away, or provided with retirement and/or insurance, leaves our country with poverty where adequate provision for rainy days had been made during productive years."

With famed criminal lawyer Clarence Darrow *(right)*; Nye at the time was Chairman of the National Recov ry Review Board. *Acme*

At a recent Washington party
Chris Albertson

Flash Gordon getting out of another scrape in one of the chapters made in 1936. Dale is played by Jean Rogers.

LARRY "BUSTER" CRABBE

Paramount Pictures signed Buster after he won the 400-meter race in the 1932 water Olympics. He finished in 4 minutes and 48 seconds compared with Johnny Weissmuller's 1924 victory of 5 minutes and 4 seconds. His first pictures for Paramount were in a loincloth: *Tarzan the Fearless* (1933), and *King of the Jungle* (1933).

Although Buster made over 30 feature films during the thirties and forties as *Billy the Kid* and a 13-chapter serial of *Buck Rogers,* his public image will always be "Flash Gordon." The two serials he made portraying the earthman who battles Ming the Merciless became so popular that they were the first and only serials ever to be shown at evening performances in first-run houses. Eventually the chapters were put together and released as two feature films. Twenty years later, they were a hit all over again on television.

In the early fifties his *Captain Gallant of the French Foreign Legion* was a success as a syndicated television series. Appearing with Buster was his son Cuffy Crabbe who played his ward.

Buster had an early morning exercise show for a while during the fifties which emanated from New York City. He still appears from time to time as a guest on a TV show, and has done parts in westerns made by his old friend Eddie Small, the movie producer.

Since the early sixties Buster has been the aquatic director of the Hotel Concord in New York's Catskill Mountains. He likes to tell a story about his climbing out of the pool one day and overhearing one lady guest say to another, "Do you see that man? My dear, I remember him when I was a little girl. He used to play Flash Gordon." "I didn't mind it so much," says Buster, "except that I swear both of those gals were older than I am."

Buster is a grandfather by his daughter, whom he often visits in Los Angeles. Cuffy is now a student at a university in Arizona and his parents live in Rye, New York. Although "Ming the Merciless" (Charles Middleton) and "Dr. Zarkov" (Frank Shannon) are dead, he still keeps in touch with the lovely "Dale" (Jean Rogers) who is married to a top Hollywood agent.

Buster, who considered a career in law before he became successful as an actor, has done very well with his company, the Buster Crabbe Swimming Pools, which are very popular in the suburbs. Another of his business interests is his boys' camp in the Catskills. Buster recently joined a New York City stock brokerage firm as a licensed representative.

Unlike many stars who deeply resent being associated with one character, Crabbe delights in the revivals of Flash Gordon. Unlike most of the serials at that time, it was made on a budget of over $300,000 which in the thirties was more than some features cost. Buster is rightfully proud of his part in the series.

The fan mail still pours in from around the world where Flash Gordon is playing in theatres and on television. Most of it lately has been from the new African nation of Ghana. All the envelopes have to say is "FLASH GORDON, U.S.A."

"Buster" Crabbe, director of water sports at The Concord, Kiamesha Lake, N.Y.

Gene with his famous horse, Champion, on his Sunday night show in 1940. *CBS Radio*

GENE AUTRY

Gene Autry is one movie cowboy who really was a westerner by birth and upbringing. Born in Texas in 1907 he later moved to Sapulpa, Oklahoma, where he worked as a telegrapher at the local railroad junction. It was during that time when he was in his late teens that he got an additional job singing on the local radio station. One of his admirers was another Oklahoman, Will Rogers, who encouraged him to continue as an entertainer.

Gene became so popular in Oklahoma that within three years the radio show was his own and was being heard in several adjoining states. Columbia Records gave him a contract, and he was off to the races with his first hit which he also co-authored, "That Silver-Haired Daddy of Mine."

In 1933 he left radio for a while to make movies, his first with Ken Maynard in *In Old Santa Fe*. His 13-chapter serial *The Phantom Empire* (1934) is a classic of its type, and is still shown among devotees of the macabre in early sound films. He made over 64 feature films for Republic Pictures (which was still called Mascot Pictures when he made his first for them, *Tumblin' Tumbleweeds* in 1935).

Gene was the first western star to show up among the Top Ten moneymakers in Hollywood. He remained in those ranks from 1937 until 1942. He was also the first star to allow his name to be associated with merchandise, and has had as many as 100 different products on the market at one time bearing his name and likeness. Another first in Autry's life was in 1950 when he became the first cowboy to be named as one of the ten best dressed men in America.

His coast-to-coast radio shows for Wrigley Gum enjoyed great popularity, beginning in 1940. Listeners were always told that Gene was speaking to them right from Melody Ranch, and that his horse, Champion, was right there with him. Actually, Gene does live on a ranch in the San Fernando Valley called Melody Ranch.

His radio and movie work were halted from 1942 until 1945 when he served in the United States Air Force, from which he emerged a Flight

124

Officer. After the war he went back to work for Wrigley on Sunday nights and formed his own independent film company, for which he was to make 46 features.

During the years Gene reigned supreme as the screen's top cowboy, his formula set the pace for many other westerns. Any Autry fan will tell you that his pictures had ample comedy relief in the person of Smiley Burnette and the tops in western ballads, such as "South of the Border." There was, however, very little dalliance with girls. If the hero found it absolutely necessary to kiss the lady it would usually come in the last scene, and even then during the clinch the camera would pan to Champion, who looked about as uncomfortable as Gene wiping off the lipstick at the fade-out.

A musical group called "The Sons of the Pioneers" supplied the backing for Gene's numbers in many of his features. A young man appearing as a member of the group, and who later became "The King of the Cowboys," was Roy Rogers.

He had married Ina Mae Spiney in 1932, niece of his first song-writing collaborator.

Some of the songs he has introduced are "Mexicali Rose" and "Here Comes Santa Claus," both of which have sold over one million copies. His rendition of "Rudolph the Red-Nosed Reindeer" brought him a platinum copy after the sales went to two and one half million records.

Gene began devoting all of his time to his investments around the early fifties. He is Chairman of the Board of Golden West Broadcasting which controls radio station KVI in Seattle, KSFO in San Francisco, and KMPC in Los Angeles. In 1964 his corporation bought KTLA, Channel 5 in Los Angeles, from Paramount Pictures.

Autry's other interests and holdings include the Continental Hotel on Hollywood's Sunset Strip, the Mark Hopkins Hotel on Nob Hill in San Francisco, 25 percent interest in one music publishing firm and 100 percent in another, a flying school, a crop-dusting service, several ranches, several oil wells, the Gene Autry Championship Rodeo shows, and Gene Autry Television Productions which has produced such series as *Annie Oakley, Range Rider,* and *Buffalo Bill, Jr.*

Chairman of the Board of Golden West Broadcasting.

In the prime of her career, in *Dragonwyck*, 1946, directed by Ernst Lubitsch, and *(below)* today.

ANNE REVERE

She has been playing old women so long that most of her fans expect her to be ancient. Anne was born in 1903 in New York City and attended Wellesley College. During the twenties she worked throughout the United States in stock and repertory.

In 1931 she made her debut on Broadway in *The Great Barrington* and then *Lady With a Lamp* the same year, appearing the next season in *Wild Waves*. In 1933 she did the play *Double Door* in New York, leaving for Hollywood to film the screen version released in 1934, starring Evelyn Venable (married to cinematographer Hal Mohr and teaching Greek at U.C.L.A.). It was Miss Revere's first motion picture and her last for six years.

In 1934 Lillian Hellman's play *The Children's Hour* was presented on Broadway with Miss Revere in the role of Martha Dobie. The theme was very controversial for the time. It was the first time a production had dealt openly with the subject of Lesbianism, and it was an enormous success. Anne's personal reviews established her as one of the top character actresses in the New York theatre. After its Broadway run she took the play on tour.

In 1937 she played Celia in *As You Like It,* and in 1939 was one of *The Three Sisters* on Broadway.

In 1940 Anne Revere was brought back to Hollywood where she made one movie after another for the next 19 years. A few of those films, which were distinguished by her performances, are: *The Howards of Virginia* (1940), *Men of Boys Town* (1941), *Flame of New Orleans* (1941), the memorable Bette Davis-Miriam Hopkins starrer, *Old Acquaintance* (1942), *The Keys of the Kingdom* (1944), *Dragonwyck* (1946), *Forever Amber* (1947), *Body and Soul* (1947), and *You're My Everything* (1949).

Miss Revere has been nominated for the Best Supporting Actress Oscar on three occasions, winning it once: her performance as Jennifer Jones's mother in *The Song of Bernadette* (1943), her role in *National Velvet* (1945), and her portrayal of Gregory Peck's mother in *Gentleman's Agreement* (1947). She won the statuette in 1945.

126

In 1951 the actress turned in another splendid performance as the mother of Montgomery Clift in *A Place in the Sun,* the last motion picture audiences ever saw her in. Anne Revere's name was one of the 300 that appeared on the Hollywood Blacklist. Although, unlike her friend and neighbor, Gale Sondergaard, she has been able to find occasional TV work and parts in Broadway plays, the actress who was once one of the highest paid and most respected character people in films is still *persona non grata* in that medium. It seemed the heads of the major studios determined that Anne Revere was no longer suitable for employment in their industry.

For a time after Hollywood had found her political associations not to its liking, she and director Samuel Rosen (her husband since 1935) ran an acting school in Los Angeles. In the late fifties the couple returned to New York City and bought a brownstone on West 104th Street, which has all of the original woodwork and fixtures of its first owner, William Burns, of detective agency fame.

Since her blacklisting she has been seen on Broadway both in Elmer Rice's unsuccessful modernization of *Hamlet* entitled *Cue for Passion* in 1958, and in *Jolly's Progress* in 1959. When Anne was given the role of one of the sisters in *Toys in the Attic* the rumor was that Lillian Hellman, the author, had chosen her merely because of their association in 1934. The fact is, the actress originally signed for the part did not work out, and though Miss Revere was a second choice, she received the Antoinette Perry Award in 1960 for her performance.

On TV, the only major roles Anne has had were in 1960 when she was seen in *The House of Bernarda Alba* and in a one-act Tennessee Williams play presented in 1961. (She had appeared in a televised drama as far back as 1939.)

Anne has kept busy over the past few years acting in plays at colleges and universities around the country. Since 1965 she has appeared from time to time in a running part on ABC Television's *A Time for Us,* a daytime soap opera. When she signed the contract she refused to comment to interviewers on her blacklisting other than to say, "I've talked about it until I am tired of hearing myself, and I expect those listening are tired too. I am very glad to be back working and hope to continue."

ABC

Irene and Vernon Castle, 1917.
Dance Magazine

IRENE CASTLE

It was a handsome young couple, named Vernon and Irene Castle, who changed the style of dancing in this country before the First World War, as much by their personalities as by the steps they created. They were the most idolized pair in America, and the dances they introduced, such as the "Castle Walk" and "Castle Waltz," became absolute crazes in ballrooms in every city and town. (While appearing in Chicago they danced "The Castle Walk" down the aisle at the city's first "tango wedding" while a couple named Florence Eizendrath and L. Montefiore Stein were united in holy matrimony.)

The greatest influence, however, that Irene Castle had on her time was not a dance or a theatrical innovation but a coiffure. She did what no other woman of that period would have dared to do and still keep her reputation —she bobbed her hair. Overnight the style became respectable, if still a bit "daring."

In the year 1914 at the pinnacle of their career the Castles were drawing an average of $31,000 a week doing one-night stands and during their fame were the proprietors of a cabaret called Sans Souci. When Madison Square Garden held an amateur dancing tournament the Castles, as the most famous and admired married couple in the country, sponsored it, assuring its success by the magic of their names alone.

It was not a change in trends or a loss of popularity that ended the Castle legend. In 1915, Vernon, who had always been an enthusiastic supporter of England, was accepted into the Royal Canadian Flying Corps as a second lieutenant. After shooting down two German planes he was promoted to the rank of Captain. In 1917 he was sent to Canada to train pilots, and when America entered the war he was transferred to Texas to do the same for American aviators. In February of 1918 Castle was killed in an air crash during a training flight.

Irene Castle continued after Vernon's death to set fashions in hair styles, clothing, and dances in films and on the stage. They had made silent films together such as *Whirl of Life* (1915) and appeared on the stage in *Watch Your Step* (1915). Alone, Irene had great success on the stage and screen both during the war when her husband was away and after she had been widowed. On Broadway she costarred with Vivienne Segal (now retired with the exception of an occasional TV appearance in southern California) in *Miss 1917*. She starred in featured films such as *The Hillcrest Mystery* (1918) and an extremely popular serial of the day, *Patria* (1917), in which she was billed as "the most popular and admired woman in America," and throughout the twenties she was a popular figure in vaudeville.

Although Irene Castle had become less active by the thirties, her popularity was sufficient to set gate records when the New York World's Fair of 1939 honored her with an Irene Castle Day. She rose to the occasion by creating the "New York World's Fair Hop."

Little has been heard of the once famous dancer since then. Most of her time and energy have been devoted to her favorite cause, a sanctuary for stray pets. From her large beautiful home in Lake Forest, Illinois, Irene operates a shelter (which she calls "Orphans of the Storm") for any and all breeds.

Dance Magazine feted her with a birthday party in New York City in one of her rare public appearances in recent years, attended by such luminaries as Bette Davis, Pearl S. Buck, and Marge and Gower Champion. Said Miss Castle, who was born in 1893, "I could have danced all night."

At her seventy-first birthday party. *Dance Magazine*

In *Thrill of a Lifetime* with Ben Blue, 1937.

JUDY CANOVA

Judy Canova, who made a career of being a hillbilly, began life in 1916 in Jacksonville, Florida. She was part of a family vaudeville team until 1934 when she landed a part in the Broadway show *Calling All Stars* with Gertrude Niesen (who now lives in retirement in Los Angeles).

Her big break came the following year in Hollywood when director Busby Berkeley gave her a bit without billing in *In Caliente*. The popular singer of the day, Wini Shaw (now living in Sunnyside, Long Island, with her husband, a box office treasurer of a New York theatre), was to sing "The Lady in Red" in a nightclub scene, and Berkeley created one of his most beautiful and extravagant production numbers around it. Just as it ended, from behind a pillar Judy appeared in a costume resembling Wini Shaw's. The moment she opened her mouth to sing all of the effect created by the original performance was destroyed. The audience howled. It is a wonder the song survived the Canova treatment to become a standard. (Thirty years later when the Gallery of Modern Art in New York City held a Busby Berkeley festival Judy's takeoff brought down the house once more.)

Judy immediately got other parts suited to her hillbilly hokum. Few knew that the absurd voice she used to butcher songs with had been trained for classical singing.

Her vignettes in important films such as *Thrill of a Lifetime* (1937) and *Artists and Models* (1937) were so popular that in the late thirties she began to make what were known as "programmers." These were full-length films made on a low budget that played the lower half of double bills. A few that Judy turned out were: *Scatterbrain* (1940), *Puddin' Head* (1941), *Singing in the Corn* (1947), *Honeychile* (1951), *WAC from Walla Walla* (1952), and *Untamed Heiress* (1954).

From the war years and on into the fifties, long after many other popular radio shows had fallen by the wayside—with the advent of television—Judy had a popular weekly half-hour radio program. One of the characters appearing with her was called "Pedro." His expression, "Pardon me for talking in your face, *Señorita*," became a household remark during the forties. Another character introduced on the *Judy Canova Show* was her "Cousin Ureenus" who used to eat chopped liver ice cream. On signing off, Judy would sing the popular song "Goodnight Sweetheart."

Variety, which began reviewing television shows in 1939, credits Judy Canova's appearance that year as being the first hillbilly act ever seen on the medium. Judy formed her own TV production company, Caravan, Inc., in 1957 but has hardly been seen with the exception of some guest appearances on the *Huckleberry Finn Show* in the late fifties.

Judy makes an occasional rodeo appearance, though she doesn't have to work anymore and chooses her roles sparingly.

Those expecting to find Judy living in the Ozarks with chickens running around her front yard would be greatly surprised by her beautifully furnished home and tasteful clothes. She lives with her second husband, a real estate broker, and her daughters Diane and Julietta in the San Fernando Valley—not far from the retreat of the widow of Herbert Yates, longtime head of Republic Pictures. Vera Hruba Ralston, the Czech ice skater-actress, known to movie fans as the Queen of the "B's," lives with her mother and 17-year-old dog.

A sophisticated Judy today.

HELEN WILLS MOODY

The girl who grew up to be the world's greatest female tennis player was born in Centerville, California, in 1906. Her maiden name was Helen Newington Wills, but she was known by her married name after she and Frederick S. Moody, Jr., wed in 1929.

Her record stands to this day. She was the undisputed Queen of Tennis not only for her game but because she had that certain something that makes the difference between the great and the near-great. She wore her famous white visored hat like a crown. Her manner was cold and calculating toward her opponents and disdainful to the press and spectators. She was beautiful, and moved on and off the courts with the authority of a champion. Helen had star quality.

Her concentration on the game was absolute, and no matter what happened or how the crowd cheered, her expression remained impassive. In no time she had been dubbed "Little Miss Poker Face."

Helen Wills Moody was the winner of the United States Women's Singles in 1923, 1924, 1925, 1927, 1928, 1929, and 1931. She played on eight Wightman Cup teams, winning 18 singles against 2 losses. She shared the United States Women's Doubles victories in 1922, 1924, 1925, and 1928.

At Wimbledon, England, where the international games are played, she won the singles eight years: 1927, 1928, 1929, 1930, 1932, 1933, 1935, and 1938, and with various partners took the doubles there in 1924, 1927, and 1930.

Helen was the victor of the French Singles four times. Her most dramatic appearance there was against the great French player, Suzanne Lenglen. The press in the United States, while rightfully proud of her, whipped the nation up to fever pitch over the match by playing on national pride, making the contest into something resembling good versus evil. Miss Lenglen and her American opponent were as different as night and day. Lenglen drank, smoked, was seen constantly in Riviera nightclubs, and was unattractive. The foreign newspapers, on the other hand, saw the Frenchwoman as chic, which she was, and fun-loving. Helen Wills Moody appeared to them to be humorless, virginal, and far too sure of herself. It was close to a national tragedy when "our Helen," as the press called her in those days, was trounced 6–3 and 8–6.

It is a great pity that such a splendid career was marred by her rather petulant behavior. A very unfortunate incident lingers in the memories of tennis fans from the Women's National Singles of 1934, which were held at Forest Hills. Mrs. Moody had beaten Helen Hull Jacobs each time they had met, the latter always taking it very well. This time Miss Jacobs had achieved one set up and had a big lead in the second when Mrs. Moody, complaining of an injured spine, defaulted the set, match, and championship by walking off the court. Although she did have an operation after that and was away from her game for a year, rumor had it that the very next day she had to be talked out of playing in the doubles by her partner because the default of the previous day would have been pounced on by the press as merely an act of female pettiness in denying her old opponent the satisfaction of a clear-cut victory.

The following year at Wimbledon, Helen Jacobs came within a breath of that victory until Mrs. Moody turned the tables in the last minutes of the finals and took the title.

Mrs. Moody has written two books, *Tennis,* which she also illustrated, in 1928, and "15–30," which was published in 1937, a year before she retired from major tournament play.

She has never commented publicly about the remarks made about her in the autobiography of the late Bill Tilden, tennis' greatest male player. If only a portion of what he related about her personality in *My Story* is true it would explain why Helen Wills Moody is remembered most, while Helen Jacobs is remembered best.

She married her second husband, Aidan Roark, in 1939 and for a while they lived in Pacific Palisades, California. They now reside in one of the most beautiful communities on the West Coast, Carmel-by-the-Sea, California, a small wooded community of wealthy residents right on the Pacific Ocean. Mrs. Roark is as aloof in retirement as she was while in the public eye. Her attitude toward her game these days seems puzzling. She does not appear at tournaments or keep in touch with players. The United States Lawn Tennis Association has never been notified that she and her husband moved a number of years ago to her present address. Also, it has been years since she subscribed to *World Tennis* magazine or communicated with them. About the only activity she participates in is Republican politics.

Helen Wills Moody in a photograph taken before her famous match with Helen Hull Jacobs at Forest Hills in 1934. *U.S. Lawn Tennis Association.* With dog "Docky," at her home in California recently (*right*). *UPI*

ANNA STEN

The famous actress' real name is Anjuchka Stenska. She was born in Russia in 1910, the daughter of a Swedish mother and a Russian ballet master. She worked as a waitress at the age of twelve, soon after her father died.

When she was fifteen the great Stanislavsky saw her in an amateur play in Kiev and arranged for her to enter the Moscow Film Academy. At eighteen she was part of a traveling troupe doing plays throughout Russia under the auspices of the Moscow Art Theatre. At first she made Russian films in the Crimea and then at the big studios in Moscow. Anna then was sent to Germany to make pictures on a German-Russian coproduction arrangement. Two of the movies she made in Russia are perfect examples of the excellent work turned out at the time by the Soviet cinema, *Girl with the Hatbox* (1927) and *The Yellow Ticket* (1928).

Anna Sten played opposite the late Anton Walbrook in the talkie *Trapeze* (1931) which had as its director the great German talent, E. A. Dupont. Another of her better pictures of that period in Germany was *Bombs Over Monte Carlo* (1931). It was, however, her part of Grushenka in *The Brothers Karamazov* (1931) that brought her to the attention of the American producer Samuel Goldwyn. The film was directed by a Russian, Fedor Ozep, who was also her husband. Before accepting Goldwyn's five-year contract she and Ozep parted, and in 1932 Anna married her present husband, the producer of *Karamazov*, Eugene Frenkes.

Anna Sten arrived in Hollywood in 1932. When she first drove down Hollywood Boulevard she thought it so strange that it must be all one large movie set.

Her first film was not released until 1934. The two-year interim was used by Goldwyn to have his new star tutored in English while he was making her the subject of one of the most intensive personal publicity campaigns Hollywood had ever seen.

Nana opened in New York's Radio City Music Hall on February 1, 1934. Her leading man was Phillips Holmes, whom Goldwyn borrowed from Paramount. The sets were lavish and Miss Sten was beautiful. Her screen debut was directed by Dorothy Arzner, one of the hottest in the business at that time. Miss Arzner faded from pictures several years later and is now directing television commercials in Los Angeles. The picture received good notices but did not fare well at the box office.

Goldwyn had originally promised Anna that he would do an American version of *The Brothers Karamazov*. Instead he gave her a production of another Tolstoy novel *Resurrection* which was called on the screen *We Live Again* (1934). Opposite her was one of the screen's most popular actors, Fredric March. Again Goldwyn spared no expense, and again the film flopped dismally at the box office.

Her third and final effort under that contract was with Gary Cooper in *The Wedding Night* (1935). It is Anna's favorite among her American movies. The picture had star names, a top production, good release, publicity, and reviews. The only thing wrong was, like the other two, nobody went to see it. The Goldwyn-Sten contract was dissolved by "mutual agreement."

Miss Sten made other films during the thirties and forties both in Hollywood and England, but none of them were great successes. In each, however, *Exile Express* (1939), *They Came to Blow Up America* (1943), and *Three Russian Girls* (1944), she was a joy to look at and turned in a good performance.

Anna Sten has been referred to as "Goldwyn's Folly" and "The Edsel of the Movie Industry." Whatever the reason for her failure to click with the public, she was indisputably a fine actress and a classic beauty. Most movie historians feel that she was oversold and improperly handled.

Miss Sten maintains both a ranch-style house in Beverly Hills and an apartment in New York City. During the war she began painting and has had one-woman shows in Los Angeles and New York which were critically and financially successful. Her first show in Los Angeles in 1962 sold out completely. Her works were sent on a European tour by the Smithsonian Institution and are in the collection of the Boston Museum.

With the exception of an English picture *The Nun and the Sergeant* (1962) and an occasional TV role Anna Sten devotes most of her time to painting. When she is in New York, however, she attends classes at the Actors Studio and promises to appear in a play for them if it is produced on Broadway. Her role in it: an Eskimo.

The Edsel of the movie industry in *Nana* for Samuel Goldwyn, 1934. A deeply suntanned Anna Sten in her Manhattan apartment recently (*right*).

Alfred Monaco

About to give the downbeat for a 1945 CBS radio broadcast.

PHIL SPITALNY

The all-girl orchestra leader received his musical training in Eastern Europe, where he was born. His expertise as a conductor was obvious to vaudeville impresarios who gave him steady employment in the pits of their houses after he came to the United States. For a while he settled down in Cleveland, Ohio, at the Allen Theatre where in a short time he became a local favorite.

In the late twenties Spitalny conceived his idea for an all-girl orchestra. He had gone to hear the debut of a fourteen-year-old violinist named Evelyn Kaye. He was so taken by her playing that he immediately thought of hiring her. As she continued to play, the idea expanded. Why not lots of girl musicians? Why not all girls? Beautiful talented girls and lots of strings. The teenager was hired and performed simply under the name "Evelyn," but not for long, for soon fan mail began to pour in describing her technique as "magic." Thus she became the only musician ever to have her instrument receive equal billing, becoming known as "Evelyn and Her Magic Violin." As he envisioned his new orchestra, a vaudeville tour would be impractical because of its size. But this was the time of the new entertainment medium known as radio. In spite of the novelty of the group being essentially visual, the all-girl concept was a radio hit, and like most innovations it inspired a number of copies. Spitalny's orchestra, however, was never seriously challenged because of the quality of its sound. Most of the members were hand picked from Manhattan's famed Julliard School of Music.

One of the first sponsors of *The Hour of Charm,* as the show was called, was a national manufacturer of chocolate. The slogan of the product was

136

"Chocolate of the highest quality for the lowest price." These were the days of live radio. The announcer walked to the microphone and told audiences from coast to coast that the program was being brought to them by "Chocolate of the lowest quality for the highest price." The studio audience howled. Spitalny doubled in two. The girls giggled. But when the announcer was so convulsed he couldn't say it correctly, it was the last straw. The contract was immediately cancelled. Although there was another sponsor ready to pick up the tab, that was the last *Hour of Charm* with a male announcer. From then on Spitalny's music was introduced by "The Voice of Charm." One of the female announcers with the program for many years was Arlene Francis.

Although Phil Spitalny was famous throughout the land, none of his radio listeners knew that he spoke with a heavy accent. Throughout his career Phil never said a word on the air, until a 1965 interview.

In the late forties, when it seemed clear that television and not radio would be the dominant medium, Spitalny decided not to make the switch, remembering that he had always promised himself that when he had attained success he would know when to quit.

Phil Spitalny and Evelyn have been married since 1950 when they moved to Miami Beach. Their home was built to their specifications—it contains not only a music room but a bathtub shaped like a violin. One of their neighbors is the former movie beauty, Toby Wing, married to the famous pioneer aviator, Richard Merrill.

For a while Phil suffered ill health after his retirement. He has recovered and is now the music critic for the Miami Beach *Sun*. Every summer Phil and Evelyn come to New York on their way to the music festivals of Europe. During their stopover an annual luncheon of all the *Hour of Charm* girls who live in the area is held in the hotel where the Spitalnys stay.

With wife, Evelyn, at a recent opening in Miami Beach. *Allen Malschick*

"The Male Shirley Temple," during a 1937 appearance on *The Eddie Cantor Show.*

BOBBY BREEN

The child actor had been around even before Eddie Cantor made him a regular on the late entertainer's weekly radio show in 1936. It was, however, that exposure on coast-to-coast radio that made Bobby Breen a star. He became so identified with Cantor that when Bobby called him "Uncle Eddie" the public actually believed that he was a nephew. On the same shows with Breen was another Cantor discovery, a young lady who was to become one of Universal Pictures' biggest money-makers during the thirties, Deanna Durbin. Now married to a film director, Miss Durbin lives in Paris shuddering at even the mention of a comeback.

In the thirties every major lot in Hollywood had a child star. RKO had Bobby. From the age of eight until his voice began to change he made films such as *Hawaii Calls* (1938), *Fisherman's Wharf* (1939), and *Way Down South* (1939). As a child star he was made conscious of budgets, overtime, bookings, grosses, etc. He had a fortune put aside for him before he was grown up, a name that is still recognized around the world, and the experience of a veteran entertainer. To Bobby, he was a boy who had everything but a childhood.

With short pants, curly hair, and a soprano voice Breen forged a sissified image that has haunted him through his service in the United States Army, two marriages, and his second career as an adult singer in nightclubs.

In his appearances today he peppers his act with songs such as "Rainbow on the River" (the title song from his 1936 motion picture). The voice is deeper now but it still has that same distinctive quality that made matrons want to cuddle him and kids want to kick him. "They expect me to come onstage still wearing short pants," says Bobby. "It takes a lot of work out there to make them believe I'm grown up. They resent it somehow. It's something I have to fight every single performance."

Breen considered several other professions after his discharge from the Army, and event spent some time in the real estate business, but show business was too much a part of him. Although the money he had made before the war was in trust waiting for him when he came of age, there remains a thinly veiled bitterness about those years, and he frankly admits that if his son were to choose a career in show business it would be a great disappointment to him.

When asked about some of his contemporaries Bobby says, "I dated Shirley Temple once, but it was only a publicity stunt. Cora Sue Collins came backstage to see me a couple of years ago when I was playing Houston, and it was nice to see her again. They tell me that Dickie Moore has an office in this building, but I never see him. I didn't see much of them even in those days. It wasn't that I didn't like them, but there just wasn't time."

Bobby Breen Productions maintains offices in the theatrical district of Manhattan booking Bobby's club act which has played Australia, New Zealand, and South Africa in recent years to excellent reviews.

Bobby's wife works closely with him, and they commute together daily from their Riverdale, New York, home. The most exciting item on the horizon for the Breens is the contract Bobby recently signed with Mo-Town Records. The Detroit firm handles some of the hottest names in Rock 'n' Roll, such as the Supremes. Breen's first record for them will be a Rock version of "Rainbow on the River."

Today as he appears in nightclubs around the world.
CBS Radio

A publicity shot taken during the 1930's at the height of his popularity on radio. *CBS Radio*

LANNY ROSS

Though not as a singer, Lanny Ross has been performing since the age of four. He began on the stage in London, and at six years was with the great actor George Arliss in his production of *Disraeli*. His own father was the well-known Shakespearean actor, Douglas Ross.

After attending Yale, receiving a degree, and being admitted to the New York Bar, Lanny decided to try his luck at singing. He had been a member of the famous "Whiffenpoofs" at Yale.

Lanny made his debut under the title "The Troubador of the Moon" on Christmas morning, 1928. His success was almost immediate and lasted longer than that of most of the singers who were overnight sensations on the infant medium, radio.

For six years he was the singing star of the Maxwell House *Show Boat,* emceed by the late Charles Winninger. Packard Motor Cars' *Mardi Gras* and Camel Cigarettes' *Camel Caravan* were two other important radio shows featuring his name during the thirties.

Lanny was as handsome and romantic-looking as he sounded over the air. In Hollywood he starred in *Melody in Spring* in 1934 opposite a young lady who had just changed her name from Harriet Lake, which is what it had been on Broadway, to Ann Sothern. His costars in *College Rhythm* (1934) were the late Joe ("You wanna buy a duck?") Penner and the lovely Helen Mack, who lives in the apartment next to Lanny's on Manhattan's East 57th Street. The feature-length Fleischer cartoon *Gulliver's Travels* (1939) featured the voices of Lanny Ross and his other neighbor, Jessica Dragonette.

In 1938 Lanny Ross was the featured male vocalist on the Lucky Strike *Hit Parade*. The top songs of the year were "Thanks for the Memory" and "Jeepers Creepers."

Throughout his career his theme "Moonlight and Roses" was the sign-off on all his network programs. Probably the most popular of all was his Monday through Friday Franco-American show immediately following *Amos 'n' Andy*.

During the Second World War Ross served on General Douglas MacArthur's staff in the South Pacific. He was later awarded the Medal of Merit.

In the early days of television Lanny had the popular *Swift's TV Variety Show* and *The Lanny Ross Show*.

Ross married Olive White, his press agent, in 1935. Their only child, a daughter, died a few years ago. In the living room of their duplex apartment are large portraits of their granddaughter and her late mother.

Lanny has taken up painting. One of his friends who encouraged him in his hobby and complimented him on his efforts is the wife of the famous art dealer, Victor Hammer, of the Hammer Galleries. She was for nearly thirty years one of the best loved women on radio, Ireene Wicker, "The Singing Lady."

Lanny Ross is active in the affairs of the radio and TV performers union, the American Federation of Television and Radio Artists, and is on the board of the scholarship fund named for the founder of the union, the George Heller Foundation.

Although he is less active before the cameras and microphones, Ross is quite well known as a producer of industrial shows. He also finds time to perform occasionally in summer stock and nightclubs around the country.

The main project taking up his time is a Broadway show which has been in the works for some time. Lanny has written the music and lyrics, and plans to have it produced under the title *Morning Town*.

Lanny is today a producer, a grandfather, and still a performer. *Augusta Berns*

In 1942, when her "peek-a-boo" sweep was the rage of the country.

VERONICA LAKE

Veronica Lake was born Constance Ockleman in 1919 in Lake Placid, New York. Her father was a college professor and, before she decided on a theatrical career, she was a premedical student at McGill University.

In 1941 she was under contract to Paramount Pictures. There was a role for a beautiful girl in one of their big pictures of that year. Since the male stars, William Holden, Ray Milland, and Brian Donlevy, would provide enough star power to assure the picture's success, the front office decided to take a chance on their starlet with the peculiar hair-do. The film was *I Wanted Wings,* and Veronica was a sensation and a brand new exciting star. She introduced the "peek-a-boo" hair-do which swept the country's beauty parlors overnight. So popular, in fact, was this new coiffure that during World War II the Defense Department of the United States made an official request of Paramount to change the hair style of their star. So many women in defense plants had emulated it that there were countless work stoppages and injuries from hair getting caught in machines. She obliged by adopting another favorite style of the time, the upsweep.

Another 1941 movie that proved Miss Lake to be a skilled comedienne was *Sullivan's Travels.* She turned in a splendid performance opposite Joel McCrea, under Preston Sturges' direction. Veronica's hair was hidden under a man's cap during much of the film, demonstrating that she was more than just a girl with a gimmick.

In 1942 Paramount took another chance on a young actor under contract to them named Alan Ladd. They had difficulty casting him because he was extremely short. So was Veronica. Together they made *This Gun for Hire.*

From then on, half of the leading ladies in Hollywood would have walked in a trench all through a picture to meet the height requirements for playing opposite the dynamic new star. The magnetic combination of Lake and Ladd was seen in three other films: *The Glass Key* (1942), *The Blue Dahlia* (1946), and *Saigon* (1948).

Another smash for Veronica in 1942 was her role opposite Fredric March in *I Married a Witch.* The following year she was in the all-star *Star Spangled Rhythm* and *So Proudly We Hail,* a popular film about women at war which had Claudette Colbert and Paulette Goddard in the cast. She made two pictures with Eddie Bracken in 1945: *Out of This World* and *Hold That Blonde,* and one with Sonny Tufts (who lives in Hollywood and appeared on a special TV show in 1966 as the trivia personality of the year): *Bring on the Girls,* followed by another picture with Tufts, *Miss Suzy Slagle* (1946).

Some of her other credits include the excellent melodrama *Hour Before Dawn* (1944) with Franchot Tone, *Duffy's Tavern* (1945), and *Isn't It Romantic* (1948).

After she left Paramount in the late forties little was heard of her other than occasional stories about her personal life—none of which were pleasant though reportedly true. In 1951 she and husband André de Toth filed voluntary bankruptcy petitions and their $120,000 Hollywood home was seized for nonpayment of taxes. At its auction there were no bidders. Following the couple's divorce Veronica moved to New York City.

She worked for a while during 1962 as a hostess in the restaurant of the Martha Washington Hotel in New York and was for a short time in 1963 a waitress in a Greenwich Village café, thereafter drifting from one odd job to another. In 1964 she appeared off-Broadway in the revival of *Best Foot Forward.* She got fine notices, and the show was a hit, but the comeback that many believed and hoped for did not happen.

Veronica still lives in New York City, but grants very few interviews. She seems anxious to work, and has done some roles in Florida during the 1965–66 season, and a low-budget movie in Montreal recently. On her return she stopped in the Midwest to visit her new grandchild.

In a New York theatre lobby recently.

BURTON K. WHEELER

The influential isolationist Senator was born in Hudson, Massachusetts, in 1882, the son of a shoemaker. After attending public schools there, he went to the University of Michigan, graduating from the law school in 1905. That same year he opened a law office in Butte, Montana. He was elected to the Montana Legislature in 1910, appointed United States District Attorney in 1913, serving until 1918, was defeated for governor in 1920 but elected United States Senator in 1922, serving four terms until 1946.

Although elected to the Senate as a Democrat, a year later he switched party affiliations and ran on the Progressive Party ticket as the vice-presidential candidate with Robert "Fighting Bob" La Follette, the presidential candidate. They received 4,822,856 popular and 13 electoral votes.

He backed the Democratic candidate, Al Smith, in 1928 and was one of the earliest preconvention supporters in 1932 of the New York governor, Franklin D. Roosevelt, as well as being instrumental in obtaining for Roosevelt the support of Louisiana's powerful "Kingfish" Huey Long.

Throughout the first few years of Roosevelt's New Deal, the Montana Senator voted for most of its measures. He balked, however, at the far-reaching effects contained in the National Recovery Act. Wheeler's leeriness of the complicated bill was proved justified when it was later declared unconstitutional by the Supreme Court.

In 1937, when F.D.R. presented the Congress with his bill to pack the Supreme Court, Wheeler split with his party's leader saying that what the President was asking for amounted to dictatorial powers and the control of all branches of government. Up until that time Wheeler had always enjoyed the strong support of labor, but thereafter he could never again count on the support of the unions—who supported F.D.R.'s attempt—and many of them opposed him for his renomination in 1946.

By 1940 Wheeler had become one of the greatest crowd pleasers on the isolationist circuit. His appearance at an America First rally was a sure guarantee of a packed house. The fever to keep America out of another war was strong enough to cross party lines and bring together such divergent forces as Socialist Norman Thomas, Republicans Senator Nye and Congressman Fish, as well as Democrat Wheeler and many others besides. However, when war with the Axis finally broke out on December 7, 1941, Wheeler supported all of F.D.R.'s wartime measures.

In the spring of 1940 Wheeler announced that he would be available for the nomination at the Democratic Convention that summer even if F.D.R. decided to seek a third term. He declared that only a noninterventionalist candidate could win in November. John L. Lewis threw his support behind him, but by the time the delegates met Wheeler was out of the running.

Wheeler was the co-author with the late Sam Rayburn of the Utility Holding Company Bill, which he handled in the Senate. The law, subsequently known as the Wheeler-Rayburn Act, was aimed at destroying holding companies that could not clearly prove the economic necessity for their existence.

Throughout his career he stormed against the trusts, including the mining interests and oil companies; he urged rigid regulation of big business. Flouting party leadership, he often sided with Senators Borah of Idaho and Norris of Nebraska, yet in 1933, when he became chairman of the Committee on Interstate Commerce, he served as front man for the Roosevelt Crusade.

During the Democratic Convention of 1944, as well as the previous one in 1940, many political observers chose Wheeler as the man, who, as a vice-presidential candidate, could bring harmony to the party. Many of Roosevelt's closest advisers, pleaded with Wheeler, as they also did in 1940, to run for the vice-presidency. Wheeler refused, and at the conventions it was Wallace and Truman respectively who were chosen.

When Wheeler stood for reelection in 1946 he was defeated. He tells it this way: "In 1946 money was sent in from New York, Hollywood, and other places to defeat me, and some of the labor and farm leaders whom I had befriended when they had few friends were the ones that beat me in the primary. However, that is life, and I have no regrets. As a matter of fact, they did me a favor from the financial standpoint and probably from a health standpoint."

Wheeler has been practicing law since 1947 in partnership with his son in Washington, D.C., with most of their work taking them before the Federal Communications Commission and the Interstate Commerce Commission. Of current events he says: "If I were in the Senate today, I would be supporting some things that the Administration wants and opposing others. I was always an independent in politics and still am. I have always felt we had no business in Vietnam, and that we can't tell every country what kind of government they are going to have. Nor can we buy the friendship of countries any more than you can buy the lasting friendship of individuals."

In his Washington, D.C., law office recently.

Addressing an isolationist rally in 1939.

George Lohr

In 1938.

GALE SONDERGAARD

Gale Sondergaard was a successful stage actress before she entered motion pictures. After studying under Jessie Bonstelle as a member of the famous Bonstelle Players, she appeared on Broadway in a number of plays. Her most important role was that of Nina, in Eugene O'Neill's *Strange Interlude*. In the original 1928 New York company the role was essayed by Lynn Fontanne, who was replaced by Judith Anderson, followed by Miss Sondergaard. That Miss Sondergaard was given so meaty a part already played by two of the most famous actresses in the American theatre is a testimony to the faith the producers had in the young actress.

In the early thirties her husband, Herbert Biberman, a successful stage director in New York for the Theatre Guild, went to Hollywood with a contract to direct pictures. At the time the Bibermans moved to California, Gale decided to give up her career—she had little interest in movies, and felt they were not the proper medium for her.

After Gale settled down in her new home and became used to a life away from Broadway, an agent asked her permission to submit her name for the role of Faith in the classic *Anthony Adverse*. Mervyn LeRoy, who was directing it at Warner Brothers and looking for a face that was unknown to movie audiences, chose her for the part. It was with little enthusiasm that the actress accepted it, though. Even when with an ecstatic LeRoy she saw the rushes she was unimpressed. The role seemed small after what she had become used to on Broadway, and her acting seemed to her to be "self-conscious."

The picture was released in 1936, the year that the Academy of Motion Picture Arts and Sciences added the category of Best Supporting Actress. Gale Sondergaard received the Oscar for her first screen role.

Although her debut role and many others she played were sympathetic ones, Gale Sondergaard is remembered as the Queen of the Heavies. She laughs today when fans refer to her as the Lady They Loved to Hate, and

146

seem to have forgotten that she was Mme. Dreyfus in *The Life of Émile Zola* (1937) and was a foil for Bob Hope and Bing Crosby in *The Road to Rio* (1947). She was, however, a menace in many a movie in the thirties and for-ties—she played the Eurasian wife of Bette Davis' lover in *The Letter* (murdering Bette in the last reel), Jimmy Stewart threatened to drop her down a manhole after she frightened Simone Simon in *Seventh Heaven*, and she was burned up in a forest after scaring little Shirley Temple in *The Bluebird*.

In 1946 she was once again nominated for the Best Supporting Actress of that year for her performance in *Anna and the King of Siam*. (The picture in which she played the role of Rex Harrison's wife has not been shown on TV because of the musical remake, *The King and I*.)

In 1948 Gale Sondergaard, along with 300 others in Hollywood, was black-listed from the motion picture industry following the famous House Un-American Activities Committee's investigation of the film industry. Her husband was a member of the group, now referred to as "The Hollywood 10," who refused to give testimony to H.U.A.C. and were sent to prison.

Since 1948 Miss Sondergaard has not made a film, television, or radio appearance as an actress though she and Herbert Biberman have been on countless panels and interview shows concerning the blacklist. Profession-ally, however, they are *personae non gratae* in the entertainment industry.

The Bibermans sold their home in the Hollywood Hills in 1965 and moved to New York City where Gale did an off-Broadway one-woman show in 1966 entitled *Woman*. In it she read works such as *The Doll's House*, concerning the emergence of woman as an independent being.

There is no apparent bitterness in Gale today. She talks easily with young fans who recognize her on the street from her old pictures now playing on *The Late Show* on TV, and exhibits a dazzling smile that belies the troubles she has known. While performing in *Woman* in 1966, her daughter died unexpectedly.

About her career she says, "Yes, I miss acting. A part of my life—a part of me, really—stopped when my work was taken away from me. I miss it every day. I miss it very much indeed."

Today, with husband, Herbert Biberman.
Edward Oleksak

In a costume by Adrian, circa 1923.

LEATRICE JOY

Leatrice Joy is her real name which seems quite fitting since everything about her is genuine. Her first name was that of her father's old girl friend, her mother had a unique way of teasing him. Joy was her mother's maiden name and predicted the pleasure she would give for so many years to her fans.

Although her career in pictures dates back to 1915, it was not until the early twenties that she became a big star. In the meantime she played an extra in one of Mary Pickford's early movies and was the love interest of both Billy West and Oliver Hardy in the slapstick comedies the two comics made after the First World War.

It was Cecil B. de Mille who made Miss Joy into one of the biggest stars of the silent era. For him she made *Manslaughter* (1922), and the original *Ten Commandments* (1923). The two worked so well together that when de Mille left Paramount to become an independent producer he took Leatrice with him. Leatrice headed an all-star cast for *Java Head* in 1923 and in 1924 she costarred in *Triumph* with Rod La Rocque, who is married to Vilma Banky and lives on their ranch in California.

When she bought a Rolls Royce in 1926 Conrad Nagel told her he thought it was extravagant. "What, darling, does 'extravagance' mean when you are making thousands of dollars a week?" she answered.

Leatrice was neither a vamp nor a sweet young thing. In most of her pictures she was the severely tailored career woman. Much of the popularity of bobbed hair during that period was due to her mannish coiffures.

Miss Joy went into semi-retirement in the thirties, living in Beverly Hills, appearing occasionally in a small film part. At that time she fostered the career of one of the best remembered Negro character actresses, Louise Beavers, who was for 12 years Miss Joy's personal maid before peeling grapes for Mae West.

In 1954 Leatrice had a supporting role in a picture called *Love Nest*. Another in the cast was a comedian who had not been too successful. His name was Jack Paar. The ingenue was played by a blonde whom Miss Joy noticed at once in spite of her small part. "She had the bearing of a real star and was gifted with that wonderfully innocent sex appeal that is so rare." Her name was Marilyn Monroe.

Born in New Orleans, there is more than a trace of a Southern drawl in her speech. The farther back into the past she goes the heavier it gets: "I'm never lonely on cold, snowy nights. I have the delightful memories of a wonderful, happy childhood, and a terribly romantic youth. Did you know that John and I eloped to Mexico? A *mariachi* band played "Alexander's Ragtime Band" as our wedding march. Still, it was romantic. Everything was then."

She is still addressed as "Mrs. John Gilbert," although she and the matinee idol were divorced long before he died in 1936. Their grandson is an eleven-year-old aspiring actor, whose agent is also a Paramount star of the silent period, Esther Ralston.

Miss Joy lives in a charming house in Riverside, Connecticut. It is right on the water and is appropriately called "The Magic Cottage." Much of the time its owner is away keeping speaking engagements at women's clubs or visiting friends in Hollywood.

Today: grandmother, lecturer, writer. *John Virzi*

LARRY ADLER

Larry Adler won a contest three weeks after he began playing the mouth organ (he never calls it a "harmonica"), at the age of fourteen. The place was Baltimore, where he was born and grew up. The year was 1928.

His mother encouraged him to "be somebody" which, for a musician, meant go to New York. In the big city he auditioned for the famous Borrah Minnevitch (of "Harmonica Rascal" fame) who told him, "Kid, you stink." Eddie Cantor, Gus Edwards, and Flo Ziegfeld thought otherwise and encouraged him to stick around until he got a break. Each was to say after Adler had made it that he had found the kid playing on the sidewalk for pennies.

Adler didn't have long to wait. By 1934 he was playing the Palace Theatre on Broadway and appearing as a guest on the radio variety shows of the day.

The elevation of Larry Adler to stardom made the harmonica respectable for the first time. Until then the instrument had been reserved for hillbilly acts and blackface performers. Kids began taking it up around the country during the Depression.

In 1935 Adler made his first trip to England. He played in the big musical success of the season, *Streamline*. In 1937 Jack Warner heard him play during an engagement at a Hollywood nightclub, and signed him up for the movie *The Singing Marine*. The director, Busby Berkeley, had no knowledge of the contract until Larry appeared ready for work. Once he heard Adler play he was delighted to change a few of the old scenes around and make what turned out to be the opening, and highlight, of the picture —the harmonicist playing for a group of Marines, including Dick Powell, around a campfire.

By the late thirties Adler was known all over the world through his recordings and movies. In 1939 he played his first symphony concert in Sydney, Australia.

The music he created, which turned the mouth organ into a sophisticated instrument, was appreciated as much by fellow musicians as by the general public. When he played the "Bolero" for its composer, Maurice Ravel listened intently and then told Larry all of the mistakes he had noticed during the piece. Heartsick, Adler asked if Ravel would at least sign the arrangement that Adler had done. "But," said Ravel, "I thought you would allow me to keep it as a souvenir!"

Composers have written works especially for Adler to play. The late Ralph Vaughan Williams and Darius Milhaud, both avid Adler fans, contributed original works to his repertoire, as did Arthur Benjamin and Cyril Scott. Only recently Ira Gershwin gave him an unpublished concerto of the late George Gershwin along with permission to perform it.

As the postwar Red scare began in 1947 Larry Adler along with his longtime friend and frequent partner in recitals, dancer Paul Draper, were accused of being Communists. On advice of attorneys and friends they sued the woman who had brought the charges for libel. The long and costly case ended in a hung jury.

From that day on Larry Adler's services, once sought after by producers in all media, were unwanted. In 1948 Adler, his wife, and three children moved to England where they have lived ever since.

Whatever his political leanings or feelings about his native land, Larry Adler entertained United Nations troops in the front lines during the Korean War in 1952.

Adler has never ceased working in England, and enjoys enormous popularity there. His concerts, benefits, TV appearances, and tours have made him as much of a drawing card there as he ever was in this country. In 1966 his appearance at the Edinburgh Festival was the highlight of the affair.

Although he still comes to the United States for a club or a concert date from time to time, his bookings are in small clubs rather than the places that used to carry his name proudly on a marquee. Neither the TV networks nor the motion picture studios seem interested in his abilities. Although he has done the musical scores for major motion pictures such as *The Great Chase* (1965) and *King and Country* (1966), it was usually under another name to protect the studios. The notable exception was the English film *Genevieve* which starred the late Kay Kendall, and received an Academy Award nomination in 1954 for the Best Original Musical Score.

Adler says of his adopted country: "England has a sense of tolerance and fair play I hope some day will be present in the United States. My friend Paul has recently moved back to New York. He tells me things have changed. I'm afraid they will have to change a good deal more than they have before I return."

At the height of his fame, 1945, just two years before he was blacklisted, and *(right)* during a recent visit to New York.

NBC Radio   *William Glenesk*

JOHN W. BRICKER

Senator John W. Bricker was born in 1893 and grew up on a farm in Mount Sterling, Ohio. He earned a law degree at Ohio State University. After serving as a First Lieutenant in World War I, he went into law practice in 1920 in Columbus, Ohio, becoming Assistant Attorney General in 1923 and Attorney General in 1933.

In 1939 Bricker was elected Governor of Ohio on the Republican ticket serving a total of three terms. His terms in office were marked by fiscal responsibility and a determination to check the expanding power of the federal government. Bricker went so far as to resist appeals by Ohio cities for emergency relief from Washington.

At the G.O.P. national convention in 1940 it was Governor Bricker who urged that the nomination of Wendell Willkie be made unanimous, following an exhausting and bitter fight between the Old Guard and the internationalists in the Republican party. When Bricker asked that all Republicans join in the cry "We Want Willkie," it was a plea for party unity and a dramatic national debut by the man who had his eye on the nomination four years thence.

The Conservative wing of the G.O.P. had been foiled in its attempt to nominate one of their own in 1936 and in 1940. In 1944, although General MacArthur's name received more than passing mention, among the professionals it was John Bricker of Ohio who was the leading contender from the Right—the war was still being fought, and MacArthur was in the Pacific. Bricker, on the other hand, was very much available for press conferences and speeches, and he controlled the powerful Ohio delegation. He had the added benefit of being endorsed by one of the most influential and skillful politicians in his party, Senator Robert A. Taft, also of Ohio. Bricker announced his candidacy on November 16, 1943.

Although Bricker was unable to capture the Presidential nomination, Governor Thomas E. Dewey of New York took on the Ohio governor as running mate. Dewey and Bricker seemed an unlikely combination, even in a profession known for its strange bedfellows—the New York Governor was viewed by the Old Guard as a liberal and an internationalist. The Dewey-Bricker ticket was defeated by the Roosevelt-Truman team, who campaigned with the seemingly logical slogan "Don't Change Horses in the Middle of a Stream." Presidents had traditionally been reelected during wartime, and the results were no great surprise.

If there is an American public official more easily forgotten than a vice-president it is the man who only ran for the office. Bricker, however, achieved fame far greater than second-in-command would ever have afforded him, merely by proposing one piece of legislation. He had been elected Senator from Ohio in 1946 on principles and promises even more to the Right of fellow Ohioan Senator Taft. He remained a consistent foe of centralized government and this country's growing involvement in international affairs. It was his fear of America's direction in world politics that led him to create the famous Bricker Amendment. The Amendment would make any treaty or agreement with a foreign country invalid if it conflicted with the United States Constitution, and made all treaties and agreements subject to two-thirds approval by the Senate.

Bricker's fear of the infringement on our national sovereignty was shared by the American Medical Association, the Daughters of the American Revolution, and an organization made up of mothers of overseas armed forces personnel known as the Vigilant Mothers for the Bricker Amendment.

Although the Amendment was defeated in the Senate by a vote of 42 to 50 on February 25, 1954, the following day Senator Walter F. George proposed a watered-down version which received the necessary two-thirds majority with a vote of 61 to 30. On the crucial motion to send the amendment to the states for ratification, however, the vote was 60–31, one less than the number needed.

The Bricker Amendment died hard. It was proposed four times in the Senate over the next four sessions. The last time it was up for a vote was 1958. It was defeated as was its author by his Democratic opponent Mike DiSalle in the senatorial elections of 1958.

No one, least of all Bricker, expected he would lose that election. He returned to law practice with his old firm of Bricker, Evatt, Barton, Eckler and Neihoff in Columbus, Ohio. One of the partners in the firm is John Day Bricker, his only son. In 1964 rumors were about in Ohio politics that Bricker would oppose Senator Stephen Young in the senate race of that year, but he chose otherwise. His continued interest in politics precludes office-holding. He refuses to say whom he would like to see as the upcoming G.O.P. presidential nominee, but when George Romney first ran for the governorship in Michigan former Senator Bricker referred to a Senate hearing years ago when Romney, then an auto executive, was queried by Bricker: "One of the most able witnesses I've ever seen," said Bricker of his witness, "an excellent choice for anything he wants." (In 1964 Bricker was solidly behind Senator Barry Goldwater.)

John W. Bricker is on the Board of Trustees of Ohio State University and Franklin College. He is a 33-degree Shriner and is active in the American Legion.

With Mrs. John W. Bricker on the campaign trail in 1944, and (*right*) during a recent visit.
Jacob Lofman

With Ann Dvorak in the popular 1932 flick *Crooner*.

DAVID MANNERS

Before leaving his home in Halifax, Nova Scotia, where he was born in 1901, Rauff Acklom changed his name to David Manners. In New York the future Hollywood leading man studied drama and worked with the Theatre Guild.

When Manners arrived in Hollywood in 1929 he was exactly what the studios were looking for. The new sound systems had ended the career of many silent stars, and the casting offices were told to find actors who could speak properly. David's stage training had provided him with the proper diction, and nature had given him the clean-cut good looks that fit so many parts being cast at the time. His first picture, and probably his best part, was in the classic *Journey's End* (1930) from the enormously successful stage play. A contract with First National Pictures resulted from that picture.

Manners was aptly named. His first name might have been "Good" considering his image at the time. Always well dressed, well spoken, and with impeccable manners, David was a perfect leading man for aspiring young actresses and older female stars who wanted nobody stealing scenes from them with mannerisms or too much sex appeal. This young man was just right and every actress wanted him in her picture. He was what girls in those days called "a good catch," playing an earnest, sincere young man with the kind of good looks that needn't worry parents unduly. David wasn't the type of fellow to let the public down—he was always the perfect gentleman with Loretta Young, Mae Clarke (who won a tidy settlement from a Los Angeles TV station a few years ago when an old woman who emceed a horror movie claimed to be she), Joan Blondell, and Ann Dvorak.

154

It is unfortunate that Manners, who made so many pictures in the thirties, was in so few that really hold up by today's standards. The only two which are shown today at art houses as cinema classics are *Journey's End* (1930) and Katharine Hepburn's first film, *A Bill of Divorcement* (1932). Although he never played a "heavy," he is associated with horror films because of his appearance in *Dracula* (1931), the original sound version, *The Mummy* (1932), in which his leading lady was Zita Johann, now living in West Nyack, New York, and *The Black Cat* (1934).

While his career in films didn't last beyond the late thirties his credit list is a long one. A few of the better pictures were: the first sound version of *Kismet* (1930) with Otis Skinner, *The Millionaire* (1931) opposite Evelyn Knapp (now Mrs. Snyder of Beverly Hills, California), *Man Wanted* (1932) with Kay Francis (next to Greta Garbo, no star has drawn a tighter curtain around her life since her retirement in the late forties. Living just off Fifth Avenue in New York's East sixties, Miss Francis refuses to sign autographs, to be photographed, or interviewed), *Crooner* (1932), *The Greeks Had a Word for It* (1932) with Ina Claire (completely retired to a very social life in San Francisco, California), and *Mystery of Edwin Drood* (1935) with Heather Angel (now Mrs. Robert B. Sinclair of Montecito, California). David also made several pictures with the lovely European star Elissa Landi (who died of cancer in 1948), *Warrior's Husband* (1933), and *The Great Flirtation* (1934), after which he lived in relative obscurity.

In 1946 he attempted a comeback on Broadway in the production *Truckline Café* but the play was not successful. Also in the cast was a young actor, Marlon Brando.

During the fifties David turned to writing. Since then he has completed three novels under the name David J. Manners. He is currently working on his fourth book.

Manners, who has never married, lives in a beautiful home in Pacific Palisades, California, where he enjoys being a Sunday painter and gardener.

Now a successful novelist.

John Virzi

During one of his first interviews after being appointed to Hiram Johnson's Senate seat in 1945.
CBS

WILLIAM F. KNOWLAND

Senator William Fife Knowland was born in 1908 in Alameda, California, the son of the owner-publisher of the Oakland *Tribune*. He attended the University of California, graduating in 1926.

After college he worked on his father's paper. He became a California State Assemblyman, serving from 1933 until 1935, and a state Senator serving from 1935 until 1939.

During the Second World War he was a commissioned officer with the United States Army. Upon his discharge Knowland was appointed by California Governor Earl Warren, an old political crony, to serve the remaining year of the term of Hiram W. Johnson, who had died. Knowland was elected to a full term on his own in 1946.

Knowland was one of the youngest and brashest senators on Capitol Hill. Usually the Senate deals with such behavior as his by ignoring the upstart, but Bill Knowland had an integrity and energy that won him friends among his colleagues and a good reputation with the press. He was reelected in 1952, and a year later, in spite of his lack of seniority, became majority leader. He served in that capacity during Eisenhower's first two years in office and thereafter as minority leader until 1957.

One of the surest signs in American politics that an officeholder has Presidential fever is when he makes a concerted effort to appear both liberal and conservative at the same time. "Middle-of-the-road" was the popular expression during the Eisenhower era, and Knowland did his utmost to seem right on the double line. He was a diligent worker on behalf of Ike's domestic programs, or at least most of them. It was in the field of foreign affairs that his natural instincts toward the Right betrayed themselves. Knowland fought hard for the Bricker Amendment, and even after it seemed dead and buried could be counted on to say a few good words about it. The China lobby in Washington had no stronger ally than the senior Senator from California. His stands for a blockade of the Chinese mainland and against the admission of the People's Republic of China to the United

156

Nations were so vehement and so often repeated that they earned him the title of "the Senator from Formosa."

When in 1957 *Time* magazine did its cover story on Knowland, Joe McCarthy's power was over, and he was only a few months away from his death (Knowland had voted against the censure of Senator McCarthy), Robert Taft had been gone for several years, and Eisenhower was in his second and final term as President. The final assessment of Knowland's potential then was that next to Richard Nixon he was the most powerful man in his party. In a way his position was more advantageous than the Vice-President's since he could be freer in his public utterances. However, as a political thinker, he was dismissed as a "young fogy."

Exactly what Knowland had in mind when he quit the Senate in 1958 to run for the governorship of California may never be known. It was then nearly a foregone conclusion that Vice-President Nixon would have the G.O.P. Presidential nomination sewed up in 1960. Knowland might have figured Nixon for a loser and, perhaps, intended to sit it out for six years and take the nomination in 1964. One thing is certain, he definitely had his eye on the White House.

The Republican governor of the Golden State at the time was Goodwin Knight, also no pal of Nixon's. Knowland and Nixon pressured Knight into running for the Senate, much against his will. Knowland then proceeded to run on a platform that included "right-to-work" laws. Both he and Knight went down to humiliating defeat at the polls. It was a beating that all but wrecked the California G.O.P. (When Nixon tried for the same post in 1962 Knight gave him nearly as much trouble in the primaries as the Democrats did in the general election.)

Knowland never again tried for public office, although just about every time a California election approaches his name is mentioned for one office or another. He took over the Oakland *Tribune* after his father retired a few years ago, and he and the paper have remained loyal to the G.O.P., with Knowland being a willing campaigner for candidates in areas where he is still popular around the state. The former Senator is a pilot and belongs to a club of civilians who have broken the sound barrier. He lives in Piedmont with his wife. They have three children.

At a recent press conference on California politics in San Francisco. *UPI*

FRED A. HARTLEY

The man who successfully coauthored one of the most controversial pieces of legislation in the last forty years, the Taft-Hartley Act, was born in Harrison, New Jersey, in 1902. Fred A. Hartley was graduated from Rutgers University, and held various municipal offices in Kearney, New Jersey, including that of Police and Fire Commissioner before he was elected to the House of Representatives in 1929.

In his first Congressional election it looked for awhile as though he had been defeated by his Democratic opponent, but after a recount Hartley was adjudged the winner. He entered the House at the age of twenty-six, just one year over the minimum required, the youngest Congressman in that session.

Hartley admits to having entered politics as a liberal, but by the thirties he had become an isolationist and voted against lend-lease and the revision of the Neutrality Act. For the first 14 years of his tenure in office he had the support of the A.F.L., which was no small consideration to a Congressman who represented an area nearly completely industrial.

Some of the legislation that Hartley was responsible for during his ten consecutive terms in office was a physical fitness bill, the franking privilege to servicemen overseas during World War II, and the extra ration of gas allotted to civilians for vacations during World War II. Like many of the isolationists the tag of "anti-Semite" was one he had to avoid at every corner. In the 1930's, after he proposed his bill to promote physical fitness, someone compared his proposals to those of Hitler. Hartley was quick to point out that the cosponsor of the bill was a New York legislator, Sammy Weiss.

During the war Hartley voted for strike control bills and opposed "portal-to-portal pay," a main objective of unions at the time. Although he had supported such legislation as a pro-A.F.L. amendment to the Wagner Labor Act during the thirties, by the end of World War II he and the unions had parted political company.

When the 80th Congress was elected overwhelmingly Republican, Hartley said: "The mandate of this Congress was to protect the public from violence, loss of output and class hatred due to increasing labor disputes, to protect the workers from political and financial exploitation by union leaders, and to save the American system of free opportunity and free enterprise." By this time he was admittedly right of Senator Robert A. Taft of Ohio.

In 1947 with postwar strikes rampant in the United States, Hartley was the youngest chairman of any Congressional committee, heading the powerful House Education and Labor Committee. The official title of the bill he wrote with Robert Taft was the Labor Management Act of 1947. It passed both chambers in early June only to be vetoed by President Truman. It is Hartley's opinion that Truman acted under political pressure by the unions rather than from conviction. On June 23 the veto was overridden, and on August 22, 1947, the Taft-Hartley Act became the law of the land.

Hartley maintains to this day that the law benefits labor unions as well as employers, and that such was his intent when he wrote it. Bridling at the suggestion that he is antilabor he indignantly points out that he is and has been a union member all of his adult life.

Supporters of the bill called it the "worker's bill of rights." *The New York Times* editorialized: "It is an attempt . . . to see to it that organized labor does not trespass as it has been doing so flagrantly upon rights of management, the individual worker and the general public."

Fred Hartley chose not to seek reelection in 1948. His district had been gerrymandered, and he was then living in another area of New Jersey. The vendetta that the unions had threatened played no small part in his decision.

Although he retired from politics, Hartley kept an office in Washington, and acted as a business consultant there and in New Jersey until 1961 when he suffered a stroke which paralyzed one side of his body. Hartley had, however, been a fine athlete during his Rutgers days, and never allowed himself to get out of condition. He responded to treatment, and by 1965 was driving his Mercedes Benz around the New Jersey countryside near his farm in Milford. He lives quietly in a large ultramodern ranch home with his wife and several Great Danes.

About Republicanism today Hartley says, "Taft was ahead of his time. He warned the G.O.P. that it would have to take the initiative in proposing social legislation. Personally, I am opposed to the [Liberal Republicanism] turn the party has taken but as a practical politician I can see that it has to be done."

In retirement now.

The Congressman in his office, 1936.
Harris & Ewing

Wishing all her fans a Merry
Christmas in 1929.

PATSY RUTH MILLER

The silent screen star was born in St. Louis, Missouri, in 1905. She was
educated at various Roman Catholic schools before her father, a drama
critic for a local newspaper, moved the family to Los Angeles when she
was in her early teens.

Patsy has appeared in films since 1920, including a small part in *Camille*
(1921) with Rudolph Valentino and Alla Nazimova, and in *Omar the Tent-
maker* (1922). The picture that made her a star, however, was the original
Lon Chaney silent version of *The Hunchback of Notre Dame* (1923)—she
portrayed the dancing girl, Esmerelda, the role that was to overshadow
everything she did after that.

Some of her credits during the silent era after becoming a star are: *Why
Girls Go Back Home* (1926), *The White Black Sheep* (1926) with Richard
Barthelmess, *Private Izzy Murphy* (1926), *Oh, What a Nurse* (1926), *Broken
Hearts of Hollywood* (1926), *What Every Girl Should Know* (1926), *Hell
Bent for Heaven* (1926), *Wolf's Clothing* (1927), *Hot Heels* (1928), *Beauti-
ful but Dumb* (1928), *Red Riders of Canada* (1928), and *No Gate Crasher*
(1928).

While turning out such pictures, Patsy was living in the style expected
of silent stars. She drove a Pierce-Arrow and gave her kid brother Winston
a Stutz Bearcat which she bought from Constance Talmadge. (Winston
Miller is now a producer-writer at his sister's old lot, Universal, which has
passed through several hands since the days of its first czar, Carl Laemmle.
Carl, Jr., son of the founder and also a producer during Patsy's era, lives
quietly in Manhattan.)

Her talkies include the all-star *Show of Shows* (1929) in which Patsy was
one of the Floradora Girls, *Night Beat* (1931), and her last, *Lonely Wives*
(1931) with Edward Everett Horton and Laura La Plante (a close friend

160

of Miss Miller's over the years, married to screen producer Irving Asher and living in an ultramodern house in Palm Desert.)

After Patsy's career in talkies failed to materialize she began to write. Throughout the thirties and forties she wrote radio scripts and magazine stories that were published in *The New Yorker* and other top publications. In 1934 and 1936 her short stories received honorable mention at the O. Henry Awards. She also wrote a novel, in 1939, called *That Flanagan Girl.* By the time she decided to give it all up Patsy had a considerable following for her work among mystery story fans.

The former star married the prominent New York importer, E. S. Deans whom she met in 1951 while on vacation in the Bahamas. They live in an enormous house with frontage on Long Island Sound in Stamford, Connecticut. Much of their time is spent traveling—Patsy has been around the world several times and at least once a year gets to Hollywood for a visit with some of her contemporaries like Helen Ferguson (now Mrs. Hargrave of Beverly Hills).

One of Patsy's neighbors and close friend is the silent star, Jacqueline Logan, now a pillar of the John Birch Society in Bedford Hills, New York. They are active in local politics together, Patsy describing herself as "a conservative Republican." She says "I was for Goldwater in 1964 and for Taft before that. You can put me down as a 100 percent constitutionalist."

Patsy is asked constantly about Valentino. At the time she made her film with him he had not yet become a household name. To the question what was he really like she replies, "Rudy was everything he wasn't on the screen. He was refined and courteous. I deeply resent some of the things I have seen written about him recently. The fact is that he was from an excellent Italian family and was a perfect gentleman and a wonderful friend to all of us who knew him."

Of the past Miss Miller concludes, "I seldom think about it, but I am grateful for having been associated with the movie industry at a time at which, I believe, it was at its peak. I guess I'm not good copy. I liked all of the people I worked with, but I haven't time to miss any of it. My life now is everything I could possibly ask for."

Today too busy for most things except traveling.

John Virzi

Jenkins during the hearings, 1954.

RAY H. JENKINS

In 1954 Ray H. Jenkins, a criminal lawyer practicing in Knoxville, Tennessee, was picked by the Senate Subcommittee on Congressional Investigations to represent that body in the famous Army-McCarthy hearings. Several months later he was the most famous attorney in the United States.

Jenkins was suggested to the Committee by Senator Everett Dirksen, whom he had met previously in another connection, and went to Washington for what he recalls as, "a more merciless, searching, cruel cross-examination that I had ever inflicted upon the most bloodthirsty murderer whom I had prosecuted in Court. They were a wily, foxy group of men. I didn't know at the time, but from time to time one would slip out of the room, and it developed that he was talking long-distance to people in Tennessee whose names I had dropped, including the members of our Supreme Court, the Court of Appeals, the trial courts, the editors of the Knoxville newspapers, lawyers, and public officials."

While Senators Mundt, Jackson, Symington, McClellan, Dworshak, and Potter were interviewing Jenkins, the F.B.I. was making a thorough check on his personal life. "Finally," says Jenkins, "when they had me hanging on the ropes, I was excused from the room, and a caucus was held. Senator Mundt called me back and smilingly said, 'Ray, you're it.'"

The battle between Secretary of the Army Stevens and Senator McCarthy had been widely publicized. The honor and integrity of both had been brought into question. The hearings, nationally televised for all to see and hear, started out to be an orderly dignified procedure but soon degenerated into a brawl, and orderliness surrendered to pandemonium. What should have been concluded within a few weeks went on and on interminably for the better part of two months.

A thick-necked, gravel-voiced man, Jenkins bent over backwards to be impartial during the stormy hearings. He was rewarded for his efforts by being accused by both sides of favoritism.

After the great battle Jenkins returned to Knoxville, and is there today still practicing criminal law. The 25,000 letters and wires he received during and after the hearings are still in storage—he has never opened one of them. Jenkins on the verdict in retrospect: "These seven dedicated senators wrote a report in effect finding both parties guilty as charged. It was a correct verdict. It reflected the consensus of opinion of the American people." And on Senator McCarthy: "I feel history will evaluate Senator McCarthy as a blustering, dynamic but reckless individual, devoid of any feeling of the consequences of the rashness in his utterances. At the same time, however, he, more than any man of his generation, alerted the nation to the one great overriding issue in the world, and to its danger—communism.

"Had Senator McCarthy been able to control his tongue, his temper, and his intemperance he might have become the President of the United States."

Today, the Army-McCarthy hearings a distant roar. *Skeet Talent Studio*

In his famous straw boater, with cane, 1931. *Maurice Seymour*

HARRY RICHMAN

The musical star, born in 1895 in Cincinnati, Ohio, was doing a vaudeville single in blackface at the age of twelve. As a teenager he was part of a team called Remington and Richman, interrupting his show business career during the First World War to serve in the United States Navy.

In the early twenties he was the accompanist both for Mae West and the Dolly Sisters (Jenny is dead and Rozicka divides her time between New York City and Palm Springs), and at the time roomed with Bugs Baer and Damon Runyon.

After appearances in *Varieties of 1922, Queen of Hearts* (1923), opposite the late Nora Bayes, and the *George White Scandals of 1926* Richman had become a big enough name to have his own speakeasy, "Club Richman" on Park Avenue.

Some of his other Broadway shows were: *Sons o' Guns* (1929) with Lily Damita (who lives most of the time in Palm Beach, Florida), *Ziegfeld Follies* (1931), *George White Music Hall Varieties* (1932), *International Review* (1933), and *Say When* (1934) with Bob Hope. His last Broadway show was *New Priorities of 1943*.

On the movie side, Richman starred in one of the earliest and most successful film musicals, *Puttin' on the Ritz* (1930), with Aileen Pringle. His other pictures were *Music Goes Round* (1936), *Stars Over Arizona* (1937), and *Kicking the Moon Around* (1938), which he made in England.

Richman figured in one of the first of the famous radio "feuds," which was broadcast in 1927 from his nightly floor show in New York. He and Nils T. Granlund engaged in a series of running arguments done for laughs and publicity. They got both, and started a trend in the new media that produced the famous Ben Bernie-Walter Winchell, and Jack Benny-Fred Allen feuds.

164

At the height of their careers in the late twenties he and Clara Bow made headlines with their on-again off-again romance. His popularity was just as great in England where he packed the Palladium and Café de Paris during several visits in the thirties.

During his engagements at the Palace Theatre he introduced two new-comers—Kate Smith and Lillian Roth.

Richman collaborated on a number of songs and introduced many others which are associated with him, such as "Laugh, Clown, Laugh" and "Puttin' on the Ritz." Three standards he wrote are "There's Danger in Your Eyes, Chérie," "Singing a Vagabond Song," both in 1930, and "Walking My Baby Back Home" in 1931.

During the forties he was a guest on every top radio show, singing and clowning with his friends Eddie Cantor, Ben Bernie, George Jessel, and Rudy Vallee. He was on many occasions the headliner in 1944, 1945, and 1946 at the Roxy, Paramount, and Capitol theatres in New York City.

After being out of the spotlight for several years Richman had a minor success in 1959 when he appeared in Miami and Las Vegas in a nightclub review, *Newcomers of 1926–68.* In 1963 he played the Desert Inn in Las Vegas and the Latin Quarter in New York as a single.

Harry Richman was married to model Yvonne Epstein, to former Zieg-feld girl Hazel Froidebaux, and to dancer Yvonne Day. He has been single since 1954.

He has been living frugally in semi-retirement in North Hollywood, California. Since the late forties when he became inactive in show business he has been spending his time visiting friends and writing his life story, recently published as *A Hell of a Life,* in collaboration with Richard Geh-man. He is in excellent health, has the companionship of a pet squirrel, and rehearses constantly, but with no intention of resuming work on a regular schedule.

Enjoying retirement in Southern California.
Clifford May

With Victor McLaglen in *Professional Soldier* (1936).

FREDDIE BARTHOLOMEW

Born in Ireland in 1924 and brought up in Wilshire, England, by his grandparents and aunt, the future child star was spotted by a studio talent scout while on a holiday in New York City. At the age of ten he was chosen for the title role in the motion picture classic *David Copperfield* (1934), in which he costarred with W. C. Fields.

Thereafter he appeared in such movies as *Anna Karenina* (1935) with Greta Garbo as the mother who walks out of his life, *The Devil Is a Sissy* (1936) with Jackie Cooper, *Captains Courageous* (1937), in which he braved torrential storms with Spencer Tracy, *Kidnapped* (1938) with Warner Baxter, *Lord Jeff* (1938) with Mickey Rooney, and *Swiss Family Robinson* (1940), making the best of a shipwreck.

Through it all he maintained such composure and good manners that he became one of the biggest box office draws throughout the entire period. But to any boy who grew up during that era Freddie will always be the personification of the sissy that he played in *Little Lord Fauntleroy* (1936).

Freddie's private life was nearly as fraught with troubles as his screen roles. In 1937 his aunt, who had raised him and was his legal guardian, was unsuccessfully challenged in the courts by his mother and father who wanted their son back once he had become one of MGM's most valuable properties. Freddie testified that he loved only "Aunt Sissy," and hardly knew his parents. That same year Millicent Bartholomew, "Aunt Sissy," appeared with Freddie again in court in an attempt to have him released from his MGM contract. The terms of the contract, which as his legal guardian she had approved at the time, guaranteed the boy $700 weekly to begin with and would be raised to $1,000 weekly by the end of a seven-year period. Since Freddie was the hottest male child actor in Hollywood at the time his aunt deemed the salary insufficient. The court ruled against her.

Freddie made no movies of any consequence after 1940. (His appearance in *Yank at Eaton* in 1942 was well received but it was Mickey Rooney's picture.) After making millions for Hollywood studios he was reduced to making B pictures such as *Naval Academy* (1941) and *The Town Went Wild* (1944) both with Jimmy Lydon (now a producer at Warner Brothers), the boy who made a career out of playing "Henry Aldrich." His roles became smaller and smaller, and the movies got worse.

During World War II he joined the Air Corps and became a United States citizen. After his discharge he toured the country on the strawhat circuit, having a minor success in the late forties and in 1947 he appeared in *Sepia Cinderella,* a Billy Daniels starrer for RKO.

In 1949 Freddie accepted a job with the New York TV station WPIX as host of an afternoon movie program. Gradually he began directing shows, and became interested in the production of television commercials. "I was a very good television director, to tell you the truth," says Freddie.

In 1954 he joined the advertising agency of Benton & Bowles, one of the largest in the world, becoming in 1965 a vice-president and assigned to one of their largest accounts.

Bartholomew's job takes him back to Hollywood perhaps a dozen times a year. The studios that used to turn out his pictures are now making the commercials and series his agency considers for purchase. Many of the technicians, however, are the same ones who knew the former actor as a boy star.

He seldom sees any of the actors he used to work with. A former child actress he recently ran into in New York and lunched with was Edith Fellows, now taking college courses in Manhattan while trying to decide whether or not to pursue her acting career. Freddie was recently surprised to learn that another MGM moppet of his era, Tommy Kelly, is the Co-ordinator of Youth Opportunities for the Santa Ana, California, schools.

Fred, as he is now called, commutes daily from his home in nearby New Jersey, where he lives with his second wife, a stepdaughter, and a boy and girl of his own. In the garage is a collection of foreign and domestic sports cars—his hobby.

In his current role at Benton & Bowles, Inc.

John Virzi

ARTHUR TRACY: "The Street Singer"

The famous balladeer was born in Philadelphia, the fifth in a family of seven children. His father was an accountant and Tracy's original goal was to become an architect. Arthur won first prizes for singing in his city and state while studying at the famed Curtis Institute of Music. In the early twenties while preparing to enter a national singing contest, a scout for the Shuberts offered him the lead in a touring company of *Blossom Time*. Traveling about the United States with that production he ran the gamut of show business available to an entertainer during those years: vaudeville, burlesque, legitimate theatre, concerts, and stock companies.

While picking up valuable experience moving around the United States, Arthur also studied the languages of the various nationals pouring into this country after the First World War. Much of his success is attributed to his ability to sing in ten different languages, from Japanese to Yiddish.

Tracy was a personality whose fame was made by radio almost overnight. He was heard on radio in Philadelphia when the medium was still at the cat's whiskers stage in 1923 and 1924. He gave it another try during 1929 and 1930 in New York, beginning for nothing and finally working up to a salary of $95.00 a week. His first sponsor was an exterminating company. In 1931 Bill Paley of CBS put him on three times a week on a six-week trial basis. By the time the fifth week came around it was obvious by the fan mail that the network had a valuable property on its hands and that the Street Singer would have to announce his real name to his fans. Up until that time he had appeared merely by title on radio.

Those were the days of titles. There was "The Songbird of the South" (Kate Smith), "The Idol of the Airlanes" (Jan Garber), and "The Red-Headed Music Maker" (Arthur Godfrey). Tracy named himself "The Street Singer." The title became so famous that many today who remember it have to think a minute before they can recall that it belonged to Arthur Tracy.

One of his early radio programs was Chesterfield's *Music That Satisfies* in 1932 which also featured Ruth Etting and the Boswell Sisters.

Arthur had appeared in Hollywood's *Big Broadcast* (1932), the first of the famous series of all-star movies, after reaching stardom on radio.

During that year Arthur's theme song "Marta" (rambling rose of the wildwood) which had sold records in the millions in the United States became a two million seller in England. Due to his initial success there he became one of the most popular singers in the British Isles, and three years later he responded to the demand and sailed for what was supposed to have been a limited personal appearance tour. Rather than being content with seeing their idol and continuing his popularity, his presence seemed to make him an even greater star. The result was that he stayed until just a few days before the outbreak of World War II. During that period he wrote and appeared in four movies, one with Lilli Palmer, one with Margaret Lockwood, and another with Anna Neagle (who is still active in England in plays and television).

The Street Singer has played the Palace and the Roxy in New York City, the Palladium in London, and given one Command Performance. He has recorded over 600 songs.

Through the forties Arthur resumed his radio shows—sponsored by Ex-Lax—made some movie shorts, and was a headliner at nightclubs in New York, Chicago, Hollywood, and Las Vegas.

In 1950 Tracy began to cut down on his theatrical activities to devote more time to his real estate holdings. He invested in Brentwood Village in Washington, D.C., and Oxford Circle in Philadelphia, and is a very popular landlord among the children of the tenants whom he takes for trips to the zoo or just for a drive in his Cadillac when he visits these cities.

Tracy attributes his success on the air to the training he got during his free and low salary days. He went without meals many times, and bought the station's engineers pints of liquor to curry their friendship and learn just how that strange contraption called a microphone worked—Tracy was a favorite of listeners right from the beginning of his Columbia trial because he had mastered the technique necessary for singing over the air.

His latest appearances were on *The Ed Sullivan Show* in 1963 and at the Concord Hotel in New York's Catskills in 1964.

The street on which Arthur does most of his singing these days is West 57th Street where he lives in a large apartment full of the antiques he collected over the years. When people ask what he is doing he tells them that he is "clipping coupons" but makes no secret that he would like very much to be back in front of an audience and is always among the first to volunteer his services for benefits.

He is presently writing his life story, in which Hollywood studios have already shown interest. The title will be, of course, *The Street Singer*.

Circa 1933, at the height of his popularity.

Today, ready and willing to make a comeback.
Maurice Seymour

In *Theodora Goes Wild* (1936).

IRENE DUNNE

One of the screen's most delightful ladies was born in Louisville, Kentucky, in 1904. She went to school at the Chicago College of Music and in 1920 made her stage debut in that city.

In 1922 New York saw her for the first time, when she appeared in the play *The Clinging Vine* which starred Peggy Wood. The next part she had was in *Lollipop* on Broadway in 1924 and was back the following year in *City Chap*. Then came *Sweetheart Time* in 1926 followed by *Yours Truly* in 1927, which starred Leon Errol. In 1928 she was in two shows: *Luckee Girl,* and *She's My Baby* with Clifton Webb and Beatrice Lillie. In 1929 she toured the United States in the role of Magnolia in Flo Ziegfeld's production of *Showboat*.

Miss Dunne then went to Hollywood. Her first motion picture was *Leathernecking* (1930), followed by *Present Arms* the same year. Her first big picture and the one that made her a star was *Cimarron* (1931), also making that year *Consolation Marriage* with Pat O'Brien. She made *Back Street* (1932), and although filmed twice since, movie buffs insist that the Irene Dunne version is the best, *Silver Cord* (1933) with Joel McCrea and *No Other Woman* (1933) with Charles Bickford, *Age of Innocence* (1934) and *Sweet Adeline* (1935). She starred in the highly successful screen version of *Showboat* (1936) and *Theodora Goes Wild* (1936), with Melvyn Douglas for which she received her first of four Oscar nominations.

When people speak of the wonderful light comedies made during the

170

thirties they are usually referring to the pictures turned out by Carole Lombard, Jean Arthur, and Irene Dunne. The three ladies made airy, sophisticated pieces of foolishness that stand up today remarkably well. In fact Miss Dunne's charm has been an embarrassment to more than one actress in a remake of one of her pictures—invariably critics would compare the new version to the original most unfavorably. (*Magnificent Obsession* in 1954 didn't have the magic Robert Taylor and Irene were able to generate in 1935, and in spite of all the money spent in 1965 on *Cimarron* it was generally agreed that Richard Dix and Miss Dunne won the West more interestingly.)

Unfortunately, some of Irene's best pictures cannot be seen on television or in movie art houses because they were remade as films or done as Broadway musicals and therefore the originals are withheld from distribution, among them *Roberta* (1935) with Fred Astaire and Ginger Rogers, and *Anna and the King of Siam* (1946).

Her other screen credits include: *The Awful Truth* (1937) with Cary Grant, *Love Affair* (1939) with Charles Boyer, *My Favorite Wife* (1940) again with Grant and his roommate at the time, Randolph Scott, *Penny Serenade* (1941) a Dunne-Grant classic tearjerker, *A Guy Named Joe* (1943) with Spencer Tracy, *White Cliffs of Dover* (1944), and from the Broadway stage *Over 21* (1945), *Life With Father* (1947), *I Remember Mama* (1948). Irene played Queen Victoria in *The Mudlark* (1950) but it was unsuccessful at the box office. Her last motion picture was *It Grows on Trees* (1952) and in 1956 she was seen on TV's *Ford Theatre* in a play.

In 1957 she was an Alternate Delegate at the twelfth session of the United Nations General Assembly. Irene always had a keen interest in politics, campaigning for Republican candidates in a number of California races. She is also active in various Catholic charities.

She was married from 1928 to a dentist, Francis Griffin, until his death in 1965. They had one daughter. Irene still lives in her West Los Angeles home. Irene has never announced her retirement, but she has turned down countless offers of movie, stage, and television work over the past decade.

Arriving at a recent opening.
Francis Young

PAULETTE GODDARD

The date of Paulette Goddard's birth has never actually been verified. Most film historians agreed that it was sometime close to 1911. Like Oscar Wilde, Marion Levee (her real name), believes that a woman who would tell her real age would tell anything. What is known about the girl from Great Neck, Long Island, is that she had an uncle named Goddard who was a close friend of the producer Flo Ziegfeld. She prevailed upon Goddard to use his influence with the impressario to get her a job on the stage. When the Great Ziegfeld hired his show girls, talent and experience were not what he looked for as they seldom had anything to do but look gorgeous. He signed the high school girl and put her into *No Foolin'* which was a hit on Broadway in 1926. Paulette played a popular headline personality of the day, "Peaches" Browning, in a skit with another unknown at the time, Claire Luce. (When asked about Paulette recently Miss Luce said, "Even then she had something. There was a vivacity and pertness that you couldn't help but notice.") Paulette became one of Ziegfeld's favorites, and the next year he put her in *Rio Rita*. She met and married her first husband around that time. He was Edward James, president of the Southern States Lumber Company, and for a while she lived with him in Asheville, North Carolina.

By 1931 Paulette had left her husband, driven to Reno for a divorce (in a Dusenberg), and arrived in Hollywood where she landed a contract with Hal Roach at $100 a week. After six months she was let go. She appeared in a few musicals of the period, such as *The Kid From Spain* (1932) with Eddie Cantor. Her parts were tiny, usually no more than a member of the chorus, as she was for Busby Berkeley in one of his extravaganzas.

How and where she and Charlie Chaplin met is as mysterious as nearly everything else about their relationship. In 1934 the comedian announced that he had found the girl he had searched for to essay the role of the waif

172

in his film *Modern Times*. They worked on the picture two years, and upon its completion in 1934 set out on a world cruise chaperoned by Paulette's mother. Their marriage was not confirmed until 1942, when the couple were divorced. According to the records sworn to at the time, they were married in Canton, China, in 1936. In the meantime she had appeared in his next production, *The Great Dictator* (1940).

Shortly after the Chaplins were divorced Paulette wed Burgess Meredith in a ceremony held in the garden of the late David O. Selznick.

During her marriage to Chaplin, Paulette had advanced her career and her bank account by shrewdly negotiated contracts, and her appearance in some important films: *The Cat and the Canary* (1939), *The Women* (1940), *Northwest Mounted Police* (1940), and *Reap the Wild Wind* (1942). Right up until it was announced that Vivien Leigh had been chosen to play the role of Scarlett O'Hara, Hollywood was all but certain that the part in *Gone With the Wind* would go to Miss Goddard.

The Burgess-Goddard liaison lasted five years. During this period the actress continued to star in such big pictures as *Kitty* (1946) and *Unconquered* (1947).

The "girl on the moon," as she was called during her time with Ziegfeld, began to fade in pictures in the early fifties. Some of her last were memorable for their ludicrous titles (which befitted their plots): *Bride of Vengeance* (1949) and *Babes in Baghdad* (1952).

In 1957 the novelist Erich Maria Remarque dedicated his book *The Black Obelisk* to her, and the following year they were married. They maintain apartments in Paris and New York—two in each city because they have not lived together since becoming man and wife.

Paulette, bedecked in part of her famous jewel collection, is a familiar face in chic restaurants and nightclubs in Paris and New York, where she spends most of her time, though in 1966 she appeared as the mother of Claudia Cardinale in the film *Time of Indifference,* from the Alberto Moravia novel.

As she appears today.

Marcelle Corday comforts Luise after the famous telephone scene in *The Great Ziegfeld*, 1936.

LUISE RAINER

Although the Viennese actress was only twenty-two when Metro-Goldwyn-Mayer brought her to Hollywood, Luise Rainer had had practical experience on the stages of Austria since she was four years old. Her debut in films was in 1935 with William Powell in *Escapade*. The audience reaction to her was very favorable, and the front office ordered the scenario department to seek vehicles that would suit her.

Luise was beautiful, talented, and charming, but also extremely mannered. Finding the right part for her was no easy matter. That the studio was able to come up with two parts in the next two years that were perfect makes her story all the more incredible.

She was chosen the Best Actress of 1936 by the Motion Picture Academy for her performance in *The Great Ziegfeld*. Her part was a very small one. She portrayed the late Anna Held in a telephone scene which not only was the dramatic highlight of the film because she made it so, but it was—and is—still referred to—a perfect example of how a good actress with a single prop can run away with a picture.

In the picture with her was William Powell as Flo Ziegfeld, and a large number of stars who had appeared for the great producer in shows over the years, all playing themselves. One was the dancer Ann Pennington, for many years a star on Broadway and famous for her dimpled knees. She lives in a Times Square Hotel not far from the theatres which used to carry her name in blazing lights.

It was *The Good Earth* with Paul Muni in 1937 that enabled Luise Rainer to become the first woman to win the Best Actress award two years in a row. It is a record that has never been equaled by any actress. The picture was the last film made by Irving Thalberg, who died before it was completed. Ironically, it was Thalberg's widow, Norma Shearer, who was favored to win the Oscar that evening for her role in *Romeo and*

Juliet. Miss Rainer was phoned from the hotel where the awards dinner was held and asked to come at once to accept the statuette.

The Culver City lot, thrilled by the publicity and prestige Luise Rainer had brought, put her to work at once in one film after another in an effort to cash in on her box-office potential. Her film *The Emperor's Candlesticks* (1937) was neither well received nor well attended. *Toy Wife* in 1938 was even worse. Both she and Spencer Tracy had to endure the silly plot of *The Big City* (1937). Her only picture of any consequence after the Oscars was *The Great Waltz* in 1938. Based loosely on the life of the Waltz King, Strauss was played by Fernand Gravet, who is still active in the French theatre. His mistress was played by the Polish soprano Miliza Korjus who received an Academy Award nomination that year and then slipped into total obscurity. Miliza is married to a Beverly Hills doctor and has recently begun to make new recordings for her own company, Venus Records.

The downward trend of the Rainer career has been founded on reasons ranging from studio politics to bad advice from playwright Clifford Odets, her husband at the time. Whatever the reason or reasons, the simple and amazing fact is that by 1939 she was finished in Hollywood.

In the early forties she appeared on a number of radio dramatic shows, and in 1942 was seen on Broadway in a play entitled *A Kiss for Cinderella*. Casting Luise Rainer was, however, as difficult in other media as it had been for motion pictures. Her forte was crying scenes, endurance of pain. These unique abilities earned her the titles of "The Viennese Teardrop" and "Austrian Whine."

After over twenty years of inactivity she has shown some interest in acting again. She came all the way from London where she lives with her husband, a prominent publisher, to film a half-hour television play in Hollywood in 1966 because the part interested her. Her leading man was another discard of M-G-M from thirty years ago, Ramon Novarro. The press questioned her upon her arrival about a comeback, but she insists that she prefers the quiet life she leads in England.

A scene from a recent television appearance. *ABC TV*

The First Lady of M-G-M in the mid-1930's.

NORMA SHEARER

Because of the many important pictures she made during the thirties Norma Shearer is usually thought of essentially as a talkie star. She was, however, a big star during the silent era also and appeared in *The Student Prince* (1927) opposite Ramon Novarro and with Lon Chaney in *He Who Gets Slapped* (1924).

Before Norma made a name in Hollywood she did bit parts as far back as 1920, after arriving from her native Canada, in such films as D. W. Griffith's *Way Down East* and *The Flapper*.

Her marriage in 1927 to Irving Thalberg, the boy wonder of the movie industry, assured her of the best vehicles and promotion Metro-Goldwyn-Mayer could offer, which was in fact the best in Hollywood. Her appearance in a film brought out the best in that studio's talents. She was gowned by Adrian. Her sets were provided by Cedric Gibbons, and in later years her brother, Douglas Shearer, supplied the best sound recording in the in-

176

dustry. Her directors, George Cukor, Robert Z. Leonard, and Sidney Franklin, were always the hottest around at the time.

Soon Norma Shearer had the unofficial title of "First Lady of M-G-M." If anyone thought that it was no more than a title they had only to ask other contract actresses such as Joan Crawford and Greta Garbo about who had the choice of roles and pictures during those years.

Wisely, Norma would not allow herself to be typecast. She played everything from high comedy to Shakespeare to Eugene O'Neill.

Norma Shearer was a contender five times for the Academy Award. She received the coveted trophy as the Best Actress of 1929–30 for her performance in *The Divorcee,* and was nominated for her performances in *A Free Soul* (1930–31), *The Barretts of Wimpole Street* (1934), *Romeo and Juliet* (1936), and *Marie Antoinette* (1938).

Thalberg died in 1936, but his widow continued taking the plum roles on the Metro lot. The pictures in which she appeared read like a list of the top productions of the thirties: *Private Lives* (1931), *Strange Interlude* (1932), *The Women* (1939), and *Idiot's Delight* (1939).

In 1942 Miss Shearer made *Her Cardboard Lover.* It was her worst film and it was her last. She announced her retirement from the screen, and has turned thumbs down on such comeback vehicles as *Mrs. Miniver* and *Sunset Boulevard.*

The same year Norma quit acting she married ski instructor Martin Arrouge, a handsome Basque twenty years her junior. Until 1960 they lived in the same huge beach house right on the Pacific Ocean in Santa Monica that she and Thalberg had occupied. Their new home in West Hollywood is the setting for many parties which are attended by Hollywood's Old Guard. Mr. Arrouge was instrumental in bringing the Winter Olympics to Squaw Valley in 1960.

Mrs. Martin Arrouge today,
better known as Norma Shearer.

RAMON NOVARRO

Ramon Samaniegoes (his real name) was born in 1899 in Durango, Mexico. Although it was never mentioned in the biographies put out by his studio, Novarro's first film was not *Prisoner of Zenda* in 1922. He had a small role in a Mack Sennett picture in 1921 called *Small Town Idol*. Even before that he played an extra in a Paramount picture in 1919 entitled *The Goat*. He and the late Wallace Beery made their film debuts together under Cecil B. de Mille's direction in a Mary Pickford starrer in 1918, *The Little American*.

Although he made important features such as *The Student Prince* (1925) and *Where the Pavement Ends* (1923), Novarro is best remembered for the title role he played in the 1926 version of *Ben-Hur*. It gave his career an enormous boost, and assured him of screen immortality, but at the same time obscured some of his other outstanding silents, *Scaramouch* (1922) and *The Midshipman* (1925).

Ramon is treated much more kindly today by film buffs and critics than he was by the studios of the twenties—despite consistently good performances and a large, loyal following, he was constantly referred to as "the second Valentino."

Ironically, unlike Rudolph Valentino, he was not limited to playing Latin lovers. (The other giant of the time who overshadowed him in the silent era, John Gilbert, did not survive the advent of sound.) It was a great accomplishment for Novarro finally to convince the producers that he was a star in his own right and to give him vehicles better than embarrassing copies of Valentino pictures, such as *The Arab* (1924).

When talkies arrived his accent was a help rather than a hindrance. M-G-M wisely had him record "Pagan Love Song," the "Moon River" of its day, which was enormously popular. In casting Novarro M-G-M gave him parts that suited a foreign dialect. In 1930 the studio let him play what he actually was, a Spaniard, opposite Dorothy Jordan in *In Gay Madrid*. He played an Oriental with Helen Hayes in *Son-Daughter* (1932), and in *Mata Hari* (1932) he played a Russian opposite Greta Garbo, to whom he posed the famous question, "What is the matter, Mata?" His role in *The Barbarian* (1933) with Myrna Loy was of lesser importance but is an example of how he gracefully made the transition from silents to sound by playing exotic roles. In 1934 he was matched with a countrywoman, Lupe Velez, in *Laughing Boy*.

Ramon has never completely stopped making films, but his roles after *Cat and the Fiddle* (1934) kept getting smaller and smaller. Even when he was given star billing, as in *Desperate Adventure* (1938), it was in a low-budget feature for Republic Pictures.

In the late forties he began turning up again in pictures. His role in *We Were Strangers* (1949) with John Garfield and Jennifer Jones was his largest and most interesting in many years and started talk of a comeback, which never materialized, appearing thereafter in such undistinguished films as *Crisis* (1950) which starred Cary Grant, and *The Outriders* (1950). In 1960 he had a role in *Heller in Pink Tights*.

Novarro never married and lives alone in a large home in the Hollywood Hills. Two consolations he has had over the past years for the descent of his star are his Roman Catholic faith and the money which he wisely invested during his peak years. In August, 1966, Novarro filed a $57,000,000 claim against the United States for rent that he says is due him on that portion of territory around the Rio Grande that the United States returned to Mexico in 1963. The land had been given to Novarro's grandfather by Mexican President Juarez. Because of the change of course of the Rio Grande in 1864 the property was occupied by the United States.

Occasionally he accepts a role on a television show if it seems right to him. He enjoys the medium which in his judgment differs greatly from feature films. During the 1966 season he was seen both with Luise Rainer playing a European nobleman, and as a foreign doctor on *Dr. Kildare*.

As he appears today.

An M-G-M publicity still of Miss Massey which appeared in a movie fan magazine in 1939.

ILONA MASSEY

The Hungarian stage and screen beauty was born in Budapest in 1912. Under her real name, Ilona Hajmassy, she sang in music halls and operettas in Austria, Germany, and Hungary until the mid-thirties when Metro-Goldwyn-Mayer brought her to Hollywood.

M-G-M at the time had under contract Nelson Eddy and Jeanette Mac-Donald, who made some of the top grossing pictures of the period. The fact that they performed together better than they got along personally was an open secret in Hollywood. It was the practice of the majors at that time to have someone waiting in the wings who could fill in for a leading star in case that personality became too difficult. In addition, Metro saw great potential in Ilona as a star in her own right. She could sing beautifully and wore period costumes very well—and was the perfect threat to hold over the head of Jeanette MacDonald.

Nelson Eddy and Ilona Massey were tried as a duo in two movies: *Rosalie* (1937), and *Balalaika* (1939). The public, which had grown used to seeing Eddy with Miss MacDonald, would not accept the new combination that seemed tantamount to adultery. Despite the MacDonald-Eddy feuds being leaked to the press on several occasions, many of their fans actually believed the couple were married.

In 1941 Ilona made a film with Binnie Barnes (wife of Columbia Pictures executive Mike Frankovitch) which was appropriately called *New Wine*. (As any connoisseur will testify, new wine is always very bad.)

During the Second World War Miss Massey was always in danger of some kind—both the F.B.I. and Scotland Yard were after her in *International Lady* (1941) but things turned out all right when the F.B.I. agent, George Brent (retired in Rancho Santa Fe, California), fell in love with her;

180

she had more problems in *Invisible Agent* (1942) but Jon Hall (living in semi-retirement in Malibu, California) was there to help her, and Bela Lugosi and Lon Chaney, Jr., menaced her in *Frankenstein Meets the Wolf-man* (1943). Also in 1943 as a change of pace Ilona Massey sang and clowned with Milton Berle and Arthur Treacher in *Ziegfeld Follies* on Broadway.

Other film credits include: *Holiday in Mexico* (1946) with Jane Powell and Walter Pidgeon, *The Gentleman Misbehaves* (1946), *Northwest Out-post* (1947), another try with Nelson Eddy, *Love Happy* (1950) with the Marx Brothers and her last film *Jet Over the Atlantic* (1959).

When in 1954 a special subcommittee of the House of Representatives held hearings in Manhattan on communist aggression in Eastern Europe, their star witness was the blonde, who testified to the rape, murder, and robbery committed by the Soviets against her people in her native land. Miss Massey had succeeded in bringing some of her family to the United States, but her hatred of Communists is still intense. During the visits of former Premier Nikita Khrushchev and Deputy Premier Anastas Mikoyan to this country in 1959 Ilona Massey was one of those who picketed in pro-test wherever the Soviet leaders made public appearances, and posed proudly for newspaper cameramen next to signs calling Khrushchev "The Butcher of Bucharest." She is a strong supporter of the Assembly of Captive European Nations and the Hungarian Freedom Fighters.

Ilona has been married successively to Alan Curtis, star of "B" pictures during the forties; to Charles Walker, owner of a fashionable Manhattan jewelry shop, and is now the wife of General Donald S. Dawson. They live in a beautiful home in Bethesda, Maryland, a few miles from the nation's capital where Ilona is both very much a part of the social scene and active in the Reserve Officers Wives' Club and though not a member of course, the Daughters of the American Revolution.

She seems to have little interest in working again in motion pictures or on the stage.

Ilona today.

In a publicity shot published in *Photoplay Magazine*, 1923.

DAGMAR GODOWSKY

While Artur Rubinstein and Leopold Godowsky played a duet in the drawing room, Dagmar Godowsky, silent film vamp, was ushered into the world in the bedroom of a Chicago hotel suite in 1897. Her father, one of the half dozen great pianists of this country, was concertizing in the United States at the time. Shortly after the birth of his daughter he accepted the position of Imperial Royal Professor of Music from Franz Josef, Emperor of Austria-Hungary, and took his family to live in Vienna.

Dagmar was brought up in a home in which the family physician was Dr. Wilhelm Stekel (disciple of Freud), and dinner guests might be Ignace Paderewski, Thomas Mann, Sergei Rachmaninoff or Gustav Mahler.

At the outbreak of World War I the Godowskys moved to the United States, settling in Santa Monica, California. Motion pictures were just beginning to come into their own, and Dagmar, who had recently discovered that she was attractive to men, embarked on a career as a vamp in movies.

She appeared in *The Trap* (1919) and her friend Alla Nazimova gave her a small role in *Stronger Than Death* (1920). She made *Red Lights* (1921), *The Altar Stairs* (1922), *The Peddler of Lies* (1922) with her leading man Frank Mayo, whom she married, *Common Law* (1923), and was given the third female lead in the Valentino starrer, *The Sainted Devil* (1923), and her last film, *Meddling Women* (1924), with Lionel Barrymore.

After two years of marriage she obtained a legal separation, but continued to live in the same house with Mayo under an arrangement Dagmar calls "a platonic marriage," but within a couple of years they were divorced. Mayo died in California in 1963 at the age of seventy-three.

Miss Godowsky then set off for New York where she had a brief run in the Ivor Novello-Constance Collier play *The Rat,* canceled on opening night because of Dagmar's encounter with a bottle of bootleg gin. Following that, under Mark Hellinger's management, she toured the Keith vaudeville circuit in the late twenties doing a dramatic sketch, and made an unsuccessful attempt to run a nightclub in Long Island, New York.

Although she was once described by a cinema magazine as "at her movie most, a minor vamp of the early twenties," her impact on the film colony during those years seems to have been considerable. She claims that it was she who introduced Rudolph Valentino to the late Natacha Rambova, that Charlie Chaplin really wanted to marry her when he was tricked into marrying Mildred Harris, and that Irving Thalberg while still little more than a clerk at Universal was nursed through illnesses with the chicken soup she made for him. During her short career in pictures she played with Helen Keller, Sessue Hayakawa, Nita Naldi, Marie Dressler, and Lon Chaney.

During the thirties she accompanied her father through the Orient, Europe, and South America on his concert tours until his death in 1938. About this time her younger brother, Leo, had developed a process for color photography, which he sold for several million dollars to the Eastman Kodak Company. We know it today as Kodachrome.

For several years Dagmar acted as personal manager for her old friend, Igor Stravinsky. In 1958 she wrote her autobiography, *First Person Plural,* in which she described herself as having been unbelievably beautiful and overwhelmingly charming. Heinrich Ivan Kuchenmeister, the powerful German industrialist, was sufficiently enamoured with Dagmar to offer to leave his wife and risk his professional career for her. At the time, a German aristocrat marrying the daughter of a world-famous Jewish family would be risking both economic and social reprisals. Hitler had just come to power and made it clear that the Jewish presence in the Third Reich was not desired. Dagmar left Germany learning later that the man she seriously considered marrying had become a Nazi. Although the book's accuracy was challenged by many, most critics agreed that it was by far the best written and most amusing of its kind.

During World War II Miss Godowsky held court in a beautiful home in Beverly Hills. She entertained politicians, her old friends from the movie colony, and the giants of the music world.

Madame Godowsky keeps an apartment in Manhattan which she deserts for Europe each summer, also taking an occasional Hollywood jaunt. Some of her close friends are David Sarnoff, Dr. Lin Yutang, Vladimir Horowitz, and the Soviet pianist Sviatoslav Richter. Since the success of her first book she has been promising friends and her publisher to do another. The title will be *I Lose Everything But Weight.*

In New York City recently.
Peter Basch

In 1923, the top comedienne on the screen, and (*below*) photographed recently in a New York hotel lobby.

CONSTANCE TALMADGE

Constance, the youngest of the three famous actress sisters, was born in Brooklyn, New York, in 1900. As a teenage girl she had beautiful brown eyes, golden hair, and one of the most aggressive stage mothers movie executives ever encountered.

Connie did extra work and bit parts in films, such as *Latin Quarter* (1914), before she got the chance to play the mountain girl in D. W. Griffith's masterpiece, *Intolerance* (1916). It was a small role and no one had ever heard of her. When it was shown in theatres, however, the part seemed much more important, a credit to Miss Talmadge's superb flair for comedy. Her next appearance was in the 14-reel epic listed as *Georgia Pearce,* a medieval French story. Two others who were to emerge as stars of the silent era, Bessie Love and Carmel Myers, appeared briefly in the film. Miss Love now lives in Bayswater, England, and Carmel Myers, a New York toiletries manufacturer, claims that she had not made any picture at that time, although one of those who recognized her at a recent screening of the film was her daughter.

Through the energetic pursuit of people in the right places, Mrs. Talmadge was quick to capitalize on the reception her daughter got from the critics and public. In 1917 Connie starred with Earle Foxe in *Honeymoon* and in 1918 she was seen in *The Gray Chiffon Veil.*

Although she made pictures for First National, Selznick, Paramount-Famous Players, and others, Connie's largest group of films were produced by Joseph M. Schenck, husband of her eldest sister Norma. Norma was the Bette Davis of the silent era and was a star second in importance only to Mary Pickford. At the peak of their careers Norma received $8,000 a week and Constance $6,000—with no income tax—making comedy less profitable than drama. The Talmadge girls were what today one calls "super stars." Their name alone assured the financial success of a picture.

Connie was unexcelled during the twenties for sophisticated screen comedy, and was very popular among schoolgirls, who copied her hair styles and clothes. It was a time of fads, and movie stars exaggerated the nonsense to match everything else in their lives. Connie and her friend Aileen Pringle once went on a corn binge for several weeks. Corn chowder, corn fritters, corn on the cob—they couldn't get enough.

Some of the many, many comedies Connie Talmadge is remembered for are: *Wedding Bells* (1921), *Lessons in Love* (1921), and *East Is West* (1922), both from New York stage plays, *Dulcy* (1923), *The Goldfish* (1924), *Heart Trouble* (1924) with Ronald Colman, *Sybil* (1926) with Chester Conklin and *Venus of Venice* (1927).

When talkies came Constance Talmadge went. Unlike her sister Norma, she didn't even try to make the change, and warned the other star against it. But Norma tried sound films, and after a brief success, and failure, she too quit. However, through Mother Talmadge and Norma's husband, the two stars remained among the richest in Hollywood. The Talmadge studios where their productions were made is now a studio of a West Hollywood decorator and set designer. The dressing rooms of the two sisters have been for years an apartment house inhabited by Estelle Winwood, famous actress of *The Madwoman of Chaillot,* among others.

Since her retirement Constance has lived quietly in her homes in Hollywood and New York. She maintains an apartment on Manhattan's Park Avenue not far from that of two other silent stars, Lillian Walker and Olga Baclanova. She is still close to her sister Natalie, who was known more as the wife of Buster Keaton than as a movie actress. Natalie lives in Santa Monica, California, a short distance from Mary Miles Minter, who has refused to be photographed, interviewed, or even to give an autograph since her career was ruined following the murder in 1922 of William Desmond Taylor, the silent screen director.

Connie has been married to John Pialoglou, Alistair McIntosh, and Townsend Netcher, and was widowed by her last husband, Wally Giblin, a Wall Street broker.

John Virzi

From left to right: Connee, Martha, and Vet Boswell at the height of their popularity, 1934. *Paul Schaeffer*

THE BOSWELL SISTERS

The Boswell Sisters, Connee (originally Connie), Vet (Helvetia), and Martha, hailed from New Orleans, Louisiana, where they began playing instruments and singing before they were of school age. They had been playing clubs around the country in the twenties before swing was the popular sound (with the exception of a few musicians). Their first record was made in 1928 for Victor (before it became RCA Victor). Two of their early hits of 1930 and 1931 were "My Future Just Passed" and "When I Take My Sugar to Tea."

"The Boswell Sound," as it is still called in the music business, created a sensation. There had been sister acts before, and many since, but it was these three Southern girls who were able to blend their voices in a way the public never heard before—they merged harmony, rhythm, and feeling to produce a musical togetherness that has been imitated but never equaled. The records they made during the thirties for the Brunswick and Okeh labels are among the most highly prized and sought-after by discophiles.

In 1930 they had a popular radio program for Camel Cigarettes, and the next year were regulars with Bing Crosby on *The Woodbury Hour*. In 1932 the Boswells were heard on Chesterfield Cigarettes' *Music That Satisfies* show. The announcer was Norman Brokenshire. All of these shows were on NBC's Red Network, and when in 1933 the girls moved over to rival CBS it was considered a major coup for Bill Paley's network, which until that time had been unsuccessful in its competition with NBC for big name talent. From then on the announcers started saying with much more authority, "This is CBS, the stars' address."

Truly musicians' musicians, the group has been praised by the top performers of their time—and since. No lesser names than Bing Crosby, Ella

Fitzgerald, and Paul Whiteman expressed admiration for the distinct qualities of their sound. Rudy Vallee was one of the earliest Boswell enthusiasts. Not only did the girls sing great but each was also an accomplished instrumentalist as well. Connee, who has been confined to a wheel chair since she suffered a polio attack at the age of three, plays just about every instrument but favors the saxaphone. Martha was usually on piano, and Vet alternated between banjo and violin.

The girls appeared together in three pictures. In 1932 they made both *Moulin Rouge* with Constance Bennett and Franchot Tone and *The Big Broadcast* with Kate Smith, Burns and Allen, and Bing Crosby. In 1934 they were in *Transatlantic Merry-Go-Round* with the late Nancy Carroll.

When Vet and Martha decided to give up show business for marriage in 1936 the team broke up. Connee, the youngest, who had been appearing as a single as well as with her sisters since the beginning, continued alone.

During the Second World War when she was entertaining troops and had to sign hundreds of autographs every day she began spelling her name "ee" instead of the original "Connie."

She has appeared recently at the Flamingo and Thunderbird hotels in Las Vegas, in New Orleans at the Hotel Roosevelt, and in New York City on *The Ed Sullivan Show* and *Perry Como Show.* Connee has been married since 1935 to Harry Leedy, who managed the sisters since they began performing professionally. They live in a large apartment on New York's Central Park West full of the paintings Connee does in her spare time.

Martha lived on a farm near Peekskill, New York, until her death in 1958. She had one son.

Vet, the second eldest of the trio, has been residing in Peekskill with her husband, who died in 1958, and daughter. Mrs. John P. Jones (her name by marriage) manages to get to the city for a visit with Connee about once a month. If the deal now pending to film the Boswell sisters' biographies goes through she will dub the musical sequences with her sister.

Two contemporaries they still see are Morton Downey and Gene Austin, famous popular singers. Downey is a director of a number of corporations living in Stamford, Connecticut, and Austin still plays a nightclub engagement now and then and resides in Las Vegas.

Connee and Vet posed recently for the only photograph taken of them together since the sister act was dissolved in 1936. *Edward Oleksak*

As "Baron von Munchausen"
in the early 1930's. *NBC*

JACK PEARL

Jack Pearl is one of the last and one of the greatest of a vanishing breed in show business—the dialect comedian. Over twenty years have passed since his heyday, and yet even now young people, who are completely unaware of the real Baron von Munchausen and the self-styled Munchausen, Jack Pearl, are still posing the famous question, "Vas You Dare, Sharlie?"

In 1932 when *One Man's Family* began and Jack Benny made his first broadcast, Jack Pearl was already one of radio's biggest hits. An example of just how fast and firmly he caught on is shown by his salary, which Lucky Strike Cigarettes raised from $3,500 to $8,500 weekly, in only five months. The absurd lies of "Baron von Munchausen" and news from his famous "Cousin Hoogo" kept audiences howling from coast to coast during the crippling Depression.

Pearl was not, however, a name made by radio. He began his career as one of the many young people who were at one time members of Gus Edwards' famous "School Days" act in vaudeville. Some of his classmates were George Jessel, Walter Winchell, and Ricardo Cortez, who is now a New York stockbroker. After his graduation to adult roles he performed in many revues, plays, and musicals on Broadway, and was many times on the bill at the prestigious Palace, the cathedral of Vaudeville. In 1927 he and Ted Lewis were starred in *Artists and Models* on Broadway. Pearl was chosen to star in the last *Ziegfeld Follies* (1931) that was personally produced by the great showman. With him in that show were Harry Richman, the late Helen Morgan, and Ruth Etting. It was the show from which Miss Etting was dropped because of a dispute between Flo Ziegfeld and her manager-husband, Moe "the Gimp" Snyder. Etting and her present husband, Myrle Alderman, are living quietly in Colorado Springs, Colorado. Moe Snyder is a businessman in his hometown, Chicago.

The character, Baron von Munchausen, became so popular that when Pearl made movies he received second billing to the Baron. One film utilized the fictitious nobleman in the title *Meet the Baron* (M-G-M, 1933), with the credits reading, "Jack Pearl as 'Baron von Munchausen.'" Costarring with him were Jimmy Durante and the late Zasu Pitts.

By the time TV came on the scene producers and networks had become increasingly cautious of comedians who told jokes in ethnic accents. Pearl, who had always been a welcome guest on the biggest shows of the thirties and forties, was offered shots on such programs as the *Ed Sullivan Show* on TV, but the censors were becoming increasingly nervous over his material. The irony of the change in standards for comedy is galling to Pearl. Never in his career was he accused of being "blue" and yet material is now permitted on television and radio that would have brought the vice squad, while dialects of Jews, Germans, Negroes, etc., are frowned upon as being offensive.

For a while he tried turning to dramatic acting, but there was little interest in his availability as an actor. "They'll let Berle, Jessel, Gleason, and Ed Wynn do serious bits but not Jack Pearl. I don't know what it is. I don't beef about not working. Thank God, I don't need to for the money anymore. I withdrew my services except as an actor, and it looks like they don't want me on those terms."

Jack lives in the East Fifties in New York City. He still keeps in touch with many of the great stars he knew and worked with in his prime. Two of his close Manhattan friends are the legendary comedy team Smith and Dale.

Asked if he resented the fact that the Baron became more famous than he, Pearl replies: "I didn't when the money was coming in, but I've got to admit that sometimes even now it bothers me a little. After all these years I get cab drivers who'll turn around and say, 'Hey, aren't you the guy who used to play the Baron?' But listen, I'm grateful, too, that they remember."

Jack Pearl today: retired.
John Virzi

Fan letters sent to her radio series during the thirties and forties were replied to with this photograph.

IRENE RICH

The popular radio and screen star was born of prosperous parents in Buffalo, New York, in 1891. While Irene was still young the family moved West after losing most of their money in a financial panic. Before entering films as an extra in 1918, Irene worked as a real-estate saleswoman.

Her first real part that year was in *The Girl in His House,* in which she had the second lead. In 1919 she was with Lon Chaney in *The Trap,* and the following year made the first of several movies with Will Rogers, *Jes' Call Me Jim.* In 1921 she made *Desperate Trails* with Harry Carey, and in 1922 played second fiddle to the star of *Brawn of the North*—Strongheart, the famous movie dog. One of Irene's most famous silents was *Lady Windemere's Fan* in 1925.

Although Miss Rich has described her screen image as "the doormat in an endless series of domestic films," she departed from that character in 1928 to essay the role of Harriet Craig in the original screen version of the prize-winning play *Craig's Wife.*

She realized her appeal was to women rather than men and chose her screen roles and her later radio scripts accordingly. Irene Rich made pictures for Warner, Fox, Goldwyn, Universal, and Pathé before the advent of sound films and afterwards went from Metro-Goldwyn-Mayer to Republic and back again.

In 1933 Irene Rich began her coast-to-coast radio program entitled *Dear John.* It was an immediate success. In 1936 *Variety* called her "The No. 1 Slim Woman of the Air," referring to her claim that it was her sponsor's product that kept her slender. Her sponsor, Welch's Grape Juice, claimed that his sales had increased 638 percent since the show began. Some of the "Dear John" scripts were written by Arch Oboler.

To promote the series and the product Miss Rich's age became one of the best documented in America. In newspaper, magazine, and radio advertisements she constantly proclaimed that although she was thirty-nine, those wonderful nonalcoholic grapes had kept her svelte and beautiful. Later it was although she was forty, although she was forty-one, and from then on the age became simply, "over forty." The radio series lasted over a decade, right into the forties.

Her sound career was less successful at its beginning. She made *So This Is London* with Will Rogers, and a few other talkies of little distinction before announcing in 1934 that she had given up Hollywood and the movies.

In 1935 she costarred on Broadway with the late George M. Cohan in *Seven Keys to Baldpate* and did not return to Hollywood until 1938 when she again began playing mothers and grandmothers in such films as *That Certain Age* (1938) with Deanna Durbin, *The Mortal Storm* (1940), and *Keeping Company* (1941) with Ann Rutherford (now Mrs. William Dozier, wife of the producer of TV's *Batman* series).

Some of Miss Rich's other credits are: Down to Earth (1932) with Will Rogers again, *The Lady in Question* (1940) with a very young Rita Hayworth, *Calendar Girl* (1947) supporting Jane Frazee (now Mrs. Tryon, of Santa Monica, California), *Fort Apache* (1948) the epic western, and taking time out in 1948 to costar with the late Bobby Clark on Broadway in *As the Girls Go* before doing one of the biggest critical and financial failures of movie history, the Ingrid Bergman version of *Joan of Arc* (1950).

An astute businesswoman, Irene ran a successful stock farm during her years on radio. She prided herself on the fact that every facet of her business showed a profit. At a time when movie names meant "box office" for personal appearances she was a familiar face on the vaudeville circuits in major cities around the country.

Irene married her fourth husband, George Henry Clifford, a wealthy New York businessman in March, 1950, living at the time in the Waldorf Towers in Manhattan. A few years later they moved to the Hope Ranch in Santa Barbara, California, a kind of senior-citizen project for retired millionaires, which has a beautiful golf course and country club. The Clifford home is set in a lovely wooded area. One of their neighbors is her sculptress daughter, with whom Irene shares her life-time supply of grape juice.

On the grounds of her home recently in Santa Barbara, California. *John Virzi*

BEBE DANIELS

The early screen star was born in 1901 in Dallas, Texas, to theatrical parents who moved to Los Angeles when she was still a baby. Bebe (pronounced "bee-bee") was educated in convent schools and played child roles in silents and for the various stock companies that were located in Los Angeles.

Before appearing in a feature picture Bebe made over 200 shorts with comedians Harold Lloyd and Snub Pollard. While dining one night with Lloyd, Cecil B. de Mille spotted her and offered her a part in *Male and Female* (1919). Some of her other early movies were: *Everywoman* (1919) with Violet Heming (a resident of Manhattan's East 57th Street), *Affairs of Anatol* (1921), *North of the Rio Grande* (1922) with Shannon Day (living in a theatrical hotel in New York City and teaching drama), and the Valentino starrer *Monsieur Beaucaire* (1924) with Doris Kenyon (living in Beverly Hills with her musician husband), *Argentine Lover* (1924) opposite Ricardo Cortez, and *Lovers in Quarantine* (1925) with the stage actor Alfred Lunt.

Even at the beginning, Bebe had the distinction of being liked as much by her colleagues as by her fans. She and Betty Compson (now running a gift shop in Glendale, California) were chosen as the two most popular stars among the stars. In 1920 movie fan magazines conducted a poll among their readers to determine the most popular film folk, and Bebe Daniels was sixth on a list headed by Mary Pickford.

In 1921 the actress was arrested for speeding and sentenced to ten days in jail. Her cell had a Persian rug on the floor, her meals were catered by an elegant restaurant—and her Stutz was parked outside. Musicians serenaded her, and just about every star in Hollywood came to visit her—among the 792 who signed her guest book were Jesse Lasky, Jack Pickford, Eddie Sutherland (now living in a New York hotel while he negotiates old films for TV), and Priscilla Dean (now living in Leonia, New Jersey). As soon as she was released she went into a picture based on her experience, called *The Speed Girl* (1921).

Bebe Daniels was probably the most versatile star in silent films. Paramount Pictures put her in westerns, melodramas, comedies, costume epics, and flapper stories. Until the advent of sound she appeared in pictures such as: *Miss Brewster's Millions* (1926), *Volcano* (1926), *A Kiss in a Taxi* (1927) with Chester Conklin, *Take Me Home* opposite Neil Hamilton, and *Feel My Pulse* (1928) with Richard Arlen.

When her studio refused to believe she could make a successful talkie she bought out her contract and went to RKO where she not only talked but sang in one of the most successful musicals in movie history, *Rio Rita* (1929). After that Bebe was a bigger star than ever and went on to make such sound films as *Dixiana* (1930), another musical, *Reaching for the Moon* (1931) with Bing Crosby in his first important part, *The Maltese Falcon* (1931), *Silver Dollar* (1932), *42nd Street* (1933), and *Counsellor at Law* (1933) with John Barrymore, directed by William Wyler.

Bebe was probably the most eligible bachelor girl in Hollywood and dated such notables as Jack Dempsey, tennis' Bill Tilden, and Rod La Rocque. She changed all that by marrying Ben Lyon on June 14, 1930, with whom she made *Alias French Gertie* (1930). They toured the United States in several plays during the thirties with time out for Bebe to do *The Song You Gave Me* (1933) in England. In 1936 the husband-wife team went to London for a three-week Palladium engagement, which was so successful that they toured the British Isles with the act until 1939, when Ben became the head of the English talent office for Twentieth Century-Fox. Even after World War II broke out the Lyons stayed on in London earning the love and respect of the English people by entertaining servicemen and civilians throughout the Blitz. In 1946 they returned to Hollywood but after a short time there decided that they had truly become Londoners, and moved back again.

In England they made feature films, *Life With the Lyons* (1954) and *The Lyons in Paris* (1956) never released in the U.S. and they had a radio show *Hi, Gang*, which ran 12 years and four years on TV.

Until Bebe had a stroke in 1963 the Lyons were one of the most popular families in England. Miss Daniels has nearly completely recovered from her illness, but is still advised by doctors not to become involved in anything that requires too much work. She is now trying her hand at writing mystery stories.

In 1926 Miss Daniels was the "good little bad girl"—playing both heroine and heavy. At the right are Ben, Bebe, and son Richard, adopted war orphan. He played Irene Dunne's boy in *Anna and the King of Siam*, and is one of London's top disc jockeys. *British Broadcasting Corporation*

Stepin worked up enough energy to lift a finger in *Charlie Chan in Egypt* (1935).

STEPIN FETCHIT

The first Negro actor to receive featured billing in movies was born in Key West, Florida, in 1902. His real name is Lincoln Theodore Perry. Little is known about his early years before reaching Hollywood, in the late twenties. He claims to have had stage experience, but no credits have ever been offered.

Stepin Fetchit fell right into the caricature created by "Amos 'n' Andy"— the Negro as funnyman. As for Stepin, he walked, talked, and thought seemingly in slow motion, and was particularly popular with audiences in spooky pictures, where the slightest creak of a floorboard would set his eyes rolling and his knees shaking.

The way in which he was treated by his friend Will Rogers in pictures they made together is a study in race relations of the period. It was perfectly acceptable for the greatly respected comedian to talk to Fetchit in much the same manner that one would address a not too bright house pet, and threats of a kick in the pants to get Stepin moving sent the audience into hysterics. With his eyes always half closed and his slue-foot gait, Fetchit played to a fare-thee-well the stereotype of the southern field hand. His delivery was very much like that of the Amos 'n' Andy character, "Lightnin'."

Although many Negroes had appeared in pictures before his arrival, Stepin Fetchit was the first to register on the screen as a personality. In the early thirties he was placed under contract to Fox Films, and set about living like a movie star—or at least as he thought a movie star should live. By his own count he owned 16 different automobiles during the decade of the thirties. One was a pink Rolls Royce, which he claims was the first in Hollywood, and no one yet has challenged his statement; another was a Cadillac limousine with a white chauffeur. His favorite automobile had a neon sign with his name across the back of it. Stepin also owned two dozen custom-made suits and 50 shirts.

He has stated that he made over $2 million, and while it is doubtful that his contract and free-lancing could have brought that much, he worked a great deal, and certainly would have done very well. The fact that the money was made at a time when prices were less than half what they are today makes his plight all the sadder—he declared bankruptcy in Chicago in 1947, with assets of $146.

Some of the films in which he appeared are: *Swing High* (1930) with the late Helen Twelvetrees, *Carolina* (1934) which starred Janet Gaynor, *The World Moves On* (1934) with Madeleine Carroll (now dividing her time between New York and Paris), *Judge Priest* (1934) with Will Rogers, *Country Chairman* (1935) and *Steamboat Round the Bend* (1935) both with Will Rogers. Stepin played the role of Joe in *Showboat* (1936) and was with Charlie Ruggles in *His Exciting Night* (1938).

In 1943 a judge in Chicago sentenced him to thirty days in jail for impairing the morals of a minor. It was during a period when he was working at small clubs and carnivals around the country in a review called *Flamingo Follies*. It was rumored that he could not find work in films because the civil rights groups objected to his portraying the Negro in an offensive manner. When asked about this Stepin said that he changed his image and his act long ago, but that people just haven't noticed the difference. He seemed to resent people associating him with "Uncle Tom," and yet in 1951 he ran an ad in *Variety* billing himself as "The Laziest Man in the World." His counterpart, Butterfly McQueen, now works about in Atlanta.

His last films were made after a hiatus of nearly 15 years. He was with Jimmy Stewart in *Bend of the River* (1952), and appeared in the Joan Crawford picture *Sudden Fear* (1954).

In 1964 Fetchit was admitted as a charity patient to the Cook County Hospital in Chicago for a prostate operation. Nothing more was heard of him until Heavyweight Champion of the World Cassius Clay, after knocking out Sonny Liston in Maine in May, 1965, announced he did it with a punch taught him by his good friend Stepin Fetchit. The former character actor was on hand to explain to reporters that he had learned the "secret punch" from another Negro champion, Jack Johnson.

It would be difficult to find a more incongruous situation than the Clay-Fetchit association. The world's perhaps most famous and most arrogant Negro, Cassius Clay, has among his entourage the Negro who probably has done more than any man today to label his race with all the things Clay isn't. If there is justification for the relationship, it is probably Stepin's conversion to the Black Muslim faith.

Sampling a piece of his birthday cake recently, served by his old friend Cal Thompson, chef at a Chicago hotel. *Wide World*

MISCHA AUER

The Sad Russian of so many movies in the thirties and forties was born Mischa Ounskowski in 1905. His father was a Czarist naval officer. The family occupied an estate 30 miles from St. Petersburg, and Mischa still remembers being able to see the spires of the churches in the city on clear days. The house and land are now a part of Finland.

After the Bolsheviks took power, Mischa was sent with the children of the Russian intelligentsia to a school in Siberia where they were to learn communism. It was a time of famine, and he became one of the roaming children of Russia—"the original company," says Mischa—who traveled together from place to place seeking food and shelter.

Finally he escaped with his mother to Southern Russia, and became an assistant apothecary to the British Expeditionary Forces, who were stationed there. During this time Mischa drove an ambulance in a typhus plague, and saw his mother die of the disease.

In 1920 his maternal grandfather, Leopold Auer, who had been violin soloist to the Czar, succeeded in bringing him to the United States. He was given the name Auer, and sent to study at New York's Ethical Culture School.

Mischa became very interested in the theatre, and during the twenties was with both Eva Le Gallienne's company and Walter Hampden's. In 1925 he appeared with Helen Chandler on Broadway in a production of *The Wild Duck*.

When talking pictures arrived Hollywood was looking for accents. Mischa went west and spent three years struggling in small parts. His early period in films includes: *The Benson Murder Case* (1930), *Women Love Once* (1931) with Lilyan Tashman, *Unholy Garden* (1931), a Ronald Colman starrer, *Arsene Lupin* (1932) with both John and Lionel Barrymore, *Mata Hari* (1932) with Greta Garbo, *The Infernal Machine* (1933), and *The Crusades* (1935). In most of them he played the heavy.

Then in 1936 his career took a sharp turn upward when director Gregory La Cava cast Mischa as the character who impersonates a gorilla in *My Man Godfrey*. He was nominated for that year's Oscar as the Best Supporting Actor and, although he didn't win, it meant the end of his menace period.

A few of the forty-odd films the Russian made after *Godfrey* are: *That Girl from Paris* (1936) with Lily Pons (semi-retired in Palm Springs, California), *You Can't Take It With You* (1938), *Hellzapoppin* (1941) with Olsen and Johnson, *Twin Beds* (1942), and *Up in Mabel's Room* (1944).

In the forties Auer began devoting most of his time to the stage. In 1941 Mischa and Jessie Matthews (now one of England's most popular soap opera television queens) were in the unsuccessful *The Lady Comes Across*. In 1942 he and his wife, Joyce Hunter, played the Loew's State Theatre on

Broadway in a very successful act with Mischa, assisted by his wife, playing the piano, telling jokes, and doing some wildly funny business with a couple of grapefruits and a lemon. He and Joyce had been married in 1941 with Mayor La Guardia presiding.

Mischa was a great favorite in summer stock, and was seen in *Twentieth Century* in 1948 playing the producer, *The Happy Time* in 1953, and *Room Service,* also in 1953.

His film and stage appearances since then have been rare. In 1958 he played with Martine Carol in the French film *The Foxiest Girl in Paris,* and his last movie to be released in the United States was *We Joined the Navy* (1962). In 1964 he starred in New York in the Lincoln Center State Theatre production of *The Merry Widow.*

Mischa, who speaks English, Russian, German, French, Spanish, and Italian, has been living in various parts of Europe for more than ten years. He moved from Paris to Spain, and after marrying again in 1965, settled down in Rome, where he plays host to visiting Hollywoodites who come away raving about his cooking.

In 1939, the year he costarred with Bing Crosby and Joan Blondell in *East Side of Heaven.*

The Mischa of the present.
Friedman-Abeles

Atlantic City, 1941.

MISS AMERICA OF 1941

At the age of four Rosemary La Planche made her public debut as the bearded daughter of the late Louise Fazenda in the silent film *The Bearded Lady of the Circus*. Later she had supporting roles in two of Deanna Durbin's biggest hits, *100 Men and a Girl* (1936) and *Mad About Music* (1938).

A native Californian, Rosemary was born in the Atwater district of Glendale and attended John Marshall High School. It was during her graduation year that she took the coveted Miss America title. Prior to that she had held the title of "Miss California" for both 1940 and 1941.

Following the Atlantic City coronation (Bert Parks did not do the honors that year), she was signed by RKO Pictures, and eventually appeared in over fifty films, either starring or featured at Columbia, Monogram, and Republic, as well as her home lot. Rosemary's credits include: *The Falcon in Danger* (1943) opposite Tom Conway (discovered in 1965 broke and despondent in a furnished room in Venice, California), *The Sky's the Limit* (1943) with Joan Leslie and Fred Astaire, *The Mexican Spitfire's Blessed Event* (1943) with blonde Marion Martin (now Mrs. Karzykoski of Santa Monica, California), *Two Weeks to Live* (1943) with Lum 'n' Abner, *Prairie Chickens* (1943), *Swing Your Partner* (1943) with Vera Vague (married to Norman Morrell, the associate producer of the Andy Williams TV show), *Betty Co-ed* (1946), *Devil Bat's Daughter* (1946), and *Strangler of the Swamp* (1946).

However, before embarking on her acting career and immediately after winning the coveted title, Rosemary was sent on a whirlwind public appearance tour around the United States. Her first stop was the now-demolished Roxy Theatre in Manhattan where her act consisted of chatting with the emcee and doing a tap dance. One of the burning questions fired at her wherever she went that year by the press was whether or not she approved of the then controversial dance called "the jitterbug." Miss America seemed to please both young and old by saying that she thought it fun to do but admitted that it was rather ugly to watch.

In 1947 Miss America became Mrs. Harry Koplan; her husband was the emcee on various radio and TV shows he produced in Los Angeles. His longest-running show was an audience participation program, on both media, called *Meet the Missus*. Very often Rosemary was part of the entertainment on the shows her husband put together, though they appeared together mostly on KNX, the CBS outlet in Hollywood. Appearing on the same station at the time was a singer from the old Kay Kyser aggregation, Harry Babbitt, who now sells land units in a senior-citizen project in Laguna, California.

Rosemary La Planche's commercials for Cuticura and Geritol are still running on the *Lawrence Welk Show* and *Ted Mack's Amateur Hour* among others, and she has appeared also acting on *The Donna Reed Show, Hennessey, and CBS Reports*.

The Koplans live in Sherman Oaks, California. Rosemary is the mother of a teenage boy and girl (the owners of a turtle, tortoise, and miniature French poodle). The former Miss America, even while raising a family, manages to keep active as an actress. Now that the children are a bit older she is seen on television quite often. She lists her hobbies as cooking, sculpturing, painting, and dancing. Her interest in art has become more than a sideline of late after she sold eight paintings in six months.

She attributes her present slender figure to dancing, a talent which gave her a number of points when she won her title. The judges must have known what they were doing in 1941, when Rosemary's measurements were 36-24-34. They are exactly the same today.

Sherman Oaks, California, today.

In 1941, one of her best years.

JOAN LESLIE

Born Joan Agnes Theresa Sadie Brodell in Detroit, Michigan, in 1925, Joan and her sister Betty were singing and dancing in vaudeville while still in grammar school. While on tour with their act in New York City an MGM talent scout saw Joan and signed her to play Robert Taylor's little sister in the Greta Garbo starrer *Camille* (1937).

Free-lancing between her *Camille* role and her first studio contract, she did *Men With Wings* (1938) in which she supported Andy Devine, *Winter Carnival* (1939) with Virginia Gilmore (a member of New York City's chapter of Alcoholics Anonymous and the ex-wife of Yul Brynner), *Two Thoroughbreds* (1939) with Jimmy Lydon, *Nancy Drew, Reporter* (1940) with Bonita Granville (now Mrs. Jack Wrather of Beverly Hills) and *Laddie* (1940).

Joan used the name Leslie from the very beginning in show business, but changed it briefly to Carmencita Johnson for her role in *High School* (1940) with Jane Withers.

The picture in which she got her big break was *High Sierra* (1941) with Humphrey Bogart. Placed under contract to Warner Brothers, Joan played opposite Gary Cooper and Dickie Moore (now a public relations executive specializing in industrial shows in New York City) in *Sergeant York* (1941), and did two films that year with Eddie Albert: *The Wagons Roll at Night* and *The Great Mr. Nobody*. From then on the studio treated her as the top ingenue on the lot. For her sixteenth birthday Jack Warner gave her a new Buick, and Joan and her family moved to Beverly Hills. But of all the things happening to her, the roles she was being assigned were the best of all.

In 1942 she was seen in two of the finest pictures produced that year: *The Male Animal* and *Yankee Doodle Dandy* singing and dancing along with Jimmy Cagney (who is retired on his farm in Martha's Vineyard,

Massachusetts). In 1943 she had a role in the excellent drama *The Hard Way* in which she played the kid sister of Ida Lupino. Joan was the dancing partner of Fred Astaire in *The Sky's the Limit* (1943) and was Ronald Reagan's girl in *This Is the Army* (1943), an Irving Berlin musical. Again in 1943 Miss Leslie and the late Eddie Cantor teamed up in *Thank Your Lucky Stars.*

In 1945 she began appearing with Robert Hutton, with whom she has remained friends through the years, in a series of films which were very popular at the time—*Too Young to Know* (1945), *Janie Gets Married* (1946), and *Wallflower* (1948).

Joan made two films with Robert Alda, *Rhapsody in Blue* (1945) and *Cinderella Jones* (1946). In 1945 she was loaned to Twentieth Century-Fox for *Where Do We Go From Here?* which had in its cast two players who were to marry years later: Fred MacMurray and June Haver.

During the Second World War Joan Leslie appeared often at defense plants and army bases to entertain the workers and the boys in service. Few Hollywood stars put in as many hours as she did at the famous Hollywood Canteen near Hollywood Boulevard and Vine Street. She was "the girl next door" or, "the girl back home" to tens of thousands of G.I.'s throughout the forties who sent for her photograph.

After her marriage in 1951 to Dr. William Caldwell, Joan found she had less time for and interest in acting. A few years after their twin girls were born she accepted a part in the Vera Hruba Ralston starrer *Jubilee Trail* (1954) at Republic and was seen in *The Revolt of Mamie Stover* (1957) but she still has no interest in a comeback. A few years ago Robert Hutton was visiting Hollywood from England where he was living and asked Joan's permission to submit her name for a running part in a television series he was discussing, but she refused.

Joan, her husband, and her teenage twin girls have been living in a large beautiful house in the Los Feliz area of Los Angeles, where she is active in Catholic charity work.

At a recent party at the Beverly Hilton Hotel in Beverly Hills, California. *John Virzi*

In a scene from one of his early talkies, *The Man I Love* (1929).

RICHARD ARLEN

Richard Arlen, who appeared in the first movie that was named Best Picture of the Year, was born in 1899 in Charlottesville, Virginia. His real name is Richard van Mattimore. During World War I he was a member of the Royal Flying Corps, and after the Armistice attended St. Thomas College in Virginia for a while, moved to St. Paul, Minnesota, where he worked as a sports writer for a newspaper, and was the swimming coach at the St. Paul Athletic Club. Following that, for a brief time he labored in the oil fields in Texas.

Arlen likes to tell the story of how he lived on 14 cents a day for over three weeks after first arriving in Hollywood and making the rounds of the studios. The only job he was able to get in movies was as a worker in a film laboratory at Paramount. He broke his leg one day in an accident on the job, and was sent to the Paramount hospital where he was spotted by a director who promised him a part once he was well again.

Richard's first important role was in 1923 when he played in *Vengeance of the Deep*. Placed under contract to Paramount, he played in a raft of silents throughout the twenties. A few of his early credits are: *Coast of Folly* (1926) opposite Gloria Swanson and *Figures Don't Lie* (1926).

In 1926, after the cameras had been rolling several days on *Volcano,* he was taken off the picture. Feeling that his career had suffered a major setback he went into a fit of depression. Another contract player, the beautiful actress Jobyna Ralston, was the one to cheer him up. They were married in 1927. That year he appeared in *Blood Ship* costarring Jacqueline Logan, and *Rolled Stockings* with Clara Bow.

Instead of his career going downgrade it went skyward when he won a role in *Wings* (1927), the picture that received the first Academy Award ever given for the Best Picture of the Year. It was directed with great authority by William Wellman, who, like Arlen, had flown during the war, and starred Clara Bow, Gary Cooper, and Charles "Buddy" Rogers (married to Mary Pickford for many years now).

Arlen was in two of the most important early talkies. The first was *Beggars of Life* (1928) which was adapted for the screen from the popular novel of the day, written by Jim Tully. Again Arlen had William Wellman as director, and this time costarred with the American actress who became one of Europe's most popular leading ladies, Louise Brooks (who writes an occasional article for cinema magazines in her home in Rochester, New York). The second was the first talkie version of the classic Western *The Virginian* (1929) with Gary Cooper and Walter Huston. In 1929 he also appeared in *Three Feathers* with Clive Brook, who now lives in England.

Few actors worked more than Arlen during the thirties and forties in sound pictures, a sampling of which are: *Touchdown* (1931) with Charles Starrett (now living in Laguna Beach, California—as do, among other neighbors, Brenda Joyce and Eric Linden), *All American* (1932) opposite Johnny Darrow (now a successful Hollywood talent agent), *Tiger Shark* (1932), *Three-Cornered Moon* (1933), *Alice in Wonderland* (1933) playing the part of the Cheshire Cat and which starred Charlotte Henry (now a secretary in a convent in San Diego, California), *College Humor* (1933) with Mary Carlisle (now managing the Elizabeth Arden salon in Beverly Hills, California), *Helldorado* (1934) with Madge Evans (who, since 1939, has been the wife of the Broadway playwright Sidney Kingsley), *Forced Landing* (1941), *Speed to Spare* (1948), and *Sabre Jet* (1953).

Richard Arlen, who has appeared in over 250 feature films, toured summers during the fifties in *Anniversary Waltz* on the strawhat circuit, and several years later appeared in two movies, *The Best Man* (1964) in a walk-on part, and *Cavalry Command* (1965). For a while in the early sixties he was the representative for Puritan Sweaters in trade shows around the United States.

Arlen, who lives in North Hollywood, is currently on a national lecture tour talking about the Hollywood he has known over the years.

In his San Fernando Valley home recently.
John Virzi

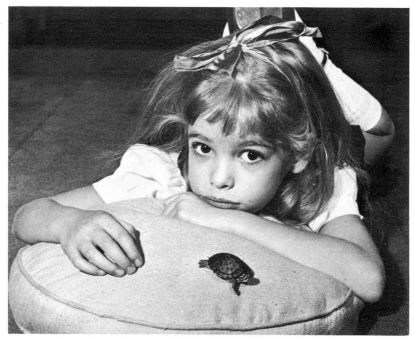

Evelyn Rudie as she appeared on the *Playhouse 90* dramatization of *Eloise* in 1956. *CBS TV*

EVELYN RUDIE

Playing the title role on the *Playhouse 90* TV dramatization of Kay Thompson's *Eloise* was Evelyn Rudie, who had never before had a large part. This was 1956, the time of live television. Miss Rudie was eight years old at the time.

Evelyn got through *Eloise* with splendid notices. Through sheer force of personality and an incredible sense of publicity she emerged more famous than the fictional child. Her press conferences from then on were better attended than those of top stars. It had been many years since Hollywood had a child star, and the press put her on at every opportunity, encouraging her to speak out on every conceivable ill in the world. A precocious little girl, Evelyn needed little prompting.

Evelyn appeared more in the papers during the balance of the fifties than in television and movies. Her personality and image were so strong that it was difficult to cast her though she appeared as a guest on many TV shows, more times than not playing herself, and just about every interviewer around had her on to say something cute.

The only two outstanding bits of work she did at that time were her appearance in the television spectacular, *The Red Mill,* and a movie, *The Gift of Love,* in which she costarred with Lauren Bacall. Both of these were in 1958.

The demise of Evelyn Rudie as an actress and public personality came one year later when the Hollywood police, the Federal Bureau of Investigation, and all the news services were alerted that Evelyn was missing. Hours later she was "found" aboard a plane bound for the nation's capital. Miss Rudie once during a casual meeting with Mamie Eisenhower had been invited to visit the White House. On the spur of the moment, without informing anyone, the moppet decided to take the First Lady up on the invitation.

Almost nothing has been heard of Evelyn since. Her parents insisted that she finish her schooling before accepting any more roles. Even her fan mail is delivered first to her father. She answered a recent note from one:

"About my plans—there is not much to tell yet, except that I'm terribly busy in college. I made straight 'A's (brag, brag) in my last year at Hollywood High School (majoring in science). In my spare time I study dancing, piano (both modern and classical), and acting, of course. I have done quite some stage work recently here in Los Angeles and also given several concerts. Films and TV are tabu for me for the time being, as it would absorb too much time, and my parents want me to go ahead with my studies first —till something really worthwhile comes along in showbiz. This may be soon—though not so soon. But—be that as it may—I try to be ready for any 'emergency.'"

Evelyn is a big girl now.

HELEN HULL JACOBS

She won the United States Women's Singles Championship in 1932, 1933, 1934, and 1935, thereby becoming the first woman to win the title four years successively. She also held the United States Women's Doubles Championship in 1932, 1933, and 1934, including the 1934 Mixed Doubles with George Loft, now living in Chicago.

Helen Hull Jacobs was born in Globe, Arizona, on August 6, 1908. She attended the University of California at Berkeley from 1926 until 1929.

Helen's first title came in 1924 when she won the National Junior Tennis Championship, repeating the victory in 1925 as well. She was a member of the American Wightman Cup team from 1927 through 1938. In 1936 it was she who brought the Crown home to America for her Women's Singles victory at Wimbledon, England. Six different times Miss Jacobs was a finalist at the games in Wimbledon, spanning 1929 through 1938.

In 1942 Helen attended William and Mary College, entered the Waves in 1943 as a Lieutenant (j.g.), and served until 1945 as a public relations officer at the United States Training School in the Bronx, New York.

In 1947 she tore the Achilles tendon in one leg, and has not played tennis since. She was in a brace over seven months because of the accident, and was advised never to attempt the strenuous game again.

Recalled to active duty in 1949, Helen served as the Public Relations Officer at the Naval Gun Factory in Washington, D.C. In 1952 she was assigned as Administrative Assistant and Public Relations Officer to the

In 1934, the year she won both the singles and doubles. *U.S. Lawn Tennis Association*

A recent pose—she has not played for many years. *Asbury Park Press*, N.J.

Naval Station in Dalgren, Virginia, and in 1953 became Officer in Charge of Enlisted Personnel (inactive) in New York City. Since 1954 Miss Jacobs has been on inactive status with the role of Commander U.S.N. (ret.).

After leaving the service Helen lived and worked in New York City. She designed sports clothes for women, and was from 1961 until recently Senior Editor of the Grolier Company, working on their Book of Knowledge.

Of the famous feuds between the two Queens of Tennis, Helen Hull Jacobs and Helen Wills Moody, Miss Jacobs said recently, "We didn't know how it started and we didn't know how to stop it. She was never anything but extremely pleasant whenever we met." They have not seen each other since 1938.

She is currently working on her nineteenth book, her first an autobiography, *Beyond the Game*, written in 1936. Some of her other books are *Storm Against the Wind* and several about a character named Judy: *Laurel for Judy*, *Judy, Tennis Ace*, and also *Young Sportsman's Guide to Tennis*. Miss Jacobs has written a number of articles which have appeared in national magazines.

Helen Jacobs is a joiner. She is a member of Kappa Alpha Theta, the San Francisco Press Club, the Berkeley Tennis Club, the All England Lawn Tennis and Croquet Club, and the English Speaking Union in London. She has never married, and lives in a midtown Manhattan residential hotel.

CARL HUBBELL

Carl was born in Carthage, Missouri, in 1903 and came to professional baseball playing with the Beaumont team in the Texas League, until 1928, when he moved up to the big leagues—and the New York Giants.

There the lean left-handed pitcher had his finest hour in a game that added nothing to the Giants' race for the pennant or winning the World Series—the 1933 season had already seen "The Meal Ticket," as Hubbell was called, pace the Giants to the National League flag with 23 victories, and the subsequent World Series began with the hero pitching two more victories (20 innings without allowing an earned run), enabling the Giants to crush the Washington Senators in five games.

It was only natural, then, for the stylish screwball artist to be the starting pitcher for the National League in the 1934 All-Star game—the vehicle for that finest hour. The American League lineup featured the five most feared batsmen in many a day—Babe Ruth, Lou Gehrig, Jimmy Foxx, Al Simmons, and Joe Cronin. They came up to the plate in that order. They went down in that order—all on strikes. Baseball had never seen a pitching exhibition like it.

Hubbell had great moments, however, before and after that game: in 1929 he pitched a no-hit game, which ended in a score of 11–0 against the Pittsburgh Pirates, pitched a straight 46⅓ scoreless innings in 1933, and was voted both in 1933 and 1936 the most valuable player in the National

League by the Baseball Writers Association. A statistical example of three great years is:

Earned Run Leader	Innings Pitched	Earned Run Average
1933	309	1.66
1934	313	2.30
1936	303	2.31

Other great moments were five straight seasons (1933–1937) when he won 21 or more games, winning 16 in a row in 1936—24 straight if you count the 8 he won at the start of the 1937 season, and in 1936 and 1937 he was the National League pitching champion, in 1936 winning 26 and losing 6, in 1937 winning 22 and losing 8. In 1940 he pitched a one-hitter in which he faced the minimum 27 batters.

In 16 major league seasons (1928–1943), all with the New York Giants, Hubbell racked up 253 victories and a lifetime earned-run average of 2.98 and a career average of less than 2 walks per game.

Had Carl not overworked his arm he would probably have gone on for several more seasons. He retired from playing in 1943, which enabled him to see more of his two sons, Carl Owen, Jr., and James. He has remained with the Giants ever since in the capacity of director of the team's San Francisco farm system, in the meantime, in 1947, being named to the Baseball Hall of Fame. Carl lives in Burlingame, California, and spends his leisure time playing golf.

After pitching a 19-inning, 1–0 victory against the St. Louis Cardinals, 1933 *(far left)*.

Working out of an office now, in Candlestick Park, San Francisco.

WHATEVER BECAME OF . . . ?

Second Series

WHATEVER
BECAME
OF...?

Second Series

by
RICHARD LAMPARSKI

CROWN PUBLISHERS, INC., NEW YORK

Acknowledgments

The author would like to express thanks to the following people who helped in the preparation of this book: Alfred Monaco, Clifford May, Peter Hanson, John Robbins, Jon Virzi, Joe Riccuiti, Bob Stewart, Don Koll, Ian McGowan, and Danny Frank. And to the following organizations for their cooperation: A.F.T.R.A., *Movie Star News, The Sporting News,* and Cinemabilia.

The photographs contained in this book are from the author's own collection, or were kindly supplied by the personalities themselves, or are part of the collections of Jon Virzi, John Robbins, Diana Keyt, and Clifford May.

Names that carry an asterisk (*) in the text appear as separate segments in Volume One of *Whatever Became of . . . ?*

Second Printing before Publication, November, 1968

© 1968, by Richard Lamparski
Library of Congress Catalog Card Number: 68–9092
Printed in the United States of America

Published simultaneously in Canada by
General Publishing Company Limited

For Mary Margaret McBride, The First Lady of Radio,
with many thanks for the help and encouragement she
gave me and the luck her friendship brought me.

CONTENTS

In Alphabetical Order

The great artist in a 1933 publicity shot for one of his frequent radio appearances. *NBC*

PAUL ROBESON

One of the twentieth century's most talented and controversial men, who was to become best known as a great singing star, was born in Princeton, New Jersey, in 1898. His schoolteacher mother died when he was only six years old. His father was a poor but highly respected minister who early in his lifetime had escaped from slavery in North Carolina. Robeson worked hard to win a scholarship to Rutgers in 1915. He was the third member of his race to be admitted to what was then a private institution. He did sensationally well. He made Phi Beta Kappa in his junior year and as a senior was selected for Cap & Skull in 1919. He excelled at track, basketball, football, and baseball, winning twelve varsity letters. By the time he graduated, the expression "Robeson of Rutgers" was well known.

To support himself while going to Columbia Law School Paul Robeson played pro football. While attending the university he met and married Eslanda Cardozo Goode in 1921. She assisted and advised him in everything he did after that. It was she who in 1920 persuaded him to play a role in *Simon the Cyrenian* at the Harlem YMCA, against his better judgment. He was asked to join the Provincetown Players, a Greenwich Village theatre group which included the playwright Eugene O'Neill.

George Jean Nathan, the dean of theatre critics at the time, saw Robeson in *All God's Chillun Got Wings* in 1924 and again the same year in *Emperor Jones* and called him one of the most thoroughly eloquent and convincing actors he had ever seen.

The following year the famous singer gave his first of many concerts. Through radio and phonograph records the name of Paul Robeson soon became known throughout the world. In 1928 he sang "Ole Man River" in *Show Boat* in London and remained to play the role of Othello in 1930.

In England, where he spent most of his time until 1939, Robeson became intensely interested in economics and politics. When George Bernard Shaw first asked his opinion of Socialism, Robeson hardly knew what the word meant. He was to state years later, however, that a "socialist society represents an advance to a higher stage of life." In 1934 he made the first of many trips to the Soviet Union and expressed his admiration for their way of life, emphasizing the lack of racial discrimination he found there. During the Spanish Civil War he sang for the Loyalist troops.

One of the highlights of his career was when he first sang "Ballad for Americans" on radio in 1939. His greatest dramatic triumph was when he played the title role in *Othello* on Broadway in 1943.

Robeson was active in civil rights before it was popular and was a founder of the Progressive Party, which nominated Henry Wallace and Senator Glen Taylor (now manufacturing toupees in Millbrae, California) for President and Vice-President in 1948. In 1949, because of his frequent statements criticizing the United States and complimenting Russia, an outdoor concert in Peekskill, New York, was interrupted by violence. Held a week later, over twenty thousand fans turned out.

The Robeson's only child, Paul, Jr., married a white girl in 1949. A year later his father's passport was withdrawn and for eight years he engaged in a legal battle to regain it. In 1946 he had testified under oath that he was not a Communist Party member, but in hearings after that he refused to answer the question, stating that it infringed upon his constitutional rights.

In 1952 he was awarded the Stalin Peace Prize, but was unable to go to Russia to receive it until 1958 when the State Department was ordered by a federal court to return his passport. While in Europe on that trip he played *Othello* at Stratford-on-Avon. The bad press he had received in this country for years made his appearances here rare, but in Europe he was still regarded for his artistry alone. His concertizing on the Continent continued through the early sixties.

In 1963 Robeson took ill and underwent treatment in an East German hospital. That year he and Mrs. Robeson, who was acting as his manager at that time, returned to the United States. His wife, who in later years had also been his spokesman to the press, died in 1965. Robeson has never fully regained his health and ever since, has lived in their apartment on Jumal Place in Harlem— with frequent trips to Philadelphia where he also maintains a home. He no longer gives interviews and letters are answered by his son, stating that his father's health does not permit him to perform or answer questions.

A rare stroll near his Manhattan home. *UPI*

Entering a federal court in 1948.

"AXIS SALLY"

Very little is known about Mildred Gillars Sisk prior to her World War II emergence on Radio Berlin, which prompted the G.I. nickname "Axis Sally."

She grew up in Portland, Maine. After attending Ohio Wesleyan College during the thirties she spent several years knocking about as an actress in New York City with no success of any note. She did no better in Europe during her few years there before Pearl Harbor. Afterward, overnight, she became a radio personality of such fame that she was known on two continents. Although her voice was not heard in America except by those who might have picked up German radio on short wave, her countrymen were informed of her regular broadcasts by the American press and in letters written home by boys serving in the European Theatre of operations.

Mildred has maintained from the time she was arrested by the Allied Forces after the fall of Berlin that she was not "Axis Sally." She claims that she had broadcast under the name of "Midge." The nickname came about, according to Mildred, when the American boys confused her with another woman who did use the name "Axis Sally." This woman, says Mildred, broadcast from Rome, and it was she whose broadcasts gave "aid and comfort to the enemy." To this day Mildred Sisk swears that she was so upset at the time over what the Rome "Axis Sally" was saying on the air that she made several strong protests to the German Foreign Office, which were ignored.

Unlike Mildred, the Roman "Axis Sally" had renounced her United States citizenship. The Italian counterpart was born in New York City to Constantine Zucca, owner of an Italian restaurant in Manhattan's theatre district. Rita Louise Zucca was prevented from reentering the United States after the war and eventually served nine months in an Italian prison. Her present whereabouts are unknown.

The Allied Occupation Forces returned Mildred to the United States in 1947, and a year later she was made to stand trial in federal court. The prosecution's case against her was much weaker than most observers expected. While ten counts of treason were brought against her, she was convicted of only one. Still, treason is never treated lightly anywhere and the single count was enough to bring her a sentence of "from ten to thirty years."

Mildred was paroled in 1960 after serving ten years in the woman's federal prison at Alderson, West Virginia. Another inmate of the penitentiary at the same time was Mrs. Iva Toguri D'Aquino, better known to G.I.'s who fought in the Pacific Theatre as "Tokyo Rose." Mrs. D'Aquino, who was a Nisei Japanese, was last known to be living with her father, a Chicago pearl importer.

During her imprisonment Mildred was converted to the Roman Catholic faith by nuns who were doing social work among the prisoners.

Upon her release she visited for a time with her half sister who lives in Ashtabula, Ohio. The two had never been close, but were reconciled during Mildred's trial when her sister read the evidence against her and decided that she was being railroaded. The sisters are close friends today. Mrs. Nieminen is fifteen years younger than Mildred.

For the past seven years "Axis Sally" has been living quietly in a small apartment that is part of a convent. Although she has not taken her vows, Mildred lives and works with the Sisters of the Poor Child Jesus who run a girls' boarding school in Columbus, Ohio. She receives a salary as a music teacher and has apparently impressed both the faculty and student body. Parents of the children attending the school are aware that the notorious "Axis Sally" is teaching their children, but no one seems a bit disturbed. When asked about her employee recently, the Mother Superior said that Mildred has been "definitely a good influence on the students." A spokesman for the diocese was quoted as saying that "She has been living a very productive life since she came here."

"Axis Sally," still rather theatrical in manner, does not like to grant interviews or to be photographed. On the rare occasions she talks to a reporter she is reluctant to discuss the past except to say in a voice that would be instantly recognized by thousands of World War II veterans: "There is no doubt in my mind that I received an unfair trial. It all happened so long ago."

At work recently. *UPI*

With Howdy Doody in 1950.

BUFFALO BOB SMITH

The man who was to become the first—and the most popular—kiddie entertainer on television got his nickname from his home town.

His first job in show business was as a member of a singing trio known as the "Hi-Hatters." In 1933, the year of Repeal, they were heard over a local radio station sponsored by a brewery. The following year the late Ted Collins brought them to New York City where they were featured on the Hudson Terraplane Show, which starred Kate Smith. Six months later Smith was back in Buffalo as staff pianist and musical arranger at WBEN. He held various jobs in local radio until 1945 when the New York City NBC station, then called WEAF, hired him to do their morning show Monday through Saturday from 6 A.M. to 9 A.M.

For two years Smith pestered the network brass to try him on the technically primitive medium of television, without success. He developed the Howdy Doody character on his Saturday morning radio program, which was called "Triple B Ranch." It was basically a quiz show for children.

"Howdy Doody Time" finally made TV on December 27, 1947, the day after New York's famous blizzard. Its time slot was 5:30 to 6:00 P.M. Monday through Friday. It was the first offering of the day on TV at that time and was preceded by the well remembered test pattern of one geometric design or another. This was before the coaxial cable had linked the East and West coasts, and therefore seen only in six eastern cities.

A few weeks after the premiere Smith suggested to the sales department that he offer a free Howdy Doody pin to any boy or girl writing in. The mail pull would be an indication of his listenership since rating services had not at that point been developed for the new medium. All the National Broadcasting Company knew was that there were approximately forty thousand television sets within the viewing area. In three days eighty thousand requests were received. These were the days when a family with a television set with its seven-inch screen made larger by a thick glass bubble in front of it was watched by as many neighbors on the block as the living room could accommodate. Still, no one had guessed that the red-haired puppet and his friends, John J. Fadozle, America's No. 1 (Boing!) Private Eye, Cornelius J. Cobb, storekeeper in the town of Doodyville, and Flub-a-Dub, Howdy's pet, had gained such popularity in so short a time. It was a success that was to continue and even increase until Smith suffered a heart attack in 1957 and switched to one show a week on Saturday mornings from 10 to 10:30.

The same year he completely sold out his interest in Howdy Doody items— tee shirts, dolls, spoons, dishes, and comic books—to NBC and took a whopping capital gain.

The Saturday show went off the air on September 30, 1960. The original Clarabell, a clown who never spoke but was handy with a seltzer bottle, was played by Bob Keeshan, now CBS's Captain Kangaroo. Judy Tyler played Princess Summerfallwinterspring until she was killed in an automobile accident on July 4, 1956. And the puppet Howdy Doody, which had three different heads available, is kept by Rufus Rose, the show's chief puppeteer. (Perhaps Howdy Doody's chief competitor was Mr. I. Magination, played and created by Paul Tripp, now hosting a local NBC program called "Birthday House.")

Since 1960 Buffalo Bob has devoted most of his time to his family. Smith has been married since 1940 to his first grade classmate. His oldest son, Ron, is a stockbroker. The second, Robin, is in medical school, and teen-ager Chris is in high school. The Smiths spend their winters in Fort Lauderdale, Florida, where they build and sell condominium apartments. They summer in Calais, Maine. Smith owns the local radio station, WQDY, and just purchased stations WOU at Houlton, and WMKR at Millinocket. During the fall and spring their home is a nine-room apartment in New Rochelle, New York, a few blocks from Smith's Wykagyl Liquor Store.

During an interview by Author Richard Lamparski in Bob's New Rochelle apartment. *Peter Schaeffer*

A famous Vandamm Studios photograph in 1934.

KATHARINE CORNELL

The First Lady of the American Theatre was born in 1898 in Berlin, where her father was studying medicine, and raised in Buffalo, New York. Her father gave up his medical practice to manage the Star Theatre in that city. In her youth, Katharine leaned more toward athletics than acting. She excelled in swimming, tennis, and ice skating, although she did study drama at the Oaksmere School in Mamaroneck, New York.

She made her debut in 1916 with the Washington Square Players in *Bushido,* and then studied and toured for three seasons with the famous Jessie Bonstelle Players. It was because of her work there that she was chosen in 1919 to play in *Little Women,* in London. That year she was introduced to Guthrie McClintic in the office of producer William Brady.

McClintic was a director who once wanted to be an actor. Miss Cornell was an actress who lacked the ambition necessary to succeed in the theatre. Following their marriage in 1921, throughout her career he supplied the drive and guidance she needed. He directed all of her vehicles after 1921, when she captivated New York audiences in *A Bill of Divorcement.*

Mostly her roles were romantic and emotional. Because melodrama and love stories were the rage of her era, she soon became a major star.

On Broadway she starred in *The Enchanted Cottage* (1923), *Candida* (1924), which she was to revive many times, *The Green Hat* (1925), her most spectacular success during the twenties, *The Letter* (1927), and *The Age of Innocence* (1928).

Dean of Drama Critics George Jean Nathan once said of her, "I would give all the other young actresses put together for her—and three-quarters of the older ones."

Undoubtedly, her best remembered role was as Elizabeth Barrett Browning in *The Barretts of Wimpole Street,* which she first did in 1931. After a year on Broadway, she took it on the road. No other actress of her time was more popular with women. She is credited by many in the theatre as being responsible for reopening "the road"—by proving to producers that plays on tour could be very profitable. Since Miss Cornell produced her own plays, under the banner of "Katharine Cornell Presents," she took all the chances but in return reaped huge profits. She revived *Barretts* over and over again. As late as 1956, she played it on television. Unfortunately, by this time the material was overly familiar, and she was too old for the role.

In 1934 she was in *Romeo and Juliet*. *St. Joan* (1936) was another personal triumph. In 1939 she played *No Time for Comedy* on Broadway and on tour. In 1941 she appeared in *The Doctor's Dilemma*, which she followed with an all-star revival of *Candida* in 1942. In 1943 she made her brief and only appearance in a movie, *Stage Door Canteen*, playing herself. In 1944 Miss Cornell talked the U.S.O. into sponsoring an overseas tour for servicemen. At first the officials thought the actress would be too "heavy" for war-weary G.I.'s, but she proved them quite wrong. Her *Antigone* was an artistic success, though it was a box-office failure in 1946. In 1947 she was in *Anthony and Cleopatra*.

During the thirties and forties she was heard occasionally on U.S. Steel's radio show, "Theatre Guild on the Air." In 1957 she headed the cast of a TV production of "There Shall Be No Night."

In 1959-60 "Kit," as her colleagues call her, made her farewell tour in *Dear Liar*. She traveled all over the nation in a trailer built especially for her.

In 1961 Guthrie McClintic died, and she has not acted since. Asked why recently, she replied: "I was nervous from the beginning, and it got worse as years went on. He always gave me the security I needed. I felt I couldn't do anything after that."

If she had any temptations to go back on her word, it became impossible after 1966 when she developed a heart condition. Her time is divided between her summer home in Martha's Vineyard and a brownstone in Manhattan's East Fifties. Miss Cornell keeps a huge dachshund named Kasper as a companion. Her only professional activities in the past few years have been some narrations she has done for National Educational Television and the recordings she has been doing for the blind for some time now.

"Kasper" and his mistress in their Manhattan home. *Larry Fried.*

Leopold (left) and Loeb (center) under arrest for their thrill killing. *UPI*

NATHAN LEOPOLD

The co-conspirator in what was perhaps the most vicious, most pointless murder on record was also the youngest student ever to graduate from the University of Chicago. He came from a wealthy family and was about to continue his education at Harvard when at the age of nineteen he and his friend, Richard Loeb, brutally murdered Bobby Franks, a fourteen-year-old distant cousin of Loeb's. Loeb was a great admirer of Nietzsche and fancied himself a "Superman." He was quite handsome and had been the youngest graduate in the history of the University of Michigan. Leopold admired Loeb's supreme confidence and intelligence and was strongly attracted to him sexually.

Their plan for the perfect crime was carried out on May 21, 1924, in a cold-blooded, awkward fashion. The victim was not even the one they had originally intended to kill. Their sole purpose in the murder was to prove that they were of superior intelligence and could not be caught. They further complicated matters by calling the victim's family and demanding ransom money, pretending that the child had been kidnapped and was still alive. They flaunted their cunning and audacity among themselves by actually aiding the police in the search for the missing boy and offering suggestions and theories to the authorities, whom they felt were bunglers and incompetents.

Bobby Frank's body was found the day after the murder and not far from it police picked up a pair of glasses, carelessly dropped by Leopold. He and Loeb denied they knew anything about the case. They claimed to have been driving all day in Leopold's Willys-Knight. They had no apparent motive. They knew the boy and had liked him. Not everyone, however, liked them. The family chauffeur, who had always found the boys insufferable, told police the car had never left the garage on May 21. Leopold said that he might have lost his glasses when he was in the area bird-watching several weeks before, yet they were spotless when found. The police separated the boys and played them against each other. Loeb, the "Superman," cracked first. Rather arrogantly they admitted what they had done.

They were young, rich, and privileged, with contemptible manners, and they had committed a heinous crime in a state that had capital punishment;

16

and being Jewish certainly didn't help. Their families obtained Clarence Darrow to represent them.

Darrow had them plead guilty and then for over one month the prosecution attempted to convince Judge John R. Caverly that the only possible penalty was the death sentence while the defense countered with testimony from doctors, psychiatrists, and neurologists. Darrow's summation lasted two full days. Since the boys had admitted guilt at the beginning, Darrow put capital punishment on trial. To the amazement of most and the disgust of many they received "life imprisonment, plus ninety-nine years each." The judge said that he kept them from hanging only because of their ages.

Darrow stated years later in his autobiography that the fees he received would not even have covered his office expenses. The Loebs and Leopolds at first made no effort to pay at all, and indicated that they felt the sentences were harsh.

In 1936 Richard Loeb was stabbed to death by a fellow inmate who claimed that Loeb had attempted to molest him sexually. Although the pair had been kept separate from the time they entered Joliet prison, there were outcries from the press about preferred treatment.

"Babe," as Loeb used to call his partner, was a model prisoner from the start. He allowed himself to be used as a test case for new drugs, and tutored other prisoners. However, when Nathan Leopold was paroled in 1958 more than a few voices of dissent were raised. He went immediately and quietly to Puerto Rico where he has been doing medical research. Although he still considers himself a Jew, he has been closely associated with the work of the Church of Brethren in curbing disease.

In 1961 he married the widow of a doctor in San Juan. Having served out his parole, Leopold is now a free man. He is the director of research for the Health Department of Puerto Rico, and is credited with helping combat tropical parasites and leprosy. Leopold is often offered as a model of rehabilitation. What spare time he has is spent writing scientific articles. When Meyer Levin's very successful book, play, and motion picture *Compulsion* appeared a few years ago Leopold filed suit claiming that he alone had literary rights to his own life. His autobiography, *99 Years Plus Life,* was published several years ago but did not do well.

A director of research today. *UPI*

The "King of Jazz" in 1928.

TED LEWIS

The High-hatted Tragedian of Song was born to an owner of a local department store in Circleville, Ohio, in 1891. His real name is Theodore Leopold Friedman. By 1906 he was featured in his home-town theatre playing the clarinet. Shortly afterward Ted ran away from home to join a carnival where he did spiels in front of the kooch-dancers, and became one of the exhibits of Dr. Cooper's Medicine Show, billed as "Wild Rosie." Ted was also the emcee.

Lewis claims it took him fifteen years to make it big in show business. In the interim he appeared in burlesque, dog and pony shows, vaudeville, and minstrels. He was once fired from Professor Oscar Ameringer's Symphony Band for jazzing up Beethoven's Fifth Symphony. At one point he teamed up with another musician named Al Lewis. Ted changed his name shortly afterward because Friedman could not be accommodated by the small marquee of a theatre. In 1911 he got his first break when he played the famous Hammerstein Theatre on West 42nd Street with his partners Duffy & Giser. Victor Moore and Will Rogers were on the same bill. By 1916 he had formed his own four-piece band and played the College Arms in Coney Island. From there he went to the fashionable Rector's on Broadway where Bonds clothing store stands today. He was a big hit and introduced his theme song, "When My Baby Smiles at Me." It was the Rector's engagement more than anything else that earned him the title many people associate with Paul Whiteman, "The King of Jazz." Lewis is the original. It was also at Rector's that he first wore the famous battered silk top hat which he won in a crap game from a cabbie. The first time he performed in it was as a joke but he has never been without it on stage since and considers it good luck. Saks Fifth Avenue once borrowed the hat to create a display around it in one of their windows.

Another big boost to his career was when John Murray Anderson asked him to fill in a five-minute spot at the Greenwich Theatre in Greenwich Village. It was supposed to be temporary until Anderson could get "a name," but Lewis was such a hit he was kept on for three years.

In 1922 he married Ada Baker, a toe dancer he had known more by correspondence than by their three or four meetings. His partners gave it six weeks. The Lewises were married first on stage in Rochester, New York, then by a city hall clerk, and again in a rabbi's home. It took. She has been his wife, friend, and manager ever since.

During the twenties he had the very successful Ted Lewis Club at 52nd Street and Seventh Avenue. The money he made there with a $3 cover charge more than offset his $150,000 loss—his *Ted Lewis Frolics* bombed in 1923 before it got to Broadway. He was also in Broadway shows such as *Artists and Models* in 1927 and played the Ziegfeld Roof. In one year he played in 150 different places in addition to his own club.

Lewis has for years enjoyed great popularity in England and has given a command performance for George V.

Some of the songs Ted popularized and introduced were "When My Baby Smiles At Me," "The Sunny Side of the Street," "Me and My Shadow," and "Cuddle Up a Little Closer."

His movies include *Is Everybody Happy?* (1929), *Show of Shows* (1929), *Here Comes the Band* (1935) with Virginia Bruce and *Manhattan Merry-Go-Round* (1937) with Ann Dvorak.

Some who were members of Lewis' band before they made it on their own are Kay Kyser (who lives with his wife the former Georgia Carroll in Chapel Hill, North Carolina, where he is a teacher and practitioner of Christian Science), George Raft, and the Dorsey brothers.

Lewis made a fortune over the years in radio, television, and nightclub appearances, right through the forties and sporadically through the fifties. He still plays several engagements a year and would have brought a show to Broadway in 1966 if Sophie Tucker, one of his co-stars, had not died before the opening. Miss Tucker was also one of his closest friends. His "shadow," dancer Eddie Chester, still works with Lewis whenever he has a booking.

The man who introduced the talking and laughing horns lives with his wife at the Majestic apartments on Manhattan's Central Park West for over thirty-five years now.

His famous top hat probably will be donated to the Ted Lewis Museum in Circleville, Ohio. The town also has a Ted Lewis Playground courtesy of the Lewises. He was voted a life member of their Chamber of Commerce in 1934 for the many plugs he has given it in his shows over the years.

In his Manhattan apartment. *Diana Keyt*

Starring in *Rose of the Rancho,* 1936.

GLADYS SWARTHOUT

The beautiful prima donna of the Metropolitan Opera and motion pictures was born in 1904 in Deepwater, Missouri, an Ozark mining town. She attended the Central High School in Kansas City and went on to Bush Conservatory of Music in Chicago from which she received a Doctorate of Music in 1923.

Gladys began singing as a very young girl at her local church. After Bush, she spent the summer of 1924 preparing for an operatic debut. She learned twenty-two roles for the 1924–1925 season of the Chicago Civic Opera Company. Gladys sang fifty performances, more than any other member of the company. After that she went to Europe for a rest and upon her return joined the Ravinia Park Opera Company and sang with them during the seasons of 1927, 1928, and 1929. By the time she left to join the Metropolitan she was considered among their top attractions.

Her debut with the Metropolitan came in 1929 as La Cieca in *La Gioconda.* She also sang the roles of Niejata in the United States premiere of *Sadko* and Cathos when Lattuada's *La Preziose Ridicole* made its bow in this country. She was very soon one of the company's leading mezzo-sopranos. Her most famous roles were in *Norma, Peter Ibbetson, La Gioconda, La Forza del Destino, Mignon,* and *Carmen.* Her repertoire contained twenty-five operas.

Paramount was anxious to have a star to compete with M-G-M's Jeanette MacDonald and Columbia's Grace Moore. They signed the singer to a lucrative contract and introduced her to the movie-going public in a barrage of publicity. Her film efforts, however, were not well received at the box office. She made *Rose of the Rancho* (1936) with John Boles, *Give Us This Night* (1936), which had a score by Erich Korngold, a book by Oscar Hammerstein II, and Jan Kiepura as her co-star, *Champagne Waltz* (1937), *To Have and to Hold* (1937) with Fred MacMurray, and *Romance in the Dark* (1938) with John Boles. Her last picture was a melodrama with Lloyd Nolan, *Ambush* (1939).

Radio, however, proved a boon to her career. She began in the medium in 1935 and appeared on such programs as the "Chase and Sanborn Hour," "Caravan," and the "Ford Sunday Evening." She also had her own program which was heard in New York City over WEAF, now WNBC, and sang everything from arias to pop songs and spirituals. For five successive years beginning in the late thirties she was named the Number One Female Singer of Classics on radio by the critics in the United States and Canada, outpolling even the popular Jessica Dragonette.* Her radio popularity made her concert tours and recordings among the most successful year after year.

Her Carnegie Hall appearance in 1942 caused critic-composer Robert Lawrence to write "a genuine mezzo-soprano, the best among present day American singers of this genre." Miss Swarthout was particularly effective in person. She was not only lovely to look at but had great chic and several times was named among the best dressed women in America.

In 1956 she underwent a very delicate and critical operation on her heart which had been damaged during a bout with rheumatic fever as a child. By 1957 she retired.

In 1958 the singer won the Heart of the Year award and became a member of the Mended Heart Club, which is made up of past major heart surgery patients.

After she left the music world, Gladys and her husband Frank Chapman divided their time between their Connecticut home and their villa set in an avocado grove in Florence, Italy. Chapman, who had given up his own singing career to manage his wife's, died in 1966. They had been married for thirty-five years. Miss Swarthout's first husband, Harry Richmond Kern, died in 1931 after six years of marriage. She has no children by either union and has never remarried.

She spends spring and summer at La Ragnaia in the suburbs of Florence "because my husband loved that place most." The fall and winters are spent in her New York Fifth Avenue apartment. She attends Metropolitan performances from time to time but never sings, "not even in the bathtub."

The former prima donna at a recent party in Florence. *Clifford May*

"The Citizen of the World" arrives in the country of his birth in 1950. N. Y. *Daily News*

GARRY DAVIS

The ex-GI who emerged from the shadow of his famous father to become known around the globe as "the citizen of the world," was born in Bar Harbor, Maine, in 1922. Until he joined the United States Air Force at the outbreak of World War II, he had spent most of his life in Philadelphia where he was known somewhat as a playboy. For awhile he was gainfully employed as understudy to Danny Kaye. The only reason for any public attention he may have received during those years was the fact that he was the son of society band leader Meyer Davis.

After mustering out of the service Davis stayed in Paris where he became interested in the World Federalist movement, which he left after becoming disenchanted.

At first the press treated him as little more than a nut with good intentions and bad taste when in 1948 he announced that he was giving up his United States citizenship and dramatized this by tearing up his passport. He would not, he said, apply for another from any country. He had formed the Association for the International Registry of World Citizens and People's Assembly and was now "a citizen of the world." He had fought one war and firmly believed that nationalism was the basis for all conflicts between nations. Through his canny sense of publicity Davis broke into the news over and over again. At one point he took refuge from authorities in Paris by retreating to the international grounds of the United Nations offices. On another occasion the gendarmes had to be called out to escort him from the grounds of the Palais de Chaillot where he had camped in a pup tent. His phrase "citizen of the world" had a ring to it and he began to attract huge crowds of war-weary young Frenchmen wherever he spoke. France's initial reaction was to give him twenty-four hours to leave the country. But it was not long before he was received in a private interview by French President Vincent Auriol. Not all his followers were starry-eyed peaceniks. His plan for the world government was endorsed publicly by such men as André Gide, Jean-Paul Sartre, Albert Camus, and Albert Einstein. The French press began referring to him affectionately as "le petit homme" and his mail reached four hundred letters per day from all over the world.

Throughout it all Davis wore his brown leather flyer's jacket with a faded decal of a pinup girl on the back.

Days of glory for Garry were short. His failure to forge his crusade into something resembling a political power is perhaps a proof of his sincerity. Had he lusted after power as he did after peace, he might have survived. By 1950 all of the steam had gone out of his movement as it broke off into countless fringe groups. The intensity of the Cold War at that time made the Davis dream seem like a wonderful but wistful bit of science fiction. In April of 1950 he returned to the United States where he was detained for four days of questioning on Ellis Island. He told reporters that he was still "a resident of the earth" and that he disagreed with United States intervention in Korea.

In Ellsworth, Maine, in 1950, Davis married the former Hollywood dancer Esther Peters in an original service he created, called "unification of love." It was announced shortly afterward by the State Department that Davis had made a formal request for reinstatement as a United States citizen. A spokesman for the government said that his application would be considered along with all others that were on file from French immigrants. Davis had entered this country on an immigration visa.

Davis and his wife drifted back and forth across the Atlantic and have now settled in Mulhouse, Alsace. In 1961 he published his book, *The World is My Country*, in which he states that the only real solution to the problems besetting the world is for the various countries to give up their sovereignty and accept a global government. Today he admits that his idea of world law is "way out" but remains firmly committed to it. "In other words," he said, "the brotherhood of man must be realized politically. I consider the problem to be essentially a spiritual one."

The firebrand of the forties supports his family—three boys and a girl ranging from one year old to fourteen years old—as the holder of a franchise for the Culligan water-softening process and a dry lubricant called Dri-Slide, which is used in industry.

The famous leather jacket that stood for many as a symbol of the hope for peace that Garry Davis instilled in his followers was given to a hobo nearly twenty years ago.

Esther and Gary pose on the land they purchased recently in Wettolsheim, Haut-Rhin, France. On the deed it is registered as "World Territory."

With Raymond Walburn (left) in *Professor Beware,* in 1938.

HAROLD LLOYD

The movie comedian whose films grossed over $30,000,000 was born in Burchard, Nebraska, in 1894.

Harold had some experience in amateur theatricals before the family moved to southern California where he attended San Diego High School. For awhile he entertained the notion of becoming a professional boxer. When the Edison Company came to town and announced that they would be hiring extras to appear in a film they were making, Harold's mother encouraged him to try out, hoping this would make him forget about the dangerous sport. It worked because immediately after graduation, his acting ambition fired by the one short job he got from Edison, Lloyd went north to Hollywood where he found occasional work as a walk-on or extra. He appeared with Jane Novak (who lives in Sherman Oaks, California, not far from her sister Eva Novak of Van Nuys). Like the characters he played later, Harold never gave up in the face of hard times or adversity. Director Ford Sterling told him that he had no talent whatever for comedy.

Then in 1915 a young man named Hal Roach, who had just inherited a few thousand dollars, thought Harold was funny and together they devised a character they called "Willie Work." Later it was changed considerably and renamed "Lonesome Luke." Their Rolin Film Company made one- and two-reelers featuring the awkward optimist who became popular the world over. In 1917 Lloyd added the now famous horn-rimmed glasses and developed the character still further for his first feature picture, *Grandma's Boy* (1917), which was a howling success.

When Lloyd and Roach amicably parted company in 1923 Harold went to Pathé where, as his own producer, he had even greater success. His revised character, always named Harold, had been refined and developed into a clean-cut, honest, very likable young man whom bullies and the world in general conspired against. Lloyd played down his natural handsome features and thereby had as many men as women rooting for him when he tried to win the campus sweetheart or free himself from some of the complicated and dangerous situations that developed in all of his pictures.

His features such as *Why Worry?* (1923), *Hot Water* (1924), *The Fresh-man* (1925), and *For Heaven's Sake* (1926) were full of sight gags, all on Harold and usually as suspenseful as they were funny. He hung from ledges of skyscrapers, braved live lions and fierce revolutionaries. He always fought clean and he always won both the fight and the girl. His leading ladies were Bebe Daniels,* Jobyna Ralston, and Mildred Davis, whom he married in 1923.

Harold Lloyd made his talkie debut in *Welcome Danger* (1929). His films were fewer after sound came in but still very successful. A few were *Feet First* (1930), *Movie Crazy* (1932), *The Cat's Paw* (1934), *The Milky Way* (1936) with Lionel Stander (who lives with his wife in the Park Lane section of London), and *Professor, Beware* (1938) with Raymond Walburn (who still does an occasional Broadway role, and lives with his wife in Gramercy Park in Manhattan), his last until *Mad Wednesday,* which he made for the late Preston Sturges in 1947.

In 1952 the Motion Picture Academy presented Lloyd with a special Oscar engraved "Master Comedian and Good Citizen." In 1962 a compilation of clips from his pictures brought raves at the Cannes Film Festival. It has been released in the United States under the title *Harold Lloyd's World of Comedy.*

One of the richest stars in Hollywood, Lloyd is still married to Mildred Davis. They have one son, Harold, Jr., who is a singer, and two daughters. Their Italian Renaissance mansion in Beverly Hills is on twenty acres of some of the world's most expensive real estate and includes a nine hole golf course, two swimming pools, a tennis court, and a bowling alley. Harold keeps in good condition by spending time at each of the sports every day. He is an expert photographer and has had articles published in trade journals on color stereo photography.

Like the character he played on the screen, Lloyd is a most friendly and unpretentious man. Much of his huge wealth is diverted to charity and a great deal of his spare time is spent working for the Shriners, which he headed for some years. When he senses that visitors to his estate are overwhelmed by the lavish surroundings, he usually points out some priceless rug or piece of antique furniture that his Great Danes have ruined.

In his Beverly Hills home. *Jon Virzi*

25

The Governor in 1944 . . .

THOMAS E. DEWEY

The twice defeated Republican presidential candidate was born in Owosso, Michigan, in 1902 over the general store that belonged to his maternal grandfather. His paternal grandfather was for many years the G.O.P. county chairman and had been a charter member of the party when it was founded. Thomas E. was also a cousin of Admiral George Dewey, hero of Manila Bay.

During his campaigns much was made of the fact that he had worked his way through the University of Michigan, from which he was graduated in 1923. Actually, Tom had a group of local boys selling magazines for him in a clever and profitable arrangement whereby he held the franchise and the boys did the selling. To hear Dewey's public relations people tell it he was a poor newsboy on a windy street corner. Quite otherwise. His father was the publisher of the Owosso *Times*.

Dewey's study of law was second to his ambition to be an opera singer. He was an exceptional baritone and when he came to New York in 1923, it was to study singing as well as to attend Columbia's Law School. While training he sang regularly in churches in and around Manhattan. He says that he also sang in a synagogue, but when questioned where, his memory fails him. His voice could not be counted on. When he developed laryngitis before a recital, Tom decided to devote all of his time and energy to law and politics.

In 1928 he married a girl who always amazed those who met her by the contrast she provided to her husband. Frances E. Hutt, grandniece of Jefferson Davis, is warm and friendly with a delightful sense of humor.

From private practice, in which he did very well after his admission to the bar in 1926, he was appointed chief assistant United States Attorney for the Southern District of New York. By this time his local politicking had been rewarded with a district captainship. Two days after F.D.R. was elected President in 1932, Dewey's superior resigned. Dewey took full charge of the prosecution of Irving "Waxey Gordon" Wechsler, a beer baron, and to the surprise of everyone, most of all the racketeers, won a conviction on charges of tax evasion. It was the first of many guilty verdicts. Dewey left the punks to his assistants. The big boys he reserved for his special skill which was not always noticeably considerate of the defendants' civil liberties. Following a return to private practice in 1933, he accepted an appointment in 1935 as a special prosecutor against organized crime. In a nearly perfect score as a prosecutor, Dewey obtained convictions against Tammany district leader James J. Hines, stockbroker-socialite Richard Whitney, Bundist Fritz Kuhn, and Louis "Lepke" Buchalter. Dewey was credited with breaking up the notorious "Murder, Inc.," and by the late thirties his reputation as a racket smasher was nationwide. He achieved his biggest courtroom victory when Charles "Lucky" Luciano was found guilty and deported to Italy.

From 1937 to 1941, Dewey was serving as District Attorney in New York City under Fiorello H. La Guardia. In his first try for the governorship in 1938 he was narrowly defeated by incumbent Herbert Lehman. His *Case Against the New Deal* in 1940 was a best seller, and he came to the G.O.P. convention of 1940 as a favorite for the nomination but lost to the gallery demands of "We want Willkie."

Dewey's basic principles seemed to change with the times and the opinion polls. Prior to World War II there were warm words from the isolationists; in his last years in public life he was generally regarded as an internationalist. As Governor from 1943 to 1954 he won badly needed reapportionment, liberalized unemployment insurance, built highways, and sponsored public housing. His heart may have been to the right but his eye was dead center on the White House.

His defeat by Roosevelt in 1944 was no surprise since the war was still on, but when he received 189 electoral votes to Harry S. Truman's 303 in the 1948 election the entire Western world shook its head in wonderment. The late Dorothy Parker cost him not a few votes when she summed up his humorlessness and conservative image in one quip—"He looks like the little man on the wedding cake."

What fooled the professionals as well as Dewey was his remarkable ability to persuade a jury or a board of directors. In small groups he exuded confidence. To the masses he appeared pompous, and in a man so young it must have seemed even more distasteful.

Dewey and his wife now keep a large apartment in Manhattan's Seventies, and a country estate in Pawling, New York. His Wall Street law firm of Dewey, Ballantine, Bushby, Palmer & Wood, in which he is still active, is one of the most prestigious and lucrative in the country.

. . . and addressing the G.O.P. Convention, 1968. *UPI*

A typical publicity pose, 1952. *UPI*

"GORGEOUS GUSSIE" MORAN

Gertrude Augusta Moran was born of Irish and German parents in Santa Monica, California, in 1924. She began playing tennis when she was twelve years old. By thirteen she had earned the name "tomboy." Ever since a boy in her class spotted her middle name on a report card, and teased her about it long and hard, she became known as Gussie. "Gorgeous" was added by *Life* magazine in the late forties when the pretty athlete began copping titles around the country.

At sixteen she was playing well enough to be considered among the more important young prospects in southern California. She had some coaching from the late Bill Tilden and Eleanor Tennant who had coached Alice Marble. But Gussie's interest slackened after Charlie Chaplin, who played with her regularly, warned her that if she continued her game as often and as hard as she customarily did, she would develop large muscles. She continued playing but less frequently, until her enthusiasm revived in 1945.

Gussie had two things against her. She had a rather late start and the rather stuffy Southern California Tennis Association gave her little help or encouragement since it frowned on her colorful clothes and flamboyant behavior.

In 1946 at the Nationals, which were held at Forest Hills, New York, a practically unknown Gussie fought her way to the quarterfinals and took a set from Pauline Betz, the only one Miss Betz lost in the whole tournament; in 1947 she and Mary Arnold Prentiss won the National Clay Court Doubles. Gussie and Pancho Segura won the Seabright mixed doubles crown in 1946, and got to the final round of the National Mixed Doubles where they lost to an Australian team of Bromwich and Brough. On the way to that final they licked defending champs Billy Talbert and Margaret Osborne Du Pont. The next year Gussie made the Top Ten of Tennis list for the first time. In the spring of 1949 she came to tackle the National Indoor Tennis Championships. She wound up on March 26 with three titles: Mixed Doubles, Women's Doubles, and the coveted Women's Singles. At Wimbledon in 1949 she was beaten after the third round by Gem Hoahing.

Gussie was a press agent's dream. She had a commercial airplane named for her. She dated just about everyone and posed for publicity pictures in every conceivable costume and position. On the front of magazines she appeared as a cover girl, and on the back, as an endorsement for cigarettes. In 1950 the American Fashion Academy named her the "best dressed woman in sports." She made up her own list of the most attractive men in sports. Wherever there was an open microphone or shutter, Gussie was there. Her really big break came when Colonel Teddy Tindling designed an outfit for her to wear at Wimbledon in 1949, which did not include panties. Gussie says she wanted something to make her look more feminine and added panties trimmed in lace. The photographers went wild and people who never saw a tennis match knew who "Gorgeous Gussie" was after that. And Gussie was pretty good at reminding them every chance she got. She has since worn leopard skin panties.

On October 26, 1950, she made her pro debut in Madison Square Garden. She also played exhibition matches and gave tennis lessons (one of her pupils was Ron Ely, star of TV's "Tarzan" series). There was talk of her going into movies but the only part she ever played was herself in *Pat and Mike* (1952) with two of her friends, Katharine Hepburn and the late Spencer Tracy. For a while she designed and manufactured a line of tennis apparel which did not include lace panties.

Gussie had a hard serve, and a good ground stroke and forehand. Her favorite partners are Pancho Segura and Pancho Gonzales (who has a tennis club and school in Malibu. He and Gussie still play). She plays at least four or five times a week. Next to tennis her favorite sport is swimming and she does plenty of it.

According to "Gorgeous Gussie," she has been married "2½ times." The "½" was annulled. In 1966, single, she moved to Manhattan and accepted a position as an advertising consultant for World Tennis and a job with Eastman-Kodel for whom she arranges fashion shows and does commercials. In 1968 she covered the Wimbledon games for Westinghouse Radio.

Gussie today, in her Manhattan apartment. *Diana Keyt*

At the height of her career. *NBC-TV*

FAYE EMERSON

The unofficial First Lady of Television was born in Elizabeth, Lousiana, in 1917. Faye Margaret lived with her father, who held jobs as varied as rancher and court stenographer, and mother in Texas, Illinois, and, finally, California where her parents were divorced when she was thirteen years old. Her mother remarried and settled in San Diego, while Faye was placed in a convent boarding school in Oceanside, California. After high school graduation, she attended San Diego State College, and appeared in several productions of the Community Players.

In 1941 she married William Crawford, a San Diego automobile dealer. They had one child "Scoop." The Crawfords were divorced in 1942.

Faye was appearing in *Here Today* in 1941 at San Diego's Municipal Theatre when she was offered contracts by both Paramount Pictures and Warner Brothers. She chose Warners and remained with them for five-and-a-half years during which time she made such pictures as *Murder in the Big House* (1942) with Van Johnson, *Mask for Demetrious* (1944) with the late Peter Lorre, *Destination Tokyo* (1944), *Between Two Worlds* (1944), her personal favorite, *The Very Thought of You* (1944) with Dennis Morgan, *Hotel Berlin* (1945) with Helmut Dantine (who resides in Beverly Hills with his wife, the daughter of movie mogul Joe Schenk), and *Danger Signal* (1945) with the late Zachary Scott.

Faye never really became a star in movies but was one of the more interesting leading ladies at a time when most films were essentially men's pictures. While at Warners her close friend, the late Ann Sheridan, induced her to bleach her brunette hair blonde. She wore her hair pulled back tightly which became her trademark.

Her first real fame came as the wife of Elliott Roosevelt whom she first met at a Hollywood dinner party. The couple were married on the rim of Grand Canyon in 1944. During part of their marriage Faye lived at the White House, with F.D.R. baby-sitting with "Scoop" and Mrs. Roosevelt reading him bedtime stories. Until she died Mrs. Roosevelt always asked Faye and her son to spend

New Year's Eve with her. After the war Faye and her husband were the first journalists to be permitted to enter the Soviet Union where they interviewed Stalin for a national magazine. They were divorced in 1950.

Faye Emerson truly came into her own on television. She was first seen on May 11, 1948, in "Tonight on Broadway." She was making her Broadway debut at the time in *The Play's the Thing*. For the next fifteen years she was probably the busiest woman in the business. She was the femcer on "Cavalcade of Fashion," a panelist on "Leave it to the Girls," and for five years beginning in 1953, on "I've Got a Secret." She wrote a thrice weekly TV column which was syndicated by United Press, and substituted for Arlene Francis (on "Home"), Garry Moore, Dave Garroway, and Edward R. Murrow (on "Person to Person") shows. Faye even had a show with her third husband Skitch Henderson on the New York NBC station in 1953 and 1954. They were divorced in 1957 after seven years of marriage.

During those years, Faye was on Broadway in such plays as *Parisienne* (1950), *Heavenly Twins* (1955), *Protective Custody* (1956), and *Back to Methuselah* (1958) opposite the late Tyrone Power. In the following summer months she toured the straw-hat circuit in *Goodbye, My Fancy, Dangerous Corner,* and *State of the Union.*

In 1963 the lady who had been chosen the best-dressed woman on TV, for no apparent reason announced that she was going to take a year's leave of absence and would travel extensively in Europe. To the surprise of everyone she never returned. Until a few years ago she lived in Klosters, Switzerland, and in 1965 bought her present four-bedroom home in the suburbs of Palma, Majorca. Faye has never remarried. No month goes by that she does not refuse a TV or movie offer. Since 1963 she has been in the United States only once for a few days on business. Her Manhattan town house is rented through her son, a real estate broker, who doubts she will ever come back to work on TV and the stage again.

At a bar in Majorca recently. *John Howard*

Battling Billy in 1941.

BILLY CONN

The man who nearly took the heavyweight championship away from Joe Louis was born in the tough East Liberty section of Pittsburgh, Pennsylvania, in 1917.

At fourteen he began to be a regular face around the East Liberty Gymnasium which was run by Johnny Ray who later became Billy's manager. At first Conn only ran errands but he soon began going a round or two invariably with older and bigger boys.

Billy flunked several times in grade school, tried the industrial school, and left for good. In a short time he was back at the gym full time.

He began to fight professionally in 1935, losing his very first encounter. It only goaded him on and in the next two years he made an important record for himself. In 1937 alone he whipped one former middleweight and four former welterweight champions. He fought the formidable ex-champion, Fred Apostoli, twice. The second time around Conn and the Italian exchanged some verbal unpleasantries which were heard over the overhead microphone of which neither was aware. Their language not only was profane but contained more than a few racial slurs. If anything, it only served to further endear Conn to Irish-Americans. He had become their hope of regaining the crown the much loved James Braddock* lost to Joe Louis not long before. Billy won both Apostoli fights and went on to take a close decision against Melio Bettina, thus winning the light-heavyweight championship.

Billy began to put on weight, with an eye on the heavyweight title held by Louis. He impressed the pros when his merciless body attack flattened Bob Pastor. Conn and promoter Mike Jacobs were determined to put the twenty-three-year-old Billy against the Brown Bomber. In November of 1940 Billy disposed of Lee Savold, a heavyweight who was then considered Louis' closest threat. Billy took a terrible beating in the process but outboxed his challenger and won on points. This was the plan he had in mind for Louis.

The famous match took place in the Polo Grounds on June 18, 1941. Everything went according to Billy's plan with the exception of the third round when Louis got in his best punch. But Billy survived it and the crowd roared.

Billy was smaller and lighter, all the odds were against him, and yet he was boxing circles around the champion. Conn went to the ring with his usual cockiness and was growing bolder with each round. Even when Joe was able to hit him Billy showed no signs of weakening. What's more he had so confused Louis and tired him that he was able to get in some very good punches of his own. By the twelfth round Billy was way ahead on points and the crowd was hysterical. He came out of his corner for the thirteenth round with all the confidence in the world. He jabbed Louis and hooked him and for a minute it looked like the Bomber was going to go down. Then, while his handlers screamed to Billy to "move," Conn went in for the kill. Billy got greedy. Louis caught him with an uppercut and while 60,071 fans watched with their mouths open Billy Conn fell to the canvas, knocked out. Had the punch come just three seconds later, the bell would have saved him. After the war they were rematched again but Billy was no longer the quick young man. Louis KO'd him in the seventh round on June 19, 1946.

Years later the two were discussing the legendary scrap and Billy said to the ex-champion, "Joe, why didn't you let me win that one? You could have sort of loaned me the crown for six months." "Billy," said Louis, looking straight at his old foe, "you *had* that title for twelve rounds."

Billy went back to the Steel capital but not to East Liberty. The Conns, four children and his wife Mary, live in a $60,000 home on Dennison Avenue in the Squirrel Hill section. Most of Billy's earnings went into a very lucky oil speculation, and was reinvested in Pittsburgh real estate, which he has since managed. Until 1967 he was the greeter at the Stardust Hotel in Las Vegas, Nevada. From time to time Billy referees a big fight. In 1967 he stopped the Carlos Ortiz-Sugar Ramos battle in the fifth round in Mexico City and proclaimed Ortiz the winner. He is not an unfamiliar face at ringside for an important fight, but swears that he really isn't very interested in the sport any longer—"there just aren't any more fighters." In the past several years he has been in the papers on occasions involving brawls with relatives and strangers. In all cases Billy was the victor.

Today he is Billy the Businessman.
UPI

Head Technocrat Scott, 1934. *UPI*

HOWARD SCOTT

Howard Scott, the leader of the bizarre economic movement that bemused and amused most of the United States during the Great Depression, was born in Virginia before 1900. Facts about his personal life and background, like a clear explanation of his scheme, were never divulged.

He has stated that on July 1, 1918, he opened his first Technology office at 107 Waverly Place in Greenwich Village, and remained through the twenties. It was not until Depression days that the Technocrats came into their own. Scott's plan promised that every workingman who labored for 4 hours per day, 4 days per week, 165 days per year would be paid $20,000 annually for his efforts. Nor would those efforts be strenuous, as Technocracy would reduce all toil to the barest minimum.

In 1932 several Columbia University professors discussed Technocracy with Scott in a formal symposium held on school grounds. As soon as the meetings were publicized the University asked Scott to leave and disavowed the Technocrats.

Explanations of how the Technate State of North America would function were few and vague. One capsule of the plan from Scott's own literature said: ". . . if sufficient energy-consuming devices are installed and total amount of extraneous energy consumer per capita reaches or exceeds 200,000 kilogram calories per capita per day, toil and workers alike will be eliminated."

During the Depression era, when they were going strong, Scott made many appearances on radio and was in the papers constantly. Chapters of Technocracy were all over the country, with an Institute of Technocracy in California. Those who took them seriously listed the Technocrats as Rightists and yet Scott has been quoted as saying that, "Marxian Communism is so far to the right it is bourgeois" when compared to his philosophy.

Although Scott has always maintained that his movement was not a political party and had no desire for political power, those who remember the gray uniforms and automobiles complete with their emblem of a circle separated by a curved line felt it had all the trappings, including a military salute, of a Fascist organization.

Walter Lippmann dismissed Scott's plans for replacing currency with energy units of "ergs" and "joules" as, "nothing but the pretentious ignorance of a crank."

Engineers, who would be the elite of the country under Technocracy, and economists have suggested that many of Scott's plans were similar to those set forth by William Henry Smyth and Thorstein Veblen, but the founder states that "We derive most of our concepts of thermodynamics and energy germinants from the works of J. Willard Gibbs."

By 1942 interest in the movement, which had dwindled greatly as the Depression subsided, was revived briefly when full page advertisements appeared in newspapers throughout the United States asking President Roosevelt to make Howard Scott the "Director General of Defense." These, said Scott recently, were placed by overenthusiastic members of his West Coast branches.

In 1948 Scott was again in the news when a former official asked the courts for an accounting of the monies Scott received for uniform sales and membership dues (at that time $6 yearly). The fallen-away Technocrat stated that there were then 8,900 members. This is the only figure ever divulged and even today Scott refuses to say how many members he has or has had.

Scott has always managed to keep something resembling an office over the last twenty years to testify that Technocracy is not dead, as many people thought he was. The last few years he has maintained some kind of a project in Rushland, Pennsylvania, which houses Technocracy's publishing enterprises. Their magazine, *The Technocrat,* is still sent out monthly to the faithful.

He boasts chapters in the Northwest, Canada, and California. In the past year ads have begun to appear in Greenwich Village newspapers promoting meetings and literature. Although over seventy years old, Scott still runs the whole show. Most of the movement's writings are by him and nothing is decided without his approval. Their slogan, after fifty years, is unchanged— "Something New Under the Sun." His followers, whose dues are now $9 a year, who would run the North American continent on the principles of engineering, do not seem troubled that their leader still has no degree in either economics or engineering.

The director in chief at his headquarters in Rushland, Pennsylvania. *The Technocrat*

At one of her regular guest appearances on network variety shows, 1933.

ETHEL WATERS

The first Negro woman to receive star billing in America was born in Chester, Pennsylvania, in 1900. At five Ethel was singing in churches. When she was sixteen she was working as a laundress and chambermaid in a Philadelphia hotel for $4.75 a week. On her seventeenth birthday, which was Halloween, two boys took her to a nightclub on Juniper Street, and encouraged her to sing; a mask she was wearing helped overcome her initial shyness. She sang two songs which went over so well that the boys convinced her to turn professional. They got her a job for $9 a week at the Lincoln Theatre in Baltimore. The money seemed fine until she learned that they each were getting $25 a week as her managers.

Throughout much of the twenties she performed in theatres, cabarets, and vaudeville. Much of her work was in the South and all of it in the Negro circuit of show business. Her material was usually "blue," but always deeply religious; she sang spirituals off stage. In 1927 she debuted on Broadway in *Africana* and in 1929 made *On With the Show*, her first movie, with Sally O'Neil, in which Ethel sang "Am I Blue?"

In 1930 she opened on Broadway in *Lew Leslie's Blackbirds* and in 1931 starred in *Rhapsody in Black,* which was so successful that versions appeared in 1932 and 1933.

When she was appearing in *As Thousands Cheer* during the 1933–1934 season, the authors Moss Hart and Irving Berlin invited her to the weekly cast parties. She agreed to attend though only as a performer.

Two of her titles were "the tawny Yvette Guilbert," and "the bronze Raquel Miller." In 1935 she was featured with Bea Lillie in *At Home Abroad*. All through the thirties Ethel was a frequent guest star on network radio programs where her color was no problem. In 1938 she had a highly successful one-woman concert at Carnegie Hall.

Perhaps Miss Waters' greatest hit was her role in *Mamba's Daughters* which opened on Broadway in January, 1939. It is also her personal favorite. She is also closely associated with *Cabin in the Sky* in which she introduced the standard "Takin' a Chance on Love" in 1940 and repeated her role in the movie version in 1943.

In 1942 Ethel and Count Basie packed them in at the Palace. In 1949 she headed the bill at the Roxy. She made such films as *Tales of Manhattan* (1941), *Stage Door Canteen* (1943), and *Pinky* (1949), a highly controversial movie on race relations at a time when the subject was considered taboo by Hollywood. For her performance Ethel was nominated for an Academy Award.

In 1950 Ethel Waters was back on Broadway in the memorable Carson McCullers play, *The Member of the Wedding*, which she also played on the road. The movie version, which was a box office failure, brought her a second Academy Award nomination. At a fade-out Miss Waters is seen in a rocking chair singing "His Eye Is on the Sparrow" which was the title of her autobiography, a 1951 best seller.

On TV she was the original "Beulah" but left the role after one season in 1950. In 1956 she made *The Heart Is a Rebel* and in 1959 was seen in *The Sound and the Fury,* her last movie. In 1960 her great weight (at times as much as 250 pounds) and worry over money brought on a heart attack. She has lived quietly ever since.

The lady who popularized such hits as "Supper Time," "Heat Wave," and "Stormy Weather" has an apartment on Orange Drive in Los Angeles. She has been married and divorced three times, but has no children. There were bad investments and tax troubles and now all her money is gone. Her few public appearances are with Billy Graham's Crusades. After attending one of the evangelist's Madison Square Garden rallies, she sang in the choir every night afterward. Says Ethel: "I heard them singing "This is My Song" and I thought I'd come home. That was the turning point in my life.

On a recent rare night out. *Jon Virzi*

Heavyweight Champion of the World in 1950. *Ring Magazine*

EZZARD CHARLES

Boxing's most colorless champion was born in the crossroads town of Lawrenceville, Georgia, in 1921, though he has always considered Cincinnati his home. Ezzard began fighting as a boy in the streets and in the ring. For three years he was an amateur and for nineteen years a professional. It was instinctive with him. He has said that for years he did not really understand the difference in the categories. "I just thought you went in and fought, and they gave you something, or not."

Charles was by no means a second-rate fighter. He simply had the misfortune of being the World's Heavyweight Champion between Joe Louis, probably the sport's most loved, and Rocky Marciano, a very popular and colorful champion. (Ezzard always admired the comic strip character Joe Palooka, who was basically a gentleman.) Charles had few enemies, but the sport promoters knew that people bought tickets to see a fighter lose as well as win; Ezzard just didn't draw crowds. He lacked the killer instinct which makes for both excitement and victories. Sports writers called him "Snooks" to distinguish him from the "bombers" and the "maulers."

Charles fought 122 times as a pro and won 96. He first came to national attention in 1948 when the twenty-year-old Sam Baroudi died of a brain hemorrhage after hitting the canvas from Charles' slugging in the fourth round in Chicago. And in December of that year he whipped Joe Baksi, which put him in the challenger class for the heavyweight crown.

Even the fight that brought him the title was dull. He outpointed Jersey Joe Walcott in June, 1949, to win the National Boxing Association's crown (not recognized in New York or London). The crowd booed both fighters in the match that had been promoted by Joe Louis. In August of 1949 he won with a T-K.O. The following August Charles and Freddie Beshore drew the lowest gate in the history of heavyweight championship fights, $28,666.00, at the

Buffalo Memorial Stadium. While 6,298 fans watched, the referee stopped the scrap in the fourteenth round, with Ezzard winning.

He held the title only two years. Even after he beat Joe Louis in September, 1950, when the former champion tried to come back in Yankee Stadium, Charles seemed to gather no glamour. Louis was much older, and tired, and it went the full fifteen rounds for a decision in Ezzard's favor. Then on July 18, 1951, he was rematched with Jersey Joe Walcott,* and the former champion KO'd him in the seventh round.

Charles fought for a few years and then returned to Cincinnati, the city that had showered him in chrysanthemums when he had come home a hero, where he became a salesman for a wholesale wine firm.

After collecting purses totaling $1,500,000, Ezzard is now working for a salary which he is very glad to get each week. He has a job with Mayor Daley's Commission on Youth Welfare. From a small office on Chicago's South Side, the former champion tries to steer Negro youths on the right path. He arranges block parties and runs films which are made for rehabilitation and self-improvement. "I jive around with the kids mostly. I try to pick the worst kid, and jive him. Sometimes it works, sometimes not." None of the boys remember him as world champion, but they all know that he was one. Even when he was on top Charles liked young people. He used to load up his big convertible and take as many boys and girls as it would hold out for a drive and a rare visit to a restaurant where they were told to order anything they wanted. For a while after leaving the ring Charles was a wholesale wine salesman, but his health has been greatly impaired by lateral sclerosis, and he really prefers what he is doing now. His financial condition he philosophically attributes to "bad investments." He still likes boxing and says that in spite of his present situation he thinks the game gave him "a wonderful life."

Recuperating from a recent illness.
Chicago Daily News

As Gilda in *Rigoletto* in 1940. *De Bellis*

LILY PONS

Lily Pons was born in Draguignan, France, in 1904 of French-Italian parents. The family was musical, the father a fine violinist, the mother a singer, and Lily and her two sisters pianists.

Lily first discovered her singing talents during World War I when she entertained soldiers but it wasn't until after a stint with the Paris Theatre des Varieties, for which she undertook ingenue roles, that she seriously considered singing as a career. Her first husband August Mesritz encouraged her to study singing. At twenty-one she began studying with the great master Alberti de Gorostiaga, who was to remain her only teacher. Within three years she made her operatic debut singing the title role in *Lakmé* at Mulhouse, Alsace. Other engagements in provincial opera houses followed in quick succession.

She was heard by Giovanni Zenatello, then scouting for the New York Metropolitan Opera, and he recommended her for an audition. Her Met debut was made in 1931 singing what was to become her most famous role, *Lucia di Lammermoor.* Also in the cast were Benjamino Gigli and Ezio Pinza. Olin Downes, then critic of *The New York Times,* said of her performance, "Her mad scene was a foretaste of full-fledged virtuosity." The public concurred apparently, for she received sixteen curtain calls. Madame Pons has always sung the mad scene a full key higher (F) than the key in which Donizetti wrote it (E Flat).

From 1931 to 1938 she sang at the Metropolitan and the Colón in Buenos Aires. In addition, she made appearances with the San Francisco, Chicago, St. Louis, and Philadelphia opera companies. She toured South America, Canada, Australia, Europe, and the British Isles.

Lakmé was revived at the Met especially for her as was *La Sonnambula.* Her repertoire also includes Gilda in *Rigoletto,* Rosina in *The Barber of Seville,* Olympia in *The Tales of Hoffman,* and Philine in *Mignon,* in addition to other coloratura parts.

She made such films as *I Dream Too Much* (1935) with Henry Fonda (one critic said it should have been called *I Scream Too Much*), *That Girl From Paris* (1936) with Jack Oakie and Gene Raymond, and *Hitting a New High* (1937), again with Fonda. During these years she appeared weekly on radio, singing with the forty-piece orchestra that her new husband André Kostelanetz conducted. They were married in 1938, just five years after her divorce from her first husband. Together they were to become the highest paid musical duet in history. Her activity at the Met during the first ten postwar years had included only thirty-four performances during that time.

Throughout the fifties Madame Pons made countless television appearances, having been on "The Perry Como Show," "What's My Line?," "The Ed Sullivan Show," and "The Show of Shows." She was once the subject of "This is Your Life," and has sung occasionally during the sixties.

In 1965 the Met feted her on the twenty-five years of her continuous activity at the house. No other soprano has ever sustained such a time span at the Met. The Met presented the famed coloratura in an assemblage of familiar arias and songs, including, of course, the mad scene from *Lucia*. Among the audience were Leopold Stokowski, Gladys Swarthout, and David Oistrakh.

Lily had no sentimental attachments to the old house. When it was being razed she was one of the few former stars not passionately in favor of saving it. She told an interviewer that the dressing rooms were impossible and that the house was hopelessly antiquated.

Lily Pons has in the course of her public career received many honors, ranging from being made an officer of the French Legion of Honor to the naming of a town after her, in Maryland, Lilypons, previously Lily Pond.

Madame Pons maintains residences in Dallas, Palm Springs, New York, and the south of France. She was divorced from Kostelanetz in 1958 and has never remarried. She has had no children. Although her engagements are scarce and have been rather poorly received in the last few years, she continues to sing. It is most unfortunate because her voice is nowhere near the lovely thing it was.

Former Metropolitan Opera stars (left to right) Bidu Sayao, Giovanni Martinelli, and Lily Pons on a TV discussion show.

Beck in 1936. *UPI*

DAVE BECK

The precursor of Jimmy Hoffa was born in 1894 in Stockton, California. His father, Lemuel, was a carpet cleaner and his mother took in washing to help support the family. In 1898 the Becks moved to Seattle. Dave left school when he was sixteen and went from one job to another. In 1914 he began driving a laundry truck. During World War I, while a member of the United States Navy, Dave flew on anti-zeppelin missions over the North Sea. After the Armistice he married Dorothy Leschender, and went back to his old job. This was during the early days of organized labor in America. Dave joined Local 566 of the Teamsters as its secretary, and in 1923 became president of the Joint Council of Teamsters. In 1927, he was made general organizer for the Pacific North West and British Columbia. Ten years later he formed the Western Conference of Teamsters. In a short time it also included the Midwest and East. In 1940 he became vice-president. He was made executive vice-president in 1947 and elected president in 1952.

Beck was the old style union leader who never avoided a fight. When Harry Bridges challenged the Teamsters for representation of the warehouse workers on the West Coast in the late thirties the formidable longshoremen battled their competition in the streets, repeatedly, but to no avail. The Teamsters won both the battles and the jurisdiction.

Since Beck ran the Teamsters as his personal fief, most of the credit for their rise must be given to him. He also had to take the blame for its faults when the legal troubles began. Four years after he assumed the presidency, the union treasury had increased by $9,000,000 and the membership by 250,000. He prided himself on the claim that his union lived up to its contracts and kept strikes to a minimum. His critics, even some within the Teamsters, attributed this to the fact that Beck was also a businessman and employer. It was an open secret that he had large holdings in such things as gas stations and bowling alleys.

By the time his serious woes with the government began, Beck had achieved respectability and was considered by many to be a perfect example of what a poor boy in America could achieve if he really tried. He was on the Washington State Parole Board and a member of the Seattle Civic Service Commission. Other status positions he had obtained were membership in the Board of Regents of Washington State University and officership in the American Legion and the Elks. Politically he was on the conservative side. His worst enemy never accused the Teamsters of any Communist infiltration.

No one seemed to question how he had become a millionaire on a union official's salary. Then a Senate investigating committee began to inquire into the sources of his personal fortune and the workings of his giant union. It was revealed that Beck had been running the Teamsters like one of his private holdings. Very few decisions on matters of contracts and investments of union funds were delegated. (When he became president, Beck turned over all organizing chores to his protégé Jimmy Hoffa, who was later to succeed him.) There was a report that Teamster money had been used to build a huge mansion in the suburbs of Seattle. This house was later sold to the union for $163,000 but Beck continued to live in it rent free, with the union paying the taxes on the property. When in 1955 the Teamsters opened their new $5,000,000 headquarters in Washington, D.C., Dave moved into a lavishly furnished office in the penthouse which had a view of the Capitol dome. Although he favored handmade suits and expensive cars, he did not drink, smoke, or gamble.

In 1961 Beck was sentenced to five years in prison for filing false income-tax returns. He was paroled after serving two-and-a-half years at the United States penitentiary on McNeil Island, near Tacoma, Washington. During his trial and subsequent appeals Beck never lost his cool. The roly-poly unionist became a model prisoner and when he was released in 1964 went right back to Seattle where he oversees his business and real estate holdings estimated by more than one source to be worth over $2,000,000. All the time he was in jail he continued to draw his yearly $50,000 salary from the Teamsters.

In 1967 Dave Beck married his second wife Helen and honeymooned in Hawaii. Beck will talk with newsmen but refuses to get into anything controversial. During the Hoffa trials and upon his imprisonment, for instance, Beck had no comment. He still refuses to discuss the matter.

With wife, Helen, on a recent vacation. *UPI*

43

Something to write home about in the 1940's.

ESTHER WILLIAMS

"The Queen of the Surf," as the M-G-M press agents dubbed her, was born in Los Angeles in 1923.

She attended the University of Southern California for awhile and did some modeling until Billy Rose hired her in 1939 to appear in his Aquacade at the Golden Gate International Exposition in San Francisco. Esther probably would have competed in the Olympics but they were not held due to the outbreak of World War II.

Metro-Goldwyn-Mayer put her under contract and gave her a few small roles such as in *Andy Hardy's Double Life* (1942) and *A Guy Named Joe* (1943), in which she supported Irene Dunne* and the late Spencer Tracy.

The Esther Williams moviegoers remember from the forties and fifties emerged in *Bathing Beauty* with Red Skelton and organist Ethel Smith (who resides in Manhattan's Parc Vendome apartments) in 1944. She never developed into much of an actress and try as she did her singing was never more than mediocre, but her pictures were loaded with catchy tunes and talented people. Esther did little more than swim or pose in a bathing suit. As it happened she did both very well. Her figure was curvaceous and in Technicolor her luscious complexion came over very well. There was not another girl in the movies who could swim so well—and could she kiss underwater!

Most of Esther's notices were terrible but they seemed to have no affect on her fans. In 1950 exhibitors named her one of the world's biggest box office draws.

Most of her pictures were musicals shot in Technicolor. They had big names, handsome leading men, and some fine underwater photography. The Culver City lot spared no expense when they put her in such vehicles as *Thrill of a Romance* (1945) with Van Johnson, *Ziegfeld Follies* (1945) with Lucille Bremmer, *Easy to Wed* (1946) with Lucille Ball, *Fiesta* (1947) with Ricardo

Montalban, *This Time for Keeps* (1947) with Lauritz Melchior, *On An Island With You* (1948) with Peter Lawford and Jimmy Durante, *Take Me Out to the Ball Game* (1949) with Frank Sinatra and Betty Garrett (living in Los Angeles with her husband Larry Parks*), *Neptune's Daughter* (1949) with Red Skelton, *Pagan Love Song* (1950) with Howard Keel, *The Duchess of Idaho* (1950), *Texas Carnival* (1951), *Million Dollar Mermaid* (1952) with Victor Mature, *Dangerous When Wet* (1953) with Fernando Lamas, *Easy to Love* (1953), and *Jupiter's Darling* (1955) with Marge and Gower Champion.

Toward the end of her career Esther made a valiant but unsuccessful attempt to climb out of the water and into dramatic roles. In 1957 NBC television presented her in the "Aqua Spectacular," the last of her bathing suit appearances. After that she did *The Unguarded Moment* (1956), in which she was sexually molested by John Saxon; with the late Jeff Chandler, she made *Raw Wind in Eden* (1958) in Italy; and after the rather tacky *The Big Show* (1961) with Robert Vaughn, she quit.

In 1957 Esther ended her thirteen year marriage to actor-producer Ben Gage. She was awarded custody of their children—two girls, Benjie, eighteen, and Susan, fourteen, and a boy, Kim, who at seventeen stands 6 feet 7 inches tall.

Fortunately, for Esther, not all her savings were invested in the ill-fated Esther Williams Swimming Pools—she can still afford to turn down movie and TV roles. She expresses very little interest in working again, but does not close the door completely to offers. "I'm perfectly content to sit in my Santa Monica home watching my kids grow up," she said recently.

When in 1967 she was inducted into the Swimming Pool Hall of Fame, Esther was accompanied by her close friend and constant companion, Fernando Lamas. As the cameras clicked and fans gawked everyone commented on how well she looked. Yes, she swims every day.

With 1928 Oympic gold medal winner Arne Borg from Sweden after induction together into the Swimming Pool Hall of Fame in Fort Lauderdale, Florida. *Ed Plummer*

45

Glenn (left) congratulates Ben Eastman who won the half-mile on the
same day Cuningham broke the mile
record, June 16, 1934. *Acme*

GLENN CUNNINGHAM

The Master Miler of the thirties was born in Atlanta, Kansas, in 1912. When he was seven years old Glenn was caught in a schoolhouse fire. His legs were so badly burned that at first doctors doubted the boy would live. For seven months he had to lie in bed while the burns turned to ugly scars. Once he was permitted to walk there was no stopping him. Each day he walked a little more around his father's farm and little by little he was walking faster. Once he had proved to himself that he could walk long distances, he began running. A little at first, and then more and more.

Cunningham's leg trouble did not end when he started running and winning races. The burns ate away the flesh and left delicate scar tissue in its stead. He was unable to limber up like most athletes. Instead, he had to prance. He was immediately labeled a show-off and was soundly booed at some meets even before they began. Once the warm-up periods were over, however, the crowds' attitude was somewhat different. Cunningham piled up a staggering record of wins during his career. On June 16, 1934, at Princeton, New Jersey, Glenn, representing the University of Kansas, broke the world record for the mile. His time was 4:06.8. The race, which was sponsored by the university, saw another record shattered. Ben Eastman of Stanford set 1:49.8 as the new standard for the half-mile.

At the 1936 Olympics, held in Berlin, he romped in second in a sensational 1,500-meter race in which Jack Lovelock of New Zealand set the world's record of 3:47.8. Two years later Glenn picked up a trophy for the mile run in New York at the Seventh Regiment Games on February 11. He was clocked at 4:15.2, breaking the 4:18.2 meet record which had stood for twenty-five years. Then in April of 1938 Archie San Romani forged ahead of him at the last minute and broke the tape at 4:23 on the Kansas University track.

Galloping Glenn was the model athlete. He never broke training in or out of season. He did not drink or smoke, and never has. But he had a great deal going for him when he was out on the track. His hearing was so sensitive that not only could he detect his opponents approaching from behind but could distinguish among them just by the sound of their feet on the cinder path. In 1936 he was admittedly out of condition when he was matched with Joe Mangan and Gene Venske. Mangan broke on top and decided to yield the lead. No one would pass him. He slowed down to a walk until the last 220 yards when all at once Glenn took off and bolted past both his opponents to win. The race has been called the Typographical Error Mile because he was clocked at 4.46.8, which looked more like a typist's mistake than a time.

Glenn hasn't run in competition since he was stationed at the Great Lakes Naval Base during World War II. Following the war, he and his first wife, a fellow student at Kansas University whom he married in 1934, were divorced. They had two children. In 1946 he married again, and has ten children by this marriage.

After graduating from Kansas University he continued his studies at New York University, and received his Ph.D. in June, 1938. Afterward he accepted a job with Cornell College in Mount Vernon, Iowa, as Director of Student Health.

Since 1946 Glenn has been a farmer. The Cunninghams have a large spread on Route 2 just outside Augusta, Kansas. The farm is very well known in those parts, but not so much for the fact that its owner is one of the all-time sport greats. Along with their herd of livestock the family has collected wild and exotic animals from all over the world. Tourists often stop to see children playing with yaks and llamas, but more often than not the children are not Cunninghams. Glenn and his wife have turned their home into a place for children from "troubled homes." They have had as many as eighty-eight boys and girls living with them at one time. The great runner is justly proud of the remarkable results the healthy atmosphere of his farm and family have produced in kids who would otherwise be kept in institutions.

In June of 1968 Cunningham appeared on "The Joey Bishop Show" and announced that not only was he broke but deeply in debt because of the great expense he has been undergoing in supporting so many children. He asked for contributions.

At home today. *Augusta Daily Gazette*

In *Polo Joe,* 1936.

JOE E. BROWN

Joe Evans Brown, the famous big-mouthed comedian, was born in 1892 in Holgate, Ohio, one of seven children of a poor family. As a boy he knew cold, hunger, and hard work. Joe taught himself acrobatics, and when he was ten years old he was accepted as a member of the Five Marvelous Ashtons, traveling with Sells and Downs Circus. His salary was $2.50 a week.

In 1906 the Ashtons broke up after their appearance at a honky-tonk house, the Haymarket Music Hall, which was destroyed by the San Francisco earthquake. Joe went into baseball, a game he has always loved and which was the background for several of his movies. He played off-seasons and summers for such semipro teams as Crowley's All Stars. He was such a cutup that the other players encouraged him to return to show business, but as a comic this time. He joined the Bell-Prevost Trio in 1914. They specialized in acrobatics at the Henderson Music Hall at Coney Island. On the bill with them was a sketch called "Change Your Act" with Victor Moore. On the same bill was a man named W. C. Fields. The trio remained together for eleven years and played just about every burlesque house and vaudeville circuit in the country. Along the way Bell dropped out and they became known as Prevost and Brown.

Joe E. was never a favorite of the intelligentsia. His comedy was rather obvious and without much subtlety, but at least it was not pretentious. He was a natural comic who needed neither gags nor gimmicks to get a laugh. He had what might be called the humor of reaction—a frustration of purpose or a confrontation with some unlooked-for situation. His face was marvellously expressive and his mouth was huge.

Joe made his Broadway debut in 1918 in *Listen Lester* which starred the late Clifton Webb. This was followed by *Jim Jam Jems* (1920), in which he co-starred with the late Frank Fay. He was in the third edition of the *Greenwich Village Follies* in 1921 along with the late Harry Langdon and Ned Sparks. The show introduced the song "Three O'Clock in the Morning." He was also in *Shore Leave* (1922) and *Betty Lee* (1925).

While he worked on Broadway he made countless screen tests at the old studios in Fort Lee, New Jersey, none of which prompted a studio to sign him. Then he came to Los Angeles with the late Ona Munson in *Twinkle, Twinkle.* An agent saw him, considered him a "natural," and talked director Ralph Ince into seeing Brown perform in the show. He was placed under contract to F.B.O.

Studios (later to become R.K.O.) and appeared in *Crooks Can't Win,* his first film, in 1922. Joe bombed in each of his first six pictures, playing dramatic parts. He clicked first in *Hold Everything* (1930) and received star billing afterward for many years. Of his seventy-five movies twenty-nine were made during his nine-year contract with Warner Brothers. Some of them were: *Circus Kid* (1928), *Sally* (1929) with Marilyn Miller, *The Tenderfoot* (1932), *Elmer the Great* (1933), his favorite role, *A Midsummer Night's Dream* (1935), in which he played the role of Flute. His pictures were the biggest money-makers the studio had for 1932, 1935, and 1936.

During World War II he set a record entertaining troops in 742 overseas shows. Congress awarded him the Bronze Star for his efforts, one of the very few times a civilian has been so honored. Joe wrote a book about his wartime experiences, *Your Kids and Mine.* His son, Don, was killed in action.

After the war he starred on the stage in the Mary Chase (who lives in Denver, Colorado) comedy, *Harvey,* for 1,680 performances in the national company and then in Australia and England. In 1951 he had a short run in *Courtin' Time,* a musical version of *The Farmer's Wife.*

During the fifties he was quite active in television. He emceed "Talent Scouts," when Arthur Godfrey was away, and "Strike It Rich," and he starred on "Circus Hour."

In 1956 his autobiography *Laughter Is a Wonderful Thing* was published. It revealed him as a man not too dissimilar from the character he had been playing for so many years.

In 1959 he re-created Cap'n Andy in *Show Boat* in the City Center production, a part he played a decade earlier on the screen. In 1959 he had the last and most outrageous line in the Billy Wilder picture *Some Like It Hot.* Jack Lemmon is seated next to him in drag. Joe E. has just asked Lemmon to marry him and Lemmon tells him that there is something he should know, that he, Lemmon, is actually a man. "Well," replies Joe, "no one's perfect." He has rarely worked since and there is no financial need for him to do so.

Always a close family man, Joe lives in Los Angeles with his wife, the former Kathryn McGraw, whom he married in 1915 at New York's City Hall after courting her by mail for months. They have a son, two adopted daughters, and a number of grandchildren with whom he spends much time. He is an avid, skilled golfer.

At the Los Angeles Country Club.

The Girl of the Year, 1938. N. Y. *Daily News*

BRENDA FRAZIER

The Girl of the Year 1938 was born in 1921. Her parents, who were socially prominent Bostonians, separated shortly after her birth. Like Brenda's beaus, friends, husbands, and relatives, they were very, very rich. It was old, quite respectable money. Or at least until 1938.

Brenda lived part of the year with her father and part with her mother. Her parents lived in different cities, moved in different circles, and called Brenda by different names. Her father, who spent most of his time in Palm Beach, called her Diana—her full maiden name is Brenda Diana Duff Frazier.

When Miss Frazier's father died in 1933 his will stated that on her twenty-first birthday she was to receive the $4,000,000 he had left her only if she did not continue to live with her mother. "Mummy," who didn't care much for him either, had the will invalidated so that Brenda got the money and Mrs. Frazier got Brenda—whom she took to live with her at the Ritz in Manhattan. As the only child of a wealthy, socially ambitious woman, Brenda was schooled at Miss Porter's and Miss Hewitt's before being sent to Munich where she attended a very chichi finishing school. Mummy chose her clothes, her dates, and her friends. When in 1937 Mummy decided that Brenda was to "come out," no amount of the girl's pleading against a debut could dissuade Mrs. Frazier.

The year was 1938. Spain was in flames and the rest of Europe was a tinder-box; Chamberlain appeased Hitler at Munich; Japanese armies swept across China; and at home continued labor unrest made Americans wonder whether the Great Depression would ever end. But the Girl of the Year was Brenda Frazier. Her pictures were in all the papers, and her name was in the columns. *Life* magazine featured her on the cover. The press saw only the waxen skin, and vivid red lips and nails of a girl whose mother had the naïveté to spend a fortune on a single party while many of her countrymen considered themselves lucky if they had enough to eat. Some readers were infuriated while others were simply amused to read of Cafe Society's antics. The important thing was that Brenda sold papers. She became a household name in homes that had never read the Cholly Knickerbocker column. The El Morocco's Jerome Zerbee photographed her against the famous zebra skin upholstery of the club's banquettes, and no one did more to make the Stork Club "in" than Brenda Frazier—whose friendship with proprietor Sherman Billingsley lasted until he died in 1967. The club's press agent, Chick Farmer (now the P.R. man for the Garden City Hotel on Long Island) made sure she got the right table and lots of attention.

The only other deb who came close to Brenda in prominence was Cobina Wright, Jr. Millions of radio listeners tuned to the "Bob Hope Show" laughed weekly at the merciless parody by Blanche Stewart and Eliva Allman playing "Brenda and Cobina."

At a time when $50 per week was considered a living wage by millions of American families, Brenda turned down a $500,000 offer to star in M-G-M films. But endorsed Woodbury soap.

After her marriage in 1941 to John Simms Kelly (known to football fans as "Shipwreck" Kelly) Brenda settled down to a quiet life on Long Island. In 1945 the Kellys had a daughter, Victoria; the marriage ended in 1956. The next year Brenda married Robert F. Chatfield-Taylor, a distant relative.

Brenda no longer lives with her second husband. The last few years of her life have been spent in a large secluded house in Medfield, outside of Boston. Although she does very little entertaining and is seldom seen in nightclubs, her life in past years has not been without incident. There was a long bout with ill health, which was the result of years spent on a near-starvation diet to avoid gaining weight; she has survived a complete nervous breakdown; and in 1961 she attempted suicide.

In 1967 Brenda and her daughter, a tall blonde girl who is very attentive to her mother, returned to Boston and took an apartment. Brenda continues to see her analyst who has been working with her for five years now almost every day.

It is doubtful that many people personally disliked Brenda—it was inevitable that a girl so rich and pretty would be envied and even laughed at during such a time in America's history. Her ways were no more extravagant nor her antics more ludicrous than those who succeed her today. Probably the worst thing that can be said about such people is that they are completely nonessential.

Brenda today. *UPI*

"Hoppy" in 1935.

WILLIAM BOYD

"Hopalong Cassidy," as he is known around the world, was born in Cambridge, Ohio, in 1895. When his parents died he left school and home in Tulsa, Oklahoma, and set out for Hollywood, spending his last nickel on a ticket to Granfe, California, where he worked as an orange packer for a year before he could save enough money to reach his destination. Arriving at the movie capital, he worked as a laborer in a steel mill and as a policeman nights while he spent his days trying to break into pictures. Bill worked as an extra for several years before he managed to get any featured roles. In 1919 he had a very small part in the Cecil B. De Mille production of *Why Change Your Wife?* It was De Mille who also gave him his two best parts in the silent *Volga Boatman* (1926) and *King of Kings* (1927) in which he played Simon of Cyrene.

During the twenties, Boyd was a popular leading man with the audiences and directors for his straightforward performances as well as with his co-stars for his easygoing manner. His greatest drawback was a famous stage actor by the same name who had played Sergeant Quirt in *What Price Glory?* Boyd tried calling himself Bill instead of William, but there was still a lot of confusion between the two. In 1931 the stage actor was arrested at a party at which there was illegal liquor and gambling. Many of the nation's newspapers ran Bill's photograph by mistake, which certainly did his career no good. When the stage actor died Boyd reverted to William.

Some of the silent pictures he made were *Road to Yesterday* (1925), and *The Last Frontier* (1926), *Dress Parade* (1927), *Night Flyer* (1928), and the D. W. Griffith production *Lady of the Pavements* (1929) with Jetta Goudal (who lives in Los Angeles with her husband, designer Harold Grieve). He might have achieved full star status had Gary Cooper not been able to make *The Plainsman*—De Mille admitted that Boyd was his second choice. Many years later he seriously considered him for the role of Moses in the remake of *The Ten Commandments.*

Boyd's talkie career limped along with such mediocre films as *The Painted Desert* (1931) with the late Helen Twelvetrees, *Lucky Devils* (1933) with William Gargan (who has retired since a throat operation left him with a mechanical voice box), and *The Storm* (1934).

In 1939 Boyd won the title role in *Hopalong Cassidy,* originally intended for James Gleason. Bill changed the character from a hard-drinking old reprobate to a westerner who was practically gallant. He took the role quite seriously and within a short time developed a huge audience of adult men who identified with the man in the black cowboy suit who could handle any trouble that arose. The Saturday matinee crowd liked him because the action was never delayed for a song or two nor did their hero have much truck with the sheriff's daughter or her like. To his friends, what was most surprising of all was that Bill actually learned to ride well; until then he had not only been a wretched horseman but disliked horses.

When Harry "Pop" Sherman stepped down after producing fifty-four features, Boyd took over in 1943 and made another twelve. He economized on them until the productions suffered in quality, and at the box office. At one point he was on the brink of bankruptcy. Then along came television and Boyd saw a chance to make a fortune. He sold his ranch, borrowed every penny he could, and bought all rights to the character. His gamble paid off handsomely. In 1951 alone the gross sales of "Hoppy" products and commercials tie-ins were $25,000,000. He made new pictures expressly for TV and took great care to keep violence at a minimum. He also toured the country with his own circus. Sixty-three TV stations carried the series, 155 newspapers ran the "Hoppy" comic strip, 152 radio stations broadcast the audio version, and 108 manu-facturers turned out products bearing the Hopalong Cassidy name. The character, the products, and the films grossed $70,000,000 in 1952, the height of the boom.

In the late 1950's Boyd sold out all his interests for a staggering profit, which he could treat as a capital gain on his income tax return. He has made several appearances since, but has a policy against kids being charged to see him. For more than a decade he and his fourth wife, actress Grace Bradley, whom he married in 1937, have lived quietly in their Palm Desert home. He seldom sees his former sidekick Gabby Hayes (who is in his eighties and is bedridden), and very seldom visits Hollywood.

In his desert home. *Jon Virzi*

Billings (left) and Tom Mooney meet in prison in 1935. *UPI*

WARREN K. BILLINGS

The co-defendant in what has been referred to as the "American Dreyfus Case" was born in Middletown, New York, in 1894.

On July 22, 1916, a bomb exploded during a Preparedness Day Parade in San Francisco, killing nine and maiming many others. Tom Mooney, a powerful and articulate labor organizer, and his twenty-two-year-old protégé, Warren Billings, were arrested and brought to trial. Mooney was sentenced to death (after Woodrow Wilson interceded this was reduced to a life term) and Billings got life imprisonment.

Some of the most influential men in the country objected strongly to the trial and the sentences. Upton Sinclair (living the past few years in ill health in Monrovia, California) and the late Theodore Dreiser were among the many who joined organizations to secure the release of the men they believed to be innocent. A Presidential commission was set up to investigate the matter and when its report was filed it stated that "The utilities sought to get Mooney and Billings." It was also found that the district attorney who prosecuted the two had knowingly destroyed evidence and that major testimony had been perjured.

Billings and Mooney, while symbols of a cause, were also victims of the era as well. Shortly after the bombing, the United States entered World War I and public attention was focused on defense and victory. During the ensuing Roaring Twenties the nation underwent a "Red Scare" second only to the McCarthyism of the fifties. In the thirties people were preoccupied with the Great Depression, but by that time the two had become so famous that many felt they might lead a workers' revolt if they were released. The press often referred to them as "radical labor leaders" which suggested to many that while they might not be guilty as charged the country was safer with them behind bars. "Believe me, it took a hell of a lot more money to keep us there than it did to put us there to begin with," said Billings recently.

Finally, California's first Democratic governor of the century, Culbert Olson, honoring an election pledge, pardoned Mooney on January 7, 1939. Mooney at once began a campaign to free Billings. However, because of expenditures and

Mooney's association with the Communists the two old friends soon fell out. When Mooney died in 1942 he had already lost much of the respect he had gained during his years in prison.

While politicans argued among themselves over the case, prisoner #10699 languished for another ten months in Folsom Prison in California. After reading the pile of evidence that should have proved his innocence, the state's Attorney General said he saw "no justification for release" and voted against it as a member of the Prison Advisory Board. He was later elected governor and then appointed Chief Justice of the Supreme Court. His name—Earl Warren.

Billings was released in October, 1939, after having spent twenty-three years, two months, and twenty-three days incarcerated for a crime he did not commit. Even then he was not given a full pardon, but only a commutation of his sentence, with the result that he could not vote or own property. It was not until 1962 when Governor Edmund "Pat" Brown granted him a full pardon that he was completely freed of the stigma of guilt. He has yet to receive a penny from the state in compensation for the years of his life that were taken away.

In October of 1940 Billings married Josephine Rudolph with whom he had corresponded for seventeen years. He opened a watch repair shop at Seventh and Market streets in San Francisco only blocks from where the bombing took place. He ran his business until 1958 when he became eligible for Social Security. The Billingses now live in San Mateo where he works two days a week in a jewelry shop to supplement the $89 a month he gets from the government. Still a strong union man, Billings is a member of the executive board of the Watchmakers' Local No. 101.

His semiretirement has allowed him to renovate the sixty-year-old house in which they live and to begin his book of personal recollections about the Mooney-Billings case. The working title is *Bum Beef,* a prison expression for an unjust conviction. In the meantime he sells autographed copies of *Frame-up,* a 1967 book on the case, making about $3 per book—an arrangement he worked out with the book's author in return for his cooperation when the book was being written.

The former cause célèbre at a recent union meeting. *Los Angeles Citizen*

One of the top-rated weekly radio shows, 1939. *NBC*

EDGAR BERGEN

The perfect stooge for his wisecracking cheeky, world-weary teen-ager dummy was rated Number One in every radio popularity poll of his day. Edgar Bergen was making $6,400 a week for his weekly radio appearance, $75,000 a year from movies, and $100,000 a year from dolls, gadgets, and so forth. And all this just one year after his radio debut!

He has rightly been called the Noel Coward of ventriloquists.

While attending Lakeview High School in Chicago, Illinois (where he was born in 1903 of Swedish immigrant parents), Bergen conceived the idea for a dummy, having long since discovered in himself a flare for ventriloquism. Theodore Mack, a master craftsman, carved a dummy to his specifications, copying the facial features of a newsboy whom Bergen knew, named Charlie. He named his dummy Charlie Mack. He changed it to McCarthy purely for the sake of euphony. The cost of the dummy, made of basswood, paint, string, and springs, was $35.

As an afterschool usher at the old Victoria Theatre, he was able to entertain at Saturday matinees. Upon graduation he attended Northwestern University, and entertained at campus functions.

After leaving college, he quickly found work since his act was virtually unique, eventually playing in almost every state. He played London, opening at the Grosvenor House, and was very well received. Following London he went to Sweden, playing before the Crown Prince in his native language.

By the time he returned to the United States vaudeville was dead, and he adapted his act for nightclubs. He was soon playing the Casanova Club in Hollywood, the Chez Paree in Chicago, and the Rainbow Room in New York City. At an Elsa Maxwell party Rudy Vallee caught his act and signed him to appear several times on his radio program, finally permanently in 1937. That same year Chase and Sanborn gave them a program on Sunday nights, with Don Ameche as emcee, and singer Dorothy Lamour. W. C. Fields joined them later.

Although Bergen and McCarthy made twelve shorts for the old Vitaphone Company between 1933 and 1935, they now went to Hollywood as full-fledged stars, appearing in such films as *The Goldwyn Follies* (1938) with Zorina, Bobby Clark, and the Ritz Brothers, *Charlie McCarthy, Detective* (1939), *You Can't Cheat an Honest Man* (1939) with W. C. Fields, and *Look Who's Laughing* (1941) with Lucille Ball, Fibber McGee and Molly, and Neil Hamilton.

In 1939 Bergen introduced another dummy, Mortimer Snerd, a country bumpkin, and sometime later another dummy, Effie, a sort of hip old maid.

Although Hollywood circles considered Bergen a sort of man-about-town, often escorting stars at various functions, he lived a quiet private life with his mother until her death in 1945. The same year he married Frances Westerman, a former Powers' model and actress. Their daughter Candice was born in 1946 and their son Kris Edgar in 1961.

Since World War II, throughout which he traveled extensively entertaining troops, Bergen was restricted to nightclubs, although he appeared on TV, sometimes without his little friends, as in the 1948 movie version of *I Remember Mama*. His last movie appearance was also a solo venture *Don't Make Waves*, with Tony Curtis and Claudia Cardinale. Beginning in 1956 Bergen and his wooden friend hosted the daytime quiz show "Do You Trust Your Wife?" for a few years.

His beautiful daughter Candice has become a star in her own right. And in 1967, she and Bergen made their legitimate stage debut at the Westbury Music Fair in Long Island in *Sabrina Fair,* playing father and daughter.

That he never made it as a straight actor disappointed him. He is somewhat resentful that the dummy became more famous and recognizable than its creator. The millionaire can well afford to nurse his grievances. Much of his money is in Hollywood real estate. He owns an entire block on Sunset Boulevard, in which his magic shop is located. He often wanders in. Even at the height of his career he was able to walk in and mingle with the customers who did not recognize him without his toupee and "Charlie McCarthy."

A family portrait: Edgar and daughter Candice.

A studio publicity still, 1938.

ELEANOR HOLM

The girl whose divorce-plaintiff fame nearly overshadowed her success as a swimmer was born in Brooklyn in 1914.

When she was only fourteen Eleanor won the the three hundred yard medley in the Olympics in four minutes and twenty-five seconds. In 1932 she set a new world's record in the Olympics with her fifty-yard backstroke. The same year she won the three hundred yard medley. Altogether Eleanor held fourteen titles in domestic and Olympic swimming meets. She won the National Indoor Junior Championship in three different categories, the National Women's Indoor Championships in five different categories, and the outdoor Junior Medley Championship. She is the only American female swimmer to have competed in three Olympic games.

In 1933 Eleanor became the wife of singer Arthur Jarrett, who traveled with her much of the time and managed her career. In 1936 the swimmer moved from the sport pages to the headlines when she was removed from the United States Olympic team of that year for breaking the strict training rules. There was a great deal of jealousy among her teammates as well as the Olympic board over the fact that she was so well known. They seemed to feel that her notoriety came close to violating the sacred amateur standing that is so closely guarded in this country. What caused the crisis was when Eleanor attended a party where she was the only team member. In plain view of the Olympic officers and their wives she drank champagne. No one accused her of being drunk but the incident was enough to have her dumped.

The press was on Eleanor's side and for awhile it looked like she might be reinstated. When confronted with the signatures of one hundred Olympic contenders from different countries asking that Eleanor be allowed to compete, the board grew even more adamant. Eleanor's amateur days were over.

In 1932 Eleanor had been named one of the Wampus Baby Stars of that year along with Ginger Rogers, the late Boots Mallory, and Mary Carlisle (now manager of the Elizabeth Arden Salon in Beverly Hills). Her movie career, however, never caught fire—she received terrible notices for her starring role in *Tarzan's Revenge* in 1938.

In 1938 she and Jarrett were divorced and a year later Eleanor married the pint-sized impresario, Billy Rose, who starred her in his Aquacade at the 1939–1940 World's Fair. The two seemed to get along beautifully for the next twelve years, during which time she hosted his frequent parties at their lavish Mount Kisco estate. In his autobiography Rose praised her to the sky in a chapter entitled "Holm, sweet, Holm." Her marriage ended her career.

In 1951 Joyce Mathews, who had been married to Milton Berle, slashed her wrists in Rose's apartment. Eleanor dropped by about that time and the "War of the Roses," as the press dubbed it, began. Eleanor, with the true instincts of a champion, retained attorney Louis Nizer. Billy locked her out of his town house. She threatened to produce a list of six of his playmates. He stated that he had a list of his own and that not all of Eleanor's transgressions had been with men. The tabloids played up the lesbian angle and ran quotes from some of the Broadway notables who knew and disliked Rose, which included just about everyone who had ever done business with him.

Just when it looked like the two parties were going to come to court, where names would be named, Rose capitulated. After three years of well reported antics and insults back and forth they settled—a Beekman Place town house, $200,000 cash, and an annual allowance of $30,000 for his former wife.

Eleanor was seen around town at nightclubs and parties for a few years and then in 1960 she quietly moved to Miami Beach where she has lived ever since. She likes the climate and finds it very conducive to the outdoor sports she still participates in regularly. Recently she wrote a booklet on swimming for beginners, which is distributed to youngsters as a public service by the Pepsi Cola Company. She has not remarried and has no children. Along with occasional traveling Eleanor works on a few committees for charities and does an interior decorating job from time to time, a knack she found she had during her Mount Kisco days.

In 1967 Eleanor filed suit against the already entangled Billy Rose estate, claiming that $20,000,000 was due her for several phony Renoirs the late producer had given her as part of their settlement.

From left to right: Johnny Weissmuller, Eleanor Holm, sportscaster Jack Whittaker, and Buster Crabbe when the three swimmers were installed in the Swimming Pool Hall of Fame in Fort Lauderdale, Florida. *Ed Plummer*

Between her two terms in Congress, she spoke
at pacifist rallies throughout the nation, this
one in New York in 1933. N. Y. *Daily News*

JEANNETTE RANKIN

The first woman to be elected to the United States Congress was born in
1880 in the territory of Montana (Montana was not admitted to the Union
until 1889).

A feminist, Miss Rankin was active in suffragette movements from her early
years when the idea of women having the right to vote was either ludicrous or
anathema to many men. Coming from a well-to-do family she was able to
devote all of her time and energy to advancing the cause of suffrage. Before she
was able to cast a ballot in a polling booth she won the right to vote and
debate in the House of Representatives.

In 1916 Miss Rankin was elected to Congress from Montana on a woman's
suffrage ticket, despite the Democratic landslide that year. Her first term in the
House was distinguished by her determined efforts to keep America out of
World War I. Even after the sinking of the Lusitania she opposed our entry and
joined with forty-nine congressmen and six senators on April 16, 1917, to vote
against the declaration of war against Germany. "I want to stand by my
country, but I cannot vote for war," she stated. The vote, which was in the
minority, did not increase her popularity and when she was up for reelection in
1918 her district was gerrymandered. Undaunted, Miss Rankin ran instead
for the senate seat, but was defeated.

Throughout the 1920's and 1930's Jeannette Rankin appeared on countless
platforms speaking for disarmament and peace. When she was not in office
she lobbied against increased military appropriations, claiming it was the
generals who had caused all the wars to justify their own existence. She has
opposed United States intervention into any conflict, however small, anywhere
in the world. "America," she has said, "has the war habit. It is a habit we must
break before we are broken by it."

When World War II broke out Miss Rankin again ran for Congress from the
state of Montana and was elected on the Republican ticket. "I've always been

a Republican," she says, "for the same reason that most people are either Democrats or Republicans—because their fathers were one or the other. Frankly, I cannot see a particle of difference between the two." Her second term which began in 1940 was ended for all practical purposes on December 9, 1941. That was the day that Jeannette Rankin became the sole member of either house to vote "nay" on America's declaration of war against Japan. Three days later she simply said "present" when her name was called in the vote to go to war against Germany and Italy. "What good would it have done to vote 'no,' " she said recently. "We were already at war against Japan. F.D.R. had what he wanted—war. He wanted to be a war President. Everything he did from the day he first took office pointed to the fact that he wanted to fight Germany." Few members of government have been treated as Jeannette Rankin was treated after those votes. Her congressional colleagues shunned her, the press ignored her, and she was publicly booed and hissed. Even many who had stood on America First platforms with her were caught up in the patriotic spirit that prevailed in the country after Pearl Harbor, and had no sympathy with her stand. "They all said that would be the last anyone would hear of me. Well, they were wrong. I have never stopped working for peace and I never will," said Miss Rankin the day after she lead a group of five thousand women in Washington, D.C. under the banner of the Jeannette Rankin Brigade to protest the war in Vietnam. That was January 15, 1968.

Miss Rankin divides her time between a ranch in Montana where she summers and her winter home in Watkinsville, Georgia. She is still available for lectures and rallies and enjoys them thoroughly. To those who find the energy and spirit of the eighty-eight-year-old spinster remarkable she says: "But you see I have to keep going. No one can let up in this effort to bring about peace. Real peace. A lasting peace. We have got to get it into our heads once and for all that we cannot settle disputes by eliminating human beings."

The Honorable Jeannette Rankin at eighty-eight. *Ben Fernandez*

Once the biggest moneymaking team in show business, circa 1945, with Bud on the right.

"BUD" ABBOTT

The straight man of one of the most popular comedy duos in show business was born in Asbury Park, New Jersey, in 1895. He was named William. His father was the advance man of a circus in which his mother performed as a bareback rider. Bud's childhood was spent in the Coney Island section of Brooklyn.

There are several versions of how and why the team originally got together. One has it that Lou Costello's straight man didn't show up one night and Abbott, who had been working in the box office, was asked to pinch hit in a burlesque theatre in upstate New York where the act was booked. Another story tells of Costello, who was a compulsive gambler all his life, losing his shirt in a poker game and Abbott bailing him out. Both agreed that they first met in a burlesque house in upstate New York, but as with most references to their private lives, Abbott and Costello could never get together on the origin of their famous partnership.

On stage few twosomes ever had the smooth rapport they developed. From the time they joined forces in 1925 until they broke into the big time in 1938, the boys moved around the country in tab shows, vaudeville and mainly burlesque. In a short time Abbott and Costello were "top bananas" on the bump and grind circuits, and worked fairly steadily. There were many disagreements between them, but no one watching their comedy routines would ever know it. Costello was short, fat and mad. Abbott was thin, dour, and easily exasperated.

In 1938 they were booked into a New York vaudeville house, where the late Ted Collins spotted them and put them on the "Kate Smith Show," which at the time was one of the most popular radio programs in America. People who would never think of entering a burlesque theatre heard them that night. The material they had developed and used over the years was completely fresh to this audience, and the reaction was national convulsions. Other top shows signed them to appear and the following year they were seen in *Streets of Paris* on Broadway. The movies grabbed them and they debuted in *One Night in the Tropics.*

Through the forties and into the fifties Abbott and Costello were the comedy kings of America on their own radio programs and in feature film after feature film. A few that helped keep Universal-International Pictures out of bankruptcy during very lean years were *Buck Privates* (1941), *Pardon My Sarong* (1942), *Lost in a Harem* (1944), *Abbott and Costello in Hollywood* (1945), *Abbott and Costello Meet Frankenstein* (1948), *Abbott and Costello in the Foreign Legion* (1950), and *Abbott and Costello Meet Captain Kidd* (1952). They were included every year from 1941 until 1951 among the top ten box office favorites in the country. Typical of how financially successful they were are the figures reported on one of their starrers: cost of production—$90,000, grossed—over $10,000,000.

In 1957, after a great success on television, they finally split. Costello was being offered as a single. Abbott, ten years older than his partner, said that he would retire to his ranch in Ojai, California.

In 1958 Abbott filed suit against Costello for $222,465.19 he claimed was owed him for a TV series they had done together. It was still in litigation a year later when on March 3, 1959, Costello died of a heart attack.

Then the Internal Revenue claimed that he owed them several hundred thousand dollars in past taxes. Within weeks Abbott, who thought he was set financially for the rest of his life, was forced to sell his ranch, the property surrounding his Encino home, and the residual rights to his TV films. Had he sold everything he owned, he could not pay the principal and interest.

About then, Abbott and Eddie Foy, Jr., announced they would team as a comedy act, but nothing came of it.

In 1964 the comedian suffered a mild stroke. In his few statements to the press these past years, he seems free of any bitterness. He seems proud of the fact that he and Costello had sold over $80,000,000 worth of war bonds in the forties, and that despite his home in Woodland Hills having become less sumptuous than he had been used to, he did not seek bankruptcy as a way out of his troubles.

What final settlement he made with Uncle Sam is not known, but he and Betty Abbott, his wife of many years, live comfortably not far from the Motion Picture Country Hospital.

Bud spents most of his time in Western attire. *Jon Virzi*

The songbird in a publicity shot from 1939.

GERTRUDE NIESEN

The musical comedy and radio star of the thirties was born to Colonel and Mrs. Monte Niesen in 1910 while her parents were returning by ship to New York from a summer in Europe. She began her vocal exercises early, crying all the way to the docks. Gertrude attended the Brooklyn Heights Seminary School between road tours of *The Vagabond King, Sonny, Good News,* and others. While in high school, she went to see a performance of *You Said It* and left the theatre determined to become a big star like the late Lyda Roberti. She began to do imitations of the Polish comedienne, becoming so good that her friends encouraged her to try out in Broadway auditions. (Some time much later, she replaced Miss Roberti as Lou Holtz's partner.) She made the rounds of booking agents who turned thumbs down on her. However, one agent's office boy tipped her off that "Feet" Edson was looking for a girl for Joe Taylor's vaudeville act. She got the job, which paid $100 a week. The year was 1931. Shortly afterward she was signed by the 300 Club in New York City.

Gertrude's big boost came when Rudy Vallee signed her to appear on radio on his Fleischmann Hour. At the time, Vallee was the hottest name on the air waves and the guest spots gave her excellent exposure. Almost immediately she landed a job singing a commercial. Since in those days all commercials were done live, Gertrude had to go from one radio station to another. This gave her a chance to meet most of the important people in the business as well as becoming a familiar voice to listeners all over America. More guest spots were offered by other top radio personalities and she was signed to a steady spot on a program featuring the late Lulu McConnell and the Isham Jones Orchestra. She gained great popularity in the medium. In one national poll, she ranked after Ruth Etting and Kate Smith.

Her popularity on radio soon made her a draw at presentation houses. As early as 1933 she received top billing at the Palace Theatre. The second attraction to play the Radio City Music Hall was Roger Wolfe Kahn's band with Gertrude Niesen.

She was known as a vocalist who could get lost in a torch song and turn right around and belt out something big and brassy. It made her a natural for

64

musical comedy. Her first show was *Take a Chance* in 1933 but she was seen only in one performance—she was understudy to a lady with notoriously good health, Ethel Merman. In 1934 she did *Calling All Stars* and in 1936 was with Josephine Baker, Eve Arden, Bob Hope, and Judy Canova* in *The Ziegfeld Follies*. In 1937 she made her only movie, for Universal, heading the cast of *Top of the Town*. She was supported by the late Mischa Auer, Ella Logan,* and Peggy Ryan (the proprietress of an ice skating and dancing school in Honolulu). A year later she headed the London cast of *No Sky So Blue*. Her biggest success was in *Follow the Girls* in 1945 with an unknown comic named Jackie Gleason. One critic said she delivered the big number "I Wanna Get Married" with "a combination of hungry appeal and desperate determination." She was with the show for 882 performances on Broadway and then took it on the road.

Gertrude played just about every top supper club in New York and quite a few around the country during her heyday. She headlined the show at such spots as the St. Regis Roof, the Versailles, and Casino de Paree. In 1947 the Zanzibar paid her $4,700 a week to star in a revue entitled *The Affairs of Vanity Fair*. She was supported by Hal Le Roy (living in Maywood, New Jersey).

The star had a way with real estate like she had with a song. Her heavy investing proved profitable even when she was still working and did not need the money. At one point, she bought a $2,500,000 Newport, Rhode Island, mansion for $21,000.

During the fifties her appearances began to fall off. When she starred for the last time in 1958 at the Copacabana, columnist Louis Sobol who had been one of her most ardent fans right from the beginning asked, "Why has she dropped out of show business?" The question remains unanswered. Sobol mused recently, "I guess she just made a happy marriage and called it quits."

Gertrude has been married for some time to the owner of the now defunct Black Orchid Club in Chicago. Several years ago she sold her island off Port Chester, Connecticut. She and her husband live on Hollywood's famed Mulholland Drive, though none of her show business contemporaries hear a word from her.

At a recent Hollywood premiere. *Jon Virzi*

During the 1940's, Mrs. Nussbaum was a household name. *NBC Radio*

"MRS. NUSSBAUM"

The most famous dialect comedienne from the Golden Age of Radio was born Minerva Pious in Odessa, Russia, in 1909. She came to this country when she was three years old and settled with her parents in Bridgeport, Connecticut. Minerva did not grow up in a neighborhood of mixed ethnic backgrounds; the only accents she remembers during her early years were those of her Russian-Jewish parents. The woman who has been called the "Ruth Draper of Radio" attributes her unique ability to keen powers of observation. "I am an inveterate eavesdropper in crowded places," she says, "and am benefited by what I hear through the aid of a sharp musical ear, plus absolute pitch."

Minerva is one of the few performers to be discovered and developed completely by radio. When she came to Fred Allen in 1933 through one of his writers, she was in her own words, "a complete amateur." She used her "Nussbaum" voice on the show for some time before "Allen's Alley" was formed and the character got a name, Pansy Nussbaum, bestowed by Allen himself. She stayed with the program until 1949, doing all the female voices. The other inhabitants of the famous Alley were Ajax Cassidy, the drunken Irishman who drew the most complaints from listeners, Senator Claghorn, and Titus Moody. But it was Mrs. Nussbaum with her absurd stories about her husband Pierre, who never appeared, that brought the most applause each week. One of her other popular characters was a woman called Blossom Rappaport.

Though Minerva Pious never became known to the general public, in the trade, she developed a reputation for being able to do any accent or dialect. The actress who can sound like a Park Avenue matron, cockney fishwife, or midwestern schoolgirl claims that the most sensitive nationalities are the Irish and Scotch. Her natural voice is so clear that she once received an award for having diction completely free of regional influences or affectations.

Radio performers, of course, were not seen and received scanty billing unless they were stars. Few listeners, therefore, realized that the lady who convulsed much of America as Pansy Nussbaum was also being heard on most of the other shows as well, playing totally different roles. On the "Kate Smith Show" Minerva was a debutante with a broad New York accent. For Al Jolson she was paired in sketches with Monty Woolley. Sammy Kaye's audiences heard her as Gypsy Rose Rabinowitz. Her straight man in those skits was Red Barber. Once she played a Jewish Camille to Charles Boyer's Armand. A few of the other programs of the day on which she was a frequent guest were "Easy Aces," the "Philip Morris Playhouse," and "Duffy's Tavern." She worked with the biggest names in the profession—W. C. Fields, Robert Benchley, Bob Hope, Bing Crosby, and Tallulah Bankhead.

Her motion pictures include *It's in the Bag* (1945) with Jack Benny and Fred Allen, *The Ambassador's Daughter* (1956), and *Love in the Afternoon* with Gary Cooper and Audrey Hepburn in 1957. During the fifties she spent most of her time living and working in France and England. She made *Joe Macbeth* (1956) while living in London.

She has been seen on Broadway in *Love in Our Time* (1941), *Dear Me, the Sky Is Falling* (1963) with the late Gertrude Berg, and *The Last Analysis* (1964).

Although Minerva has never married, she has a foster son who was orphaned during World War II. One of the first things she did for him was to have the twelve-year-old Italian fitted with an articulated artificial leg. She lives in a hotel in Manhattan's theatrical district and appears from time to time on such TV shows as "Merv Griffin" and "Les Crane." She has also done character parts on "Edge of Night" and "Another World." She is currently to be seen with Louis Jacobi in a TV commercial for Traveler's Insurance.

Minerva in her hotel room in Manhattan.
Diana Keyt

In 1930 Charles Farrell and Janet Gaynor were the most popular movie pair in the world.

CHARLES FARRELL

The male half of talkies' first "screen lovers" was the only son of an old New England family. He was born on Cape Cod in 1902, and matriculated at Boston University where he majored in business administration. Before he could receive his diploma the school required one year of vocational training. He was assigned the position of business manager for a prominent actor of the day who was touring the Orpheum circuit. The glamour of the theatre got to him in a short time, and he was hooked. From then on it was an actor's life for Charles.

His first job in movies was an extra in the Pola Negri* film *The Cheat* (1923). He did bit parts in six more pictures before Paramount took a chance on him as "the boy" in *Old Ironsides* (1926). In 1927 he starred in *Street Angel.*

Farrell heard that Frank Borzage was slated to direct the movie version of the stage play *Seventh Heaven.* Since he knew the director personally, he went to see him. He hoped to put in a good word for a friend he thought would be ideal for the lead. To his surprise, Borzage gave him the role instead. The part of Chico was considered a plum even before shooting began, but no one guessed that the 1927 production would be the phenomenal success it turned out to be. (That was the first year of the Academy Awards which were not called "Oscars" until Bette Davis named the statuettes for one of her husbands, who is now a Los Angeles advertising executive.) Awards were won by co-star Janet Gaynor for Best Actress, Borzage for direction, and Benjamin Glazer for screen adaptation.

Miss Gaynor had been his leading lady before, in *Street Angel,* but when they were paired in *Heaven* as the appealing waif and the young street cleaner who fell in love in Paris, audiences around the world wept. The film's theme music, "Diane," which accompanied the silent feature was a great addition. Not until Jeanette MacDonald and Nelson Eddy appeared in the mid-thirties was the popularity of Farrell and Gaynor equaled.

Charles and Janet continued as a duo in a series of features which enjoyed great popularity, but never equaled *Seventh Heaven.* Some of their vehicles were *The First Year* (1932), *Tess of the Storm Country* (1932), and *Change of Heart* (1934). Farrell made some on his own, such as *City Girl* (1930), *After Tomorrow* (1932) opposite Marion Nixon, *Girl Without a Room* (1933), *The Big Shakedown* (1934) with Bette Davis, and *Fighting Youth* (1935). His popularity began to slip in the mid-thirties, and he began to take lesser roles in such pictures as *Moonlight Sonata* (1937) with Ignace Paderewski, *Just Around the Corner* (1938) with Shirley Temple, and *The Sun Never Sets* (1939) with the late Basil Rathbone. By 1941 he was working for Monogram, the "B" studio, in *Deadly Game*. Two years earlier he had re-created his role of Chico on Broadway, with Milli Monti as Diane, but it failed to revitalize his career.

Since 1934 Charles had gone regularly to Palm Springs. The climate was good for his hay fever, and he was an avid tennis player. He and Ralph Bellamy built a few bungalows and tennis courts which eventually became *the* chic private club in the resort town. They called it the Racquet Club. Bellamy sold out early, before it mushroomed into a project that netted as much as $500,000 a year for Farrell.

In 1952 Farrell made a comeback on TV in "My Little Margie," which began June 16, 1952, as a summer replacement for the "I Love Lucy" series. Despite bad reviews it proved so popular it was continued for 128 segments, and was in syndication for many years after it went off the CBS network. Farrell and his co-star, Gale Storm, even did a radio version of the show for a couple of seasons. Charles had a series of his own after "Margie" went into reruns, called "The Charlie Farrell Show." He played himself, the manager of the Palm Springs Racquet Club.

Although Farrell has not been active on television or in pictures for a number of years, his whereabouts are well known to the movie colony. During the fifties, for seven years Farrell was the mayor of the town. In 1959 he sold his interest in the Club for $1,000,000, but continues to manage it. Since 1931 he has been married to silent star Virginia Valli who is a devout Catholic. They have no children. Charles gave up polo a few years ago, but he is still one of the best tennis players on his courts.

At the Racquet Club in Palm Springs, California. *Jon Virzi*

With Jean Gabin in *The Human Beast,* directed by Jean Renoir.

SIMONE SIMON

The girl with the most redundant name in movies was born in Marseilles, France, in 1914. Although it was rumored that she was the daughter of Marion Davies by William Randolph Hearst, her early life seems well documented to prove otherwise. Simon with her mother and stepfather, moved to Madagascar when she was three years old. Before settling in Paris in her teens she attended schools in Berlin, Budapest, and Turin.

In June of 1931 Mlle. Simon was sipping coffee on the terrace of the Café de la Paix one afternoon when she was noticed by the exiled Russian director Tourjansky, who offered her a part in a movie he was about to make in Paris. She debuted opposite the opera singer, Muratore, in the picture *Le Chanteur Inconnu* that year. Continental audiences took an immediate liking to the girl with a kittenish quality that made her seem very feminine, and that made men act very masculine. In her French films *Un Fils d' Amerique* (1932), *Le Petite Chocolatiere,* and *Les Yeux Noirs* (1933) her directors, Tourjansky and Marc Allegret, made the most of her impish appeal. By the time Hollywood took notice, La Simon had become known as "la sauvage tendre," which Twentieth Century-Fox press agents translated as "Europe's Sweetheart."

Simone was one of Hollywood's most spectacular failures. There are two versions of how she accomplished that dubious distinction. According to her studio who brought her over in 1935, she was uncooperative, temperamental, and refused to master English. She was replaced by Claudette Colbert in *Under Two Flags* (1936), a role which would probably have made her an American star overnight. According to Simone, it was the fault of the studio. Darryl Zanuck, she said, cast her in unsuitable roles and Ernie Westmore attempted to change her coiffure and makeup in order to "glamorize her." She quarreled constantly with her directors. In spite of her disfavor with the front office she managed to turn a small part in *Girls' Dormitory* (1936) which starred the late Herbert Marshall and Ruth Chatterton to such good account that the studio was deluged with fan mail for her. She registered again the next year in *Seventh Heaven* in dramatic scenes with Jimmy Stewart and Gale

Sondergaard.* In 1938 she was seen in *Josette* with Don Ameche and then in *Love and Hisses* with Walter Winchell and the late Ben Bernie. That year she brought charges against her former private secretary who had forged her name on more than $10,000 in checks. The defendant took the stand and told how Miss Simon had arranged for gold-plated keys to the front door of her houses as gifts to her "particular friends." While all America guessed, only one name appeared in print, George Gershwin.

History would seem to belie her being a failure as an actress because after her $2,000 per week contract ended and she returned to France, she made a number of good pictures. *The Human Beast* (1940) was such a hit that Hollywood offered her another chance. She returned in 1940 and made *All That Money Can Buy* (1941), a screen version of *The Devil and Daniel Webster* which starred Walter Huston, and followed that with *Tahiti Honey* (1943). Two of her United States films made during her second visit, *Cat People* (1942) and *Curse of the Cat People* (1943), have become minor classics among horror-film buffs. In 1944 she and Kurt Kreuger made *Mademoiselle Fifi* (1944).

Her attempted American comeback during the early forties included a few vaudeville appearances and a legitimate musical, *Three After Three,* with Stepin Fetchit,* which never made it to Broadway.

While she never regained the status she had enjoyed in Europe during the 1930's, the actress continued to make movies. In England she appeared in *Temptation Harbor* (1947) and *Extra Dry Day* (1956). In Italy she did *Donna Senza None* (1949). In France she has been seen in *La Ronde* (1950), *Le Plaisir* (1951), and *Pit of Loneliness* (1954) in which she played a lesbian.

She is still a Parisian, and has yet to manage a change of name by marriage, although her friendship with a Frenchman with several million dollars and a wife is well known in theatrical and social circles. Her favorite pastime is playing gin rummy. She appeared in Paris in 1966 in the play *La Courte Paille* opposite Jean Meyer, but friends say it is only an exercise in ego. She wanted to prove that she was still attractive and as good an actress as people remember. She was.

Leaving her Paris apartment. *Jon Virzi*

Detroit's top Tiger in 1938. *UPI*

HANK GREENBERG

The right-handed hitter who overcame extreme awkwardness as an athlete to be twice voted the most valuable player in the American League was born in 1911 in Greenwich Village. He moved to the Bronx when he was seven where he attended public schools. In 1927 he played first base with the James Monroe High School team but had a reputation as a "tanglefoot," one who gets in his own way. Classmates remember him as being much better on a basketball court or a soccer field than on the baseball diamond. After high school graduation in 1929, he studied at New York University for a year.

Greenberg's first contract with the major leagues was signed in 1930, and he became a Tiger. There had been a bid from the Yankees but the Detroit team, according to *The New York Times,* offered a bonus of·$9,000. During his entire first season he played in only one game and failed to hit. The Tigers farmed Hank to Hartford in the Eastern League, then to Raleigh in the Piedmont League where he batted .314. In 1932 he batted .318 for Evansville in the Three-I League and .290 for Beaumont in the Texas League.

In 1933 Greenberg was back with the Tigers. That year he played first base and batted .301. In 1934 he was batting .339. By 1936 he was at .348. They shifted him to the outfield in 1940, and he batted .340. The reason for the change was that the team wanted to get Rudy York's bat into the lineup.

In 1941 he became Private Henry Greenberg in the United States Army. In 1945 he was discharged as a captain in the Army Air Corps and went back to Detroit as an outfielder. He batted .311 that season. In 1946 he was moved back to first base and his hitting dropped to .277.

The Tigers sold Hank to Pittsburgh in the National League in 1947. He played first base and batted .249 for a salary of $60,000.

On August 23, 1947, the Polo Grounds held a "Greenberg Day" with all cash gifts going to the Rehabilitation Institute of New York University, one of Hank's favorite charities. He retired the following year when he became the general manager of the Cleveland Indians at the same salary he had been drawing on the playing field in Pittsburgh. He already had large holdings in the ball team.

During his career he played in 1,394 major league games and hit safely 1,628 times. His lifetime batting average was .313 with 331 home runs to his credit. In 1938 he came within two of tying Babe Ruth's record of sixty in a season. Greenberg was a player in two all-star games and four World Series.

After being chosen the most valuable player in the American League in 1935 and again in 1939, Hank was elected to the Baseball Hall of Fame in 1956.

Although he never became a batting champion for his league, Greenberg led at different times in home runs, triples, doubles, runs batted in, runs scored, and total bases.

Hank left his post with the Indians after the 1957 season. From 1959 to 1961 he served as vice-president of the Chicago White Sox. Since that time he has served on the board of directors of several large corporations. His money was well invested and there will never be any need for a benefit for Hank Greenberg.

In 1946 he was married to the daughter of the department store mogul, Bernard J. Gimbel. They were divorced in 1959. Hank, who has not remarried, lives in a beautiful home in the exclusive Cleveland suburb of Shaker Heights.

Two of Hank's three children are students at Yale. Neither is very enthusiastic about baseball, although both play. The oldest boy excels at football and is considering playing pro-ball after graduation. The younger Yalie is a fine soccer player.

After Greenberg gave up the national pastime he took up tennis and plays as much as four times a week. One of his frequent partners when he is on the West Coast is Pancho Segura. He rates himself "a B player. I can't beat the good guys but I'm good enough to play with them."

Steve Greenberg takes a little professional advice from his dad. Falmouth won. *UPI*

A publicity portrait taken in 1937, shortly after Madeleine came to the United States.

MADELEINE CARROLL

The beautiful and talented blonde movie star was born Madeleine Bernadette O'Carroll in 1906 in West Bromwich, England.

For a brief time she was a teacher before making her debut on the London stage in *The Lash* in 1927. The following year she made her first film, *The Guns at Loos,* and did *The Constant Nymph* in the West End. In 1929 and 1930, respectively, she was seen by Londoners in *Beau Geste* and *French Leave.*

Madeleine Carroll had a rare and valued quality depicting affluence and breeding. One close-up and from the eyes everyone knew here was an intelligent woman of great composure. In the clumsy costume of an early settler in C. B. De Mille's *North West Mounted Police* (1940) or a sarong in *Bahama Passage* (1941) she still looked like what she was—a lady.

Her early movies included *Young Woodley* (1930), *Sleeping Car* (1933) with the late Ivor Novello, and *The World Moves On* (1934), in which her co-star was Franchot Tone. In 1935 Alfred Hitchcock picked her for the lead in the great suspense film *The 39 Steps.* The late Robert Donat was male lead. Hitchcock used her again, in 1936, for another successful thriller, *Secret Agent* which co-featured the late Peter Lorre. Both films were made in England.

In Hollywood Madeleine followed up her rave notices from the Hitchcock pictures with meaty roles in Ronald Colman's version of *The Prisoner of Zenda* (1937) and *The General Died at Dawn* (1937) opposite Gary Cooper. That next year she and a young contract player named Tyrone Power starred in *Lloyds of London* with Freddie Bartholomew.*

In 1938 the late David O. Selznick cast her opposite Henry Fonda in the highly controversial *Blockade,* a film about the Spanish Civil War which was sympathetic to the Loyalist cause, thus earning the condemnation of the Roman Catholic Church.

Before leaving Hollywood for London where she spent most of the World War II years Madeleine made *My Son, My Son* (1940), *Virginia* (1941), and

My Favorite Blonde (1942) with Bob Hope. At the height of her fame a group of American servicemen voted Madeleine Carroll as the girl they would most like to be marooned on a desert island with. When informed of the honor Madeleine replied in that soft English accent, "I'm very flattered but if I'm ever cast away I hope the man is a good obstetrician."

Although she became a United States citizen in 1943, following the death of her sister in the blitz, Madeleine always remained loyal to England. She was very active in the Allied Relief Fund and worked tirelessly for the American Red Cross. For her efforts she has been honored by the American Legion and French government, and in 1948 the National Conference of Christians and Jews named Madeleine Carroll the "Woman of the Year."

Her only appearance on Broadway was for the very successful run of *Goodbye, My Fancy* in 1948. To the disappointment of many, the role in the motion picture version went to Joan Crawford.

Unfortunately, her pictures after the war were for the most part disappointing. She made *An Innocent Affair* (1949) and *Lady Windermere's Fan* (1949). Because of her beautifully modulated voice she was welcomed back to radio drama where she had always been very effective. In 1950 on TV's "Robert Montgomery Presents" she turned in a stunning performance in Somerset Maugham's *The Letter*.

Madeleine has been married and divorced four times. She married her first husband, Philip Astley, in 1931. In 1942 she divorced the producer, Henri Lavorel, to marry Sterling Hayden. They were divorced in 1946. Her marriage in 1950 to Andrew Heiskell, the publisher of *Life* magazine, lasted over a decade. During their marriage they maintained a town house in Manhattan and an estate on Long Island.

During the past six years Miss Carroll has spent most of her time in Paris and London, and is only an occasional visitor to New York.

In 1964 Miss Carroll was replaced by Arlene Francis in the play *Beekman Place* during its pre-Broadway road tour. Her agent maintains that her comeback needs only a script that meets with her approval.

With shipmate Ferdinand Gravet, fellow Parisian and former film star, on a recent visit to the United States. N. Y. *Daily News*

In 1939, at the height of his fame.

BILLY GILBERT

The world's most famous sneezer was born in 1894 in a dressing room of the Hopkins Theatre in Louisville, Kentucky. His father was a leading tenor with the Metropolitan Opera and his mother was also a member of the company. The family settled in Los Angeles until Billy was ten and then moved to San Francisco. At the age of twelve Billy went on his first road tour with a show. At eighteen he left home for good to become an actor.

He does not recall the first time he used his famous sneezing act on stage, but his reputation for the bit began many years ago when he was playing a theatre in Wilkes Barre, Pennsylvania. There were only thirty people in the audience and none of them seemed interested in what was happening on stage. Then Gilbert went into his sneezing routine and milked more laughter than had been heard all evening. The next day the local critic ignored the play completely and gave Billy's sneezes a rave notice.

Although he is best known for his years as one of Hollywood's great funnymen, Billy was a headliner in both burlesque and vaudeville before he began making movies.

His first picture was *Noisy Neighbors* (1929) and he has made over three hundred since. At the beginning he worked as both an actor and writer in comedy shorts. Two of his best remembered are the Laurel and Hardy starrers *Their First Mistake* (1932) and *Them Thar Hills* (1934). Co-starring in both was "the ever popular" and late Mae Busch. During the thirties and forties he was one of the most popular and highest paid character actors in Hollywood. He played with W. C. Fields in *Million Dollar Legs* (1932). Some of his other credits are: *Flying Down to Rio* (1933), *Here Comes the Band* (1935) with Ted Lewis, *One Hundred Men and a Girl* (1937) which introduced Deanna Durbin, *Happy Landing* (1938), a Sonja Henie* vehicle,

76

Outcasts of Poker Flats (1937) with Jean Muir, *His Girl Friday* (1940), and *Anchors Aweigh* (1945) and *The Kissing Bandit* (1949) both starring Frank Sinatra.

Had he made no other films Billy Gilbert would be a movie immortal for his off-screen sneezes in the Walt Disney classic of 1937, *Snow White and the Seven Dwarfs*. The dwarf whose sounds he dubbed were, of course, "Sneezy." The other gem of his career was his portrayal of "Herring," a thinly disguised imitation of Field Marshal Hermann Göring, in the Charles Chaplin masterpiece, *The Great Dictator* (1940).

Most of Billy's professional efforts were devoted to television and the stage during the fifties. In 1952 he starred in the musical *Buttrio Square* which was fated to close before it reached Broadway. Later, however, the producers of *Fanny,* who had heard of his fine performance, put him into the role of Panisse, originated by Walter Slezak. The critics wrote glowing notices. The same year, 1956, Billy played on TV in the spectacular "Jack and the Beanstalk" and followed that in 1957 with many appearances on Shirley Temple's "Fairytales." He has guest starred on "Arthur Godfrey Time," "My Little Margie," the "Ed Sullivan Show," and "The Gary Moore Show."

In 1963 Billy suffered a slight stroke and for over a year could not speak at all. Now, he says, "I talk as much as ever. Maybe more." His last picture was *Three Weeks in a Balloon* (1964).

Over the years Gilbert has bought several apartment buildings in Beverly Hills and a small factory in Los Angeles. He and his wife, the former actress Ella McKensie, whom he met in 1937 when they made a picture together at RKO, entertain such friends as Robert Cummings, Rudy Vallee, and Ken Murray in their North Hollywood home. Ella McKensie appeared in the famous *Our Gang* comedies. Billy points out that although she is many years his junior, "We have the happiest of marriages. I live the life everyone hopes they will lead when they reach my age."

At home with wife and young friend.

"The Great Dane" under contract to M-G-M in the forties.

LAURITZ MELCHIOR

The foremost heldentenor (heroic tenor) of his day began his phenomenal career as a baritone. He made his operatic debut in 1913 with the Royal Copenhagen Opera Company, singing the role of Silvio in *Pagliacci*. His teacher at the time, the American singer, Mme. Charles Cahier (who also coached Marian Anderson), aware of her pupil's extraordinary range and detecting a certain restraint in his singing, urged him to become a tenor and thereby give fuller vent to his voice.

From his birth in 1890, Lauritz Melchior, who has been called The Great Dane, was slated for the traditional family vocation of educator, but the family was also musical, and because the boy showed unusual promise (he was a soprano in the English church at Copenhagen), his father encouraged him. However, money was lacking. The family housekeeper offered to finance his musical education. She had in effect taken the place of the children's mother ever since the mother's death in Lauritz's infancy. This lady, Miss Kristine Jensen, had recently written a cookbook which became a best seller of its day.

Lauritz was eighteen when he began to study music seriously. Four years later he was admitted to the School of the Royal Opera, and the following year he made his aforementioned debut.

Melchior's first appearance as a tenor was in 1918, singing the role of Tannhäuser, which resulted in an appearance at Covent Garden, in London. There he met and became close friends with the British novelist, Hugh Walpole, who later helped him with money, advice, and encouragement. Then, too, Marconi, the inventor, invited the young singer to appear on the first worldwide radio broadcast—from the Marconi Experimental Station in Chelmsford, England, on July 30, 1920. Singing with him was the famed late Dame Nellie Melba. His English sojourn also won him a coveted invitation from Siegfried and Cosima Wagner to study Wagnerian roles at Bayreuth, where he made his first appearance as Siegfried in 1925.

Melchior's American debut was in 1926 when he sang Tannhäuser at the Metropolitan Opera. He was to remain with the company until 1950, when he quit over a dispute with manager Rudolf Bing. His last performance at the famed opera house was his seventy-first Lohengrin and his five hundred and thirteenth appearance in the twenty-four-year affiliation. Other roles included Tristan, the two Siegfrieds, Parsifal, together with non-Wagnerian parts, his favorite among these being Othello, Le Prophet, and Canio in *Pagliacci*. During these years he also appeared in the capitals of Europe and cities in the United States. He worked with dramatic sopranos Freida Leider, Kirsten Flagstad (with whom during the Depression era he consistently set box office records), Marjorie Lawrence, Lotte Lehmann, and Helen Traubel, among others.

After an appearance on the "Fred Allen Show," he was signed to a Hollywood contract. His pictures include *Thrill of Romance* (1945), *Two Sisters from Boston* (1946), *Luxury Liner* (1947), *This Time for Keeps* (1947), and *The Stars Are Singing* (1953).

In 1952 he made his vaudeville debut with an appearance at the Palace Theatre. Shortly after that he was featured in Guy Lombardo's Jones Beach extravaganza, *The Arabian Nights*. Since then he has done mostly concert work, occasionally appearing on TV or in nightclubs.

His first wife was Inger Nathansen, with whom he had two children. She died in 1924. The following year he married the German actress Maria Hacker, with whom he also had two children. Miss Hacker specialized in stunt pictures and they met when she literally fell out of the sky and at his feet in a parachute jump. Their marriage was a long and happy one. He always referred to her as "Kleinchen" (little one), and she took care of all his financial affairs. "I make the noise," he used to say, "she make the business." A year after her death in 1963, Melchior married Mary Markham, whom he had known for eighteen years. She had been his secretary and is thirty-four years his junior.

Today Melchior is as robust as ever, his 6 foot 4 inch frame still suits his 240 pounds. However, he is slightly deaf "from having listened to too much Wagner." He has only lately gone on safaris to such places as Mozambique to indulge another passion of his—big game hunting. Having become an American citizen in 1947, Melchior resides permanently in California. He is not retired completely from music, for he is continually giving auditions to prospective heldentenors. Those showing promise receive a scholarship grant from the greatest of them all, Lauritz Melchior.

During a recent interview. *New York Times*

Under contract to Columbia Pictures
during the forties.

EVELYN KEYES

No less an authority than Cecil B. De Mille said of Evelyn Keyes that she was "natural and unspoiled." It was this quality that the blonde beauty with the large moist eyes conveyed on the screen in countless wholesome roles.

Evelyn, when yet a child, was taken, along with her brother and three sisters, by her widowed mother from Port Arthur, Texas (where she was born in 1917), to Atlanta, Georgia. There she was brought up and educated, learning to play the piano and going to dancing school at an early age.

She had hoped for a career in ballet, but circumstances found her in the chorus line of a second-rate nightclub. A year later, in 1935, in a beauty contest sponsored by Universal Studios, she won a free Hollywood trip, including a screen test. She returned home to the chorus lines.

One night, she worked with the bandleader Ted Fiorito, who wrote a glowing letter of introduction to a top Hollywood agent, and off she went once again and got nowhere with the letter. Nevertheless, she soon got her break when she connected with Jeanie MacPherson one of De Mille's former top writers for over thirty years. Through her, Evelyn was signed to a personal contract.

Her first film was a small role in De Mille's 1938 version of *The Buccaneer* starring Fredric March. That same year she did *Union Pacific* (also for De Mille), *Dangerous to Know*, *Men With Wings*, *Artists and Models Abroad*, and *Sudden Money*. In addition, she landed the role of Suellen, Scarlett's sister in *Gone with the Wind*, which was responsible for a long-term contract at Columbia. Her first picture for them was a Rita Hayworth starrer, *The*

Lady in Question (1940). The following year she won her first real recognition in the leading feminine role in *Here Comes Mr. Jordan,* which starred Robert Montgomery. Then followed such films as *The Adventures of Martin Eden* (1942) with Glenn Ford, *Nine Girls* (1944), *The Jolson Story* (1946), the part that she is best remembered for as the wife of Larry Parks, *Johnny O'Clock* (1947) with Dick Powell, and *The Mating of Millie* (1948) with Glenn Ford. In 1949 she made her most dramatic picture *Mrs. Mike* with Dick Powell. The following year she did *The Prowler* with Van Heflin, and, in 1951, *The Killer that Stalked New York.*

Of her husbands, two were top movie directors, Charles Vidor and John Huston. She also had a long and very intense relationship with the late Michael Todd who gave her a cameo part in his modern classic *Around the World in 80 Days* (1956). Her last marital venture, at the time of her last film appearance, seems to have been a spectacular success in that she accomplished what neither Lana Turner, Ava Gardner, or Kathleen Winsor could do. She managed to stay married to Artie Shaw for over a decade.

Not long ago she told an interviewer that she doesn't miss Hollywood a bit. During the McCarthy era she had become thoroughly disgusted with a system she never had much respect for. The interest by fans in her pictures amuses more than flatters her. The other day one phoned her and asked if he was speaking to Evelyn Keyes. "My God," she replied, "I haven't seen her in years!"

Much of Evelyn's time is spent in their country home where she works on a mystery novel with a Hollywood background. They also keep an apartment in Manhattan.

With her husband, Artie Shaw, at a recent New York premiere. *Metro-Goldwyn-Mayer*

The photograph of George Weyerhauser circulated throughout North America by law-enforcement agents. *UPI*

THE WEYERHAUSER BABY

The Weyhausers were an immensely wealthy family, operators of the country's largest lumber company in the area of Tacoma, Washington. The company manager was John Phillip Weyerhauser, Jr., father of four children, the third of whom was to become the victim of one of the more sensational kidnappings of the thirties, the era of the big snatch, as it has been called.

On Friday, May 24, 1935, nine-year-old George Weyerhauser left school to have lunch at home, as usual. He did not make it home nor did he return to school.

That evening a special delivery letter arrived at the Weyerhauser house. It was a demand for $200,000 in small bills for the safe return of the boy. There were also instructions to place an advertisement in the personal columns of a local paper if the family meant to comply. The letter was signed Egoist. Weyerhauser told the police, already summoned when the boy failed to show up at home that noon, that he would pay the money. The tragic Lindbergh case was fresh in everyone's mind. Within the next four days Mr. Weyerhauser followed a series of intricate instructions delivered via telephone by a woman from various prearranged stations. On the fifth day a farmer and his wife answered the knock at their door and were confronted with a little boy who was by that time the most famous child in America. Said George to the startled pair, "I'm George Weyerhauser, the boy who was kidnapped."

To the police and F.B.I. agents (who had by then also been summoned on the case), the boy related an eerie story. Upon his way home that Friday noon he had been seized by a man and made to get into the trunk of a car. He spent the next four days of his life variously in two covered pits shackled to a stake, chained to a tree, and locked in a closet. He told of two men who fed and cared for him during the ordeal, but he had seen nothing of the woman who had called his father.

Two days after the boy's release, one of the bills (the serial numbers had been listed and distributed throughout the country by the F.B.I.) showed up in Portland, Oregon. Three days later several more were passed in Salt Lake City. Agents were then placed in all big stores to check all paper money taken in.

Before long in one of the stores where they were staked out a bill showed up. It had been offered by a young lady of nineteen who gave her name as Margaret Von Metz of Ogden, Utah. Upon checking the address the police found a man named Julius Thulin who claimed to have a granddaughter who had recently been married to one Harfon Von Metz Waley. This man proved to be an ex-convict with various prison records for burglary and robbery. Upon checking another local address, which had been given them by the girl, the agents found Waley. In the store of the furnished room was a partially burned roll of bills amounting to $3,700. Waley said the money had been given to him by a man who had driven him and his wife from Denver to Salt Lake City. He had thought the money was counterfeit, he added, and had no idea it was part of a ransom.

Meanwhile, in Butte, Montana, a detective recognized a man wanted for bank robbery. His name was William Dainard Mahan. Mahan escaped but left behind $15,500 of the ransom money in the car he abandoned.

In the meantime, Waley and his wife confessed to the crime and took authorities to a wooded area outside Salt Lake City where they dug up $97,000 in an oilcloth sack. The F.B.I. caught Mahan in San Francisco with $7,300 of the money with him. At the trial it was revealed that Waley had been born near Tacoma, knew the Weyerhausers were very wealthy, and plotted the snatch with Mahan while in prison. Waley pleaded guilty and was sentenced to forty-five years is prison. Mahan pleaded guilty, and was sentenced to sixty years in prison. Margaret, whose defense was that she had been unware of the crime until after it had been committed, did not convince the jury and she got twenty years. Her whereabouts since her release in 1948 are unknown.

During the Second World War George Weyerhauser served in the United States Navy and attended Yale afterward. He is the manager of the Springfield, Oregon, branch of the family business. George lives in Springfield with his wife and two children, neither of whom ever talk to strange men. He has vivid recollections of the four-day nightmare.

There still remains a big mystery. Approximately $74,000 of the ransom money has never turned up.

A businessman now. *UPI*

In 1927, salary: $3,500 a week.

BETTY COMPSON

Born in 1897 in Beaver City, Utah, with a name of Eleanor Luicime Compson, the future film star made her debut in Salt Lake City playing the violin in the orchestra of a local vaudeville house for $15 a week. When the manager gave her a chance to do a solo the family didn't have money for a costume. She went on in the rags of a street urchin. She billed herself as the "Vagabond Violinist." The audience loved it and mother and daughter were hooked.

Though still in her teens, Betty and her mother traveled up and down the West Coast playing a theatre one week and working as domestics the next until in 1915 she landed a job with Al Christie, the comedy director-producer of silent one-reelers, for $40 a week. Slapstick was in but Betty wisely avoided doing it, and although she had made twenty-eight Christie comedies when other offers came to her, she had not been typecast. The offers were welcome because Christie fired her in 1918 when she refused to make a personal appearance.

In 1919 she made *The Terror of the Range,* a serial. It was the last minor effort for many years. The same year she was cast with two other relatively unknown players in *The Miracle Man.* When the film was released Betty emerged along with Thomas Meighan and Lon Chaney as a major star. Three years later she made another blockbuster, *The Little Minister.*

Her silent films include: *Rustle of Silk* (1923) with Anna Q. Nilsson and *The White Flower* (1923) with Arline Pretty. Betty then made several films in England. On three of them Alfred Hitchcock was assistant director. In 1926 she came back to Hollywood where she made *Wise Guy* with Mary Astor. Eileen Percy was with Betty in *Twelve Miles Out* (1927). A very young Loretta Young supported the blonde star in *Scarlet Seas* (1928). The same year she made one of her best silents, *Docks of New York,* which had Olga Baclanova as its other star and Josef von Sternberg as its director.

On October 25, 1927, Betty married one of Hollywood's all-time greats, director James Cruze, who made *The Covered Wagon* (1923). Their palatial home, Flintridge, was the scene of some of the most lavish parties the movie capital has ever seen. After seven years they separated, reconciled, separated again, and after a few more years were divorced.

She made talkies when other silent stars were terrified over their voices. *The Barker,* in 1928, with Dorothy Mackaill was a smashing success. She had a whole new career ahead of her. In 1929 she and Sally O'Neil sang "Let Me Have My Dreams" in *On with the Show.* While her contemporaries starved in the new medium, Betty flourished—for awhile. She was indiscriminate about the roles she accepted. If a studio met her salary demands she would make the picture. Although she worked steadily through the thirties and into the forties, her billing soon slipped from star to bit player. Some of the cheapies that were her downfall were *Virtuous Husband* (1931) with Elliott Nugent (living on Manhattan's East 57th Street), *West of Singapore* (1933) with Margaret Lindsay (living in West Los Angeles), *Laughing Irish Eyes* (1936) with Evalyn Knapp, *Torchy Blane in Panama* (1938) with Lola Lane (a real estate dealer in Pacific Palisades, California), and *Cowboys from Texas* (1939) with Duncan Renaldo (semiretired to his estate on the Hope Ranch in Santa Barbara). In 1940 she had a meaty role in *Strange Cargo* but most of her part was cut out in the final print. Her old friend Alfred Hitchcock gave her a part in *Mr. and Mrs. Smith* (1941) and in 1946 Betty made her final movie, *Claudia and David.*

During the thirties she married producer Irving Wineberg who took her on a successful vaudeville tour of the Far East. Shortly after returning to the States, they were divorced. Betty tried to sell her own line of cosmetics for awhile and was briefly the manager of a woman's apparel shop in Beverly Hills. During World War II she met and married an ex-boxer, Silvious Jack Gall, who began a successful business of manufacturing ashtrays for hotels, clubs, and so on, which still prospers today. They lived in a large home which had belonged to her late mother in the foothills of Glendale, California. Since her husband's death in 1962, she lives there alone.

In Glendale, California, today. *Jon Virzi*

Putting the audience on in 1945.

JACK OAKIE

The master of the doubletake was born in Sedalia, Missouri, in 1903 with the name Lewis Delaney Offield. When he decided to go on the stage he took the name Oakie for Oklahoma where he had gone to school.

Jack bummed around vaudeville before he made it to Broadway in *Innocent Eyes* (1924) which starred the legendary Mistinguette. Its chorus line included the late Nancy Carroll and a girl named Lucille le Sueur, later to become Joan Crawford. Jack had a habit of playing practical jokes which the management found impractical. He was fired. In 1925 he got a job in *Artists and Models* and in 1926 was in *Peggy Ann*. The late Lulu McConnell was in both.

Paramount Pictures signed him to a long-term contract after he made *Finders Keepers* in 1927. Wesley Ruggles, a top director of the day, thought highly of Oakie's comic ability and put him into campus comedies. When sound came, these turned into musical comedies. Jack fitted perfectly as the round-faced young man who seldom got the girl but always got the laughs. He co-starred with the late Helen Kane (whose husband Dan Healy, "The Night Mayor of Broadway," lives in Jackson Heights, New York) in *Sweetie* in 1929. In a short time Oakie was one of the studio's most popular players. Others of the more than one-hundred features he made during the thirties and forties are *Million Dollar Legs* (1932), *Too Much Harmony* (1933) with Bing Crosby, *Alice in Wonderland* (1933) with Charlotte Henry, *Looking For Trouble* (1934) with the late Spencer Tracy, *If I Had a Million* (1932) with Wynne Gibson, *Big Broadcast of 1936, Florida Special* (1936) with Sally Eilers, *Thanks for Everything* (1938) with Jack Haley, *Tin Pan Alley* (1940) with John Payne, *Footlight Serenade* (1942), *On Stage Everybody* (1945) with Peggy Ryan, and *When My Baby Smiles at Me* (1948) with Betty Grable.

He was a guest on many of the network radio variety shows of the era, and in the late thirties had a program of his own for a while called "Jack Oakie's College."

Undoubtedly, his greatest plum came in the role of Mussolini in *The Great Dictator*. Bosley Crowther said of his performance in the acidic satire on Fascism, "Oakie ranks alongside Chaplin." Chaplin was the star and director but it was Jack who was nominated that year (1940) as the Best Supporting Actor.

Oakie was noted for his superb mugging and smooth delivery of wisecracks. Off the screen he was also pretty good at making caustic comments that did not always provoke laughter. He was also known in the business as an inveterate scene stealer. His best remembered bit was his famous "triple fade" which was actually a double take with one more take thrown in to milk the laughs. His timing was perfection.

Director Ernst Lubitsch called him "the best comedian in Hollywood." His first wife, actress Venita Varden, called him "jealous, quarrelsome, and abusive," when they were divorced on grounds of mental cruelty in 1938 after only two years of marriage.

His appearances in pictures dwindled greatly from the mid-forties on. He showed up in *Wonderful Country* in 1959 and *The Rat Race* in 1960 after an absence of eight years. The semicomeback was spurred by his part in the TV drama "The Battle for Wednesday Night" for which he received rave notices. His sole appearance previous to that was in a cameo part in *Around the World in 80 Days* (1956).

In 1960 his home town honored him with a parade and the dedication of a plaque. Senator Stuart Symington was one of the eulogists.

In 1963 he reportedly turned down $1,000,000 to play an ex-vaudevillian in a TV series. In spite of the enormous sum, most who know Jack believe the story. He has shown little interest in working hard for many years and has long been known to be one of the richest actors around. He was quoted sometime ago as saying that he bought A.T.&T. stock and General Electric when they were "American Smoke Signals and General Candle." He has lost his hearing almost completely, and a hearing aid does not help him.

For over twenty years he has been married to the former actress Victoria Horne. They live in a large home on Devonshire Drive in Northridge which Jack bought from Barbara Stanwyck after she divorced the late Frank Fay. Like Andy Devine, he has long been active in San Fernando Valley affairs and, also like Devine, has done very well in real estate in that area.

The white-haired comedian today. *Jon Virzi*

When she became a blonde in the late thirties. *NBC*

FRANCES LANGFORD

The blonde who was voted America's number one female singer in 1938 was born in Lakeland, Florida, in 1914 with a dark complexion and raven hair. Her mother Annie Newbern was a concert pianist. Frances majored in music at Southern College and sang in the Glee Club and school plays. She aspired to an operatic career but a tonsillectomy in 1930 changed her voice from a lyric soprano to a contralto.

In 1932 she was signed for thirteen weeks on a Tampa radio station by a cigar manufacturer after he heard her at an American Legion party. Rudy Vallee gave her a guest spot on one of his shows originating from New Orleans which was her first coast to coast program. Shortly afterward she was signed for the Phillips Magnesia program. On November 7, 1933, she opened on Broadway in the Peter Arno musical *Here Goes the Bride,* which ran for all of seven performances.

Shortly after making her legit debut, Frances was asked to perform at a party honoring Cole Porter. She sang "Night and Day" and was signed to a movie contract by Walter Wanger without even being tested.

Included in her film credits are *Every Night at Eight* (1935), which was her debut with Alice Faye and George Raft, *Collegiate* (1936) with Jack Oakie and the late Joe Penner, *Broadway Melody of 1936, Hollywood Hotel* (1937) with the Lane Sisters (Lola is a realtor in Pacific Palisades, California, and a neighbor of sister Rosemary; Priscilla is married to Joseph A. Howard, a building contractor, and lives in Andover, Massachusetts); *Too Many Girls* (1940) with Lucille Ball and Richard Carlson, *Hit Parade of 1941, Campus Rhythm of 1941* with Johnny Downs, *Girl Rush* (1944), *Bamboo Blonde* (1946), and *The Glenn Miller Story* (1954).

Frances was much bigger in radio than in movies. In 1939 she was the singing star of the Texaco Star Theatre with Ken Murray and Kenny Baker, and radio editors picked her as the "All-American Girl." In 1941 she began her long and very successful association with Bob Hope. She was the vocalist on his Pepsodent radio series and toured all the theatres of war with his famous troupe, from Cape Bon to Algiers to Bizerte, and Kairouan and Leyte. The singer was chosen by G.I.'s as the "No. 1 Girl of World War II," civilians picked her as Queen of the Campus City College of New York and Annapolis made her an honorary midshipman. At the end of the war she wrote a national news column, *Purple Heart Diary,* covering some of her experiences interviewing injured servicemen in hospitals around the world. Her most treasured award was a citation reading, "To Miss Frances Langford, with appreciation, for a grand job in North Africa. [signed] Dwight D. Eisenhower."

After the war she played nightclubs and had great success with the radio and TV series she did with Don Ameche entitled "The Bickersons." She was the star and hostess of two spectaculars, the first in 1959 with Bob Hope and Julie London, and the second the following year featuring Johnny Mathis and Don Ameche.

The singer who began her career as the "Moonglow Girl" and was once described by critic George Jean Nathan as "my dream girl" alternates her retirement years in Milwaukee, Wisconsin, and Jensen Beach, Florida, with her second husband Ralph Evinrude, Chairman of the Board of Evinrude Outboard Motor Company. They spend their winters in their Florida resort where Frances is sometimes coaxed to come on stage at "The Outrigger," their nightclub, to sing a few of the songs she has been closely associated with during her career: "You Are My Lucky Star," "I'm In the Mood For Love," and "Music, Maestro, Please."

Frances was divorced from actor Jon Hall (who lives in Malibu Beach, California) in 1955 after seventeen years of marriage. She married Evinrude the same year. She has no children.

Frances doesn't consider herself completely retired and occasionally she and Ameche get together on a TV guest spot to do their "Bickerson" skits. In 1952 she entertained U.S. troops in Korea and last year sang for the boys in Vietnam. When at home the Evinrudes do a lot of deep-sea fishing and traveling about on their yacht, the Chanticleer. Audiences are still amazed by her figure which she attributes to considerable exercise in her gym, and daily swimming.

Aboard the Evinrude yacht the *Chanticleer.*

One of the world's great voices in
1930. *RCA Records*

LOTTE LEHMANN

The great soprano from the Golden Age of opera was born in 1888 in Perlberg, Germany, where she and her brother spent their early years. Her father was secretary to the Ritterschaft, a benevolent society, and eventually he was transferred to Berlin where Lotte attended Ulrich High School to train for a teaching career. A friend of Lotte's mother noticed the girl's voice and suggested that she be given vocal coaching. Her teacher was the renowned Emma Tiedke. Later she studied at the Gerster School and the Berlin Conservatory of Music.

In 1909 she was engaged for the Hamburg Opera at the same time that Otto Klemperer was making a name for himself as its conductor. Lotte debuted as the third boy in *The Magic Flute*. She was promoted to larger parts and then went to the Vienna State Opera where she was to achieve a singular success in the company of Leo Slezak (father of Walter), Maria Jeritza, and Richard Mayr. Her first role in Vienna was Agathe in *Freischütz*. Some of her other roles were Octavian in *Der Rosenkavalier, Manon,* and *Il Trittico*. Puccini signed a photograph to her after her performance in *Il Trittico,* addressing it "to the incomparable Angelica," which she played in his opera.

In 1922 Lotte went to England and appeared at Covent Garden where she sang the role of Marschallin in *Der Rosenkavalier*. Years later *The New York Times* music critic Harold Schonberg said, "One of the authentic 20th century operatic myths is Madame Lehmann in the role of Marschallin." She returned to Vienna and sang Christine in Strauss's *Intermezzo* in its premiere in 1924 and sang *Fidelio* for the first time in her career. In 1928 she made her first appearance in the Salzburg Festival.

After the death of her husband whom she had married during her days in

Hamburg, she came to the United States and made her debut at the Civic Opera House in Chicago in 1930 singing Sieglinde in *Die Walküre*. She then embarked on a highly successful American concert tour.

In 1934 she signed with the Metropolitan and debuted again as Sieglinde with Lauritz Melchior as Siegmund. Her most popular Wagnerian roles were Eva, Elizabeth, and Else, but Marschallin was always her greatest. She continued as one of the Met's leading prima donnas until 1945, after which she limited herself almost exclusively to concert work.

In 1951 at the age of sixty-three Madame Lehmann ended a singing career that had spanned forty-one years. During the intermission of a New York Town Hall recital she announced her retirement amid cries from the audience of "No! No!" Her final song of the evening was Schubert's "To Music," after which she broke down in sobs. The audience climbed onto the stage to bid the artist a tearful, emotion-packed farewell.

Madame Lehmann has written four books: *Eternal Flight* (1938), a novel; *Midway in My Song* (1938) an autobiography; *More than Singing* (1945), on interpretation, and *My Many Lines* (1948), a study of her roles.

She returned to the Metropolitan in 1962 to direct a new production of *Der Rosenkavalier*, but she has not sung publicly since her retirement. Even for friends she declines to sing anymore. "My voice is a shadow of myself," she says, "and I hate to have shadows around me." Since 1964, "just to keep up," she has devoted her time to teaching a few pupils at Santa Barbara, California, where she makes her home on the Hope Ranch. During the summer months she produces operas at Santa Barbara's Music Academy.

A young soprano once said to her, "It must be awful for such a great singer as you to realize that you've lost your voice." "No," she replied, "What would be awful is if I *didn't* realize it."

Madame Lehmann in her garden.
Santa Barbara News Press

The pudgy Crown Prince with his father just after Carol was restored to the throne in 1932. *UPI*

KING MICHAEL I OF RUMANIA

The former boy king was born in Sinaia, Rumania, in 1921. Shortly after his birth his father Carol II who had had one morganatic marriage before he wed Michael's mother, was banished from the country by Ferdinand I, Michael's grandfather. Carol's cavortings with his mistress, Magda Lupescu, * had become too flagrant even for the jaded society of Bucharest. In 1928 Queen Helen divorced Carol. The year before, Michael became king upon the death of Ferdinand. Because of his age a regency was established which lasted until 1930, when Carol and the Lupescu returned to Rumania to take the throne from Michael who was demoted to crown prince. To a great extent due to the influence of Lupescu, Carol aligned his country with France just as war clouds were gathering over Europe. His chief opponent was the Fascist Iron Guard who hated his mistress in part because she was Jewish.

In 1940 Michael, now nineteen, was returned to the throne via a coup d'etat engineered by Marshal Ion Antonescu. Carol and the Lupescu fled the country and never returned. Although Michael had a passionate dislike for the Lupescu he also wanted no part of Hitler, whose troops now occupied Rumania. Officially his country was now fighting with the Axis but Michael was careful to remain aloof from politics during this time. Although he was only a figurehead anyway while Nazis governed the country, the young king took great pains to avoid any involvement with the Germans, hoping his people would draw the correct conclusion. Hitler needed the king as a front and Michael felt relatively safe. In August of 1944 when the German armies were being driven from Russia, Michael's forces made their move and by another coup d'etat overthrew Antonescu and declared alliance with the Allies. After the war, however, the Communists were able to force Michael's abdication and in 1947 the king went into exile in England, assuming the title of Prince of Hohenzollern. He was able to take very little money with him and it was only through the help of the English Royal family that he and

Princess Anne of Bourbon-Parma, whom he married in 1948, were able to get by until Michael was able to establish himself. For a time they had to live in a haunted house, but the former king proved an excellent flyer and became a test pilot for one of the large aircraft manufacturers. They lived decently but hardly in a kingly manner. Queen Helen, who lives in Italy, was able to send her five grandchildren, all girls, to good schools, although she too, is not really wealthy.

In recent years Michael has done rather well from his inventions in the aeronautical field. In 1963 the New York firm of Droulia and Company announced that Michael would be their Swiss representative. He has avoided any association with Rumanians in exile, thus being able to stand above their constant squabbling among themselves, and will not take any Rumanian investment accounts.

Michael was subjected to a great deal of criticism when he did not attend the funeral of his father in 1952. Although he was genuinely fond of Carol he felt that he could not appear without becoming involved with the Lupescu, who had married Carol three years before and now insisted on being addressed as Princess Elena. Aside from a rather run-down castle on the Riviera, his father left him nothing. His fortune, which was in the millions, went to the Lupescu.

While his life as a stockbroker living in Versoix with offices in Geneva is far removed from the court of Bucharest, his interest in the internal politics of Rumania has remained keen. His employer emphasizes that Michael insists his associates address him by his first name but royalists who visit him regularly call him "Your Majesty" and have never been corrected.

The man who harbors dreams of a restoration to the throne of a country in which he has not set foot for over two decades, is the son of a German by a Princess of Greece. Perhaps he hopes that he might be crowned during his third reign. Something neither he nor his father ever managed.

With Greek Princesses Irene (left) and Sophie
on a recent trip to Athens. *UPI*

In *The Glass Menagerie,* on Broadway, in 1945.

EDDIE DOWLING

The dean of the American theatre has been prominent as a songwriter, vaudevillian, musical comedy star, director, playwright, producer and dramatic actor.

He was born Joseph Nelson Goucher in 1894 in Woonsocket, Rhode Island, of a French-Canadian father and an Irish mother, whose maiden name he adopted for professional use. One of seventeen children, he learned to shift for himself at the age of eight, singing Irish ballads for pennies in front of bar rooms. His first job, at ten, was as a cabin boy on a coast steamer, then going to a similar position on a transatlantic ship, the Mauritania. In addition to his regular duties, he sang for the passengers. At the advice of an English vaudeville producer he joined the St. Paul's Cathedral Choir in London, and for some years, until his voice changed, toured with the group throughout the British Isles and the Continent.

Returning to America, he broke into vaudeville as a handy man at the old Keith Theatre in Providence, and eventually did a single song and dance routine. Within three years he was a headliner.

In the circuits he met and married Ray Dooley (of the famous British music hall family). After their marriage in 1911, they toured together, though not as a team.

In 1917 Dowling made his Broadway debut in an Erlanger production of Victor Herbert's operetta, *The Velvet Lady.* He helped rewrite it, including the composition of two songs. He was featured in 1917 in *The Ziegfeld Follies,* as was his wife—and Eddie Cantor.

In 1922 he had the first of a long string of successes, the musical comedy *Sally, Irene, and Mary,* in which he directed, produced, co-authored, and starred. It ran for three seasons on Broadway and, continued on the road. In 1926, performing all the same functions, he did the musical *Honeymoon Lane,* in which he introduced a manicurist he met in a Washington barber shop— Kate Smith. And Dowling's understudy was Bob Hope.

Dowling followed with *Sidewalks of New York* (1927), *Thumbs Up* (1934), and *At Home Abroad* (1935). Following *Thumbs Up* Dowling's wife retired from the stage.

In 1936 with Margaret Webster he co-produced Shakespeare's *Richard II,* a first in this country since the days of Edwin Booth. The star was Maurice Evans.

In 1938 Dowling did his first dramatic play, Philip Barry's *Here Come the Clowns,* co-starring with Madge Evans. In 1938 he introduced Paul Vincent Carroll to Broadway when he produced *Shadow and Substance,* starring Cedric Hardwicke and Julie Haydon. He followed this with Carroll's *The White Steed* with Barry Fitzgerald. Both these plays won the New York Drama Critics' Circle Award as the best foreign plays of their respective seasons.

In 1939 he did Saroyan's *The Time of Your Life,* starring with Julie Haydon. Newcomers in the cast were Celeste Holm, William Bendix, and Gene Kelly. This was the first play to win both the Drama Critics' Award and the Pulitzer Prize. Two years later he did two short plays, Chesterton's *Magic* and Saroyan's *Hello Out There.*

In 1945 he did *The Glass Menagerie,* thereby introducing Tennessee Williams to Broadway, and brought Laurette Taylor out of retirement to co-star with him and Julie Haydon. The play won the Drama Critics' Award.

In 1951 he did the unsuccessful *Angel in the Pawnshop,* co-starring Joan McCracken. The following year Dowling returned to the musical stage and took over the lead in the musical *Paint Your Wagon.*

Dowling was active in early radio, introducing to the air such stars as Jack Pearl,* Al Goodman and his Orchestra, Paul Robeson, Will Rogers, and Helen Morgan. And in the 1940's he emceed "We The People." He appeared on television as early as 1944 when he piloted the WOR series "Wide Horizons," an aviation program.

Dowling was the founder of the U.S.O. camp shows. Today he is deeply involved in the Eddie Dowling University Theatre Foundation, which produces plays at schools throughout the country.

The Dowlings have been living quietly in East Hampton, Long Island. Eddie produces an occasional industrial show, taking part in summer stock occasionally when roles appeal to him. He seldom comes into Manhattan but when he does there is usually a visit to the Lambs Club. Rae Dooley comes to town even less frequently. They had two children, one married daughter and a son killed in Argentina on assignment for Time-Life.

The famous showman today. *Howie Price*

Butterfly with the late Vivien Leigh
in a scene from *Gone with the Wind*,
1939.

BUTTERFLY McQUEEN

The Negro pixie who achieved movie immortality through her role in *Gone with the Wind* (1939), was born in Tampa, Florida, in 1911. Her father was a stevedore on the Tampa docks and her mother worked as a domestic. The slight British tinge to her high-pitched voice comes from the neighbors. They were from Nassau. Her mother sent her to Augusta, where she received her early education from Catholic nuns at St. Benedict's Convent.

Deciding to go on the stage, Butterfly moved north to Harlem and joined Venezuela Jones' Negro Youth Group in Harlem in 1935. After she danced in the "Butterfly Ballet" in a production of *A Midsummer Night's Dream* people began calling her "Butterfly." She has never used Thelma, her real name, since.

She debuted on Broadway in December of 1937 in George Abbott's *Brown Sugar* which ran for only four performances. The critics, however, were impressed. And so was Abbott. In his next production the following year he tailored a part in it just with Butterfly in mind. *What a Life* was a smash hit and she played it on Broadway and on the road.

When the late David O. Selznick acquired the screen rights to Margaret Mitchell's *Gone with the Wind* Butterfly asked for the role of Prissy, and was told that she was wrong for the part, and too old. Two years later her agent presented her with a contract. Butterfly had serious misgivings about the way the book treated Negroes. She considers it her best work, but wonders whether it was a backward step; in one scene, Rhett Butler refers to her as "a simple-minded darkie."

Butterfly's performance in the civil war epic made a big impression on audiences as well as the studios but she never capitalized on it. Over the years she has turned down a succession of what she calls "handkerchief head" parts. Selznick used her two more times in *Since You Went Away* (1944) and *Duel in the Sun* (1946). She played Joan Crawford's cook in *Mildred Pierce* (1945). Her memories of *Cabin in the Sky* (1943) are mostly unhappy ones. Rochester teased her unmercifully, Lena Horne treated her with contempt, and director Vincente Minnelli was nice to her face but cutting when she was not present.

She began to drift from job to job. She was for a time a paid companion to an old lady on Long Island, sold toys in Macy's Department Store, was a cab dispatcher in the Bronx, an operator of a little restaurant, and manager of a little theatre group at the Y.M.C.A. She has attended U.C.L.A., Los Angeles City College, and Southern Illinois University.

Much of the money she saved from her movie roles went into a one-woman concert she produced at Carnegie Hall in 1951. It was a financial disaster.

In 1957 Butterfly moved back to Augusta where she gave music lessons for awhile and had her own radio program. She returned to Manhattan briefly in 1964 to appear in the musical *The Athenian Touch* which had a short run off Broadway. Her big song was called "No Garlic Tonight." She went back to Georgia as a hostess at the Stone Mountain Memorial which is a complex of museums whose statuary honors the Confederacy. After that she guided tourists on strolls through a plantation mansion for several years. She is currently suing the owners, claiming that she was not paid for the photographs of her they used for publicity purposes.

She returned to Harlem in 1967 and waited tables awhile. M-G-M asked her to tour with their revival of *Gone with the Wind* in return for expenses. When the reissue premiered in New York, Butterfly was not in attendance.

In 1968 the producers of *Curley McDimple,* a musical spoof of Hollywood in the thirties, had a part written into the off-Broadway production especially for her.

Miss McQueen, who has never married, says she would like to be able to live in Africa six months of the year, although she has never traveled farther than Mexico. She works in her spare time helping with cleanup projects in her neighborhood and coaching young Negroes at a community theatre on West 125th Street.

Interviewed by the author at WBAI-FM, in New York City. *Frank Altman*

"Blondie" and "Dagwood" in 1941.

PENNY SINGLETON

The actress who became known the world over as "Blondie" was born in Philadelphia, Pennsylvania. Her uncle is former Postmaster General James A. Farley. Her real name is Mariana Dorothy McNulty and her real hair coloring is brunette.

After attending the Alex McClue School and Columbia University she performed as a singer and acrobat in Broadway in *Good News* (1928), *Follow Through* (1929), *Walk a Little Faster* (1932) with Bea Lillie, and *Hey Nonny, Nonny* (1932) before Hunt Stromberg, Sr., brought her to Hollywood. Although she had contracts with both Warners and M-G-M, her only significant part before that of Blondie was in *After the Thin Man* (1936), in which she played a nightclub dancer. Throughout the tenure of both contracts she fought continually against being cast either as the "other woman" or as a menace.

Her name, hair, and luck were all changed in 1937 when she married a dentist, Dr. Lawrence Singleton. She had a book of childrens' verse published that year under the name Penny Singleton, and decided to use it professionally as well. And the girl originally signed for the part of Blondie, Shirley Deane, took ill.

Blondie (1938), the original feature film, was made by Columbia Pictures on a low budget and released as a programmer. The radio serial which went on the air in 1939 as a summer replacement was called "silly" by *Variety*, which also remarked, "It is impossible to predict anything but a minimum audience to a minimum engagement." The public thought otherwise. Penny in the meantime divorced Dr. Singleton in 1939, and in 1941 married her present husband, Bob Sparks, who was for a time the producer of *Blondie* movies.

The Bumsteads became one of America's favorite families. The show included a little boy, Baby Dumpling, who became Alexander during the war, about the same time their cartoon daughter Cookie was born. The radio shows lasted over seven years.

Theatres around the country reported excellent audience reaction, and some advertised the pictures as the featured attraction. A few of the films that endeared the efficient young housewife and her bungling hubby to America were *Blondie Brings Up Baby* (1939), *Blondie Has Servant Trouble* (1940), *Blondie Goes to College* (1942), *Blondie Knows Best* (1946), *Blondie's Secret* (1948), and *Blondie's Hero* (1950). The series was dropped in 1943 but the public complained and the studio revived it in 1945.

Although Penny made a few other features such as *Go West, Young Lady* (1941) with Glenn Ford, *Swing Your Partner* (1943) with the Late Louise Fazenda, and *Young Widow* (1946), the Blondie image eventually prevented her from continuing her career after the radio series and movies were discontinued. In the early fifties she worked in nightclubs and presentation houses doing songs and patter to good reviews but audiences kept waiting for Arthur Lake to come onstage. In 1952 she headlined the show at the Thunderbird Hotel in Las Vegas.

Since playing Blondie, Penny has been active in the American Guild of Variety Artists, the theatrical union representing dancers, singers, and so on, in nightclubs and on stage in ice shows and presentation houses. She served two terms as president in the fifties but by the early sixties was battling AGVA's officials at board meetings and finally in the courts. In 1962 she testified before a house committee on union activities that AGVA was writing "sweetheart contracts" which compelled girls working in strip bars to mingle with the customers, thus encouraging prostitution. That year Penny was suspended from membership. Undaunted, she sued the members of the executive board demanding that they account for money from the treasury. One officer countersued for $1,180,000 in a libel action. When it was finally settled, out of court, Penny was again a member of the union, and is now a vice-president and executive secretary. In 1966 she came to New York where she led a strike by the famous Rockettes, the first in their history, against Radio City Music Hall. It lasted twenty-seven days.

She lives in Los Angeles with her husband and their two daughters, neither named "Cookie."

"Blondie" an important AGVA leader today. N.Y. *Daily News*

In the costume she wore on opening night, March 13, 1911, in *The Pink Lady*.

HAZEL DAWN

Hazel Dawn was the kind of star Alice Faye used to portray in movie musicals of the 1930's. At the age of seventeen she had Broadway at her feet. There were stage door Johnnies wearing Inverness capes and carrying long stemmed roses. The still popular the "Beautiful Lady Waltz" was "her" song and across the street from the New Amsterdam Theatre, where she was playing, Murray's Restaurant proclaimed a new drink in her honor—the Pink Lady Cocktail. Overnight she had become known as "The Pink Lady," the title of her hit musical.

Success, however, is sometimes harder to overcome than failure. Her acclaim in the title role of that Ziegfeld production was so great that she was never able to shake the public image that was forged and she remained typecast in the minds of theatregoers throughout her career.

Ironically, Hazel has never had a Pink Lady, nor any other alcoholic beverage. She was born a Mormon and, although she admits to having a few cups of coffee and tea, has remained faithful to her strict religious upbringing.

Her family took her to London where her sister, a promising singer, was to study voice. The impresario Paul Reubens discovered her and changed her name from Letout to Dawn.. She debuted in London in *Dear Little Denmark* in 1909.

In 1913 she was set for the lead in *The Little Café* but at the last minute she was replaced by the girl friend of the producer Klaw Erlanger. All Broadway heard about the shabby trick that had been played on her and when she walked on stage opening night in a lesser role the audience gave her a five-minute ovation.

Her bad experience with *Little Café* made her sign a movie contract with Famous Players. Some of her silent films are: *One of Our Girls* (1914), *Niobe* (1915), and *The Lone Wolf* (1917), in which the late Bert Lytell made his screen debut.

Three of Hazel's stage vehicles were considered at the time very racy and ran into considerable trouble with the censors which in the long run proved to be good publicity for the shows. They were *Up in Mabel's Room* (1919) with Enid Markey (like Hazel, a New Yorker and still a friend), *Gertie's Garter* (1921), and *The Demi-Virgin* (1921).

For over a decade Hazel Dawn was one of Broadway's top leading ladies. In 1916 she appeared with Elsie Janis, Leon Errol, Van & Schenck, and Marie Dressler in *The Century Girl*. It was produced by Flo Ziegfeld and had music by Irving Berlin and Victor Herbert. She introduced the song "Valencia" in *Great Temptations* (1916). In the cast of that show was a relatively unknown violinist-comic by the name of Jack Benny. In *Nifties of 1923* she did a parody on *Rain*. There were *Keep Kool* (1924) and *Ziegfeld Follies of 1925*, which had as its ballerina a soon-to-be silent star named Lina Basquette (owner of the country's top kennel of Great Danes in Chalfonte, Pennsylvania).

In 1927 Hazel became Mrs. Charles Groehl. Her only Broadway appearance after that was in *Wonder Boy* which Jed Harris produced in 1931. The play came in with rave notices from its out-of-town tryouts and a huge advance sale but had been so oversold that when the curtain went up opening night Hazel says "it was like a cold wind swept that stage. I still can't understand what happened. It was my only flop."

The Groehl family moved to California in 1935. Her husband, a mining engineer, died in 1941. In 1947 Hazel returned to New York to launch her daughter as an actress under the name Hazel Dawn, Jr. After a brief but very promising career the girl married a doctor and now lives in a New York suburb with her husband and five sons. Hazel's other child, a son, is a commercial photographer in Florida.

From 1953 until she retired in 1964 "The Pink Lady" enjoyed another kind of stardom. She was undoubtedly the most popular receptionist in New York in her job with the J. Walter Thompson advertising agency's casting department. Her sympathetic encouragement and good advice to those waiting nervously for auditions is still legend among New York actors.

Hazel is still seen constantly by New York theatregoers but now she is one of them. "I try to see all the shows," she says. "I am really enjoying life and am able to do what I want. I can't think of any people I would rather be around than theatre people. I have many, many friends and my grandchildren and my health. I've been very lucky and I'm very grateful."

In her seventies, a grandmother, and still in the pink.

Weighing in after winning the Hialeah Park Inaugural Handicap, his third victory on January 7, 1944. *UPI*

TED ATKINSON

The jockey with over three thousand wins to his record was born in Toronto, Canada, in 1916. His full name is Theodore Francis. His father, a glass engraver, eventually settled the family in Brooklyn. Ted went through a succession of jobs selling papers, mowing lawns, and peddling flowers. Although Atkinson had little formal schooling, he read prodigiously and acquired considerable knowledge, which led to his being dubbed "The Professor" by his fellow riders. Before turning to the track he worked for a Brooklyn chemical plant, pasting labels on bottles for $8 a week, which he worked into $35 a week for packing bottles and doing odd jobs.

The 5 foot 2 inch 100-pounder progressed to chief bottle packer, only to be barred from the job by the union.

A truck driver for the firm introduced Ted to the late Silvia Cucci, a jockey, and Ted soon found himself at the Greentree Stable in Red Bank, New Jersey, as a valet. Before departing Brooklyn for Red Bank, however, Atkinson made a quick trip to the Van Cortlandt Park riding academy and formally introduced himself to his first horse.

A long apprenticeship followed in which Atkinson went through the daily chores of cleaning out stalls, walking, and breaking yearlings. He left Greentree because only experienced jockeys would ever ride its Thoroughbreds in competition.

Atkinson drifted to Ohio and after months of disappointment finally got a mount aboard Musical Jack. That was on May 18, 1938, at Beulah Park, Ohio. He admits to making every mistake in the book while guiding his horse to his first victory. But the triumph gave him some much-needed confidence and, by the year's end, he had piloted thirty-six winners.

The following year, still playing the "leaky roof" circuit, he met Martha Shanks, a North Randall, Ohio, farmgirl whose father was a harness horse enthusiast, and shortly thereafter (in 1940) they were married.

In 1940 Atkinson tried the New England circuit for the first time. He rode ninety-five winners that year and the following season he rode his first stakes winner, War Relic, in the Massachusetts Handicap at Suffolk Downs. Later in 1941, he was astride War Relic when the colt defeated Whirlaway in the Narragansett.

He made the big move to New York in 1943 and success on the major circuit came quickly. In 1944 he won his first national championship, riding 287 winners, the most he ever rode in a single season. Two years later he again captured the national title, with a 233 total. After this season Greentree Stable signed him to a contract as a regular rider, succeeding Eddie Arcaro, a position he maintained for eleven years.

Atkinson wore the pink and black silks while astride such outstanding campaigners as Straight Face, Hall of Fame, Tom Fool, Capot, and One Hitter.

One of Atkinson's biggest regrets is that Tom Fool, "the greatest horse I ever rode," was not sound enough to be a starter in the Kentucky Derby of 1952. The virus that sidelined the Horse of the Year in 1953 probably cost Atkinson a victory in the Derby which, strangely enough, is one of the few major American racing fixtures to have eluded him. In November of 1957 he was installed as one of the twelve present members of the Jockeys' Hall of Fame.

Ted's last race was in January, 1959, at Tropical Park. The jockey who ranks with Sir Gordon Richards, Johnny Longden, and Eddie Arcaro* as the only jockeys ever to ride three thousand winners, lives with his wife and two children in Palantine, Illinois. Since a back ailment caused his retirement, he has worked as a New York Patrol Judge from 1959 until 1960. During that time he was also Assistant Clerk of Scales and Assistant Paddock Judge and Entry Clerk. Since April of 1961 he has been State Steward at Chicago racetracks.

Riding a desk today. *Clifford May*

The idol of the bobby-soxers in 1940.

ARTIE SHAW

The *enfant terrible* of the swing era was born Abraham Isaac Arshawsky in 1910 in New York's Lower East Side, where his Jewish immigrant parents were in the dressmaking business. Straitened circumstances led to their moving to New Haven, Connecticut. He managed to save up enough money as a grocery store errand boy to buy a secondhand saxophone, with five free lessons. He took only two, and they constitute Shaw's entire formal musical education. Soon after he was booked with a young banjo player traveling the New Haven area, appearing on so-called "Amateur Night" shows. After this, followed his own four-man, $8-a-night Pan Novelty Orchestra, and a job with the Johnny Cavallaro Orchestra. He was fourteen years old. His first "professional" job was as first alto sax with the Olympia Theatre Orchestra in New Haven. The grind proved too much for him. He joined the Joe Cantor orchestra in Cleveland and left New Haven for good.

After a year with Joe Cantor, learning to arrange and orchestrate, and writing for other bands as well, he moved to Cleveland's top band, the Austin Wylie Orchestra, remaining for two years.

A job with his first "big name" band, Irving Aaronson's Commanders, came in Hollywood, at nineteen. From then on he moved from orchestra to orchestra—Andre Kostelanetz, Howard Barlow, Peter Van Steeden, Richard Himber, Red Nichols, Paul Whiteman, and Freddie Rich.

The break came in 1935 at a musicians' benefit at the Imperial Theatre in New York City. Shaw got together a small group to fill in between the big band performances. He composed a piece for clarinet, viola, cello, guitar, string bass, and drums entitled "Interlude in B Flat." The reaction was immediate and electric—from fellow musicians. But not from the general public. He formed a more orthodox band, which caught on, and won him a contract with RCA Victor. The record company changed his name from Art to Artie.

The first record was a swing version of Friml's "Indian Love Call," with Tony Pastor singing. Victor had more than a hit. The flip side happened to have "for quiet contrast" an old Cole Porter song that had not gone anywhere. The song: "Begin the Beguine." In 1939, he won the *Downbeat* title of "King of Swing," replacing Benny Goodman, and landed a radio contract with NBC to play on the Robert Benchley Old Gold program. However, the sponsor and station, deluged with angry protests over his interview comment that "all jitterbugs are morons," readily accepted his "voluntary resignation." At this time he made his two Hollywood pictures, *Dancing Co-Ed* with Lana Turner, and *Second Chorus* with Fred Astaire and Paulette Goddard.

At the very peak of his popularity and earning some $500,000 annually, he announced his retirement. (Shortly before, Shaw had been stricken with a usually fatal blood disease, granulocytopenia.)

The following year, he organized a band. His first new record was "Frenesi," an immediate hit.

He enlisted in the Navy in World War II, and toured the South Pacific with a band for two years entertaining the troops. Medically discharged because of "operational fatigue," he underwent analysis for a year and a half, and retired to Norwalk, Connecticut, and began to write. In 1952 his book *The Trouble With Cinderella* was published, which was fairly well received.

The following year he was called before Representative Velde's (Republican, Illinois) House Un-American Activities Committee and admitted to having been a "red dupe," and recounted three persons he had seen at Communist recruiting meetings in 1946.

In 1954 he organized the Gramercy Five, another combo that failed to find an audience. He claims he has not touched the clarinet since. He lived on the Costa Brava in Spain while writing three more books, one of which, *I Love You, I Hate You, Drop Dead,* was published in 1962. That same year, Victor Records, in commemoration of their twenty-fifth year of association, presented him with eight gold discs. The eight over-one-million records: "Dancing in the Dark," "Back Bay Shuffle," "Summit Ridge Drive," "Frenesi," "Nightmare" (his theme), "Traffic Jam," "Begin the Beguine," and "Stardust." Also, in 1964 he produced a rather fine motion picture, *Seance on a Wet Afternoon,* starring Kim Stanley. In addition to his Manhattan apartment, he lives in a twenty-two room mansion in Lakeville, Connecticut, and enjoys a financial independence arising from royalties on his recordings. There he shoots, reads, and writes.

Mr. Shaw's marital excursions have made considerable news. Among his eight wives were Lana Turner, Ava Gardner, Kathleen Winsor, and the present Evelyn Keyes.

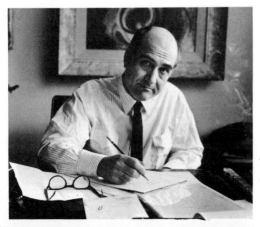

The "King of Swing" in abdication.
Diana Keyt

In 1937.

DOLORES COSTELLO

The actress who was the daughter of one of America's greatest matinee idols, and the wife of another, was born in Pittsburgh, Pennsylvania, in 1906. Her mother was leading lady (on stage) to father Maurice Costello (he was also one of the earliest, most popular leading men of the silent screen). As children, she and her sister Helene played in many of their parents' plays. Dolores made her debut at the age of five playing a little boy. Both girls played child roles in their father's movies.

Despite their famous name, the Costello sisters did not seem able to break into movies when they became young ladies. Exasperated, they came to New York City, where Dolores had some success as a model. One of the artists she posed for was the famous James Montgomery Flagg. In 1924 the girls landed roles in the George White Scandals of that year. *Scandals* ran on Broadway for over a year, and then went on the road. In Chicago a talent scout for Warner Brothers spotted them. They were placed under contract and sent to Hollywood, where once again there seemed to be no parts for them. Then one day, John Barrymore saw Dolores emerge from a car at the studio. Barrymore had seen her years before on the Costello estate on Long Island when he came to visit her father, but she was only a child at the time. Even before Warner told him who she was, the Great Profile said he wanted her for his leading lady in *The Sea Beast,* a screen adaptation of *Moby Dick.* In addition to the sheer pleasure of being manhandled by the heartthrob of millions of women, it was a guarantee to stardom.

Barrymore and Costello, two of the period's greatest names in the American theatre, made the picture in 1926. Though Dolores' role was nonexistent in the classic, it was added to the screenplay to assure a love interest. Their scenes together were torrid, and in a short time they announced their engagement. The wedding had to wait until 1928 when his divorce from Michael Strange became final. Together they made the screen versions of *Manon Lescaut*

(1926) and *When a Man Loves* (1927). Her other silents included *A Million Bid* (1927), *Glorious Betsy* (1928), *Tenderloin* (1928), *Madonna of Avenue A* (1929), and *Glad Rag Doll* (1929).

She became much less active in pictures after her marriage. In 1932 their son John, Jr., was born, and the following year they had a girl, Dolores. In 1934 their marriage, which because of John's drinking was never very stable, broke up after Barrymore phoned his wife to say goodbye and good luck. Somehow she managed to maintain a semblance of dignity while her husband cavorted around the country with his protégée Elaine Barrie.* The Barrymores were divorced in 1935. Dolores received $163,000 in securities and $850 monthly alimony.

Her credits in sound pictures include *Show of Shows* (1929), *Breaking the Ice* (1931) with Bobby Breen,* *Yours for the Asking* (1936), *Little Lord Fauntleroy* (1936) with Freddie Bartholomew,* *Girls on Probation* (1938) with Ronald Reagan and Jane Bryan, *Whispering Enemies* (1939), *The Magnificent Ambersons* (1942), and *This Is the Army* (1943), her last.

In 1939 Dolores married Dr. John Vruwink, with whom she lived in New York City until their divorce in 1951. The same year she attempted a comeback on stage in *The Great Man.*

Before her father's death in 1950, he sued her for an increase in his allowance. In those days she also was supporting her sister, who had been hospitalized for some time; Helene died in 1957. After her second divorce Dolores moved to California where her daughter had her arrested on a drunk and disorderly conduct charge.

For a number of years now, the former actress has resided with her teenage grandson on a ranch in Del Mar, California. She is occasionally visited by her son, but otherwise has little contact with Hollywood. Visitors are greeted by an array of dogs, which herald their arrival.

In a rare interview, Dolores said, "Whenever I think of John, it is with great compassion."

On her ranch in Del Mar, California.
Jon Virzi

In 1912, dancing "The Dying Swan" at the Metropolitan Opera House. Toscanini conducted.

ANNETTE KELLERMAN

The first woman to wear a one-piece bathing suit and to attempt to swim the English Channel was born in Australia in 1888.

Crippled by polio shortly after birth, Annette had to wear large steel braces about three times the weight of those used today. She was, however, determined not to allow her affliction to break her health or her spirit. Through exercise, perseverance, and sheer will power she learned to walk without the aid of braces or canes. Not content simply to be able to get around like others, Annette continued her strenuous exercises and by 1905 while astounded onlookers stood by she made a perfect dive off the pier at Ramsgate into the waters far below. After picking up a few local swimming awards she debuted at the Theatre Royal in Melbourne in a diving act, which was booked immediately for a London theatre. Audiences were amazed by the girl billed as "The Perfect Woman with the Form Divine."

The three main elements of her fantastically successful act were: (1) After the story of her childhood as a cripple was told the lady proceeded to go underwater and remained there for 2½ minutes, (2) It was the first successfully presented aquacade on stage, and (3) Her costume was a one-piece bathing suit, nothing short of a sensation at the time. Annette became the darling of the music halls.

Her United States tour got off to a well publicized start when in 1907 she was arrested by Boston police for daring to appear on Revere Beach wearing a one-piece bathing suit in plain view of decent citizens. Although many church and women's groups demanded that she be banned entirely, there were enough who felt otherwise to pack the theatres where she appeared.

In 1909 Annette made several attempts to swim the English Channel. Once she got over three quarters across before giving up, declaring that no woman had the "brute strength" required. Gertrude Ederle* proved her wrong in 1926.

Annette married James R. Sullivan in 1912, in Danbury, Connecticut. He managed and publicized her from then on.

In 1914 she was starred by Universal Pictures in *Neptune's Daughter,* a great box office success, which was followed by *Daughter of the Gods* in 1916. No stand-ins were needed. Portions of the films were used in *The Love Goddesses* in 1965, a movie made up of clips from the pictures of femme fatales from Theda Bara to Marilyn Monroe.

For the next fifteen years "The Diving Venus," another of her titles, made seven world tours on which she made a seventy-five foot dive into a forty-ton glass tank of water for paying customers from Shanghai to Buenos Aires. Her mail-order plan for beauty and health was advertised well into the thirties and was a great financial success in all the countries where she had appeared.

During World War II Annette and her husband, James R. Sullivan, spent a lot of time in Australia where she produced shows to entertain United States troops stationed in the South Pacific. She is probably best remembered during these years for her idea to have those at home send the Sunday funny papers to the boys overseas.

In 1949 M-G-M filmed Annette Kellerman's life story in color, starring Esther Williams. Made as a musical, *Million Dollar Mermaid* was a box office smash, and introduced the song "Baby, It's Cold Outside."

In 1956 the Sullivans revisited Australia to see the Olympic Games, and have lived there ever since. Their summers are spent in Sydney and they winter on the famed Gold Coast in Queensland, the surfer's paradise.

Although retired for forty years, "The Diving Venus" swims every day of her life. She is presently working for the Red Cross in aiding United States troops in Vietnam. In a recent letter to the States she said: "My past is past. The present keeps me very busy. I have continued to lecture, swim a half mile daily, do ballet practice, and I love to take long walks. We travel constantly."

Annette has never had a child. She is still married to James R. Sullivan who has never learned to swim a stroke.

Annette became a United States citizen in 1912 and spent much of the time since in this country, most of it in the Sullivan home in Pacific Palisades, before moving to Australia.

Now in her eighties, "The Diving Venus" swims every day. *Sydney Sun*

In 1936, in *It's Love Again*.

JESSIE MATTHEWS

Her pictures were the only successful musicals ever made outside of Hollywood until the Beatles did *A Hard Day's Night* (which was directed by an American) in 1964.

"Princess Personality," as a reviewer once called her, was born in London in 1907. At the age of ten she debuted on the English stage in the title role of *Bluebell in Fairyland*. Trained in classical ballet, Jessie was seriously considering an offer to dance with Anton Nolan when the great impresario Andre Charlot gave her a job in the chorus of his *Charlot's Revue of 1924*. She had been in *The Music Box Revue* the year before.

For awhile Jessie only danced in the show, but soon trouble developed with the understudy to Gertrude Lawrence, the star. The understudy's voice was poor and her temperament worse. Jessie got to understudy Miss Lawrence in London and on Broadway, and often was allowed to do one of her numbers.

In the next *Charlot Show* in 1926 Jessie was the star. She followed that with *Vanities of 1927* and *One Dam Thing After Another* the same year. In 1928 she did *Jordan* and *This Year of Grace*. Her musicals were light and silly and exactly what the public wanted in the lush twenties. In 1929 Jessie starred with the late Jack Buchanan and Tilly Losch (a resident of Manhattan's East Side) in *Wake Up and Dream*. Probably her best remembered stage show was *Evergreen* which she did in 1930. In 1931 and 1933 she was in *Hold My Hand* and *Sally Who?* respectively.

"The Dancing Divinity," another of her titles, began her picture career in 1933, a year in which she made *The Good Companions* with the late Edmund Gwenn, *There Goes the Bride,* and *Friday the 13th*. Some of her movies, including her best one, *Evergreen* (1935), played the Music Hall in New York City at a time when foreign films were little more than curiosity pieces that usually played the second half of double bills or grimy little art houses in Greenwich Village. Gaumont-British, which had experienced serious financial troubles at the time, signed Jessie, and was able to pay off all their debts with her grosses. She made one picture after another for them. Some were not very good, but all were financially successful. Her credits include: *It's Love Again* (1936), in which she co-starred with Robert Young, *First a Girl* (1936), *Gangway* (1937), *Head Over Heels* (1937), and *Climbing High* (1939).

There was much talk of her coming to Hollywood. She seemed the perfect partner for Fred Astaire. The English studio, however, had a firm contract with her and refused to let her go. She says today that she worked so hard in those years she was not even aware that offers from Hollywood had been made. She never made a film outside of England.

Broadway had not seen her in quite some time when she signed to do *The Lady Comes Across* in 1941. England was being blitzed, her third marriage was on the rocks, and the overwork of many years caught up with her. Jessie had a complete and severe nervous breakdown and left the show before it came in. Broadway never saw her again, nor did any other audience for many years.

In the fifties Jessie began to do an occasional play. In 1955 she produced *The Policeman and the Lady* and in 1958 she toured Australia in several plays. The same year she surprised and delighted her fans all over the world as the mother in M-G-M's *Tom Thumb*. Not long after Jessie got the part of Mrs. Dale on England's most popular radio serial, "Mrs. Dale's Diary," heard five days a week over the B.B.C. Almost everyone agrees that Jessie added several dimensions to the "Mrs. Dale" character. It has become more popular than ever, since she took it over.

In 1965 Huntington Hartford's Gallery of Modern Art presented "A Tribute to Miss Jessie Matthews," including a retrospective showing of her motion pictures and a twice a day in person appearance of the actress-singer-dancer whose pert smile lightened the Depression for so many moviegoers.

Along with her radio work she finds time for an occasional cabaret appearance. Unmarried for many years now, Jessie lives in the Northwood section of London with her sister Rosie.

Still acclaimed by her English public. *Gallery of Modern Art*

"Blondie" and "Dagwood Bumstead" celebrate Christmas in 1945. *CBS Radio*

ARTHUR LAKE

"Dagwood Bumstead" (as he was known to millions) was born in 1905 in Corbin, Kentucky. He attended school for a while in Nashville, Tennessee, but most of his boyhood was spent traveling with his family. His father and his father's twin brother had an aerialist act called "The Flying Silverlakes." His mother was a stage actress, known as Edith Goodwin. Although his parents would not permit him to perform when they were playing circuses, Arthur and his sister Florence became part of the act as soon as it switched to vaudeville and was renamed "Family Affairs." They toured the South mostly until the act broke up in southern California.

Arthur's last name was shortened to Lake by his producer, Carl Laemmle, Jr., when he went into movies. His first role was in *Jack and the Beanstalk* (1917), after which he went into a number of Franklyn Farnum westerns. During the twenties Arthur and Florence worked on the stage and in silents whenever there were parts for adolescents. One of Arthur's best known pictures during that period was *Skinner's Dress Suit* (1925).

In 1924 Arthur Lake began making *Sweet 16* comedies which typecast him as a teen-ager, a part he played until he was into middle age. In 1928 he portrayed the title character in the silent version of *Harold Teen*. The following year he had the juvenile lead in the color musical *On With the Show,* in which he sang "Don't It Mean a Thing To You?" His first sound film was *Air Circus* (1929).

Arthur and Florence made a musical short, *Glad to Beat You,* for Vitaphone in 1934, but movie roles were few and he toured the vaudeville circuits in order to earn a living between films. He had parts in *Silver Streak* (1934) with Charles Starrett, *Orchids to You* (1935) with Jean Muir (the blacklisted actress lives in Ossining, New York), and *Topper* (1937).

Arthur played the original role of Dagwood, and stayed with the series in motion pictures, radio, and television. When Penny Singleton left the radio version after seven years, Mrs. Lake, the former Patricia Van Cleve, took over the role and continued for the remaining five years the series was on the air. When it became a TV program in 1954, Blondie Bumstead was played by Pamela Britton for the short time it ran. It premiered in January and was dropped in December. In July of 1958 it commenced again, but this time it lasted four months.

The part of the pugnacious neighbor, Herb Woodley, was played by radio's original "Great Gildersleeve," Hal Peary (who lives in Redondo Beach, California).

When *Blondie* came along in the form of a movie in 1938, Arthur was very grateful. He has never complained about being so closely associated with the character that the public could not accept him as anything else. He was hired once for another picture by a producer he had convinced otherwise. Halfway through production they both agreed he had played the part as if it were the character Dagwood. After 1939, in the few movies he made which were not *Blondies* he played parts very much like creator Chic Young's character.

He used to entertain ideas of becoming a scenarist or director. The closest he came was when he made a travelogue on Guatemala in 1950. After the 1954 "Blondie" TV series was canceled, Arthur and his wife had a short-lived situation series called "Meet the Family." Naturally, Arthur played the dopey but likeable husband.

The Lakes, who have been married over thirty years, are the parents of two children. Their home is many times the size the Bumsteads occupied on Shady-lane Avenue in the series. It is set on a short street in Santa Monica only a few yards from the Pacific Ocean. It was in Santa Monica that Arthur, following his retirement, opened a bar which lasted all of six weeks.

Along with his large earnings acquired during his heyday, the Lakes were well remembered in the will of Marion Davies who had a great affection for her niece—Arthur's wife. One of Patricia Lake's trinkets that would be beyond the Bumstead family budget is a $600,000 cabochon cut-star sapphire necklace.

"Dagwood" today. *Jon Virzi*

In the title role of *Tosca*, 1921.
Metropolitan Opera Company

MARIA JERITZA

One of the most talented and temperamental divas of this century was born in Brünn, Austria, in 1887.

When she debuted in 1910 as Elsa in *Lohengrin* at the Olmutz Opera House, it was under her real name, Mitzi Jedlicka. By 1912 word of her artistry had reached Emperor Franz Josef who attended a performance of *Die Fledermaus* at a summer resort—just to hear for himself. It is doubtful whether it was only the big, glorious voice of the soprano that brought the old man. Like most of her fans, he was taken as well by her beauty. Few opera singers at that time were beautiful. If one had a voice there was no need. Maria Jeritza not only had a great voice, but she was so lovely to look at she could have been a stage star without bothering to sing a note. Maria's personality was something else.

Her Metropolitan debut in 1921 was less than spectacular only because the vehicle she appeared in was the now virtually forgotten opera *The Dead City* by Erich Wolfgang Korngold. Though her personal notices were excellent, it was not until American fans heard her in such operas as *Carmen, The Girl of the Golden West,* and *Thaïs* that she became the popular star that she remained until her retirement from the Met in early 1932.

Jeritza was more than a great beauty with a superb voice. She was also a remarkable actress. Puccini asked her to sing the title role in the premiere of *Tosca.* It was she who first sang "Vissi d'arte" from a prone position, a tradition still followed by many of those essaying the role.

Her repertory was large and the salaries she commanded were huge. Fans threw flowers onto stages wherever she appeared. But while critics and public were wild about her those who appeared with Jeritza often were simply mad at her. The diva's behavior was outrageous. Whenever opera lovers or musicians discuss scene stealing and onstage tricks of the trade the name of Maria Jeritza is sure to be brought up. It is said that a Polish soprano who was the brunt of one of Maria's jokes during a performance in Vienna spat in her face in full view of the audience. Her followers seemed to adore her antics. Her contemporaries made no effort to hide the fact that they did not enjoy working with her. Her temper was nearly as impossible as her professional manners.

Those who did not have to suffer her unpredictable behavior were devoted admirers. Perhaps her greatest fans were those who composed the music she sang. Puccini adored her. The great impresario Max Reinhardt starred her in *Belle Hélene* in 1911 and the following year Richard Strauss asked her to create the title role in his *Ariadne auf Naxos*. Critics wrote of her "luminous intelligence," and "enthralling vitality."

After leaving the Metropolitan Jeritza continued to concertize for a number of years in the thirties and made occasional appearances throughout the country at concerts, and with small opera companies, with great success. It is unfortunate that she marred what would have been a nearly flawless career by appearing in the forties and early fifties when her voice was little more than a suggestion of what fans remembered or could hear on her old phonograph records.

At the end of her career Madame Jeritza appeared once more at the Metropolitan in the role of Rosalinde in *Die Fledermaus* in 1951. *The New York Times* music critic, Harold Schonberg, wrote: "The fabled creature made her entrance looking young, looking as though she had commanded the years to go away. And they crept away, ashamed to touch her."

In 1948 Jeritza married a millionaire manufacturer, Irving J. Seery, her present husband. Previously she had been married to Baron Leopold Popper De Podharagh, an Austrian industrialist; and the Hollywood director, Winfield Sheehan, who died in 1945. Her marriage to the Baron was dissolved in the twenties.

Mr. and Mrs. Seery live in a mansion enclosed by a tall brick wall on Elwood Street in Newark, New Jersey. She still attends the Metropolitan regularly.

In 1967 her homeland honored her with the Golden Ring of the City of Vienna, one of Austria's most coveted awards to artists. When the eighty-year-old prima donna arrived for the presentation her fans were again titillated by what one paper described as a moment in which "the gemutlichkeit was as thick as whipped cream." She looked remarkable and was as flamboyant in manner as ever.

At a recent reception in her honor at the Austrian Consulate in New York. *New York Times*

In 1939, the top male star on the RKO lot.

TIM HOLT

Tim Holt is probably the only movie star born in Beverly Hills. The year was 1918 and his father was Jack Holt, a leading man in the silent era and a successful character actor during the thirties and forties.

When Tim, whose real name is Charles, was ten years old he played his father as a boy in *The Vanishing Pioneer* (1928). His late father never encouraged him to go into movies and Tim did not seem a bit interested in doing so until he graduated from the Culver Military Academy. Up until then about his only mention of Hollywood was when people asked him about his girls and he would complain that whenever he took one home she lost interest in him and got a crush on his dad because he was a movie star.

After the Academy, he joined the Westwood Theatre Guild and got a part in a play produced by and starring Mae Clarke (who still makes an occasional appearance on television). Walter Wanger caught the show and signed him up. Tim's first role was the radio operator in *History Is Made at Night* (1937) with Jean Arthur and Charles Boyer.

His home lot put him in a series of westerns at a time most cowboy stars were middle-aged. He never looked particularly tough and could not sing a note. Still, in a very short time the volume of mail from fans addressed to "Tim Holt, R-K-O" was second only to the queen of the lot, Ginger Rogers. The horsemanship Tim had learned at military school was put to use in a string of oaters that were all money-makers. The only trouble the studio had with their young star was that leading ladies who looked as young as he were hard to come by.

Most of the pictures Holt made during those years are best forgotten. A few of the cheapies, western and otherwise, were: *The Renegade Ranger* (1938) with a young starlet named Rita Hayworth, *Spirit of Culver* (1939) with

116

Freddie Bartholomew,* *Come on Danger* (1941), *West of Tombstone* (1942) with Charles Starrett (now a resident of Laguna Beach, California), and *His Kind of Woman* (1951) with Jane Russell.

When he did manage to break out of the casting rut, however, it was to make a blockbuster. The two really good westerns he made were a couple of the greatest ever made by anybody: *Stagecoach* (1939) and *My Darling Clementine* (1946).

Tim and Terry Kilburn (unmarried and living with his mother in Santa Monica) were part of the *Swiss Family Robinson* (1940). Orson Welles used him in *The Magnificent Ambersons* (1942), which would have been a masterpiece had it been edited by the director rather than the front office. Tim and Bonita Granville (the wife of broadcasting millionaire Jack Wrather) were two of *Hitler's Children* in 1943, the first film to be advertised by a radio saturation campaign. The prize role of his career, however, came in 1948 when John Huston cast him as Curtin in one of the best pictures of all times, *The Treasure of Sierra Madre*.

In 1942 Tim enlisted in the Air Corps. He was discharged in 1945 as a major. He continued to make movies but that fresh boyish quality he had been able to project before the war was gone.

Holt's first two marriages ended in divorce. In 1950 he moved to Hurrah, Oklahoma, where he lives now with his third wife and their three children, Jack, Bryanna, and Jay. For a while he was the sales manager of a radio station in Oklahoma City and the host of a local TV program. Recently he joined Jamco, Inc., a multi-industry company, as an executive.

Meanwhile, back at his ranch in Hurrah, from where he commutes to his office daily, Tim keeps in shape by daily horseback rides. He by no means considers himself retired from films and wants to be ready when a part is offered him. His last movie was *The Time Machine* in 1960.

At his office in Oklahoma City, Oklahoma. *Cliff May*

A scene from one of their two-reelers made in 1922.

SMITH AND DALE

"Dr. Kronkeit and his patient," as they have been known to audiences for over 70 years, were born Joseph Seltzer and Charles Marks in New York City in 1884 and 1882 respectively. Smith was one of thirteen children and had to leave school at the age of twelve to help support his family. He and Dale met one day in 1898 when Dale was riding his bicycle north on Eldridge Street at the same time that Smith was cycling east on Delancey. They have always referred to their first encounter as "a smasher." After a voluble argument a local merchant who was watching with great amusement told them they reminded him of the famous comedy team Weber and Fields. Within two months the pair had worked up a routine doing a buck and wing dance.

Their first tour was of the so-called beer-hall circuit starting from the Chatham Club in Chinatown and ending at Tom Sharkey's on 14th Street. Their act consisted of their dancing while dressed in tattered pants and sweaters.

Dale's brother, who was the manager of the Palace Garden on 13th Street and Third Avenue, got them a job there. They took on the noted honky-tonk pianist Mike Bernard who stayed with them until 1901 when they formed a troupe with Jack Coleman, Johnny Lenhart, Frank Martin, and Will Lester called the Imperial Vaudeville and Comedy Company. They played the Catskills when the Borscht Belt was in its infancy, but most of their engagements were one night stands. It was during this period that they took on the names of Smith and Dale.

A printer had one hundred cards on hand for a team called Smith and Dale that had split before the job was finished. He offered them for only 25¢ each. Unable to resist such a bargain, they took the signs and became Smith and Dale.

In 1902 they joined the Avon Comedy Four with a skit called "The New School Teacher" which went over so well that it became a staple of their act for years. The group went on tour "playing every town in which the train stopped."

In 1914 the Four sailed for England where they were the first all-American act to play the Finsbury Park Empire.

In 1915 they created their classic skit, "A Hungarian Rhapsody." It was in this act that "Dr. Kronkeit" was first introduced. Some of their other popular routines were "S.S. Malaria," "Venetian Knights," "The Last National Bank," "False Alarm Fire Company," and "Real Estators."

In a career that has bridged the Spanish-American War with Vietnam, Smith and Dale have been in every phase of show business. They made silent two reelers, played vaudeville, burlesque, appeared in Broadway shows, revues, and were on radio and television. A few of their shows were *Why Worry* (1916) with Fanny Brice, *The Passing Show of 1919, 1920, and 1921, Mendel, Inc.* (1930), *Crazy Quilt* (1932), *The Sky's the Limit* (1935), *Summer Wives* (1936), *Laugh, Town, Laugh* (1942), and *Old Bucks and New Wings* (1962). On radio they guested with Kate Smith, Rudy Vallee, Ben Bernie, and Al Jolson, and Ed Sullivan had them on several times during the past fifteen years. When the Palace Theatre reverted to a two-a-day vaudeville policy in 1951, Smith and Dale were on the first bill. A few years later they were back at vaudeville's cathedral supporting Judy Garland.

Although in the past two decades, it is more their dated brand of humor that has limited their appearances than their advanced ages, the two have remained close friends. In 1962 when they were told that there was only one role open on a "Trials of O'Brien" TV segment they tossed a coin to see who would do it. Smith won. They are not only alert but actually want to work. Someone asked Smith not long ago if he ever intended to retire and was told: "Yes, every night when I go to bed." Most of their contemporaries have either died or are in complete retirement.

Smith, a widower, resides at the Actors Home in Englewood, New Jersey. Dale lives with his wife on Manhattan's West Fifty-fifth Street.

In 1948 the Lambs Club gave the pair a Golden Anniversary night in their honor and in 1967 they celebrated their seventieth year in show business by doing some of their old skits at the club.

The famous partners at a recent meeting at the Lambs Club. *New York Times*

The Number One box-office attraction in 1926 and 1927.

COLLEEN MOORE

The superstar of the silents was distinctive right from birth in Port Huron, Michigan, in 1902. She had one blue and one brown eye. Her real name was Kathleen Morrison. Her father was a successful engineer.

Colleen maintains that D. W. Griffith did not discover her and that she did not appear in *Intolerance* (1916) as a dancing girl, that they did not even meet until her career was well established. According to her, Griffith arranged for a screen test at the persuasion of her uncle, Walter Hovey, who was then city editor of the Chicago *Tribune*. Hovey was later immortalized by Ben Hecht and Charles MacArthur in their play and film *The Front Page*.

Colleen had a real flair for comedy. She began with *The Bad Boy* (1917) and then made *The Busher* (1919) with Tom Mix. She was with Mix in *Wilderness Trail* (1919) and opposite Sessue Hayakawa in *The Devil's Claim* (1920), opposite John Barrymore, then at the height of his career, in *The Lotus Eater* (1921) and in *Forsaking All Others* (1922) with Cullen Landis. The same year she made *The Ninth Commandment* with James Morrison.

Colleen hit her stride in flapper roles. She made *Flaming Youth* (1923) with Ben Lyon who was with her again in *Painted People* (1924), which had Clara Bow also in the cast. By the time of *The Perfect Flapper* (1924), her Dutch boy bob was the rage throughout the world and her salary was $12,500 a week. The same year she starred with Wallace Beery and Ben Lyon again in Edna Ferber's *So Big*. Her two best remembered vehicles were *Sally* (1925) with Leon Errol and *Irene* (1926). Both were adapted from Broadway hits and the latter had sequences in primitive technicolor and the hit song "Alice Blue Gown," which was played on the piano or organ in theatres running the film.

Along with talent and energy Colleen had the advice and assistance of John McCormack, a onetime studio press agent who became the production head of First National Pictures. She and McCormack were married the day after her twenty-first birthday.

Colleen's drawing power at the box office continued until the advent of sound. Her pictures such as *Ella Cinders* (1926), *It Must Be Love* (1926) with Mary Brian, *Naughty But Nice* (1927), *Orchids and Ermine* (1927), in which Mickey Rooney played an adult midget, and *Lilac Time* (1928) with Gary Cooper were well received. *Lilac Time* had sound effects and a synchronized musical score playing the lovely "Jeannine, I Dream of Lilac Time."

Colleen had a good voice and some meaty roles in a few of her talkies, but somehow it was just never the same. She and Neil Hamilton (the police commissioner on TV's "Batman") did *Why Be Good?* (1929) and a young actor named Fredric March was brought from Broadway to support her in *Footlights and Fools* in 1929. She scored in *The Power and the Glory* (1933) with the late Spencer Tracy and Helen Vincent. William C. deMille was associate producer and "Mickey" Neilan was director for the screen adaptation of *Social Register* (1934), which had been a Broadway vehicle for Lenore Ulric. However, it was a flop. Her final effort *The Scarlet Letter* (1934) was also a failure.

After divorcing McCormack in 1930 Colleen married Albert P. Scott, a New York stockbroker, in 1932. Two years later that marriage was also dissolved. From 1937 until his death in 1966 she was the wife of Homer P. Hargrave, a partner of the brokerage firm Merrill, Lynch, Pierce, Fenner & Smith. They lived together in Chicago where Colleen made quite a social splash. Her doll house on which she lavished over $435,000 over the years has been displayed for many charities. It was built in 1935 and is now on permanent loan to the Museum of Science and Industry in Chicago. Decorated by Hollywood set designer Harold W. Grieve, the house features running water and electric lights. Some of its furniture is carved from precious stones.

Colleen spends much of her time in Rome with trips to Chicago, Hollywood, and New York at least once a year. In 1968 she published her autobiography, *Silent Star,* in which she stated that if she had it all to do over again she would do exactly the same. A staunch Republican, Colleen is the godmother of Governor Ronald Reagan's daughter.

With Mervyn Le Roy today.

In 1947, her face and figure interested more than skating enthusiasts.
Bruno of Hollywood

BARBARA ANN SCOTT

For a little Canadian girl who had a chronic ear ailment and was left fatherless at three, Barbara Ann did all right—she became a world skating queen.

When she was only ten years old the pert blonde won the Canadian Junior Championship. The year was 1939 and Barbara Ann was the youngest ever to win that gold medal. The next year she became the Junior Lady Champion of Canada. Four years later Barbara was crowned Senior Lady Champion of Canada, a title she was to hold from 1944 until 1948. In between there were other victories such as the North American Championship from 1945 to 1947 and the European Championships won in Davos, Switzerland, in 1947 and Praha, Czechoslovakia, in 1948. She took the World Championship in Stockholm, Sweden, in 1948 and again the next year in Switzerland. When in 1948 Barbara Ann Scott was proclaimed Ladies Figure Skating Champion at the Olympics no one was very surprised. Her score was 163.756.

Barbara found smoother skating on the ice than off. Her amateur career was colored by several well publicized controversies. In 1947 when she was training for the European competitions, the European skating authorities passed a rule allowing only Europeans to enter. The officers backed down after a public outcry of "sour grapes," but their fears were well founded because, of course, Barbara won that year and the next. Her other tussle with officialdom was when her home town of Ottawa gave her a welcome—60,000 cheering fans and a new Buick convertible with the license plate No. 47UI signifying her 1947 skating triumphs. Olympic chief Avery Brundage cited the gift as improper and demanded that she return it in order to maintain her amateur standing. After taking the 1948 Olympic title for Canada, however, she was given another car which, having decided to turn professional, she kept.

After turning professional she appeared in *Rose Marie* on the London stage and signed to headline Ice Capades of 1950 when it was still being produced by John H. Harris, a sports promoter with a reputation in the skating world for pettiness and personal abuse of employees. Harris was not able to hold names long. Sonja Henie* and Dick Button have skated for him, but for very short periods. When Arthur Wirtz asked her to star in his Hollywood Ice Revue she jumped at the lucrative offer as well as at the more pleasant atmosphere in his company. Barbara brightened that show for four highly successful seasons beginning in 1952.

During her last year with Wirtz Miss Scott met a Madison Square Garden press agent named Tommy King. They were married on September 17, 1955. After retiring, the Kings moved to Chicago where her husband is now an executive with the famous Merchandise Mart.

The Kings have no children, which has left Barbara with sufficient time to pursue sports and business activities. In the Chicago suburb of Glencoe she owns the Barbara Ann Scott Beauty Salon. She has changed sports and has developed into a top equestrienne. The Kings own two horses and Barbara shows them regularly in and around the Illinois-Wisconsin circuit. In 1966 she garnered sixty-four ribbons and twenty-one first places. She and her husband, once a professional basketball player, are avid golfers, and Mrs. King has been flying her own plane for several years. All this activity has kept her measurements and weight just the same as when she was setting attendance records in skating arenas everywhere.

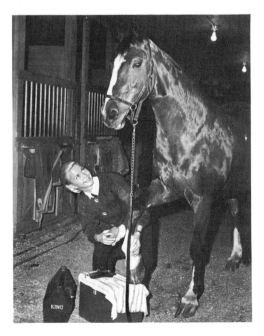

Grooming her bay gelding, Regal Tipper, who won twelve first-place ribbons in the past year.

123

Tarzan's son, with friend "Cheetah" in 1939.

JOHNNY SHEFFIELD

The world's most envied boy-actor was born in Pasadena, California, in 1931. His father was Reginald Sheffield, an English-born actor, who had played the title role in the 1923 silent film version of *David Copperfield*. The family claims a distant relationship to another John Sheffield, one of England's Poet Laureates, and to America's Benjamin Franklin.

Johnny weighed only four pounds at birth and was sickly during the first three years of his life, but his father was a firm believer in exercise and nourishing food and had his son as hale and hearty as any boy his age by the time he was five.

His first role was a plum. He was chosen to play the part of the grandson in the original company of *On Borrowed Time,* a play which began its out-of-town tryouts in Los Angeles before opening on Broadway in 1938. It starred the late character actor, Dudley Digges.

Metro-Goldwyn-Mayer let it be known that it was looking for a boy about seven years old who could not only act the part of a child brought up in the jungle, but one who could go through the grueling paces required of the part. Thanks to the exercises he had been used to since he could walk and the swimming he had learned at the same time, Johnny was hired. When his father told him that he was to play the role of Boy, the adopted son of Tarzan, Johnny yelled "Yip-eeee!" Along with his regular schooling and memorizing of lines for the pictures the young actor was given further swimming lessons by one of swimming's all-time greats, Johnny Weissmuller, who was also to play Tarzan in the films they made together.

In 1939 they made *Tarzan Finds a Son* and *Tarzan in Exile*. As all Tarzan fans know, Boy was found by the Ape Man when he survived a plane crash in the jungle. He was raised by the King of the Jungle and Jane, the King's

124

mate. Some of the other romps Johnny had in the role on the back lot of the Culver City studio were *Tarzan's Secret Treasure* (1941), *Tarzan's New York Adventure* (1942), *Tarzan Triumphs* (1943), *Tarzan's Desert Mystery* (1943), *Tarzan and the Amazons* (1945) *Tarzan and the Leopard Woman* (1946), and *Tarzan and the Huntress* (1947).

Johnny made a few movies in which he appeared in something other than a loincloth: *Little Orvie, Lucky Cisco Kid,* both in 1940 (Duncan Renaldo who portrayed the Cisco Kid for so many years has retired to the Hope Ranch in Santa Barbara, California), and *Million Dollar Baby* (1941) with Priscilla Lane (now Mrs. Joseph A. Howard of Andover, Massachusetts).

After leaving the Tarzan series, Sheffield went to Allied Artists where he starred in his own series as Bomba, the Jungle Boy. The first film was made under that title in 1949. Some of his others were *Bomba and the Lost Volcano* (1950), *Bomba and the Jungle Girl* (1952), and *Bomba on Panther Island* (1953). The pictures did very well as low budget programmers which played mostly as the second half of double bills and as the Saturday matinee feature for kiddies, but when they were re-released for television a whole new generation discovered the character and the fan mail poured in.

In the mid-fifties, however, Sheffield left movies and enrolled as a pre-med student at U.C.L.A. So completely did he divorce himself from his former profession that neither of the studios he worked for even had an address to forward his fan mail. Although he never finished college, neither did he return to making pictures. After leaving school he married, became a father, and added a great deal of weight.

His earnings during the forties and early fifties had been well invested in real estate in Santa Monica, Pacific Palisades, and Malibu. Other than looking after his holdings Johnny does not do much these days besides play with his two sons and swim in the Pacific Ocean, which his Malibu home is set along.

"Boy" as a man—a rather pudgy one at that. *Jon Virzi*

"Spit" in the movie version of *Dead End,* in 1937.

LEO GORCEY

The leader of the Dead End Kids, East Side Kids, and Bowery Boys was born in New York City in 1917. His mother was Irish Catholic, his father Russian-Jewish, an actor, Bernard Gorcey, who played the role of Papa Cohen on Broadway during the twenties in *Abie's Irish Rose.*

Leo came by the accent that was to make him over one million dollars quite naturally during his boyhood in the Washington Heights section of New York City. It was somewhat more refined than the location of *Dead End,* but not much.

During the Depression, Gorcey considered himself lucky when he was able to work as an apprentice in his Uncle Rob's plumbing shop on 23rd Street for the weekly salary of $6. He complained to his father about being refused a raise. The elder Gorcey suggested that he try out for a part in the Sidney Kingsley play which was then being cast. There were a number of parts in *Dead End* for tough-talking young street hoodlums. This was the first time Leo had ever considered following his father's profession. He won the part of Spit who was more or less the leader. The others were Sidney Lumet (now a top Hollywood director), Huntz Hall (who commutes between New York and Florida, and does an occasional TV role. He has a son at Yale), Bernard Punsley (now a Beverly Hills obstetrician), Billy Halop (who works as a male nurse and lives in Pacific Palisades, California), Gabe Dell (a top Broadway comedian and member of Actors' Studio), and Bobby Jordan (who died in 1965). Leo's salary was originally $35. After several critics singled him out as being the best of the group he asked for a raise, which was refused. "There are hundreds of kids on the streets of New York who can play this role," the playwright told Leo. "Ya," answered Gorcey, "well, go out and find one." His next paycheck was for $50.

Samuel Goldwyn bought the screen rights and hired Gorcey and the others (with the exception of Lumet) to re-create their roles. The picture, directed by William Wyler, was released to rave reviews in 1937.

The kids were put under contract to Warner Brothers where they made some of their best pictures. They were with Humphrey Bogart in *Crime School*

(1938), Jimmy Cagney (retired on his farm in Martha's Vineyard) in *Angels With Dirty Faces* (1938), and Ronald Reagan in *Hell's Kitchen* (1939). In 1940 they went to Monogram Pictures where they remained until 1955, by which time it had been changed to Allied Artists Pictures. Some of the "B" features they turned out during those years were *Ghosts on the Loose* (1943), *Bowery Bombshell* (1946), *Bowery Battalion* (1951), and *Bowery to Bagdad* (1955). Leo received star billing over the others in most of the cheapies they made and always was able to command the largest salary. That he was admittedly "the worst actor of the bunch" amuses him greatly. At present there is a possibility of an animated cartoon series utilizing their voices. The project, which was initiated by Huntz Hall, is being discussed by them, but Leo's interest is strictly financial.

When Leo's father, who had played the role of the sweetshop owner "Louie" in many of their films, was killed in an auto accident in 1955, Leo called it quits, and has remained close to his ranch. His only effort of any consequence since then was a small part in *It's a Mad, Mad, Mad, Mad World* (1963).

Leo wrote a book, *Original Dead End Kid Presents Dead End Yells, Wedding Bells, Cockle Shells, and Crazy Spells,* which was published in 1967. It told mostly of his four unsuccessful and expensive marriages.

Leo has custody of his two children, a boy and a girl, who live with him and his mother on the ranch he has owned for many years in Los Molinos, California. The Brandy Lee Ranch has Herefords, pigs, and chickens, with Leo holding forth as gentleman farmer and local celebrity. Not only does he claim not to miss Hollywood, but maintains that he never liked it. Asked what he does with his time he said recently that he thoroughly enjoys his outdoor life and liquor.

His famous manner of speech is as pronounced as ever. Very little of Gorcey's personality has changed since he left Washington Heights for Hollywood and Broadway. When the New York boy who hadn't been to his home town in over twenty years visited Manhattan in 1968, his clothes were so outlandish he was refused service in a neighborhood bar. In his pictures, Spit might have gotten tough with the barkeeper. Nowadays he just makes a joke of it and goes on his way without bothering to show them the loaded revolver he keeps tucked inside his belt.

Huntz Hall, author, and Leo Gorcey (left to right) during Leo's first visit to New York City in over twenty years. *Diana Keyt*

In 1943, America's Number One child star.

MARGARET O'BRIEN

The 1944 special Academy Award winner was born Angela O'Brien in Los Angeles in 1937 to her Irish father and Spanish-Italian mother, dancer Gladys Flores. Her first movie was made for the U.S. government and had James Cagney as her co-star.

Metro-Goldwyn-Mayer put her under contract and she attended their Little Red Schoolhouse on the Culver City lot. The studio chose her parts carefully and Margaret played them for all they were worth. In 1941 she made *Babes in Arms* with Mickey Rooney and Judy Garland. The following year she really came into her own in *Journey for Margaret*.

Miss O'Brien was not funny like Jane Withers or pretty like Shirley Temple, but she had other qualities which she used with the skill of a veteran. Like all child actors she could cry on cue, and when the occasion called for it she could be unbearably cute. And when the scene did not allow for tears or cuteness Margaret, while other actors delivered their lines, could hold her own just by being so itsy-bitsy the audience couldn't take its eyes off her. She had a distinctive acting style which is still imitated today by moppets on television, particularly in commercials.

One of the most precocious children the screen has ever produced, she was published at eleven years of age. Her book was called *My Diary* which she not only wrote but illustrated. She guested on many radio variety shows of the day trading lines with such performers as Bing Crosby and Edgar Bergen. Bob Hope and other comedians had jokes about her. As the nation's top child star, she made numerous public appearances in which she did readings.

While her movie plots differed greatly, M-G-M found a formula which showed her off to the best advantage. Her big scenes usually were with men rather than women, and old men rather than boys. Van Johnson was all right to pose with for publicity pictures because she was too young to make the bobby soxers jealous, but character actors such as Lionel Barrymore, Wallace

Beery, Charles Laughton, Walter Brennan, and Edward G. Robinson were much preferred.

Though it lasted only a decade Margaret made a goodly number of films: *Madame Curie* (1943), *Jane Eyre* (1944) with Peggy Ann Garner, *Lost Angel* (1944), *Thousands Cheer* (1943), *Canterville Ghost* (1944), a memorable musical with Judy Garland and Tom Drake (who is now attempting to reactivate his career after a long bout with alcoholism), *Music for the Millions* (1944), *Our Vines Have Tender Grapes* (1945), *Bad Bascomb* (1946), *Three Wise Fools* (1946), *Tenth Avenue Angel* (1948), *Little Women* (1949), and *Her First Romance* (1951) which attempted to establish her as a teen-age star. The change of image never worked.

In 1955 in another try to reestablish her career, she made *Glory*, about which one critic said, "The only glory in this one can be found in the title." "Glory" was a horse.

Perhaps Margaret's most dramatic and best remembered scene took place in 1947 when her mother married orchestra leader Don Sylvio. Mrs. Sylvio said that her daughter "turned on the tears" and refused to kiss her new stepfather. The morning after, Margaret and her mother left together. There was a reconciliation but the marriage was doomed.

In 1958 *Life* did a cover story on her new career in television—she repeated her role of Beth in a musical version of "Little Women," with mostly good reviews, and starred in a "Studio One" production. Margaret's only picture in the last twelve years was *Heller in Pink Tights* (1960).

Since 1959 she has been married to Harold Robert Allen, Jr., a commercial artist with a Los Angeles advertising agency. They have no children. Margaret occasionally leaves Sherman Oaks to do stock versions of *Under the Yum Yum Tree, Barefoot in the Park, A Shot in the Dark,* and *A Thousand Clowns*.

Under California's Coogan Law most of Margaret's money was put in trust for her. In 1977 she will be able to spend the principal and interest of the $1,000,000 she earned during her childhood.

A big girl now. *Jon Virzi*

In 1935, still one of the world's greatest tenors.

GIOVANNI MARTINELLI

The great tenor from the Golden Age of Opera was the first of fourteen children born to a cabinetmaker in Montagnana, Italy, in 1885. He apprenticed in his father's trade and studied the clarinet. When he was drafted for three years into the Italian Army, his skill with the instrument landed him a cushy job in the band.

While in military service Martinelli and a friend used to imitate phonograph records. His friend would play an instrument and Giovanni would sing. By chance, a vocal coach heard him and took the young soldier to Milan where a group of operatic managers, after hearing him, decided on the spot to finance his training as soon as military service had ended. He made his debut in a Milan concert in 1910.

Early in Martinelli's career the great composer Giacomo Puccini heard of him and brought him to Rome where after an audition he was assigned the role of Dick Johnson in his *The Girl of the Golden West*. While in the Italian capital he met Arturo Toscanini and Guilio Gatti-Casazza. Both were to leave shortly for positions with the Metropolitan Opera Company in New York City —Toscanini as conductor, and Gatti-Casazza as general manager.

In 1913 Martinelli married Adele Previtali and together they sailed for the United States where his friends were to welcome him as an addition to the Metropolitan roster. He made his Met debut on November 20, 1913, in *La Bohème* in the part of Rodolfo.

It is a great tribute to his artistry that Martinelli was so well received by critics and fans, for at the time Enrico Caruso's well deserved reputation eclipsed all other tenors. Without developing a public or private rivalry between the two, Martinelli soon had a large and loyal following all his own. He and Caruso found they had much in common and developed a close friendship, which lasted until Caruso's death in 1921. Both Italians, both tenors from poor families, the two nearly had tragedy in common as well.

Caruso's last performance was in *La Juive,* which Martinelli performed three years later. Martinelli, after that final curtain, was stricken with typhoid fever, lingering near death for several days. His return to the Metropolitan a number of months later was one of the most memorable nights in the history of the now demolished house. Tickets were hawked at outrageous prices. When the curtain rose on *Pagliacci* every seat was filled and standing room had been sold out to capacity. Martinelli's entrance in the role of the clown brought thunderous applause, and with each aria the cheers grew, causing the production to be interrupted over and over again. When he stood before them at the final curtain Martinelli received a standing ovation from the audience, which was more than a welcome home to one of their favorites—his performance that night was one of the highlights of his career.

Although when he joined the Met he had a repertoire of only seven roles, by the time of his twenty-fifth anniversary with the house he was proficient in fifty-seven parts. He is credited with popularizing *Othello,* an opera which until then had been unsuccessful.

Martinelli's career is remarkable not only for its heights, but for its great length as well. When he left the Metropolitan at the end of the 1945–1946 season critics still marveled over his voice. At their peak most tenors have a rather short number of years. Giovanni's voice, however, was strong without a sign of a crack or quaver well into his fifties.

Even after leaving the Met he did not retire. In fact he has never actually left opera. He has performed in many roles during the past twenty years in cities all over the world and still turns out a recording now and then. As late as 1967 he essayed the role of Emperor Altoum in *Turandot* in Seattle.

Now a widower, Martinelli spends his summers on Lake Como ("to be near the home of Verdi"), other months he is in his luxurious hotel rooftop apartment half a block from Carnegie Hall. He attends Metropolitan performances and takes a keen interest in young singers, having several pupils in New York and London whom he coaches. He is the father of two girls and a boy but is the only musician in the family.

As he appears today. *Diana Keyt*

Dizzy Dean at the height of his career. *UPI*

DIZZY DEAN

The boy with the big right arm from the cotton fields of Arkansas who achieved fame as the zany big-league strikeout artist was born in Lucas, Arkansas, on January 16, 1911. He was one of five children of impoverished cotton-pickers. His mother, who died when he was three, named him Jay Hanna after Jay Gould, the fast-dealing Wall Street financier and the famous publisher Mark Hanna. At six, Diz changed his name to Jerome Herman to honor the father of his sick and dying friend. At six, along with his younger brother Paul (or "Daffy," who played with him on the Cardinal team), he was working in the fields, traveling with his brothers and his father from state to state. The boys learned to play baseball from their father, who had played third base professionally in Hartford, Connecticut. He had fashioned his own bats and balls for the boys out of scrap.

Diz joined the army at sixteen, and remained until nineteen, taking a job with the San Antonio Public Service, pitching for the team when he was not assisting reading gas meters. A St. Louis Cardinal scout who saw him play signed him on the spot, and he was shipped to St. Joseph in the Western League where his clowning kept the fans rolling in the aisles while he racked up 17 wins out of 25 starts.

He quickly moved up to the Texas League, in Houston. At an exhibition game against the Chicago White Sox, his great pitching antagonized the big leaguers, but his clowning was too much for the manager of the Sox, who kept screaming, "That dizzy kid is making fools of us." The name stuck. Before the year was out, the Cards brought him up to the major leagues. That was 1930. His first appearance during spring training in 1931 was as a relief pitcher, but as the season got under way he was returned to Houston, winning 26 out of 36 for the year. Following his return to Houston, he met his wife,

Patricia Nash, who has been with him ever since. Recalled by the Cards in 1932, Dizzy was paid $3,000, as he was in 1933. In 1934, he was increased to $7,500 as a result of his 30 wins, increased in 1935 to $18,500, and for 1936 and 1937 combined, $27,500.

On July 7, 1937, in the All-Star game in Washington, a line drive smashed into his left foot. In pain, Diz continued to pitch until he wrenched his arm, and was never the same.

Starting in 315 games, he won 150, and lost 83. He was averaging 22 wins yearly, and 1934, his best year, he took 30 games, losing only 7. However, following his injury, he won a mere 13, in 1937, and was sold in 1938 to the Chicago Cubs, winning 7 and losing 1 that year.

In 1940, after a brief return to the Texas League, he was recalled by the Cubs late in the season to win 3 out of 6. In 1941, he took a job as a broadcaster for the St. Louis games for the Falstaff Brewing Company as a result of having befriended the Falstaff president's invalid son years earlier. He was a great success, joking and clowning between innings and during the action. Some time later, when he came to New York to do the TV broadcast for the Yankees, his employers tried to teach him the king's English, but he continued to fracture it with lines like "he slud into second." In 1952, his life story was the basis for the movie *Pride of St. Louis,* and in the following year he was voted into the Baseball Hall of Fame. By 1958 Diz was ready to throw in the towel on his $62,500-a-year CBS broadcasting job on the big league's Game of the Week.

These days, when not golfing, he delights audiences at dinners with his hilarious malapropisms. He has put on weight, but it suits a man with oil and real-estate holdings in the Southwest. Diz no longer drops water bags from hotel windows. Not long ago, he was so outraged over an estimate he got from a floor-covering store in Phoenix, Arizona, where he was until recently living on his ranch, that he bought the company. He now lives with Pat in Wiggims, Mississippi, and still broadcasts, this time for the Atlanta Braves.

"Ole Diz" during a recent interview.
UPI

His antics in the fifties were watched on television by millions. *NBC TV*

PINKY LEE

The lisping comedian who became a household name through television during the fifties was born in St. Paul, Minnesota, in 1916. From the time he was five years old he was taking dancing, singing, and xylophone lessons. When he was thirteen Gus Edwards made him part of his famous "School Days" act which toured American vaudeville houses. Pinky had to leave when his voice began to change. Returning to school, he had written a serious essay, which he read aloud. The other kids howled with laughter. It was then that he realized just how funny his lisp made things sound. He claims that the impediment is inherited. All of his cousins lisp and have for generations.

By the time Pinky was old enough to go out on his own in vaudeville, the medium was in the doldrums. For a while he teamed up with another young man to do a sailor act. Their agent explained that the act lacked sex appeal. They hired a girl named Dotty. The agent suggested that Pinky, whose real name is Pinkus Leff, take the name Lee and that the act be called "Port, Lee [the two sides of a ship] and Dotty." From then on he was Pinky Lee.

During the thirties he accepted a job in burlesque from Harold Minsky. At first he felt that it was a great comedown, as he had played Loew's State and the Palace, but jobs were few and far between. Burlesque was something that performers came from. One didn't go into it unless one were on the way down. He toured the Eastern and Western Wheels (burlesque terms for circuits) for producer Milton "Be a Booster for Milton Schuster" Schuster.

In 1932 Pinky married Bebe Dancis. The ceremony was in court, after which they were wed at a religious ceremony in St. Paul, and twenty-five years later the Beverly Hills Chief of Police married them again. For this ceremony they were required to take blood tests.

By 1942 Pinky was getting top billing at Earl Carroll's Hollywood theatre-restaurant. He stayed on until 1946 and appeared in the movie *Earl Carroll Vanities* (1945). His first and by far his best was in 1943 when he played the burlesque "banana" in *Lady of Burlesque* with Barbara Stanwyck. Some of his other films were *Blonde Ransom* (1945), *That's My Gal* (1947), and *South Caliente* (1951) with Roy Rogers.

Pinky was an early, big hit on TV. His situation comedy series "Those Two" began on NBC-TV on November 27, 1951, which ran for two years. His first co-star was Martha Stewart who was later replaced by Vivian Blaine. After "Those Two" went off, Pinky switched to a kiddie format with equal success. Betty Jane Howarth was his companion on that program which ended when he collapsed on the air. Many reports called it a heart attack. The truth is, Pinky's sinuses had become so bad that they had poisoned his entire system. Following doctor's orders, he moved to Tucson, Arizona, where the climate improved the condition greatly. In 1966 he returned to Los Angeles and one of the biggest disappointments in his life when, after an expenditure of $183,000 by the producers, *Little World, Hello,* a musical in which he was to have starred, closed out of town. The book was based on the life of the late comedian Jimmy Savo and it was Savo's widow who prevented the show from continuing by exercising an option in the contract.

Pinky and his wife of thirty-five years live in a large, luxuriously furnished apartment in a new development in Culver City, California. They have two children and a grandson. None of whom lisp.

He would like to end his career with a Broadway show, something he has aspired to all his life. He considers himself semiretired, but will work when parts appeal to him, and only for short periods. In 1967 he went out for ten weeks with the Ann Corio show, *This Was Burlesque.*

Interviewed by the author during a
recent trip to Manhattan. *Clifford
May*

In 1937 "Our Gang" posed on the Hal Roach lot. From left to right: Carl "Alfalfa" Schweitzer, Billy "Buckwheat" Thomas, "Spanky" McFarland, Darla Hood, Porky Lee, and Baby Patsy.

DARLA HOOD

The distaff member of the screen's best remembered series of comedy shorts, *Our Gang,* was born in Leedy, Oklahoma, in 1931. Her father was the banker in their town of five hundred. Darla was an only child, whose mother was determined that her daughter was going to be a success in show business. When Darla was only three, Mrs. Hood enrolled her for dancing and singing lessons which were given in Oklahoma City, necessitating a 150-mile round trip once a week.

In 1935, Kathryn Duffy, Darla's coach, took her to New York City on a trip. One night they were dining at their hotel, the Edison, in Times Square, when the orchestra leader asked Darla if she would like to lead the band. The tot guided the group through a number, to the delight of the audience. Afterward Miss Duffy and Darla were joined by Joe Rivkin, a talent scout for Hal Roach Studios. They were looking for a "little sweetheart" for the mischievous boys in their *Our Gang* series. Darla was tested in New York, signed to a nine-year contract, and sent to Hollywood where she was joined by her mother. Mr. Hood commuted as much as possible from Leedy. From 1936 until 1945 Darla appeared in over 150 of the famous shorts.

The "Gang" was tutored on the Roach lot by Mrs. Alma Reubens, who recently died in Hollywood. When the series was sold to Metro-Goldwyn-Mayer they attended the famous "little red schoolhouse" on the M-G-M lot.

Although Darla holds happier memories of Hollywood than most child stars, she admits that being the only girl among a group of preadolescent boys was often quite lonely. While the boys were always nice to her, most of the games they played excluded girls and more often than not she was left alone with her dolls.

Few *Our Gang* pictures were made during World War II because of the shortage of film, which was reserved for feature pictures. By the time they were ready to revive them Darla was too mature for the role. In 1945 she left the group and enrolled at Fairfax High School in Hollywood from which she was graduated as an honor student. She planned to continue her studies at the University of Southern California but Ken Murray offered her vocal group, "The Enchanters," a job in his famous *Blackouts of 1949* which had a long run in Hollywood before it went to Broadway. In 1950 she started the first of four seasons as Murray's leading lady on his TV series. After that Darla made numerous appearances in nightclubs in Las Vegas, San Francisco, and New York.

In 1957 she became the wife of music publisher, José Granson. Darla has a stepdaughter, Robin (18), and two children of her own, Brett (10½) and Darla Jo (8). In 1963 they moved from Los Angeles to Englewood Cliffs, New Jersey. In September of this year they moved to North Hollywood, California.

Darla still receives a great deal of fan mail from children about as old as her own, who watch the series on television under the title of "The Little Rascals." They usually want an autographed photograph. She sends out old stills from the thirties because she has found that the kids are disappointed when they discover she is a grown woman. Nearly all want to know about the other members of the "Gang." Carl "Alfalfa" Schweitzer was killed January 12, 1959. "Buckwheat" Thomas has made a career of the United States Army. "Spanky" MacFarland is the secretary-companion to a Hollywood star. "Porky" Marlowe lives in Duluth, Minnesota.

Asked if her children are impressed that their mother is in the shorts they watch on TV she said, "They take great delight in calling me in from the kitchen to show me how my ruffled panties are showing under what I guess was the first miniskirt in the movies."

Darla works quite often on TV but is seldom seen. Most of her jobs are for dubbing or voice-over work. The best known is probably the Chicken-of-the Sea commercial in which she sings the mermaid jingle.

Author Richard Lamparski interviews the adult Darla Hood. *Clifford May*

A publicity picture of the 1930's.
Metro-Goldwyn-Mayer

RICARDO CORTEZ

A few years ago a book on motion pictures was published that announced with waspish glee that the great Latin lover of the silent screen was really Jake Stein, "a plain American." It is true that Ricardo Cortez's first name was Jacob, though his last name was Krantz. It is also true that he was not born in Spain but to Jewish parents in Vienna in 1899. However, he was anything but "plain."

Cortez came to Hollywood and clicked at a time when Rudolph Valentino was proving to be very difficult. Paramount had placed him on suspension and were looking for another actor with "bedroom eyes" who could replace him if he failed to return to the lot or, after his return, to be held over his head as a threat.

Rival studios were offering the swarthy sex appeal of the late Antonio Moreno and Ramon Novarro* to a public that could not seem to get enough of the dark, brooding virility these stars projected. Moreno, however, was older than the others and his career went back as far as 1913. Novarro got better parts than Cortez but Cortez lasted much longer than Moreno or Valentino and matured more gracefully than Novarro.

Some of the silents in which he had the ladies in raptures, both in the audience and on the screen: *Feet of Clay* (1920), *Sixty Cents an Hour* (1923), *The Spaniard* (1925), *The Swan* (1925), *The Eagle of the Sea* (1926), *The Sorrows of Satan* (1926) with Lya de Putti who choked to death on a chicken bone in 1931, and *The Private Life of Helen of Troy* (1927) with Maria Corda.

When Greta Garbo was brought to this country from Sweden by Metro-Goldwyn-Mayer they borrowed Cortez from Paramount to play opposite her in *The Torrent* (1926), her first American picture. It was the first and last time that anyone was billed over Greta Garbo in any film she made in America.

Cortez underwent more than the usual trauma suffered by all silent stars when talkies proved to be permanent. Not only was he like all the others unsure of how well his voice would record or match the image in the minds of his fans, but he was faced as well with a crisis in his personal life. His wife, the lovely Alma Reubens who had been a star in pictures before and after his career caught fire, was a hopeless drug addict. Cortez had tried his utmost to cure her of the habit. She died in 1931.

Cortez then concentrated on his career and changed his image. He emerged as the suave heavy and in very short time became the kind of man audiences love to hate. He was the head of the mob, the doctor who bilked old ladies, the lawyer who could get you out of any jam. He made dozens of movies during the thirties, among them *Big Business Girl* (1931), *Thirteen Women* (1932) with Irene Dunne,* *Torch Singer* (1933) opposite Claudette Colbert, *Wonder Bar* (1934), in which he made a fool out of Dolores Del Rio while Al Jolson's heart broke, *Secret Agent* (1935) with a young blonde who was about to become famous as Bette Davis, *The Walking Dead* (1936), in which he got his comeuppance from Boris Karloff whom he sent to the electric chair in the first reel, and *Broadway Bad* (1933) with Ginger Rogers and Joan Blondell.

He continued acting in movies into the forties with such features as *Free, Blonde and 21* (1940), *Romance of the Rio Grande* (1941), *Tomorrow We Live* (1942), and *Make Your Own Bed* (1944).

In 1948 Cortez (his brother Stanley Cortez is the cameraman who distinguished such films as *The Magnificent Ambersons* (1942) and *Night of the Hunter* (1955) with his cinematography) tried his hand at directing with *The Inside Story* starring William Lundigan. His last on-screen performance was in a small but memorable part in John Ford's *The Last Hurrah* (1958).

After he began to lose interest in acting, and it was clear that his career as a director was not developing, Ricardo Cortez began to take a serious interest in the stock market. Having done quite well manipulating his own holdings and those of several friends, he joined one of the top brokerage houses in New York where he has developed a large and grateful clientele as a customer's man.

Though the former Latin lover is retired from acting, he has not tired of actors. He can be found quite often at the Lambs Club exchanging stories with contemporaries.

Cortez resides just off Fifth Avenue in the East Seventies only a few blocks from a movie star of the thirties, Johnny Downs, who works as a doorman-elevator operator.

At a recent party with the character actress Ethel Griffies. *Warner Bros.-Seven Arts*

A typical Barnes pose, in 1941. *John Robbins*

BINNIE BARNES

No one ever shot a furtive glance or delivered a caustic comment as well as the actress who was born in London in 1905 with the name Gertrude Maude Barnes. She is of English-Italian descent. Her father was a bobby, and one of Mother's three husbands. Binnie was one of seventeen children in the family.

Her first job was as a milkmaid, which must have made quite an impression because she soon left it to learn nursing at London's Great Northern Hospital. She then became an assistant in a draper's shop but claims to retain a great fondness for cows. When she saw "Tex" McLeod doing a rope spinning act at the Cosmos Club, she got a job working with him. Together they toured South America for a year. By 1928 Binnie had gone out on her own billed as "Texas Binnie" Barnes. She twirled a rope and spun tales about the great cattle ranges of the West she had never seen.

In 1929 she began her stage career with the late Una O'Connor and Charles Laughton in Sean O'Casey's *Silver Tassie*. Her big break came when she got the part of Fanny, the cabaret singer, in Noel Coward's *Cavalcade*. Binnie was brought to Hollywood to repeat her performance in the film version, but the studio decided against her and gave the role to Isabel Jewel.

Miss Barnes returned to England and was cast as Catherine Howard in *The Private Life of Henry VIII* (1933). Charles Laughton won the Academy Award for his portrayal of the title role, and Binnie was seen for the first time by United States audiences. She was brought back to Hollywood, and this time they had work for her. Lots of work. She began with Universal in *There's Always Tomorrow* (1934), which starred Lois Wilson (on AFTRA's board, and a Manhattan resident). Binnie made twenty-six two-reel comedies in England with Stanley Lupino, father of Ida and a top comedian of his day, and *The Private Life of Don Juan* (1934) with Douglas Fairbanks, Sr., before moving permanently to the movie capital.

Whether menacing the hero or trying to break up a marriage, Binnie excelled at both brittle dialogue and looks fraught with vitriol. She managed to bring

140

subtlety and nuance to some very heavy-handed scripts. During the thirties and forties she made *The Lady Is Willing* (1934) with the late Leslie Howard; *Diamond Jim* (1935), in which she played Lillian Russell; *Sutter's Gold* (1936); *The Adventures of Marco Polo* (1938); *Three Blind Mice* (1938) with Loretta Young (who resides in Manhattan, where she is a consultant to a fashion house); *The Divorce of Lady X* (1938) with Laurence Olivier; *Daytime Wife* (1939) with the late Linda Darnell and the late Tyrone Power; *Til We Meet Again* (1940); *The Man from Down Under* (1943); *The Hour Before the Dawn* with Veronica Lake * (1944); *It's in the Bag* (1945) with the late Fred Allen and Jack Benny; and *If Winter Comes* (1948). Her last pictures during this period were *Fugitive Lady* (1951) and *The Decameron Nights* (1952).

From 1931 until 1936 she was the wife of Samuel Joseph, an art dealer and publisher. In 1940 she married former U.C.L.A. All-American football hero Mike Frankovitch, who at the time was a sportscaster. The next year Binnie made the papers when she threatened to sue Columbia Pictures Corporation after being duped by director Alexander Hall into doing a scene in black lace bra and panties for *This Thing Called Love*. According to Binnie, she had been assured that she would be seen on the screen in silhouette. Her new husband was most annoyed, but they both wished that Binnie had let the whole thing drop when newspapers around the country printed a still from the scene showing Binnie in her unmentionables. Twenty years later Mike Frankovitch was one of the production heads of Columbia. They released Binnie's last and only picture in many years, *The Trouble with Angels* (1966). Binnie played a nun. A "Donna Reed Show" was her one excursion into TV in 1963.

The Frankovitchs adopted twins, who are now in the United States Army. The couple have a beautiful home on Hillcrest Drive in Beverly Hills. Binnie says she likes to work only once in a great while, and hasn't the time to miss acting because of all her duties as the wife of a studio executive. "I raise orchids," she said recently, "do gardening, and work on church projects. That's about it." Those are activities for when she is at home. A great deal of the time she travels with her husband, which she likes very much because of the theatre in New York and visits to London, her home town.

A nun in her last motion picture, 1966. *John Monte*

In *The Egg and I*, 1947. *Universal Pictures*

MARJORIE MAIN

In 1890 one of the finest character actresses this country ever produced was born in a small town in Indiana. Her father, a minister, took a dim view of actresses, but somehow his daughter managed to attend a dramatic school for a few years. She changed her name from Mary Tomlinson to Marjorie Main.

She traveled the country for a few years on the Chautauqua circuit, in vaudeville and stock companies. By the time she met and married Dr. Stanley L. Krebs in 1921 Marjorie had developed some excellent sketches and a solid reputation in her profession. While not a star by any means, she played the Palace Theatre and could hold her own with some of the best scene stealers of the day.

Her psychologist husband and she toured the United States together. He gave lectures and she handled the details. In the mid-twenties the Krebs settled in New York City and Marjorie decided to try her luck in the theatre. In 1927 she was with Barbara Stanwyck and Hal Skelly in *Burlesque* and played Mae West's mother in *The Wicked Age*. Her real break came in 1933 when she got a large part in *Music in the Air*. It was the first of three stage vehicles which she was to repeat on screen. The film version (1934) was made with Gloria Swanson and the late Douglass Montgomery but Marjorie's part was far less important than it had been on stage. Her next play was the smash hit *Dead End* in 1935. She stayed on Broadway with it for over a year and did the film in 1937, playing the mother of a gangster (Humphrey Bogart). The scene in which she slaps his face and cries "Ya dirty yellow dog" was so moving that the studios gave her one role after another in which she lived in a tenement with her bad-boy son. Also in the picture was Wendy Barrie, now the hostess of a syndicated radio series.

Marjorie's last stage appearance was in *The Women* in 1936 and again Hollywood made use of her when it was filmed in 1939.

In over eighty films beginning with a bit part in *House Divided* (1932), Marjorie Main never gave a bad performance. She saved many a bad picture and made the good ones better. During the fourteen years she spent under contract to M-G-M such stars as Jeanette MacDonald and Nelson Eddy were delighted to have her liven up their vehicles, such as *Naughty Marietta* (1935). She worked with Barbara Stanwyck in *Stella Dallas* (1937) and supported Clark Gable in *Test Pilot* (1938) and *Honky Tonk* (1941). Ronald Reagan had Marjorie with him in *Angels Wash Their Faces* (1939) and one year later she made *I Take This Woman* with the late Spencer Tracy. Cinema societies still run *The Dark Command* (1940) for the memorable performance she delivered in it. In 1941 she appeared in her first color picture *Shepherd of the Hills*.

Some of Marjorie's other important roles were in *Meet Me in St. Louis* (1944), which also had Lucille Bremmer (now Mrs. Rodriguez of La Jolla, California) in the cast, *Murder He Says* (1945), *The Harvey Girls* (1946), *Summer Stock* (1950), *Rose Marie* (1954), and *Friendly Persuasion* (1956).

In *The Egg and I* (1947) she portrayed Ma Kettle and was nominated for an Academy Award, after which she commanded a salary as large as many stars. She and the late Percy Kilbride made such an endearing pair as the eccentric farm couple they were featured together in nine Ma and Pa Kettle films which in spite of their low budgets and rather raucous humor were some of the biggest money-makers Universal International studios ever made. Her last picture was *The Kettles on Old MacDonald's Farm* (1957).

Marjorie never remarried after the death of her husband in 1935 and is now retired. Although she entered a profession her father did not approve of, she has remained throughout her life deeply religious. She is a firm believer in the Moral Re-Armament movement. She does not smoke or drink and never has.

She is justifiably proud of her career, but seems quite content to spend her time these days enjoying her homes in Los Angeles and Palm Springs. Probably the least pretentious actress in Hollywood, Marjorie does her own cooking and housecleaning which she considers good for her, mentally and physically. It is certainly not for economic reasons. Hard work and frugality were imbued in her as a child and like her midwestern accent, they have never left her.

As she appears today—always smartly dressed. *Jon Virzi*

"The Toy Bulldog," 1920.

MICKEY WALKER

The Toy Bulldog, which is how he was known during his career in the ring, was born in Kereighhead, New Jersey, which is the Irish section of Elizabeth. Mickey attended Sacred Heart School through the eighth grade, which was the end of his formal education. He then became a pin boy at the Elks Club Bowling Alley in Elizabeth and moved from that to a boiler shop of the New Jersey Central Railroad.

His first fight was on Washington's Birthday in 1918 at the local Y.M.C.A. It became so fierce, it had to be stopped.

By 1924, Mickey was getting $20,000 to box Harry Greb at the Polo Grounds. From then on Mickey would have his most colorful and successful years, under the management of "Doc" Kearns, who had also been Jack Dempsey's manager. In 1925 they made a fifty-fifty deal with a handshake and never had a word of disagreement about money after that. Kearns was noted for being a tough bargainer and he had a great deal of money for the Bulldog. Together they spent it all. After Kearns took over, his first fight that year was $100,000 to defend his welterweight crown at the Polo Grounds against Dave Shade. Mickey won in fifteen rounds. In May of 1926 he lost the title to Pete Latzo in Scranton and a month later Joe Dundee KO'd Walker in the eighth round in New York. Mickey thought he was finished. Kearns thought otherwise. On December 26, 1926, Mickey met Tiger Flowers in Chicago for the Middleweight Championship, which Flowers had taken from Greb. The gate was $77,127, the largest Chicago had seen. Mickey won a decision. He got a $110,000 guarantee to fight British Middleweight champ Tommy Milligan in England. Walker took not only the fight with a ten-round knockout but a bet of $440,000 besides. He yearned for a crack at the heavyweight crown and after beating Wilson Yarbo in Cleveland, felt he deserved one. He knocked out Mike McTigue and took a ten-round decision from Paul Berlenbach. After making over a million dollars in a few years he was forced to take $10,000 to fight Tommy Loughran in 1929. Walker lost that one, but his finances were so low that he was happy for the money. In July of 1931 he battled Jack Sharkey in Ebbets Field. The gate was $238,831. A crowd of 33,156 people watched Mickey fight Sharkey, the 2 to 1 favorite, to a draw. King Levinsky followed in 1932, and decked him in the first round of their fight but Mickey won that one, and he then beat the Basque Paolino Uzcudun the same year. Mickey might have gotten the chance at the heavyweight crown he longed for if he hadn't lost a decision in Cleveland to Johnny Risko. Instead he fought the former champion, Max Schmeling,* in Long Island City in 1932. Kearns threw in the towel in the eighth round. Toward the end of 1933 he made a try at the Light Heavyweight title when he fought Maxie Rosenbloom. He lost by a close fifteen-round decision. Then he had a draw in his fight with Bob Godwin in 1934 and lost a ten-round decision to Young Corbett in August of that year. Kearns and Mickey parted company. Kearns had advised him to quit.

But the Toy Bulldog was broke again and so he made a few more tries. He had a draw, lost a decision, and won over a guy rated as a bum. Then he knocked out Paul Pirrone in Philadelphia. He made eight more tries in 1935 which was his last year. The finale to one of boxing's most colorful careers came with a KO from Eric Seeling in 1935.

In his seventeen-year career in the ring, Walker had 141 fights. No one ever complained about going away without their money's worth.

He was always a ladies' man and used to date such lovelies of the day as Lilyan Tashman and Norma Talmadge, both long dead. After he saw Somerset Maugham's *Moon and Sixpence,* he began to paint. His primitives were given a one-man show at a Manhattan art gallery in 1944 and *Esquire* Magazine published many of them in color in one of their issues that year. Mickey has tried to sell his life story to Hollywood on several occasions, without success. In 1967 he retired from his executive position with National Distillers Corporation and now receives a pension. He has four children by previous marriages, and ten grandchildren. Mickey works closely with the poverty program in New Jersey speaking before high school audiences on the art of boxing, refereeing bouts between the youngsters, and advising on recreational facilities.

The man who was twice a world champion, holding the Welterweight title from 1922 until 1926, and the Middleweight title from 1926 until 1931, now lives on East Fifty-second Street in Manhattan with his fourth wife.

Former champions (left to right): Tommy Loughran, Mickey Walker, Jack Dempsey, and Georges Carpentier reminisce at a recent party at the Gallery of Modern Art in New York City. *Paul Cordes*

The forties.

SONNY TUFTS

The actor whose name has become a joke was born into Boston society in 1911. Sonny's father was a banker. His great-uncle, Charles Tufts, was founder of Tufts College in Boston. The first Tufts arrived in the United States from England in 1638. Bowen Charleston Tufts, III, which is his real name, went to Phillips-Exeter and then broke with the tradition of his family by enrolling at Yale rather than Harvard. He was a member of the school's most exclusive and secret senior society, Skull & Bones, and a member of the famed singing group, The Wiffenpoofs. One of his classmates was Winthrop Rockefeller.

During his years at the university Tufts had altogether five different bands, which he led at Yale and neighboring colleges. Sonny was also the vocalist for each group. His best received, most often sung numbers were "Sweet Sue" and "Egyptian Ella." He spent six months studying voice in Paris before World War II broke out, and trained for another three years on his return and even had an audition at the Metropolitan.

In 1938 he landed a part in the musical *Who's Who* on Broadway, which he followed in 1939 with *Sing For Your Supper*. Sonny sang at supper clubs and hotels such as the Glass Hat, the Belmont Plaza, the Beachcomber, in Manhattan, and the Patio, in Palm Beach.

Lex Thompson, a millionaire sportsman who had been a year behind Sonny at Yale, suggested he try his luck in Hollywood and offered to back him financially. Tufts signed a contract with Thompson for a weekly salary in return for a percentage of his future earnings. Another friend, Jack Donnelly who was a Hollywood hotel manager, introduced him to Joe Egli, Paramount's casting director. Sonny screen-tested in a scene from the Charles Boyer film *Love Affair* in which he felt uncomfortable and played the whole thing as a gag. The result was a Paramount contract and a role in *So Proudly We Hail* (1943), in which he played Kansas under Mark Sandrich's direction.

College football injuries kept him out of the war and there was a great short-age of younger leading men because of the draft. Tufts was 6 feet 4 inches with blonde hair and blue eyes. He caught on as a well-meaning but fumbling big guy and never changed his image. The films in which he appeared were *Government Girl* (1943) with Olivia de Haviland, *I Love a Soldier* (1944) with Paulette Goddard, *Here Come the Waves* (1944), *Bring on the Girls* (1945), *Miss Susie Slagle's* (1946), *Swell Guy* (1947), and *The Seven Year Itch* (1954). In the late forties as the stars returned to Hollywood and younger men came up Tufts was nearly finished.

In 1950 several ladies accused him of having bitten them in the thigh. One, the dancer-stripper Barbara Gray Atkins, sued him for $25,000. Two weeks later dancer Marjorie Von sued him for $26,500 in a similar action. Miss Von claimed a three-inch contusion. There were more arrests for drunkenness. Once he was found by police unconscious on the sidewalk, being nursed by a shapely blonde.

In 1951 the former Barbara Dare, a Spanish dancer Tufts had married in 1938, sued him for divorce. They had been separated for two years.

In 1963 Sonny played the father of Doug McClure in the TV show "The Virginian." Seventeen years ago he had played the McClure role in the movie version starring Joel McCrea.

Tufts has made two hard tries at a comeback. The first was in 1955 when he got the male lead in *Ankles Aweigh,* a musical with Betty and Jane Kean. Just before the Boston opening, he was dropped because his part "just didn't come off." In 1959, after staying sober for a year, he lost the part of Jim Bowie that he wanted so badly in John Wayne's *The Alamo.*

In 1966 he was a "trivia guest" on a TV special. The same year he was a guest on the Merv Griffin Show. As he walked on comedienne Totie Fields suggested that he sit down before he fell over, and the band played "Show Me the Way to Go Home." After taking a lot of kidding, he said to one of the guests, "You're really a young Sonny Tufts." It got a big laugh except from the actor he said it to—Tab Hunter.

Sonny is unmarried and lives in Hollywood. He says he made and spent over $2,000,000 and had a lot of fun doing it.

The sixties. *Jon Virzi*

A publicity still from 1928.

FAY WRAY

The girl King Kong took such a shine to was born on her father's ranch, "Wrayland," in Alberta, Canada, in 1907. While still a small child, she moved with her parents to Los Angeles, and attended Hollywood High School where she took part in the annual Hollywood Pilgrimage Play.

The first time Fay tried to get into the movies her mother accompanied her to the casting office of Century studios. She was refused rather curtly. Just as they were leaving the lot a producer spotted the teen-ager and offered her a small part in a comedy. She continued to do bits and extra work until Erich von Stroheim picked her from a line of bathing beauties in 1926 to star in his lavish production, *The Wedding March*. It was a choppy but memorable silent film with some splendid photography. It was released in 1928 and Fay became a star.

Fay had no faith in her career in talkies. When she made *The Texan* with Gary Cooper in 1930 they both thought they had no future in the medium. The same year she co-starred with Richard Arlen in *Sea God,* and then appeared with Ronald Colman as her leading man in *The Unholy Garden* (1931). In 1933 she was seen in such thrillers as *Vampire Bat* and *Mystery of the Wax Museum* with Glenda Farrell. Her co-stars, Joseph Schildkraut, and Leo Carrillo in *Viva Villa* (1934) are dead, as is Constance Bennett who headed the cast of *The Affairs of Cellini* which Fay did in 1934 with Fredric March. The next year she went to England where she starred in two films, *Alias Bulldog Drummond* and *The Clairvoyant* with the late Claude Rains. Her pictures were mostly programmers after that. In 1936 she was in *They Met in a Taxi* and *Roaming Lady*. In 1937 she starred in *Murder in Greenwich Village* and *It Happened in Hollywood*. Toward the end of her career she was reduced to playing in such "B" films as *Smashing the Spy Ring* (1939), *Navy Secrets* (1939), and *The Wildcat Bus* (1940).

Fay Wray was assured of movie immortality the day she accepted the role in *King Kong* (1933), although she claims she had no idea of the plot when the contract was signed. The superb special effects and fine photography made believable the story of a mammoth gorilla who falls in love with a pretty redhead. It is one of the largest grossing pictures in cinema history and has been revived by R.K.O. over and over again. In one theatre in Africa it played over twenty years.

Fay never succeeded on Broadway despite her valiant efforts as an actress and playwright. Her first try was in 1931 in *The Brown Danube* and again the same year her first husband John Monk Saunders, wrote *Nikki* for her. It was sold to the movies, but the late Helen Chandler got the role. In 1939, a year after her divorce from Saunders, Fay collaborated with Sinclair Lewis on *Angela Is 21,* but it never made it to Broadway. Her last play was *Golden Wings* in 1941.

In 1942 Fay married the scenarist Robert Riskin who wrote *It Happened One Night.* There was a rumor of a serious romance with Howard Hughes but the Riskin marriage squashed the speculation. Upon this second venture into matrimony, Fay announced that she was retiring from the screen. Not until after Riskin's death in 1955 did she accept another part.

Part of the reason for her reactivated career in the fifties was the sale of *King Kong* to television. Once again she was "a name" to young people who were not even born when the picture was originally shown. Her comeback was less than sensational. She did a few TV programs and played Jane Powell's mother in *Small Town Girl* (1953). Her last film was *Hell on Frisco Bay* in 1955.

In the past few years Hollywood's most menaced lady has spent a lot of time traveling. She has never remarried and lives alone in her home on Tigertail Road in the Brentwood section of Los Angeles. It hangs over a cliff and has a spectacular view of the city. The fan mail still pours in from around the world where *King Kong* is still being shown in theatres and on TV. Most of it is from adolescent boys.

In her Brentwood home. *Jon Virzi*

A publicity shot from 1939.

ANDY DEVINE

The gravel-voiced comedian was born in 1905 in Flagstaff, Arizona. His grandfather was Admiral James Harmon Ward, one of the founders of Annapolis and a tutor of Admiral Dewey. Andy's father was the owner of a hotel. While at Santa Clara University, he made quite a name as a football player. He also attended Arizona Teachers College for awhile. After leaving school he played pro football for a time and was also a lifeguard, telephone lineman, and news photographer.

Andy came to Hollywood in 1925 with the purpose of becoming a movie actor. His first job was as an extra in *The Collegians* (1927). He was doing quite well as a featured player, with such credits as *Red Lips* (1928) and *Hot Stuff* (1929), when the talkies came in. Most people in Hollywood, including Andy, felt that he had no career in sound films because of his very peculiar voice, which he has had since childhood. He had been playing with a curtain rod pretending it was a horn, when he fell, driving the rod through the roof of his mouth. For a full year he couldn't speak at all. When he finally did talk it was a duotoned sound with more than a slight wheeze. In 1931, however, he got a comedy part in *The Spirit of Notre Dame*. The raspy quality of his voice coupled with his girth and natural comic ability enhanced his effect. From then on his voice was a very valuable trademark.

Most of Devine's pictures were made during his seventeen years under contract to Universal. Some of those from the thirties and forties were *All Quiet on the Western Front* (1930), *Tom Brown of Culver* (1932) with Tom Brown (who resides in Sherman Oaks, California), *Dr. Bull* (1933) with Will Rogers, *Gift of Gab* (1934) with Edmund Lowe (now a resident of the Motion Picture Country Hospital), *Chinatown Squad* (1935) with Valerie Hobson (married to John Dennis Profumo, the central figure in the international scandal), *Coronado* (1935) with Johnny Downs, *Way Down East* (1935) with Rochelle Hudson (who is a realtor in Los Angeles), *Romeo and Juliet* (1936), in which he played Peter, *A Star Is Born* (1937), *In Old Chicago* (1938) with Alice

Faye, and *Stagecoach* (1939), probably his best role. Andy was a frequent guest on Jack Benny's radio program, usually featured in the "Buck Benny Rides Again" skits. In the early forties he was a regular on "Al Pierce and His Gang" and did many guest stints on "Lum 'n' Abner."* He continued with pictures, appearing in *Ali Baba and the Forty Thieves* (1944) and *Sudan* (1945). He became less active thereafter turning out such clinkers as *Michigan Kid* (1947) and *Ranchero* (1948). In 1951 he made *The Red Badge of Courage.*

For six years beginning in 1951 Andy played Guy Madison's sidekick Jingles on the "Wild Bill Hickok" TV series. He wisely accepted a meager salary while insisting on a 10 percent share of the gross. It turned out to be most profitable role he ever played.

In 1957 Andy made his stage debut playing "Cap'n Andy" in Guy Lombardo's production of *Show Boat* at Jones Beach, repeating the role in 1958 at the St. Louis Municipal Opera House. Andy had his own TV series "Andy's Gang," which was syndicated in 1956 and 1957. In 1966 he was seen on five episodes of "Flipper." In 1967 he did *My Three Angels* at the Cherry County Playhouse in Traverse City, Michigan.

His last features have been *The Man Who Shot Liberty Valance* (1962), *How The West Was Won* (1962), *Zebra in the Kitchen* (1965), and *The Ballad of Josie* (1967) with Doris Day. It was so bad it played as the second half of double bills.

For a few years he was the honorary mayor of Van Nuys, California, where he had bought a five-acre ranch at a time when the whole area looked like a location for one of his westerns. Today he spends most of his hours in his home in Newport Beach, California. Unlike many of the old residents of the San Fernando Valley, Andy doesn't complain about the shopping centers and apartment houses that have been built everywhere. Whenever anyone asks about them he laughs and says he can't say much since most of the land they are built on was sold by him.

The comedian has been married since 1933 to Dorothy Irene House. Their two sons, Denny and Tod, appeared with their father in *Canyon Passage* (1946).

A judge in his last movie, *The Ballad of Josie. Universal Pictures*

In the 1930's, his was one of the best known voices on radio and phonograph records. *NBC Radio*

MORTON DOWNEY

Although he was known variously throughout his long career as "The Golden Voiced Irish Tenor," "The Irish Troubadour," and "The Irish Nightingale" among others., Morton Downey was not from Ireland at all, having been born in 1902, in Wallingford, Connecticut. His father, who had been born in Ireland, was Wallingford's fire chief and a tavern keeper.

Downey began singing in small clubs and smokers to supplement his wages as a candy butcher on the New Haven Railroad. But his first professional appearance, at the age of nineteen, was in a little theatre in Sheridan, where he was picked out by a talent scout for Paul Whiteman. He thus became the first band vocalist per se, for until then all singers were expected also to play an instrument. The step was so unheard of that he was given a dummy saxophone in order to look like a bona fide member of the orchestra. He left the band in 1926 when he was signed by Ziegfeld for *Palm Beach Nights* in Florida.

Following this he went on his own to London, singing at the Kit Kat Club and at the Café de Paris. From London he went to Paris, Berlin, and the French Riviera, gaining an international reputation.

Upon his return to New York City, he opened his successful Delmonico Club, where he entertained and hosted the café society of the day.

Hollywood beckoned in 1929, and he made *Syncopation,* in which he sang the hit song "I'll Always Be in Love with You" to his co-star Barbara Bennett (of the famous acting family including father Richard and sisters Constance and Joan) whom he married on completion of the picture. He made another film that year, *Mother's Boy.* His only other film was made in 1930, *Lucky in Love.* Movies, however, did not seem to be suitable for him. For one thing he tended to be heavy, which seemed to make him an unlikely romantic lead. Radio on the other hand offered him his greatest success, and when he was

152

signed by CBS in the early thirties he competed favorably with the champs of the day. He sang successively for Camel, Woodbury, and Pall Mall, and at the peak of his career he received as many as 95,000 fan letters a week, earning, with theatre and nightclub appearances, as much as $250,000 a year.

During the New York World's Fair of 1939–40, he was the featured singer at Billy Rose's famous Aquacade. The following year he was signed by the Coca Cola Company for a daily radio program, singing with the Raymond Paige Orchestra. Thus began a lucrative association. He was soon to become president and director of the Coca Cola Bottling Company of New Haven (only one of his many business affiliations over the years, for Downey is or has been on the boards of such organizations as the Coronado Publishing Company, the American News Company, the Federal Bank and Trust Company, part owner of Sortilege, and many others).

His first TV appearance was in 1947, and two years later he had his own show on NBC, sponsored by a carpet company. In 1952 he was again sponsored by Coca Cola, which signed him to an exclusive five-year contract covering all radio and TV appearances.

His marriage to Barbara Bennett ended in divorce in 1941 after twelve years of home life and five children. After a bitter court dispute he won custody of the children. The battle was renewed in 1951, shortly after his marriage to heiress Margaret Boyce Thompson Schulze, the daughter of Margaret Schulze Biddle. However, Barbara, who in the interim had remarried, lost again. Barbara died in 1958. Three years later Margaret's first marriage to Prince Hohenlohe of Poland was annulled by the Catholic Church, and Downey and she were married in a religious ceremony. Following breast surgery, she died in 1964 at the age of forty-two, twenty years younger than her husband.

In recent years, his professional activity has been nil. The professional Irishman is much closer to the horsey set than to his former colleagues in show business. Morton has not remarried and lives on a large estate in Wallingford, Connecticut.

The widower in his Connecticut home. N.Y. *Daily News*

Circa 1932.

GENE AUSTIN

The man who wrote and recorded "My Blue Heaven"—one of the biggest selling records of all time—was born in Gainsville, Texas, in 1900 and raised in Louisiana.

Gene had been knocking about in vaudeville and making phonograph records since 1923, but when he walked into a studio and cut "My Blue Heaven" on September 14, 1927, he was still a pretty obscure performer. It had no special arrangement and no elaborate accompaniment. What is more, radio had at that time come into its own and was the medium from which new stars were merging. The record business was in serious trouble. In spite of all these obstacles, the song hit and hit big—for 7,000,000 copies, and it provided him with the first gold record ever awarded. It is now in The Smithsonian Institution. It was over twenty years before Bing Crosby's "White Christmas" pushed it from first place as the biggest-selling record of all time.

Today's generation mostly knows Gene as the man associated with "My Blue Heaven," but he didn't stop there. He penned and performed such standards as: "Five Foot Two, Eyes of Blue," "Ramona," "When My Sugar Walks Down the Street," "Those Wedding Bells Are Breaking Up That Old Gang of Mine," "That Lonesome Road," "How Come You Do Me Like You Do, Do, Do," and "Sleepy Time Gal."

Austin caused less swooning than Vallee, Crosby, and Columbo, who followed him and to some degree copied his style. (His weight problem worked against him in personal appearances.) He sang regularly on radio during the thirties, but he never really clicked on the air, and by 1937 when he became the regular vocalist on the "Joe Penner Show" the recording business had been in the doldrums for some time.

Gene took it philosophically. He was still able to write songs and his royalties were huge—his records, altogether, have sold over 87,000,000 copies. He made brief appearances in such pictures as *Gift of Gab* (1934), *Sadie McKee* (1934) with Joan Crawford, and *Klondike Annie* (1936). In the latter he wrote a song at the request of the star, Mae West, who told him she wanted something "Chineseie and yet sexy." What he came up with was one of her greatest numbers, "I'm an Occidental Woman in an Oriental Mood for Love." He also made a series of one-reelers for RKO.

In the late thirties when he was traveling the country making personal appearances his advance man was the colorful promoter, Colonel Tom Parker, who twenty years later hit it big managing another southern boy by the name of Elvis Presley.

Gene likes to travel and gamble which is what he has been doing since he went into semiretirement in 1940, making occasional club appearances. It may account also for the fact that he has gone through four wives. Fortunately, many of his songs have become standards and he can afford the extravagance that he is known for. In 1947 he located in Las Vegas which is still more or less his home base, although the only house he has there is an elaborate trailer named "My Blue Heaven." Also, for a few years, he had a gambling casino by that name.

In 1957 NBC presented a one hour dramatization of Austin's life in which the star was played by George Grizzard. There has been talk of a movie on him, but nothing firm.

In 1962 Gene headed the ticket in the Nevada gubernatorial elections, with Jimmy Durante's old partner, Eddie Jackson, as a running mate. They were defeated by the late Rex Bell, former cowboy star who was married to Clara Bow. Before that, Gene had campaigned in Louisiana for another singer-composer, his friend, Jimmy "You are My Sunshine" Davis, who was elected governor.

The man who once sent RCA Victor stock soaring by his string of hits can still be persuaded to sing a little at clubs in Las Vegas and New Orleans. Now a grandfather and well off through his royalties, though still traveling and gambling around the country, Gene is often kidded about the incongruity of his life, considering that his first and biggest hit was about the coziest song ever written. He just laughs and repeats what he has been saying for years, "I never want to nest anywhere."

The author of "Yes, Sir, That's My Baby" surrounded by current admirers in a Las Vegas nightclub. *Bernie Foyer*

In 1926, one of the most promising stars under contract to the director Thomas Ince, who was killed mysteriously aboard William Randolph Hearst's yacht.

JACQUELINE LOGAN

The smoky-eyed beauty of the silent screen was born in Corsicana, Texas, in 1904. Her father was a popular architect and her mother, who had a brief career in opera, did vocal coaching.

She was taken to Colorado Springs for her health where she took courses in journalism from future baseball commissioner Ford Frick (now one of her Westchester County neighbors). Her mother continued giving voice lessons. One of her pupils was Lowell Thomas.

Jacqueline set off to an uncle in Chicago, presumably for college. Instead she got a job dancing in the stage production of a local theatre, lying about her age. Her uncle was furious, resulting in her being let go. Again she lied and traveled to New York City with a theatrical troupe, landing a small part in *Flora Dora,* a Broadway musical of 1920. She was seen by Flo Ziegfeld who offered her a job dancing on his famous Ziegfeld Roof, replacing Billie Dove who had just gotten a Hollywood contract. There were also many modeling jobs including the prestigious Dobbs Girl in Alfred Cheney Johnston photographs and a Johnny Hines' comedy short. Soon she was given a screen test, which she made with another unknown named Ben Lyon (married to Bebe Daniels*).

In 1921 Associated Producers put her opposite Monte Blue in *The Perfect Crime,* which included a lovely blonde child actress named Jane Peters, later known as Carole Lombard. In 1921 she supported Mabel Normand in *Molly O* and had superstar Thomas Meighan as her leading man in *White and Un-married.* Milton Sills protected her in *Burning Sands* (1922) and Ricardo Cortez was with her in *Sixty Cents an Hour* (1923). Leatrice Joy* headed the cast of their C. B. De Mille film *Java Head* (1923). In 1925 she played opposite the late Richard Dix in *A Man Must Live* and the following year Jacqueline and William Powell made *White Mice* in New York and Cuba. She and the late Louise Fazenda were in *Footloose Widows* in 1926, the next year she co-starred with Richard Arlen* in *Blood Ship.* Her other leading men, all of whom are deceased, were Lionel Barrymore, John Barrymore, Antonio Moreno, and Lon Chaney, Sr.

C. B. De Mille chose Miss Logan for the coveted role of Mary Magdalene in the religious classic, *The King of Kings,* which holds the record for audiences. It alone has been shown somewhere in the world every day since it was first released in 1927. Dubbed voices have been added. Not only does the film now carry the voice of the lady who played the silent part but the major editing also was done by Jacqueline before the talkie version was released.

Jacqueline never really made it in the new medium. She was a member of the all-star cast of the early musical *Show of Shows* (1929), after making several early and successful sound films for Columbia.

She went to England and received good notices for stage performances, such as in *Smoky Cell.* Her English picture *Middle Watch* was given a Command Performance and she was signed by British International to write and direct. When *Knock-Out* (1931), which she wrote, and *Strictly Business* (1931), which she wrote and directed, were hits, she returned to Hollywood hoping to continue her career behind the camera. Harry Cohn, production head of Columbia Pictures at that time, admitted they were good films but was unwilling to sign a female to direct. Jacqueline appeared in a few Broadway plays such as *Merrily We Roll Along* and *Two Strange Women* before she married in 1934 and retired completely.

She has been living in Westchester County ever since but she and her industrialist husband were divorced in 1947. Her winters are spent in Florida where she visits with her old friends Lila Lee* and Dorothy Dalton. The rest of the year Jacqueline and her prize Great Dane from the Lina Basquette Kennels are to be found in Bedford Hills, New York. All of her time is devoted to what she feels are her civic duties: "I am concerned about the One Worlders and the Treason Traders who are disrupting the Constitution and selling us down the river. It isn't easy to be a patriotic dissenter. It helps to be a member of the John Birch Society."

Today a fighter for right-wing political causes. *Ing-John*

Doing her theme song from Dohnán-yi's "Children's Suite," 1931. *NBC*

IREENE WICKER: "The Singing Lady"

The petite radio pioneer was born in Quincy, Illinois. She studied journalism, drama, and mythology at the Universities of Florida and Illinois. Thereafter she settled down in Chicago which at that time was the center of radio in the United States, and married a business executive. After having two children, a boy and a girl, Ireene went into radio.

She began her broadcasts for children over WGN in Chicago in 1931. In six months the program was picked up by the Blue Network. (At that time NBC had a Red and a Blue Network, the latter becoming ABC after the Justice Department forced the split.) Her first sponsor, and the one that stayed with her for many years, was Kellogg cereals. Someone in the company's advertising agency suggested that she have a title and they hit on "The Singing Lady." At that time in radio, titles were very popular. Many artists dropped theirs, such as Lanny Ross,* who was billed for a time as "The Troubadour of the Moon." Ireene, however, was as well known for her title as for her real name throughout all her years on radio.

Her name was originally spelled Irene, but when she was about to go into radio an astrologer told her that by adding an "e" she would reap great rewards.

A generation of children and many adults who refuse to admit it were mesmerized by the lady who told them of princes, dragons, Indians, and animals that spoke. Ireene took her material from the classics, folklore, history, and well-known fairy stories. They were usually instructive and had a moral, but were always beautifully told. More times than not the programs would contain portions which were sung by Miss Wicker. On the network for over twenty years, "The Singing Lady" won every major award in broadcasting, including the coveted Peabody Award.

Then in 1950 at the height of the McCarthy hysteria, a Right Wing newsletter ran an article stating that Ireene Wicker had once signed a petition sponsoring Benjamin Davis, a New York Communist politician. And in case that did not prove that "The Singing Lady" had been subverting the minds of American children for two decades, they accused Miss Wicker of having loaned her home in 1945 to aid the refugees of Spain who had fled Franco.

Ireene's lawyer obtained a court order to examine the petition in question which contained over thirty thousand names. Her name was not included. As for the Spanish refugees, what *Counterattack,* the publication that had brought the charges, neglected to mention when accusing her of aiding the Loyalist cause in Spain was the fact that her home was opened as a benefit for any child in or out of Spain who was in need. Lest there still be doubts, Miss Wicker's counsel reminded *Counterattack* that in 1939, at the time of the Hitler-Stalin Pact, she signed the necessary paper for her only son, Walter, to join the RCAF. The boy was underage and needed his parent's consent. He was killed in action in 1942.

The reply of the paper that had set out to rid the arts of subversives was: "*Counterattack* wishes to repeat that we did not call Miss Wicker or any other person mentioned in the report a Communist or a Communist sympathizer."

Suddenly, in spite of conclusive proof to the contrary, one of radio's most popular performers was "controversial." The TV show she had signed to do was canceled. Three years later she had another one on ABC television, but it did not last long.

Ireene divorced her first husband in 1936. Five years later she married the director and owner of one of the most successful and prestigious art galleries in the country, Victor Hammer. Her daughter is married and lives in Connecticut. The Hammers travel a great deal. In 1966 Ireene toured Asia and Europe. Much of their winters are spent in Palm Beach, Florida. They live in a palatial co-op on Fifth Avenue overlooking Central Park. It is filled with priceless art, and their toy poodle.

She does a program on Sunday mornings over WNYC in New York.

Beneath a $450,000 Renoir in her Manhattan apartment. *Diana Keyt*

In 1947, in *Out of the Blue.*

ANN DVORAK

Ann McKim (her real name) was born in New York City in 1912 to Anna Lehr, a well known stage actress of the time, and Sam McKim, then a director at the old Biograph Studios. Ann's early schooling was at St. Catherine's Convent in Manhattan. Later she attended Page School for Girls in Los Angeles. In 1920 her parents were divorced, and Ann stayed with her brother. It was fourteen years before she saw or heard from her father again. By that time she had changed her name to Dvorak, which was her mother's maiden name. (She had used Anna Lehr for a short time, but gave it up when she signed a contract with R.K.O.)

During an interview in 1934 Miss Dvorak said that she would like very much to see her father again, but had no idea where he was. She asked readers to send her any information they might have, resulting in six immediate replies from men claiming to be her father. A seventh letter turned out to be the real Sam McKim. He was living in Philadelphia, and seldom went to the movies.

Ann's first jobs in Hollywood were as a chorus girl in early musicals. For a while she was a dance coach at M-G-M. After Page School she had written, directed, and acted in a few plays, but her only ambition was to be an actress. Her friend Joan Crawford introduced her to Howard Hughes who was looking for a girl to play in his production of *Scarface* (1932). Hughes put her under contract at $250 a week. After the picture was made he sold her contract to Warner Brothers. At first she had no objection. Then while making *Three on a Match* she discovered that the child actor Buster Phelps was earning twice her salary. She demanded a raise, which was refused because they had paid Hughes a goodly profit on her contract. She had recently eloped with the British actor Leslie Fenton, and now they went to Europe together, leaving Warners to think it over. When she returned a year later, it was with a boost in salary and the respect of almost every contract player in Hollywood.

Whether it was revenge or just poor judgment, the studio either gave her bad parts or bad pictures, or both. In film after film either she was over-shadowed by superstars or saddled with a hopeless plot. Although Bette Davis' performances in the two films she made with Ann, *Three on a Match* (1932) and *Housewife* (1934), seem ludicrous today, Miss Davis came away with all the attention. Even her leading man, the late Paul Muni, in *Scarface* and *Dr. Socrates* (1935), seems dated on the TV "Late Show" while Ann's underplaying and controlled intensity prove her a far better actress than believed. She made believable lines that most actresses would have choked on in clinkers such as *Away to Love* (1933) with Maurice Chevalier and *Murder in the Clouds* (1934) with Lyle Talbot. She supported Jimmy Cagney in *The Crowd Roars* (1932) and *G-Men* (1935). Some of her other leading men were Dick Powell, Errol Flynn, David Manners,* Pat O'Brien, Rudy Vallee, Douglas Fairbanks, Jr., and the late Richard Barthelmess.

In 1940 Ann went to England to be near her husband, and stayed on in London through the blitz. While there she made *This Was Paris* (1942) with Ben Lyon, *Escape to Danger* (1944), and *Squadron Leader X* (1942). Ann was divorced in 1944, and returned to Hollywood. In 1947 she married dancer Igor de Navrotsky. The marriage ended in divorce four years later.

In 1948 Ann starred on Broadway in *The Respectful Prostitute,* which ran for 314 performances before it went on the road. Her postwar movies were not much better than those she made while under contract. In 1947 she was in *The Affairs of Bel Ami* and with Henry Fonda in *The Long Night.* Her screen career ended in 1951 with *I Was An American Spy* and *Secret of Convict Lake.*

With her third husband, architect Nicholas Wade, she changed her primary residence from Malibu to Honolulu in 1959. Her husband had planned to live in Italy where he had designed several theatres. (Ann agreed, providing they spend two weeks in Hawaii before deciding!) Much of their time is spent traveling in Europe and the Orient, with long stays in their Malibu house. The Wades have no children. They are avid bibliophiles, and have a large and very valuable collection of first editions dating back as far as 1703.

At home today.

One of Hollywood's top leading men in the forties.

DENNIS MORGAN

The Hollywood leading man of the 1940's was born in 1910 in Prentice, Wisconsin, of Swedish parents. He acted in Marshfield High School plays and sang in the Glee Club. While attending Carroll College in Waukeska, Wisconsin, he was a member of the football team. At both the Wisconsin Conservatory of Music in Milwaukee and the American Conservatory in Chicago he studied voice. During his Chicago days he roomed with another hopeful, John Carroll (who is involved in a construction company in Slidell, Louisiana).

Morgan's first break came when he got a job singing at the Palmer Hotel in Chicago. After that he was for a time a radio announcer on station WTMJ and did a couple of seasons in stock. While traveling with an operatic group, for which he sang *Faust* and *Carmen* he came to the attention of the late Mary Garden who arranged for him to have a screen test at Metro-Goldwyn-Mayer. He was placed under contract and sent to the Culver City lot.

For two years he did absolutely nothing, but continued to draw a very good salary. Finally, they decided to have him sing "A Pretty Girl Is Like a Melody" in the now famous finale of *The Great Ziegfeld* (1936). Dennis was amazed at the premiere when he saw himself on the screen mouthing words that another voice was singing. Without his knowledge the studio had Allan Jones's voice dubbed in.

Morgan left M-G-M and went to Paramount where he was usually cast as a heavy, wearing a mustache. He then went to Warner Brothers where he fared no better, although they did drop his real name, Stanley Morner, for Dennis Morgan. Some of his films were made under the name Richard Stanley. The Burbank studio put him into one "B" film after another until Sam Wood took a chance on him for *Kitty Foyle*.

Dennis had heard that the director was looking for someone to play the part of a society snob. When he went to see Wood at RKO, he was offered the part of the young intern but flatly refused to play anything but the rich boy. Finally he got the role and Warners agreed to loan him out for the picture.

It was a tremendous success and a great boost to his career. His co-star Ginger Rogers won an Academy Award for her performance in the title role in 1940.

He returned to his home lot in triumph and was rewarded with some plum roles in such movies as *God Is My Co-Pilot* (1945) and *My Wild Irish Rose* (1947). When he was not working on a picture he was making personal appearance tours in which he sang the songs from some of his films. His film credits include *Waterfront* (1939), *Bad Men of Missouri* (1941), *The Hard Way* (1942), a memorable feature with Ida Lupino and Joan Leslie,* *Captains of the Clouds* (1942), *Thank Your Lucky Stars* (1943), *Christmas in Connecticut (*1945) with Barbara Stanwyck, *My Wild Irish Rose* (1947), *To the Victor* (1948), and *The Lady Takes a Sailor* (1949) with Jane Wyman. Probably his best remembered role was as the Red Shadow in *The Desert Song* (1943) with Irene Manning (living in Los Altos Hills, California, with her husband, missile scientist Maxwell W. Hunter II).

He was teamed with Jack Carson in several films, notably *Two Guys From Milwaukee* (1946). They were close friends off the screen and remained so until Carson died in 1963. Morgan had tried to join the comedian's vaudeville act during his period in Chicago.

When his movie career seemed over in the 1950's Morgan did quite a lot of television work. He was seen on NBC's "Star Stage," CBS's "Stage 7," and ABC's "Crossroads." He played a prominent role in the TV version of "Stage Door." In 1960 he had his own series for a short time, "21 Beacon Street." From time to time over the past decade he has been seen in low budget feature films such as *Uranium Boom* (1956) and *Rogue's Gallery* (1967).

Morgan has been married for many years to his high school sweetheart, Lillian Vedder. Most of his time is taken up with his extensive business holdings. Always very astute on money matters, Dennis had his last Warner Brothers contract written so that he received a salary of $25,000 a year until 1966 rather than pay huge taxes for a few years during his heyday.

A successful businessman today. *Paramount Pictures*

"Painting the Clouds with Sunshine" from the part-color "talkie" *Gold Diggers of Broadway* (1929), also featuring Nick Lucas.

ANN PENNINGTON

"The Dimpled Doll of Broadway" was born in Wilmington, Delaware, in 1893. When she was still a child her father, an executive with the Victor Talking Machine Company, moved the family to Camden, New Jersey, where one of Ann's neighbors was a girl who became one of Broadway's greatest comediennes, Rae Dooley (who lives with her husband, actor-director Eddie Dowling, in East Hampton, Long Island).

The famous pouting smile was first flashed at audiences in *The Red Widow* in 1911. The next year she appeared in Chicago in *A Polish Wedding*. By 1913 "Penny," as her friends call her, was in the Ziegfeld Follies. Her long dark hair and big brown eyes were so effective the great showman signed her again for the *Follies of 1914,* which had as its stars W. C. Fields and Mae Murray. In 1916 Ann again was in Ziegfeld's famous revue along with Marion Davies and Fanny Brice, who became her best friend. When Brice's racketeer husband, Nick Arnstein (who lives in Los Angeles where he draws a check every week for the use of his name in *Funny Girl*), was in trouble Penny came to the rescue with $20,000 in jewels, which were hocked for bail money.

She starred briefly in *Miss 1917,* a musical that ran only forty-eight performances in spite of a score by Jerome Kern and Victor Herbert. Ann's rehearsal pianist was a young man named George Gershwin.

In 1918 Ann Pennington was back in the Follies sharing billing with Will Rogers, Marilyn Miller, and Eddie Cantor.

The deliciously cute little dancer found time to make a few movies for Famous Players. A couple were *Susie Snowflakes* (1916) and *Sunshine Nan* (1918).

Another Broadway impresario of the era, George White, induced Ann to star in his *Scandals of 1919,* and then again in 1920 and 1921. In 1932 she starred in *Jack and Jill,* but the following year was back with Flo Ziegfeld for his *Follies.* George White won her back and she showed her famous dimpled knees in the *Scandals* of 1926 and 1928.

In 1930 Ann was one of *The New Yorkers* along with Fred Waring, and Clayton, Jackson, and Durante. The following year she was seen on Broadway in two shows, *Broadway Personalities* and *Everybody's Welcome*, both less than a smash hit. Demand for her services had begun to wane. In 1936 she was seen in M-G-M's *The Great Ziegfeld* in a small part, in which she played herself.

By 1937 the girl who had been photographed by Steichen, praised by George Jean Nathan, and squired by Jack Dempsey was the headliner of a second rate Broadway nightclub known as the Paradise. Her next booking, the same year, advertised her act as a "striptease." Although what she did was a few of her old dance routines, Ann permitted the show to be promoted otherwise. The trade papers shook their heads sadly, but admitted that "Penny" was still quite a little hoofer.

George Jessel showcased Ann in his *Little Old New York* show at the 1939 World's Fair. After that she toured in 1942 in *Hellzapoppin* and *The Student Prince* in 1943. That was it.

Since her retirement the "Dimpled Doll" has tried living in Florida and Hollywood, but always ends up back in Manhattan. Always, in fact, in hotels smack in the middle of the theatre district. Unmarried, after many well publicized romances with well known men, Ann lives alone. Her pastime is horse racing and when they're running "Penny" can be found at the nearest track just about every day.

She was one of those stars as greatly loved by her profession as by her fans. Her punctuality and good disposition were nearly as legendary on the Great White Way as her legs. She no longer gives interviews: "I see my contemporaries on TV sometimes and I think 'but how could you?' We're so old now. Young people do not know us and it must depress those who remember. I'd rather be thought of as the way I used to be."

Someone once asked Ann Pennington what was her favorite thing that had been written for her. She replied that it wasn't a song or a skit, but a line— "Pay to the order of Ann Pennington."

The radiant smile is unchanged. *Jon Virzi*

In 1929, with Universal Pictures.

LAURA LA PLANTE

The blue-eyed blonde who was for a number of years the top female star on the Universal lot, was born in St. Louis, Missouri, in 1904. At fifteen she began playing bit parts in Christie Comedies. In 1920 she was given what seemed at the time to be her big break when she won the part of the daughter in the "Bringing Up Father" series. The only trouble was that the series flopped and Laura returned to walk-ons. Not until she played with Charles Ray in *The Old Swimmin' Hole* (1921) did the producers begin to take notice of her all-American good looks and flair for light comedy.

Most of her pictures were made during her long contract with Universal. At first they cast her as Tom Mix's leading lady and opposite William Desmond in his serials *Perils of the Yukon* (1922) and *Around the World in Eighteen Days* (1923).

What makes Laura's success tale so extraordinary is that at the time it was more desirable to be the exotic than it was to be the girl-next-door.

Her two most outstanding films were the spooky classic *The Cat and the Canary* (1927) and the part talkie *Show Boat* (1929), for which she dyed her hair brunette to play the role of Magnolia. Other films were *Smoldering Fires* (1924) with the late Pauline Frederick, *Teasers* (1925), *Silk Stocking* (1927), *Scandal* (1929), *The King of Jazz* (1930) with the late Paul Whiteman, and *Lonely Wives* (1931).

Why Laura La Plante did not continue long in talkies is a mystery. Her voice proved to be as pleasant as her appearance and *Show Boat* was a blockbuster. But in 1932 she went to Europe. In Riga, Latvia, Laura divorced her first husband, director William Seiter, whom she had married in 1926. (Seiter's widow, silent star Marion Nixon, lives in Beverly Hills.) Shortly after, she became the wife of producer Irving Asher in Paris. Their wedding

166

was witnessed by New York City's ex-mayor Jimmy Walker and his wife, Betty Compton, on June 19, 1934.

The Ashers made their home in London for the next ten years and Laura did an occasional play there, but no films. After returning to Hollywood in the forties, Asher continued to produce motion pictures. They lived in Beverly Hills. The only hint of a movie comeback for her was in 1943 when Myrna Loy announced that she wanted out of her Metro-Goldwyn-Mayer contract. Laura was seriously considered for the role of Nora Charles in the *Thin Man* series. But she did not make a screen appearance until 1956 when she accepted the role of Betty Hutton's mother in *Spring Reunion*. Fans and critics alike agreed that the only thing wrong with her return was that she looked too young for the part. The same year teamed with silent star Aileen Pringle she debuted on television in a dramatization of a suffragette's race for the presidency of the United States at the turn of the century. It was called "She Also Ran" and was produced for "Bell Telephone Time."

In the past year the Ashers have spent nearly all their time in their home in Palm Desert, a resort community not far from Palm Springs. (Anna Q. Nilsson, the silent star, lives fairly nearby in the senior citizen project of Sun City.) Both their children were born in England. Tony, who is an executive with a Los Angeles advertising agency, finds time to write songs. One of his efforts hit the best seller charts around the country and was chosen by Broadcast Music, Inc. as one of their Ten Best of 1966. It was called "Wouldn't It Be Nice?" and was performed by the Beach Boys. His sister, Jill, is the assistant creative director at the same agency and is married to a lawyer. Laura is not yet a grandmother.

Laura swears that she does not miss making movies and has no plans at present for appearing in a new one. She likes living in the desert and is trying to adapt herself to sand blown in her house by thirty to forty mile per hour winds.

At her swimming pool in Palm Desert, California.

In 1930, with First National Pictures.

BILLIE DOVE

In New York City in 1903, one of the most beautiful ladies of the silent screen was born. Her name was Lillian Bohny. She was educated in private schools in Manhattan. When she was only fourteen James Montgomery Flagg sketched her, calling her one of the most beautiful girls in America. She did a great deal of modeling for artists and photographers and at fifteen was hired by Florenz Ziegfeld although she could neither sing nor dance. Ned Wayburn taught her the rudiments of being a showgirl. The showman paid her more than any of the other girls in his Midnight Revue on the Amsterdam Roof, just to sit in a hoop and dazzle everyone. She did little more in his production of *Sally* in 1921.

Cosmopolitan Studios gave her a bit part. She appeared briefly in *Get Rich Quick Wallingford* and *At the Stage Door*. She left for Hollywood and was replaced in Ziegfeld's roof show by Jacqueline Logan. Right away Billie landed a featured role in the Constance Talmadge* vehicle, *Polly of the Follies* (1922). Much of her early success has been attributed to Christie Cabanne who saw her potential as a leading lady.

Billie Dove was the first actress ever to receive a color screen test. It landed her the part opposite Douglas Fairbanks, Sr., in *The Black Pirate* (1926). She had "a peaches and cream complexion," which came over beautifully even in black and white.

From 1923 until 1929 the star was married to director Irving Willat. The marriage ended in divorce.

Along with those films in which she played Tom Mix's leading lady, Billie made *Country Girl* (1922), *All the Brothers Were Valiant* (1923), which was directed by her husband and co-starred Lon Chaney, *The Folly of Vanity* (1925), *The Lone Wolf Returns* (1926), *The Tender Hour* (1927) with Ben

Lyon as her co-star and George Fitzmaurice as director, *Heart of a Follies Girl* (1918), and *Her Private Life* (1929).

Billie's voice was passable and she was able to continue in pictures after sound arrived. Some of her early talkies were *A Night at Susies* (1930) with Douglas Fairbanks, Jr., *The Age for Love* (1931), which was produced by Howard Hughes, and *Cock of the Air* (1932) with Chester Morris.

In 1930 at a Hollywood party someone pointed out to Billie a young millionaire producer named Howard Hughes. Billie says the initial impression he made on her was that his clothes were very sloppy. At the time, Hughes was making headlines by spending millions of dollars on *Hell's Angels,* junking the first version and spending millions more on a second. Hughes was intrigued by the luscious star who, unlike most actresses at the party, had not thrown herself at him. He began to send her dozens of white roses and extravagant presents. Part of his courting was done in an airplane he flew himself. Finally the two began dating and within weeks were the talk of Hollywood. Hughes announced that he would produce her future films. Billie stated recently that she found him much too erratic to take seriously for a long period of time. At the height of their affair he would disappear for days without warning or explanation.

The girl whose Hollywood career really began with *Polly of the Follies* ended her years as an actress with *Blondie of the Follies* (1932), which starred Marion Davies and Robert Montgomery.

In 1933 Billie married multimillionaire Robert Kenaston. They live in a beautiful home in Pacific Palisades close to Zeppo Marx. Their children Robert Alan and adopted Gail are married. Billie's retirement upon her marriage was complete except for a small part in *Diamond Head* in 1962, in which she played a nurse.

Mrs. Billie Dove Kenaston in front of her California home. *Jon Virzi*

During a radio broadcast in the late thirties on NBC. *Metronome Magazine*

HORACE HEIDT

The popular orchestra leader of yesterday was born in Alameda, California, in 1901. For the first thirty years of his life nearly everything went wrong. His mother bought him a piano, but he hated to practice. While a student at the Culver Military Academy, he finally became interested in a musical career. He attempted to join the Culver Jazz Band but was rejected. The late "Red" Nichols auditioned also and made it.

While at the University of California, he promptly fractured his back during a football game and was told he was finished in that sport forever. While recuperating Horace heard Guy Lombardo on the radio and decided to form a group of his own.

Horace Heidt and his Musical Knights played one night stands at theatres and hotels up and down the West Coast. Between engagements Heidt worked in a real estate office and as a service station attendant. There were many "Knights" during those years since the orchestra had to be disbanded over and over due to a lack of bookings. Finally, they got a national tour for the Fanchon Marco circuit of theatres.

By 1930 Heidt and his men had arrived at the legendary Palace Theatre in Manhattan. The emcee was Ken Murray and although they were second to last on the bill, just playing the Palace was a big boost to Heidt's career. Next they went to Paris and the Riviera and rested on past laurels. When they returned the following year they had rehearsed so little that their second Palace engagement was a complete flop.

But Heidt hit his stride in radio. His first success in the medium came in 1932 with "Answers by the Dancers," a show of dance music mixed with informal interviews from the Drake Hotel in Chicago. Two years later he came up with "Treasure Chest," one of the first giveaway programs in which couples from the audience who were celebrating their wedding anniversary competed for prizes. In 1935 he changed the format to include couples who were about to be married and brides and grooms fresh from the altar. The title was changed to "Anniversary Night with Horace Heidt" and was so popular the National Broadcasting Company carried it on both their Red and Blue networks on Saturday nights. His "Pot o' Gold" show which began in 1938 was the first to give away large amounts of money and was an overnight sensation. The Musical Knights supplied the music and there were big-name guests, but the real appeal was the long-distance call to somebody somewhere in the United States who just might win the "Pot o' Gold." The gimmick worked so well that movie-theatre owners complained that it cut attendance. The movies grabbed the title and made a feature about it in 1941 starring Paulette Goddard* and James Stewart. Everyone thought it would go on forever, but the Federal Communications Commission declared it in violation of its rules and eventually forced it off the air.

Heidt started many successful careers. A few who admit that their association boosted them professionally are: Art Carney, Dick Contino, the King Sisters, Gordon MacRae, Al Hirt, Frankie Carle, and Alvino Rey.

Heidt utilized his knack for discovery on radio, television, and on the road in his "Youth Opportunity Program." Boys and girls with no experience whatever were given a chance not only to perform before an audience, but to act as stage manager, publicist, or advance man. Many of the top paid people in the entertainment industry today acknowledge the training they got as part of the company that toured the nation from 1948 until 1953.

In 1953 Horace decided to devote all of his time to the real estate holdings he had been acquiring in southern California during his lucrative years in show business. His twin boys, Jack and Jerry, are respectively: the youngest vice president in the history of California's Union Bank, and the operator of a real estate business in Los Angeles. Horace, Jr., is a student at Stanford University and Hildegard is studying art.

Heidt is the resident landlord of a 170-unit apartment complex in the San Fernando Valley, which has proved so profitable that he is planning others. His neighbors (among them silent stars Eva Novak and Chester Conklin*) like him so well that he is now mayor of Van Nuys, California.

His Honor the Mayor beside a miniature Van Nuys Street.

As a cavalry officer in 1937.

JOHN BOLES

The popular leading man of the 1930's was born into an old southern family in Greenville, Texas, in 1900. His father was a prosperous banker and cotton broker. John went to the University of Texas with the intention of studying medicine, but performed in student theatrical productions.

John, who was something of a linguist, shipped out to France in 1914 as a volunteer with United States Intelligence, returning as a lieutenant. While in France he had become seriously interested in show business. After singing at the Y.M.C.A. canteen, several ranking officers suggested that he try it for a living. He returned to Texas briefly after the war but left for Paris where he studied with Jean de Reszki and Oscar Seagle.

When he came back to the United States he lived in Manhattan, and supported himself by giving French lessons at a girls' school. Every extra penny went to vocal lessons.

His first show was *Moonlight* which opened at the Longacre Theatre in 1923, followed with *Little Jessie James* (1923) with Miriam Hopkins. He also played opposite the late Gerald Farrar in the diva's only operetta. Another of his Broadway efforts was *Mercenary Mary* in 1925.

While appearing in *Kitty's Kisses* (1926) he caught the attention of the superstar of the silents, Gloria Swanson. She was looking for a leading man to play opposite her in *The Love of Sunya*. The movie was made at the old Cosmopolitan Studios on Manhattan's 122nd Street. On March 12, 1927, his was the first feature to play at the famous Roxy Theatre. For a decade afterward John Boles was one of the most popular leading men in motion pictures.

Boles had several very advantageous qualities. He was not a pretty boy so that men didn't resent him, and women found him believable and attractive. He was a reliable and untemperamental actor and could play a well-bred, intelligent man without appearing to be a stuffed shirt. When talkies came in he was more popular than ever, since many silent stars could not speak very well, much less sing like him. Musicals were definitely the thing and John

172

played opposite Bebe Daniels* in *Rio Rita,* the picture that reactivated her career in 1929. The following year he introduced the song "It Happened in Monterey" in the lavish *King of Jazz,* and starred in the first sound version of *The Desert Song* (1929).

Female stars of the time loved working with a man whose ego would not clash with theirs. Some of the ladies who requested his services in their films were Barbara Stanwyck, Kay Francis, Joan Bennett, Lillian Harvey, Loretta Young, Rosalind Russell, Irene Dunne,* and Vivienne Segal.

John made many pictures during the thirties. A few examples of his best work are *Back Street* (1932), *Age of Innocence* (1934), *Music in the Air* (1934) with Gloria Swanson and the late Douglass Montgomery, *Craig's Wife* (1936), *Child of Manhattan* (1933) with the late Nancy Carroll, *A Message to Garcia* (1936), and the classic *Stella Dallas* (1937).

By the 1940's he was reduced to working for Monogram in such low-quality films as *Boy of Mine* (1941) and *Between Us Girls* (1942).

He did some stage work after the movies had no roles for him. In 1940 he starred in a revival of *Show Boat* in Los Angeles with Guy Kibbee, Helen Morgan, Norma Terris, and Paul Robeson. His return to Broadway in 1943 as Mary Martin's leading man in *One Touch of Venus* was a great success. His stage presence and voice were far from rusty. In the presentation houses he sang such favorites as "The Desert Song," "Waiting at the Gate for Katie," and "Rio Rita." In 1950 he was Gertrude Niesen's leading man in *Gentlemen Prefer Blondes* in Los Angeles and other cities. His last film was *Babes in Bagdad* (1952) which he made with Paulette Goddard.*

He has been married for the past forty years to the former Marceline Dobbs. They have two grown daughters, Frances Marceline and Janet. Although he does not have much interest in working anymore, he is still represented by the William Morris Agency.

The Boles divide their time between their homes in Los Angeles and Texas. The money he made during the thirties and forties was wisely invested in real estate which has made him a very rich man. John has one of the largest collections of swing music in Hollywood.

A distinguished realtor today. *Jon Virzi*

The original "It" girl at the height of her fame.

AILEEN PRINGLE

The original "It" girl of the silent screen was born to well-to-do parents in San Francisco in 1895. Under her real name, Bisbee, she attended Miss Murison's School in her native city, Madames of the Sacred Heart in Paris, and the McKenzie School in London. While in England she met and married Sir Charles Pringle who sometime later became Governor General of the Bahamas. Against the wishes of her husband and parents she debuted in the West End in *The Bracelet* in 1915. George Arliss saw her and later gave her a role in his play *The Green Goddess* on Broadway. Aileen made films long before she landed a Hollywood contract in 1922. As far back as 1920 she appeared in a movie called *Honor Bound,* made on a low budget in Fort Lauderdale, Florida, with an unknown mustached Italian actor named Rudolph Valentino.

Elinor Glyn, author of the popular Ruthenian romantic novels of the time, was asked who in America possessed the quality she had defined in her book *It*. She replied: "Rod La Rocque, Aileen Pringle, and Rex the Wonder Horse." While Aileen did not do *It* and Clara Bow capitalized on the publicity from the picture, it was she who was chosen by Miss Glyn to portray the Queen opposite Conrad Nagel (who lives on Manhattan's West Fifty-seventh Street) in *Three Weeks* (1924). The same year she and John Gilbert starred in another Glyn epic *His Hour*. Some other Pringle silents were *Souls For Sale* (1923), *The Christian* (1923), *Soul Mates* (1926), *Tea For Three* (1927), *Beau Broadway* (1928), and *A Single Man* (1929).

Aileen and her husband agreed to a very friendly separation after her decision to become an actress. Although they were not divorced for over twenty years, they never again lived together. Her only other marriage, to writer James Cain, in the forties, lasted eleven months.

Another of her titles was the "Darling of the Intelligentsia," and it was not always bestowed as a compliment. Aileen saw far more of writers than stars and her parties were attended by such names as H. L. Mencken, who was one of her more serious admirers, Joseph Hergesheimer, and Rupert Hughes. Until his death in 1966 her closest friend was Carl Van Vechten, author of *Nigger*

Heaven. She told all who would listen that she found the Hollywood intellectual climate suffocating and the natural climate boring, she thought little of Hollywood movies and the shop girls and merchants who starred in and produced them. The studio publicity department called her "highly uncooperative." She found Irving Thalberg "sneaky" and many of the other powers at M-G-M "vulgar." Aileen Pringle's career was ruined not by the advent of sound or bad pictures but by herself. Hedda Hopper thought the only explanation was her behavior. She could and should have been a major talkie star. Her voice was excellent and chic middle-aged stars such as Ruth Chatterton and Ina Claire were all the rage in the thirties. Instead Aileen continued for the whole decade making one atrocious picture after another. Her series with Lew Cody at M-G-M was bad but nothing to compare with her later sound films such as *Are These Our Children* (1931), *Piccadilly Jim* (1936), *Thanks for Listening* (1937) with Pinky Tomlin, and *John Meade's Woman* (1937), in which her part consisted of being pushed into a swimming pool while wearing an evening gown. Its star, Francine Larrimore, lives a few blocks away from Aileen today.

Although she says she wants to act again, her attitude has changed very little. Since her last film she has not worked professionally, though in 1959 she was asked to read for a part in the William Inge play, *A Loss of Roses.* When told that they were looking for a Nita Naldi type she asked them why they didn't simply hire Nita Naldi, who was living at the time.

After the death of her mother fifteen years ago, Aileen moved from her large Spanish house in Santa Monica, close to silent star Mary Miles Minter, to a small apartment in Manhattan on East Fifty-seventh Street.

She is still a sophisticated, beautifully dressed woman. She reads a great deal, sees most of the plays and movies, and is very active socially when her back, which has for years been a source of great pain to her, is well. One of her areas of knowledge is food. She is a superb cook and considers herself a gourmet. Many a waiter has been startled to hear the former star order her own meal and that of her male escort who "had no palate."

In Manhattan recently. *Jon Virzi*

Her voice and diction helped make her a star in her first "talkie," *The Awful Truth,* in 1929.

INA CLAIRE

When people complain that the theatre is not what it used to be they usually mean that there are no Ina Claire vehicles or Ina Claires around to act in them.

The actress, who was throughout her career the epitome of the well-heeled, well-bred woman, was born Ina Fagan in Washington, D.C., in 1895. With her mother as a chaperone she debuted in vaudeville at the age of twelve. In 1909 she opened in New York with an impersonation of the great Scottish entertainer, Sir Harry Lauder, that brought the house down. It also brought a lot of attention to the svelt teen-ager by producers of legitimate shows. In 1911 Ina appeared in *Jumping Jupiter* on Broadway and followed it with *The Quaker Girl.* In 1913 she starred in the London company of the Broadway smash *The Girl from Utah.* She played the part that had been originated by Julia Sanderson (Frank Crummit, Julia's husband and co-star, is dead, and Julia lives quietly in a Springfield, Massachusetts, hotel, gives no interviews, and permits no photographs).

Flo Ziegfeld featured Ina in his *Follies of* 1915 and 1916, but it was her role in *Polly With a Past* in 1917 that firmly established Ina Claire as one of the brightest comediennes in the country.

In 1919 she married critic James Whittaker, and had enormous success that same year in *The Gold-Diggers.* Ina and Whittaker were divorced in 1925.

Some of the drawing-room comedy-drama plays in which she dazzled audiences were: *Bluebeard's Eighth Wife* (1921), *The Awful Truth* (1922), *Grounds for Divorce* (1924), and *The Last of Mrs. Cheyney* (1925).

No one ever delivered a witty line on stage better than Ina Claire, but, unlike most actresses, when the occasion arose for a retort she did not need a playwright around to give her dialogue. During her brief (from 1929 to 1931) marriage to the silent screen idol, John Gilbert, a reporter asked her how it felt being married to a celebrity. "Why don't you ask my husband?" was Mrs. Gilbert's reply.

In 1929 she joined the parade of stage stars to Hollywood to replace the many silent stars whose voices made them unsuitable for sound pictures. She clicked right from the beginning and enjoyed great success in *Rebound* (1931), *Royal Family of Broadway* (1931), and *The Greeks Had a Name for It* (1932). But the stage remained Ina's first love and when S. N. Behrman wrote *Biography* (1932) for her she rushed back to the great White Way and her greatest triumph. Throughout the thirties she was seen in such plays as *End of Summer* (1936) with Osgood Perkins, father of the actor Tony Perkins, and *Once is Enough* (1938). Her two final pictures were *Ninotchka* (1939), in which she held her own with Great Garbo, and *Claudia* (1943) with Olga Baclanova.

After her marriage in 1939 to attorney William R. Wallace, Ina grew less and less interested in working. She did *The Fatal Weakness* on Broadway in 1946, but her kind of parts were simply not being written or at least produced.

Ina Claire is best remembered as the beautifully groomed sophisticate men desired and women envied. Year after year her name appeared on the "Ten Best Dressed" list.

If it was Ina Claire's intention to retire on a hit she did very well for herself. In 1954 she bid adieu to Broadway after a highly successful run in T. S. Eliot's *The Confidential Clerk*. One critic called her "a line drawing of the Twenties . . . delectable beyond belief."

For a while the Wallaces maintained a huge estate in Hillsborough, near San Francisco. Several years ago they gave it up and moved to an apartment on Nob Hill where Ina holds court to California society and a smattering of her old friends from the theatre. The lady who introduced the shingle bob hairdo to American women in 1929 as well as many clothing styles is equally imaginative in the decor of her home. Friends who have visited with her say that the flat on Sacramento Street could easily serve as the setting for one of Ina's urbane comedies.

She will not read scripts or discuss her career with reporters. The life of a matron seems to suit the former star very nicely. From outward appearances Ina Claire is very happy. If she has any problems at all they are certain to be elegant ones.

Still *soignée,* at a recent display of theatrical memorabilia in San Francisco. *San Francisco Chronicle*

All sweetness and light, the early thirties.

JANET GAYNOR

The actress who won the first Academy Award for Best Actress was born Laura Gainor in Philadelphia, Pennsylvania, in 1906. Her early years were spent in the city of brotherly love and Melbourne, Florida. By the time she was old enough to attend high school her family had moved to San Francisco.

After graduation in 1924 Janet pestered her mother and stepfather until they brought her to Hollywood. At first she worked as an extra in shorts and westerns. Then Winifield R. Sheenan gave her a contract with Fox Studios. Her first feature was *The Johnstown Flood* (1926), in which she played a very sweet little country girl beset by a number of tragedies but always brave, true, and, of course, pretty. This was essentially the character she played throughout her career in films.

On the night of May 16, 1929, at a dinner in the Hollywood Roosevelt Hotel, Janet received the first Oscar in history. The practice at the time was to give awards for several rather than just one performance. Her statuette was for her roles in *Sunrise* (1927), *Seventh Heaven* (1927), co-starring Charles Farrell, and *Street Angel* (1928).

When she wed attorney Lydell Peck in 1932 the couple was flooded with fan mail telling them that their marriage could not possibly work out, and urging Janet to wait until Charles Farrell's marriage to silent star Virginia Valli broke up, which they felt was unavoidable. The Pecks were divorced in 1934. The Farrells are still together.

Janet made such tear-jerkers as *Adorable* (1933), *Paddy, the Next Best Thing* (1933), *Change of Heart* (1934), *Carolina* (1934) with Lionel Barrymore and Warner Baxter, *Servant's Entrance* (1934) with Lew Ayres, *The Farmer Takes a Wife* (1935) with Henry Fonda, and *Small Town Girl* (1936) with Robert Taylor. One of her best talkies was *State Fair* (1933) with Will Rogers and Stepin Fetchit.*

David O. Selznick cast her in *A Star Is Born* opposite Fredric March. It was a smashing success that gave her another Oscar nomination in 1937, and it still holds up as one of the best pictures of its kind ever made. The musical version with Judy Garland made years later suffered greatly by comparison.

In 1938 after completion of *Young in Heart*, which along with *Seventh Heaven* is her favorite film, Janet announced that she was retiring from motion pictures. A year later she married Gilbert Adrian, Hollywood's most famous and successful designer. Their son, Robin, was born in 1940. Much of her time in retirement was spent with her husband on their two-hundred-acre ranch in Brazil.

In 1951 she and Farrell were co-starred once again in *Seventh Heaven* over Lux Radio Theatre. Two years later she appeared on a segment of TV's "Medallion Theatre" in a soap opera plot called "Dear Cynthia." Later in the 1950's she did a few more TV programs such as "General Electric Theatre" and "Robert Montgomery Presents." Her last movie was *Bernardine* (1957), which was Pat Boone's film debut. After Adrian died in 1959 Janet appeared on Broadway for a short time in the play *Midnight Sun*. It was unsuccessful and after that, rather than return to the Brazilian ranch she found "desolate now," she did a great deal of traveling.

In 1964 at the age of fifty-eight Janet Gaynor married Paul Gregory, a producer many years her junior, with whom she had been partners in several of his plays. Although Gregory is active in Hollywood, Janet denies any plans for a comeback either in television or motion pictures. Her demure manner on celluloid hid her true nature as an astute businesswoman. The year before her retirement she made $252,583, which made her the highest paid actress in Hollywood at the time. She admitted to having saved over $1,000,000.

Still active on the Hollywood social scene. *Jon Virzi*

Crooning in 1946.

DICK HAYMES

The troubled troubadour of the forties was born in the Argentine in 1918 to a cattle rancher of Scotch-Irish descent and an American girl who after running away from her Santa Barbara home had toured Europe as a singer and dancer. After his parents separated in the twenties, Dick went to school in Switzerland part of the year and spent the other part with his mother Marguerite who ran a dress shop in Rio de Janeiro. In his late teens they lived in Paris and London for a few years before Dick came to Hollywood in the thirties. His first trip to the movie capital was during his summer vacation from Loyola University in Montreal. After his band, The Katzenjammers, failed he joined Johnny Johnston's band as a vocalist at $25 a week. He also did short stints with the Bunny Berrigan, Harry James, and Tommy Dorsey orchestras. His top salary during that period was $50 a week. He sang on radio, did one-night stands, and worked as an extra in westerns to earn a living. In 1938 he had a small part in *Dramatic School* which starred Luise Rainer.*

It was not until 1943 that Dick Haymes hit the big time. Bookers and agents knew him by a growing reputation for a smooth, romantic delivery of love ballads, but the public had hardly heard of him when someone took a chance and showcased him in Manhattan's Martinique. It was the time of the crooners and Dick was one of the very best. The recording companies offered him their best songs. Twentieth Century-Fox signed him to a fat contract. His recordings of "Little White Lies" sold 2,250,000 copies. A Frank Sinatra disc has yet to achieve a million sale.

Hollywood was churning out big, colorful musicals and Dick clicked from the very beginning. His handsome features and "dreamy" voice were featured in *DuBarry Was A Lady* (1943), *Irish Eyes Are Smiling* (1944) with June Haver (who is retired in the San Fernando Valley with her husband, Fred MacMurray), *Diamond Horseshoe* (1945) with Betty Grable, *Do You Love Me?* (1946) with Jeanne Crain (who lives in Newport Beach, California, with her husband Paul Brinkman and her six children), *One Touch of Venus*

180

(1948), and *Up in Central Park* (1948) with Deanna Durbin, and *St. Benny the Dip* (1951). Dick's greatest hit was *State Fair* (1945), the only musical Rodgers and Hammerstein ever wrote for the screen. In it he introduced two songs which have become standards, "That's For Me" and "It Might as Well Be Spring."

His studio built a "boy next door" image for him. He had all the things at the time associated with movie stars: a pretty wife (Joanne Dru) who was also an actress, a private plane, several cars, his own radio program, and screaming teen-age girls following him wherever he went. He experienced his first bad publicity when it was revealed that he had avoided the draft by claiming an exemption as a citizen of a neutral country. He thereby forfeited his right to become a United States citizen. His first wife Edith Harper had their marriage annulled in 1938 after a few weeks. Following his split up with Joanne Dru, Dick married Nora Eddington who was previously married to Errol Flynn. In 1953 Dick married Rita Hayworth, and was nearly deported when he followed "The Love Goddess" to Hawaii without permission from the immigration people. Mrs. Haymes number 5 was Frances Makris who was followed by singer Fran Jeffries. Dick nearly made a comeback in nightclubs with Miss Jeffries. His reviews were excellent but about the time the bookings started, the marriage began to disintegrate. She married his best friend, director Richard Quine. Although Dick and Fran, by whom he has a daughter, keep in touch, Quine and Dick have not spoken since the divorce.

In 1960 with debts of nearly $500,000 Haymes declared bankruptcy. His last movie was *All Ashore* in 1953. During his marriage to Rita Hayworth their furniture was repossessed for nonpayment and their landlord sued him. In 1964 he moved to Ireland and became a citizen shortly thereafter. He and his seventh wife, model Wendy Smith, keep a small apartment in a London suburb but spend most of their time in Dublin when Dick is not on tour playing clubs in Africa, England, and Australia.

With Mrs. Haymes at their London wedding reception. *London Daily Express*

In *Samson and Delilah* (1949), under Cecil B. De Mille's direction.

VICTOR MATURE

The most famous Hollywood glamour boy of the early forties was an only child, born in 1916 in Louisville, Kentucky, of immigrant parents. His mother was French; his father, a scissors grinder, Austrian. He was wild and rebellious as a youth, quitting school at the age of fifteen. For a number of years he worked at various jobs, his most successful being a candy salesman. Later he ran a restaurant, lost $600 and sold out and headed for Hollywood.

He was twenty years old when he arrived. Supporting himself with such odd jobs as lawn mowing and dish washing, he started out in small roles at the Pasadena Playhouse, gradually rose to leads, doing some 150 parts in all. Then, in 1939, Frank Ross, vice-president of the Hal Roach Studios at the time, saw him in the Ben Hecht play *To Quito and Back* and signed him to a seven-year contract with options. His first screen appearance was in the small role of a gangster in *The Housekeeper's Daughter* (1939) starring Joan Bennett. Thirty thousand fan letters poured into the studio after his debut, and he was given the leads in *One Million B.C.* and *Captain Caution*. That same year, 1940, saw him in *No, No Nanette,* starring Anna Neagle.

In 1940, he accepted the role of the "hunk of man" in *Lady in the Dark,* starring Gertrude Lawrence. (The play was to catapult another comparative unknown to stardom, Danny Kaye.)

He appeared in *The Shanghai Gesture* (1941) playing Dr. Omar, chief aid to Madame Gin Sling—The Hayes' Office substitute for Madame Goddamn. Ona Munson played the nefarious Madame. Also in the cast were Gene Tierney and Walter Huston. With his Broadway success, his salary was upped from $450 to $1,750 per week. Later he did *I Wake Up Screaming* with Betty Grable and *My Gal Sal* with Rita Hayworth, both for Twentieth Century-Fox, who by then had bought up half his contract.

In 1942, he surprised all by joining the Coast Guard, seeing fourteen months of active duty before he was put into the branch's revue, *Tars and Spars,* which played film-vaudeville houses across the country. He was to spend almost four years in the Coast Guard.

After the war Fox signed him to a new contract giving him $3,000 a week. This was the period of his best films: John Ford's *My Darling Clementine* (1946), in which he played Doc Holliday to Henry Fonda's Wyatt Earp, *Kiss of Death* (1947) with Richard Widmark (making an auspicious film debut), and *The Cry of the City* (1948).

In 1949 De Mille borrowed him for *Samson and Delilah,* co-starring Hedy Lamarr. Other super productions came in 1953 when he did *The Robe,* and *Demétrius and the Gladiators* (1954). (Both were produced by Frank Ross.)

When his contract with Fox expired in 1954, Mature free-lanced, making adventure pictures—*Shark-fighters, Zarak*—and substandard spectacles—*The Tartars* and *Hannibal.* Usually made abroad, they were on a salary-percentage basis (as was indeed 1 s TV series, *The Big Circus,* of which, in addition to his salary of $175,000, he owned 10 percent), and despite their poor quality he made a lot of money. Mature's last screen appearance was *After the Fox* (1966), playing an egotistical middle-age movie star reduced to playing in cheap Italian spectacles. He was never better. His income must have afforded him all the satisfaction he needed, for he never really took his career seriously.

The Beefcake King now lives on a ranch near San Diego, with his fourth wife, Britisher Joy Urwick (twenty years his junior) whom he married in 1959. Mature plays golf and lives like a country gentleman, going to Hollywood only on business (he has varied interests in real estate and such things) and to visit friends. "I had a ball there when I was younger—but what do I want with it now?" he says. "I guess I've grown up."

On a recent visit to Italy. *United Artists*

In the silent version of *Romeo and Juliet*.

BEVERLY BAYNE

The distaff side of the screen's first "love team" was born Beverly Pearl Bain in Minneapolis, Minesota, in 1895. At the age of eight her family moved to Chicago. She was in her third week as a freshman at Hyde Park High School when she and a friend, Grace Taylor, decided to visit the Essanay Studios. Chicago was then the center of motion picture production and the girls were intrigued with the glamour of the new medium. A director was struck with her dark beauty and offered her a role in *The Loan Shark* (1912). Her friend, a blonde, got nothing more than a tour since in the early stages of moving pictures blondes did not photograph well. The cameras made everyone look older, so leading ladies were nearly always in their teens. Asked about her salary requirements, Beverly, who was at the time receiving a weekly allowance of 25¢ said, "How about $35 or maybe $30, but at least $25." She was paid $25 at first, then raised to $35 and within six months was making $350.

Beverly starred in over 500 movies before she retired. Many were one and two reelers. She was teamed with another Essanay player, Francis X. Bushman. They were an immediate success and continued for several years as a team. Although they were married in 1918 it was kept secret from the public. At that time any star who was known to be married was washed up as a romantic actor. They starred together in such photoplays as *Under Royal Patronage* (1914), *One Wonderful Night* (1914), *The Diplomat Service* (1916), and *Social Quicksands* (1918). One of their starrers, *Ladies' World* (1911) had a young lady named Gloria Swanson who was later signed by Essanay. Their greatest triumph was the first movie version of *Romeo and Juliet* (1916) which made them superstars. The duo commanded huge salaries and formed their own company, Quality Pictures. When Louis B. Mayer headed Metro Pictures he induced them to star in a serial *The Great Secret* (1917), paying them $15,000, a colossal sum at the time. After their marriage was revealed, Bushman's career continued (he had been married once before), but Beverly spent more time at home.

The Bushman-Bayne marriage ended in a bitter divorce in 1924. They had one son, Richard Stanbury Bushman. Neither the wife nor the son ever saw or heard from the actor thereafter. In 1941 the son had his name changed legally to Richard Bayne. The father died in 1966, the son, in 1967.

Beverly Bayne made movies after her divorce but never again was a star of the magnitude she achieved with Bushman. In 1925 she was seen in *Graustark*. She did very well on the vaudeville circuits during the twenties, touring mostly for Keith-Orpheum, and in 1927 she starred in *The Road to Rome* on stage which she followed with *Once in a Lifetime* (1931), *As Husbands Go* (1932), and *The Shining Hour* (1934). Her last movie was *Seven Keys to Baldpate* in 1935 with Gene Raymond. In the thirties she also did some radio work and magazine writing on diets and beauty aids.

In 1942 she portrayed Phyllis Thaxter's mother in *Claudia* in the Chicago company. In 1946 she and Jean Parker were seen in the short-lived play *Loco* on Broadway.

Her second husband Charles Hvass, a New York manufacturer of road-building equipment, whom she married in 1937, died in 1953, and she has not remarried.

In 1956 Beverly and her son, who had never married, moved from their home in Pleasantville, New York, to Scottsdale, Arizona, which she always refers to as "The West's most Western Town." She lives there alone today near her long-time friend, Reta Berry, the widow of Wallace Berry, whom she knew fifty years ago at the Essanay Studios. Beverly travels occasionally to Hollywood where she visits with Mary Pickford and Buddy Rogers at Pickfair and to Florida to see her old friend, Olga Petrova, who lives in Clearwater. Another Floridian, one of the screen's earliest Tarzans, is Gene Polar, a resident of Hollywood.

After the death of her son Beverly seriously considered a return to the stage or a try at television, but she claims that she just cannot bring herself to leave Scottsdale.

Two former silent stars meet in Florida: Olga Petrova (left) and Beverly Bayne. *Clearwater Sun*

In a 1928 publicity shot.

CLAIRE WINDSOR

In an era when it was taboo for film stars to be married the blonde actress featured her infant son in most of her publicity.

She was born in 1897 in Cawker City, Kansas, and educated at schools in Topeka and Seattle. After a year of marriage to William Bowes, Claire left him and moved to Los Angeles, where, to support her little boy, she took a job at $5 a day as an extra at Lasky Studios. She considered herself very lucky if the casting director used her three days a week.

She was introduced one day to Lois Weber. The female producer-director-writer was at that time, in 1920, one of the most respected star-makers in Hollywood. She was looking for a girl like Claire for *What Do Men Want?* When rushes of her proved successful, Claire was offered a contract for $150 a week for the first year with a raise to $350 for the second.

Her name was changed from Clara Viola Cronk to Claire Windsor. "They called me Claire," says Miss Windsor, "because I was so fair, and Windsor because I was patrician."

In 1922 Claire was chosen as a Wampas Baby Star, roughly equivalent to our Deb Star Ball of today.

Claire worked for nearly every major lot until the end of the silent era. Going from First National to Tiffany, Fox, M-G-M, Paramount, Universal, and Goldwyn, she made such movies as *The Blot* (1921) opposite the late Louis Calhern, and in a great boost to her career teamed with one of the leading male actors of the time, Bert Lytell, imported from Broadway where he was already well established as a star, in *Born Rich* (1924), which had Doris Kenyon (retired and living in Beverly Hills) in the cast. She then made *Souls for Sables* (1925), *Money Talks* (1926) with the late Owen Moore, *Dance Madness* (1926), *The Claw* (1927), and *Bugle Call* (1927) with the top child star of the day, Jackie Coogan (who makes an occasional TV appearance and lives in the San Fernando Valley).

In 1925 Claire Windsor and Bert Lytell were married. The liaison lasted two years. (Lytell died in 1954. He had been the Shepherd of the Lambs Club and President Emeritus of Actors Equity.) Claire was one of the many silent stars who could not make the transition from silents to sound, and after her divorce, she made several attempts at a comeback in the new cinema, but they were hardly first class efforts. Mayfair Pictures released *Sister to Judas* (1933), in which she played with John Harron. The following year she and Johnny Mack Brown made *Cross Streets* for Invincible.

Most of the former star's money is invested in Los Angeles real estate. She lives in one of her own apartment buildings on Orange Drive in the heart of Hollywood. Claire has never remarried and claims she does not wish to work again. Having visited movie and TV sets in the past years she feels that the tension is much greater than in her day. Her son, Bill, works in the planning department of the Douglas Aircraft Company in Santa Monica.

She says, "I am very busy with creating oil paintings and designing my own clothes, which I also make."

In 1966 the star who has lived quietly for so long was again in the news when Lita Grey published one of the most tasteless tomes in the annals of Hollywood, *My Life With Chaplin*. She named Claire Windsor as one of her former husband's women. Miss Windsor's reply to the insinuation was "I have not read Lita Grey's book. Had she asked me I would have told her that I thought Chaplin was a great artist. He helped to start my career by taking me out about four or five times, which gave me nice publicity. I doubt I will ever read it. I'm too busy."

At an interview with the author.

With "Asta" and Myrna Loy in *Another Thin Man*, 1939.

WILLIAM POWELL

Myrna Loy's celluloid husband was born William Horatio Powell in Pittsburgh, Pennsylvania, in 1892.

After receiving many compliments for his performance in a Christmas school play Powell was hooked on acting. Thanks to money lent him by a wealthy aunt he was able to go to the American Academy of Dramatic Art in New York City, where his classmates were Edward G. Robinson and the late Joseph Schildkraut.

From 1912 until 1916 he appeared on Broadway and in touring companies in such plays as *The Ne'er Do Well* and *Within the Law*. During the long run of the latter he met and married a member of the cast, Eileen Wilson, in 1915. They were divorced in 1931. He had a full year's run in the musical *Going Up* in 1917, which was followed by several flops and then a season in stock. When Samuel Goldwyn offered him a part in *Sherlock Holmes* (1922), Powell was delighted at the chance to play with the great John Barrymore, who had the title role, and Carol Dempster.

In 1923 William was with Jetta Goudal in *The Bright Shawl*. In most of his silent films, as during his stage career, Powell was cast as the heavy. Some of those he menaced were the late Clara Bow in *My Lady's Lips* (1925), Lois Wilson (Gloria Swanson's closest friend and a Manhattan resident) in *The Great Gatsby* (1926), Evelyn Brent in *Love's Greatest Mistake* (1927), and Doris Kenyon in *Interference* (1928).

His years on the stage had given Powell a fine, distinctive voice which was put to good use in early sound pictures, delivering retorts and wisecracks as a detective or an attorney. It was his portrayal of Philo Vance in *The Canary Murder Case* (1929) with Louise Brooks (unmarried and living in Rochester, New York) that set his new image of the dapper and very clever gentleman. While making *Man of the World* (1931) with Wynne Gibson he met and married Carole Lombard. They were divorced two years later.

Evelyn Knapp (now Mrs. Snyder of Beverly Hills) was his leading lady in

High Pressure (1932). Gangster John Dillinger came out of hiding to see Powell and Myrna Loy in *Manhattan Melodrama* (1934) and was shot down by federal agents outside the theatre. The same year Powell was teamed with Myrna Loy in *The Thin Man,* which earned him a nomination for an Oscar— five more Nick and Nora Charles pictures were to follow and six others in which Powell and Loy were co-starred. She was Mrs. Charles in all the *Thin Man* pictures but one, which he made with the late Elissa Landi. Many of their fans believed they were actually husband and wife, or at least in love. They were and still are good friends.

The real love of Powell's life in those days was Jean Harlow, whose untimely death in 1937 sent him into a long period of deep depression. They made *Libelled Lady* together in 1936.

Powell portrayed Flo Ziegfeld in *The Great Ziegfeld* (1936), for which he received another Oscar nomination and in *Ziegfeld Follies* (1946). In between there were: *My Man Godfrey* (1936), *The Baroness and the Butler* (1938), *I Love You Again* (1940) with Edmund Lowe (for some time now a patient at the Motion Picture Country Hospital), and *The Youngest Profession* (1943). In 1947 he received his third Academy Award nomination for his brilliant performance as Clarence Day in *Life with Father*. The same year he co-starred with Ella Raines (the wife of Major Robin Olds, head of the Air Force Academy in Colorado) in *The Senator Was Indiscreet*. Then he made *Mr. Peabody and the Mermaid* (1948) and *How to Marry a Millionaire* (1953). His last film and one of his best was *Mr. Roberts* (1955), in which he played the ship's doctor.

Since 1940 Powell has been married to Diana Lewis, a former actress. Although he hates to stir from his beautiful home in Palm Springs, a good part in a picture would get him back to Hollywood. He certainly does not have to work as the money he made during the era of low taxes was well invested. Powell has an only child William, Jr., by his first wife. A number of years ago the actor successfully underwent a series of serious and delicate operations for cancer.

In Palm Springs. *Jon Virzi*

In 1933, a weekly feature on the
"Eddie Cantor Show." *NBC*

RUBINOFF

The man who was once the best known violinist in America was born in
Grodno, Russia, in 1896. At the age of five he was playing the balalaika so
well that the town's music master offered to give him free lessons. His parents,
who had wanted him to become a barber, invested the equivalent of $3 in a
small violin and within a few years their son won a scholarship to the Warsaw
Conservatory. After graduating he came to this country and settled with his
family in Pittsburgh.

His professional career began in the steel capital's Cameraphone Theatre in
1912. He worked fairly steadily during the next fifteen years, but was less than
a "name" when he managed to get a week's booking at the Paramount Theatre
in Manhattan. Rudy Vallee, who prided himself on being able to spot un-
discovered talent, took Rubinoff under his wing. Within a short time (1931) he
was signed as the featured soloist on "The Eddie Cantor Show," the most
popular variety show on radio, heard weekly on NBC. Overnight Rubinoff's
name became a household word (he never used his first name—David—professionally).

Although he had been in this country since he was fifteen years old, Rubinoff
never lost his heavy Slavic accent. He practically never uttered a word on the
air. Once the red light over the control booth went out, however, he was
anything but shy. His aggressiveness with the ladies led him into court on more
than one occasion. In 1937 Peggy Garcia, a hat check girl whom the violinist
had met in a Harlem nightclub, sued him for $500,000 in a breach of promise
action. The tabloids played up testimony about the great musician's lavender
pajamas and quoted Miss Garcia as stating that "Dave is a great petter." The
plaintiff lost sympathy when it was disclosed that she had been married when
she was twelve years old. Another time in 1943 the widower of a lady who had
been acquainted with Rubinoff sued for alienation of affection.

In 1937, a year before his near fatal illness, he was applauded by 225,000
people in Chicago's Grant Park. During his career four Presidents complimented

him on his performances. He shared billing with Al Jolson, Jack Benny, Jimmy Durante, and Maurice Chevalier. Near death in a Detroit hospital he looked back on a full and financially successful life. Rubinoff survived, but by the time his recovery was complete his box office appeal began to fade.

For a man who had made as much as $250,000 a year in the middle of the Great Depression his activities during these past years must have been a bitter pill. The brochure he sends out from his Detroit office lists his recent engagements at such places as the Romulus, Michigan Kiwanis Club, and the local high school of Ashland, Ohio. His repertoire is more varied than most jukeboxes. He might begin the evening with the "Warsaw Concerto," seque into "Fly Me to the Moon," and conclude the program by playing the themes from the most popular TV commercials.

Rubinoff took himself much more seriously than did his fellow musicians. Actually, he was a good violinist but nowhere near the caliber of a Heifitz or Menuhin. What he can rightfully be proud of, if he would admit it, is that his commercial approach to the classics on radio programs with a vaudeville format introduced a great many people to music they would never have heard ordinarily.

In 1962 he announced dramatically after a concert in Plattsburg, New York, that he was retiring.

Until 1965 Rubinoff had occupied an apartment in a second-class hotel in downtown Detroit. When he decided to move to another location in Detroit, he attempted to take the paneling from the living room walls and the plumbing from the bathroom. The management objected and he was again in court and in the papers. Before a settlement was reached someone reminded the court that the maestro had always been "high strung."

Five years after his retirement he was still playing. Thanks to his son, Lieutenant Rubin Rubinoff, who was stationed in Korea with the United States Army in the summer of 1967, the aging artist entertained the troops with his own composition, "Fiddlin' the Fiddle," in Seoul, Korea.

The maestro today with his Stradivarius, insured for $100,000, which he purchased in 1930.

In 1924, Carol portrayed Nancy Montague in *America*.

CAROL DEMPSTER

The lovely heroine of D. W. Griffith pictures was born in Duluth, Minnesota, in 1902. Her parents moved to Los Angeles when she was a baby. In the summer of 1915 Carol was a student at Denis Shawn's dancing school. Griffith was shooting his masterpiece *Intolerance* (1916) and called for some of the girls to perform as dancers. Carol was among them. He used her again when *The Greatest Thing in Life* opened at Clune's Auditorium in 1918. Griffith staged a live prologue to his picture for the Los Angeles opening in which Carol danced again. Although she does not remember him, the archives of the Museum of Modern Art show that Rodolpho di Valentina was also a player in that production. Of course he later became known the world over as Rudolph Valentino.

Griffith became quite smitten with the lovely brown-eyed girl and soon she replaced Lillian Gish in his affections, as well as in some of his films. In her autobiography Colleen Moore is rather bitchy about the relationship and dismisses Carol as a girl with "a thin, sharp face. . . . She couldn't act and he was unable to teach her to do so." Quite a few film buffs disagree. One is William K. Everson, one of the world's leading authorities on motion pictures. In one of his books he named her as one of a handful of silent stars who rank as all-time greats. Her acting he rated as "superb" and compared her performance favorably to Garbo in *Isn't Life Wonderful?* (1924).

Nearly all of Carol Dempster's efforts were under the direction of D. W. Griffith. Not all of them were commercially successful. It has been suggested that the director used the profits from his Lillian Gish films to finance those with Miss Dempster. Whatever his purpose, the Dempster vehicles hold up remarkably well today. Her films are *Scarlet Days* (1919), *The Girl Who Stayed Home* (1919), *Way Down East* (1920), in which she had only a bit part, *The Love Flower* (1920) with Richard Barthelmess, *Dream Street* (1921)

192

with Tyrone Power, Sr., *One Exciting Night* (1922), *The White Rose* (1923) with Ivor Novello and the late Mae Marsh receiving top billing, *America* (1924) with Neil Hamilton who was with her again the next year in *Isn't Life Wonderful?*, *Sally of the Sawdust* (1925) with W. C. Fields and Alfred Lunt, *Sorrows of Satan* (1926) with the late Adolph Menjou and Lya de Putti, and *That Royal Girl* (1926) with W. C. Fields again and James Kirkwood. Carol had a part in a non-Griffith movie *Sherlock Holmes* (1920), which starred John Barrymore.

A great many people in Hollywood thought that Griffith and Carol would marry. One of them was Griffith. Instead Miss Dempster walked out of her contract which had three years left to run and announced her retirement. Rather than continue her acting career she choose to marry the wealthy young investment banker Edwin S. Larsen. Neither had been married before.

Since most of Carol's films were made in the East she was never really a part of the Hollywood community. Many of the greats of her era she has never even met. Today she sees Charles Farrell and Virginia Vallee during the winters, which the Larsens spend in their Palm Springs home. One of their closest friends is Lily Pons, who lives in Palm Springs most of the year. Occasionally Carol hears from Neil Hamilton who lives in Los Angeles.

From her retirement until 1965 Carol lived with her husband on their estate in Connecticut. They also maintained an apartment in Manhattan. Mr. Larsen has been retired since 1932 and in the years since then the couple has traveled extensively. In 1965 they sold their home and moved to La Jolla, California. They have no children.

Quite recently Carol said, "I just never think about my days in pictures. I am always very surprised that anyone remembers me. It was so long ago. So many of my movies were so sad. Maybe my fans would like to know that in real life Carol Dempster had a very happy ending."

At her La Jolla, California, home.
Clifford May

Punishing the parquet in 1938.

ELEANOR POWELL

The girl who was crowned the World's Greatest Female Tap Dancer in 1936 by the Dancing Masters of America was born in Springfield, Massachusetts, in 1913. Her mother, thinking that dancing lessons might help her daughter gain some poise and overcome her shyness, had enrolled her in a ballet class.

When she was only thirteen Gus Edwards saw her doing acrobatics on the beach at Atlantic City and asked her mother's permission to put her into the show he was producing at the Ritz Grill. In her late teens she went to New York determined to get into a Broadway show, but found that all of the jobs went to those who could tap. After some lessons from Jack Donahue and a lot of private practice she landed a spot in *Follow Through* in 1929. In 1931 she was in *Fine and Dandy,* and the following year Flo Ziegfeld gave her a part in *Hot Cha,* which starred Buddy Rogers (who lives with his wife Mary Pickford at Pickfair in Beverly Hills). While appearing in *At Home Abroad,* the Bea Lillie starrer, Eleanor suffered a collapse from overwork and had to withdraw completely after missing several performances, which she considered "worse than death."

When she was signed by Metro-Goldwyn-Mayer from her Casino de Paree engagement in 1935 Eleanor was still rather shy and certainly not pretty by Hollywood standards. Metro made her undergo extensive dental work, gave her voice lessons, and unleased its beauticians on the new contract player. It was a very glamorized Eleanor who tested for a featured role in *Broadway Melody of 1936.* The late Louis B. Mayer saw the test and gave her the lead. Playing a dual role, Eleanor did an imitation of Katharine Hepburn as well as a couple of dazzling tap numbers and emerged a brand new very big star. The studio rushed her into *Born to Dance* (1936) with Jimmy Stewart as her leading man and five hundred chorus boys to back her up in the finale. The next year they put her with Ilona Massey* and the late Nelson Eddy in *Rosalie* and with Robert Young in *Honolulu.*

As Ruby Keeler* became inactive, Miss Powell inherited her mantle, which meant that mothers around the country took their little girls to dance classes

194

in hopes that they would become another Eleanor Powell. Some other pictures she brightened were *Broadway Melody of 1938* with Robert Taylor, *Broadway Melody of 1940* in which she held her own with George Murphy and Fred Astaire, *Lady Be Good* (1941), *Ship Ahoy* (1942), the original title of which was *I'll Take Manila*, *As Thousands Cheer* (1944), and *Sensations of 1945*.

At the height of her career Eleanor made as much as $125,000 a picture, adding huge sums from personal appearances at the Roxy, Loew's State, and Capitol, and London's Palladium. Eleanor made many appearances on radio variety programs and even cut some records for RCA for which she tapped out her numbers from *Broadway Melody of 1936* and *At Home Abroad* with Tommy Dorsey's orchestra backing her. Most of her routines she developed herself.

In 1938 she received her first and last unpleasant publicity when the late news hen Dorothy Kilgallen began her column, "Eleanor Powell's handsome male secretary can do most anything." The article ended with the young man's telephone number. Reached for comment, he said that there was nothing between them and that he only wanted to marry a little home girl. He did— Lynn Bari, followed by Judy Garland. His name was Sid Luft.

Eleanor retired shortly after her marriage to Glenn Ford in 1943. The only work she did after that was a TV series entitled "Faith Of Our Children" which ran for three years beginning in 1955. It was a religious series more like Sunday school, which won five Emmies and many other awards. In 1959 the Fords were divorced. Eleanor has not remarried.

In 1961, when she was forty-eight, her only child, Peter, talked her into a comeback. It was the kind that most performers only dream of. She looked great, and her dancing brought the house down at Las Vegas' Sahara and Manhattan's Latin Quarter. The act ran fifty-five minutes, during which she was assisted by four young men. It was however a very expensive production and few clubs could afford it. Then, too, Eleanor did not really care to continue, and wished to continue her church work. Formerly a Presbyterian, Eleanor is now a member of a religious group called The Symposium. As associate preacher she advocates their creed of "faith a-go go" and "love a-go go."

An associate preacher today. *Jon Virzi*

From *The Best Years of Our Lives.*

HAROLD RUSSELL

The only man to win two Academy Awards for one performance was born in Sydney, Nova Scotia, in 1914. When he was six, following the death of his father, a telegraph manager, the Russell family moved to Boston. He attended public schools there and in nearby Cambridge, graduating from high school in 1933. He then went to work for a chain store, where he soon became manager of the meat department.

Russell volunteered for paratroops service, qualifying as an instructor, and specialized in demolition and explosives. He had made more than 50 jumps before D-Day on June 6, 1944. While the Allied forces were invading Normandy, Russell, a master sergeant, was showing a group of inductees how to pull the fuse on a hand grenade, when it went off.

Harold recovered from the blast at Walter Reed Hospital, but he had lost both his hands. He was fitted for artificial limbs and hooks, and began to exercise and train for rehabilitation. He was selected by the Surgeon General to portray himself in a documentary film entitled *The Diary of a Sergeant,* which told how an amputee had overcome the loss of both hands. The twenty-minute movie was shown at military hospitals and war-bond rallies. It was at a rally in Hollywood that director William Wyler saw Russell in the short.

Wyler was under contract to producer Samuel Goldwyn to direct a motion picture from a story by McKinley Kantor entitled "Glory for Three." It concerned three servicemen and the problems they encountered on their return to civilian life. Dana Andrews played a flyer, Fredric March an army sergeant, and there was a third role of a spastic sailor. After Wyler saw Russell, he and Goldwyn decided to change the script and make the character an amputee.

The movie was made under the title *The Best Years of Our Lives,* and was a smash success financially and critically. Wyler insisted that Russell not be coached in acting, for he wanted a completely natural performance. None of the male cast wore makeup.

When Harold was nominated as the Best Supporting Actor of 1946 he had stiff competition from Claude Rains, Clifton Webb, William Demarest, and Charles Coburn. The Academy board members felt that he had practically no chance of winning, and voted to give him a special award on the evening of the Oscar presentations. His special award, "for bringing hope and courage to his fellow veterans," was presented to him by Shirley Temple. Russell was backstage receiving congratulations from the other nominees when someone pulled him back onstage and he learned that he had been voted the Best Supporting Actor as well.

Russell never seriously considered continuing a screen career. While touring the country for the picture, he received two offers of parts in other movies, but turned them down. In 1946 he married and returned to Boston, where he opened a public-relations office. He is a graduate of Boston University.

In 1949 his autobiography *Victory in My Hands* was published, and has been translated into twenty languages. At one point in the book he states his philosophy: "It is not what you have lost but what you have left that counts."

Russell was the National Commander of the AMVETS in 1949, 1950, and 1960. He is the only National Commander to serve three terms. He is now the president of Tag-A-Bag Company, and in 1962 was named by President Kennedy Vice-Chairman of the President's Committee on Hiring the Handicapped. President Johnson appointed him Chairman on April 18, 1964.

People often recognize Russell as he travels around the country on business trips and to lecture. He often runs into Hollywood people he knew during his time at Goldwyn Studios. Upon meeting new people he invariably extends his right hook which he feels puts people at their ease. "People accept your disability if you accept it," he says.

Russell divides his time between Washington, D.C., where he has offices as the Chairman of the President's Committee, and Wayland, Massachusetts, where he lives with his wife and two children Jerry and Adele Rita. On his mantle sit the envy of many actors—two Academy Awards.

Harold lends a "helping hand" to a fellow AMVET.

The Orchid Lady in 1925.

CORINNE GRIFFITH

"The Orchid Lady of the Screen" was born in Texarkana, Texas, in 1896. She was educated at the Sacred Heart Academy in New Orleans where she was chosen Queen of the Mardi Gras. After her picture appeared on the cover of rotogravure sections of newspapers around the country she was signed to a contract with Vitagraph Pictures. Her early films were made in the East so that when she arrived in Hollywood in the early twenties she was already a star. Very few of her contemporaries though had ever met her. Even in an era of great beauty Corinne was outstanding. Her delicate coloring and features earned her the title of "The Orchid Lady," and her beach house in Malibu was described as "orchidaceous." Five hundred movie editors throughout the country were polled, and voted her "The Most Beautiful Woman in the World."

Her silent pictures include *The Last Man* (1916), *Doctor Love* (1917), *Miss Ambition* (1918) with Betty Blythe (who is a resident of the Motion Picture Country Hospital in Woodland Hills, California), *Adventure Shop* (1919), *Human Collateral* (1920), *It Isn't Being Done This Season* (1921), *Received Payment* (1922), *Common Law* (1923), *Black Oxen* (1924), *Declassé* (1925), *Mademoiselle Modiste* (1926), *The Lady in Ermine* (1927) with the late Francis X. Bushman, *The Garden of Eden* (1928), and *Saturday's Children* (1929). Her career was exceptionally long, but it ended with talkies. Her studio had so little faith in her that they paid off in full the remaining time left of her contract.

Miss Griffith, however, did not give up so easily. Even today she bridles when anyone refers to her as a "silent star." Although Corinne made several sound movies, none was a great success. In 1930 she made *Lilies of the Field* with John Loder (who lives in the San Luis province of Argentina) in Hollywood and then went to England where she did *Lily Christine* in 1932. In 1934 Radio Pictures gave her the female lead opposite Otto Kruger in *Crime Doctor* but she was released from her contract and paid off, with another actress replacing her. *The Mistress of the Close-up*, another of her titles, was so impossible over "her lighting" and "her scenes" (in what was supposed to be a man's picture), that the studio gave up on her.

After she was let go from the film, she toured in *Design For Living*. While away she rented her Beverly Hills home to Jeanette MacDonald whom she later sued for $1,018, claiming the singing star's dog ruined some of her furniture and draperies.

In 1936 Corinne married George "Wet Wash" Preston Marshall, owner of the Washington Redskins and a laundry empire. They lived in Washington, D.C., until 1958 when the marriage ended in divorce. While they were together Miss Griffith wrote six books, the two most popular being *My Life with the Redskins* (1944) and *Papa's Delicate Condition* (1952). Her first husband was actor-director Webster Campbell to whom she was married from 1920 until 1923 and her second was Walter Morosco, a producer who was her husband from 1933 to 1934.

Although the former star took a beating in the 1929 stock market crash, much of her $10,000-a-week salary was put into southern California real estate which has made her a millionairess many times over. She has bought, sold, and traded property until now she is one of the largest landowners in Beverly Hills.

Corinne had married Broadway dancer-singer Danny Scholl, who was then thirty-eight. After thirty-three days, during which Miss Griffith claims the marriage was never consummated, they went to court for a divorce. Scholl testified that he had married his wife believing that she was only fifty-two. He also complained that she bossed him constantly and preached Christian Science to him. When called to the stand the actress swore that she was only fifty-two, had never made a silent film, and that the real Corinne Griffith had died in the mid-thirties. She had only been her stand-in.

In spite of her age Corinne Griffith is never idle. She has according to her own count made over five hundred speeches on behalf of her pet project, the repeal of the personal income tax, which she refers to as "legalized thievery." In one of her early pictures she played a czarina. Her politics today are a bit right of the last czar.

Being interviewed after a recent robbery. *UPI*

Socking it to them on the Bob Hope radio program in the late forties. *NBC*

FRANKIE "SUGAR CHILE" ROBINSON

The pint-sized pianist who amazed and entertained millions during his short career in show business was born in 1940 and raised in Detroit, Michigan. When he was eighteen months old an aunt gave the Robinson family an old piano which was completely ignored until Frankie discovered that by touching the keys he could make sounds. His fingers were too short to reach from one key to another so he began striking the notes he wanted with his tiny fists. When a relative who knew something about music heard the child play he suggested that the elder Robinson listen to what his son could do. The father exclaimed, "I have and I can't stand it!"

Frankie had a natural talent for music and did not have to take lessons. When his parents showed no interest in a career for him friends and relatives started taking him to bars where he played for amazed customers. When some of the audience began dropping change on top of his piano, Mr. Robinson, who was an iceman, showed more appreciation for his son's talent. Stage shows were at that time common in large motion picture houses. The first theatre he was taken to for an audition dismissed the act because of Frankie's age. Phil Brestoff, in 1945 the musical director of the Michigan Theatre in Detroit, heard the boy by chance and put in a good word for him. Audiences confirmed his belief that the five-year-old was a real talent.

Although Frankie's biggest novelty lay in his youth, radio audiences were also enthusiastic. Overnight anyone hearing the name Frankie "Sugar Chile" Robinson knew that he was a preschool age Negro boy who could bang out boogie-woogie with the best of the professionals. He sat on more famous knees than anyone in America. Kate Smith, the Queen of network radio, had him on her show regularly. He was one of Danny Kaye's favorites. Bob Hope took

Frankie with him when he played the Palladium in London. True to show business tradition, "Sugar Chile" managed to steal the spotlight and sometimes the show from some of the most seasoned performers in the business. He was tiny, talented, and very cute.

One of Frankie's favorite stories about his days in the big time is when he was told that the King and Queen of England were in the audience and were looking forward to his act. He got so nervous he had a nosebleed right in the middle of it.

In 1946 at the age of six he had a contract with Metro-Goldwyn-Mayer and a $100,000 bank account. He appeared in *No Leave, No Love* (1946) with Van Johnson. This was his only movie. His managers felt he could make more money in personal appearances around the country. They were right and Frankie has no regrets. He said recently that in his time Negroes were hopelessly typecast in movies and besides, he enjoyed the excitement of a large audience.

The child prodigy dropped out of show business in the early fifties and settled down in Detroit. He and his father, who never delivered another cake of ice, own a grocery store in the Negro section of the motor city. The only time he plays the piano is at his parish church, but even that still draws a big crowd.

His only contact with his old profession is an occasional letter from one of the stars he has worked with. He swears he does not miss it a bit and has no regrets except for the fact that he suspects all the girls he dates are interested in his money. It had been put in trust and is now providing enough money from the interest alone for him to live on it. On top of that he has an investment in a therapeutic bath solution which is proving quite successful. Says Frankie, "I am a very happy man."

One thing about the boy wonder that has changed very little is his height. He is 4 feet 5 inches.

Behind the counter at his grocery store on St. Aubin Street, Detroit. *Detroit News*

Much sought after in the mid-thirties.

VIRGINIA BRUCE

The blonde star of the thirties was born in Minneapolis in 1910 with the name Helen Virginia Briggs. Her mother was an amateur golf champion of North Dakota for three years. Her insurance broker father, took the family to Fargo, North Dakota, where she attended high school, and thereafter was transferred to Los Angeles.

Virginia planned to attend U.C.L.A. but while touring a movie studio, director William Beaudine and his publicity man Harry Wurtzel saw her and Beaudine signed her to a personal contract at $25 a week. Her first film was with Madge Bellamy (who owns a scrapyard in Ontario, California, and lives under her real name Margaret Philpot). Virginia had a bit part as did Jean Harlow. Her second try was in the Helen Twelvetrees starrer *Blue Skies* (1929). Next came *Love Parade* (1929) with Jeanette MacDonald and Maurice Chevalier. Virginia had one line.

Through her friend Jack Harkrider, a designer of the Ziegfeld shows, she became one of the Goldwyn Girls in the Eddie Cantor picture *Whoopee,* the film that brought director Busby Berkeley to Hollywood in 1930. Harkrider helped get her a Broadway showgirl job in *Smiles,* which was produced by Flo Ziegfeld and starred Fred and Adele Astaire* in 1930, which was followed by another Ziegfeld production, *America's Sweetheart*. It lasted six months. She then departed for Hollywood to do a screen test at Metro-Goldwyn-Mayer with newcomer Robert Young. After a few small roles they put her in *Downstairs* (1932), which was written by and starred the great lover of the silent screen, John Gilbert. They fell madly in love during the shooting and were married as soon as it was completed. After the birth of their daughter Susan Ann in 1933 Virginia retired from the screen. One year later her retirement and her marriage ended. The Gilberts were divorced and she made *Jane Eyre* (1934). When he died in 1936 Gilbert left his ex-wife and their daughter the bulk of his $250,000 estate. In a flurry of activity Virginia appeared in fourteen movies in only sixteen months.

A partial list of her pictures are *Slightly Scarlet* (1930) with Evelyn Brent, *Mighty Barnum* (1934), in which she played Jenny Lind, *Metropolitan* (1935) opposite the late Lawrence Tibbett, *The Great Ziegfeld* (1936), in which she played Audrey Dane, *Women of Glamour* (1937) with Melvyn Douglas, *Let Freedom Ring* (1939) with Nelson Eddy, *The Invisible Woman* (1941) with John Barrymore, and *Careful, Soft Shoulders* (1942).

Virginia Bruce and J. Walter Rubin, the director-producer, first met when she arrived in Hollywood but they "didn't know it was love" until he directed her in *Bad Man of Brimstone* (1938). Upon completion of the picture the two were married on December 18, 1937. Virginia retired soon after, and her Metro contract expired. A son Christopher was born in 1941. Rubin died in 1942 leaving an estate of $50,000 in cash and securities.

In 1946 she married Ali Ipar, a twenty-three-year-old Turkish writer-producer who had just been inducted into the United States Army. She was then thirty-five. In 1947 he returned to visit his extremely wealthy father in Turkey and was denied reentry by the United States immigration authorities. A long legal battle ensued and he was finally readmitted in 1948. In 1951 her husband was called into the Turkish Army but Turkish law denies a commission to any Turk married to a foreigner. Virginia obligingly divorced him. He was discharged in 1952 and they were remarried. In the meantime Virginia and her children had lived with Ipar's family. In 1961 Ali was arrested in Turkey and spent nineteen months in prison, charged with a debt of over $3,000,000. While he was encarcerated his permanent resident visa expired which caused no end of trouble with the United States State Department.

With the exception of a film made in England in 1952 and *The Night Has a Thousand Eyes* (1948) with the late Gail Russell, she has remained retired. However, in 1960 she played Kim Novak's mother in *Strangers When We Meet*. Since then she has lived quietly in her beautiful home in Pacific Palisades, California.

As a southern California matron. *Jon Virzi*

The Hungarian beauty in 1923.

MITZI

The famous musical star whose real name was Marishka Hajos was born in Budapest, Hungary, in 1891. Shortly after she was able to talk the child began doing imitations of everyone and everything she came into contact with. From the age of four she appeared in Budapest theatres doing her imitations, singing and dancing under the billing of "the wonder child, Mitzi Hajos." She was taken to Vienna where her uncle secured a good manager who got her better billing and wages. Mitzi became so popular in Central Europe that the Emperor himself, Franz Josef, and Archduke Ferdinand, whose assassination touched off the First World War, came to see her on several occasions.

When she was only twelve years old she was brought to this country by the famous agent William Morris, who made a specialty of importing top European acts.

Morris presented her first in *The Barnyard Romeo* in 1910. That next year she was seen in *La Belle Paree* with Al Jolson, and toured in *The Spring Maid* in 1912. For her first few shows she hardly understood a word of what she was saying or singing.

Most of her vehicles were produced either by Henry W. Savage or J. J. Shubert. Savage felt that her last name should be dropped because it would never be mastered by Americans. It is correctly pronounced "Hoy-ousch." In such productions as *Her Little Highness* (1913) and *Pom-Pom* (1916) she was billed simply as Mitzi and it stuck. Her biggest hit was *Sari* in 1914 which introduced the famous "Sari Waltz." Jerome Kern wrote *Head Over Heels* for her in 1918. Sidney Greenstreet was her leading man in *Lady Billy* in 1920 and Stanley Lupino, father of Ida Lupino and a well known English stage star, was with her in *Naughty Riquette* in 1923. After *The Magic Ring* in 1926, Savage decided that the cost of musicals was prohibitive (*Ring* came in at $50,000. Minimum cost for a musical today is $600,000) and Mitzi went to the Shuberts. Her shows were light and airy with lots of music, singing, dancing, and an abundance of Mitzi. Arthur Treacher was with her in *Mad Cap* in 1928.

Another child star, Mitzi Green (wife of movie executive Joe Pevney and a resident of Newport Beach, California), was named for the Hungarian headliner after her parents had appeared in a Mitzi starrer.

By her own admission Mitzi never had much of a voice and has never had a lesson in her life but there was so much energy and personality packed into her 4 foot 10½ inch frame that she never had any trouble putting over a song. European stars were all the rage in those days and she was a particular favorite of the period.

In 1927 Mitzi became a Christian Scientist, with the usual fervor of a convert, and she neither smokes nor drinks.

In her entire career, which ended on Broadway with an unsuccessful revival of *Sari* in 1930, she missed but one performance; Mitzi, along with most of the audience, was unable to make it to the theatre in St. Joseph, Missouri, for a matinee because of a fierce snowstorm.

She was married to actor Boyd Marshall from 1920 until his death in 1950. They had no children. Following 1930, after leaving the stage she worked in the Shubert offices until 1952 when she was retired—"they made me quit. I just loved my work." In the spring of 1968 she moved from her Jackson Heights apartment into a home in Danbury, Connecticut. Mitzi sees many Broadway shows, particularly musicals. She comes into Manhattan at least once a week to have her hair done, see a matinee, and lunch at Schrafft's. She admits to missing her work in the theatre both on and behind the stage. "I'd work in a show tomorrow if I really felt the part was right for me, but listen, I'm no kid anymore and I know it." One aspect of show business that she does not long for is the attention of the public. "I just hate being stared at," she says in the still heavy Hungarian accent. "I know that's crazy for an actress and I never minded on the stage, of course, but on the streets and restaurants! It is something I never got used to. Now no one knows me and that's just fine."

Having a soda recently in Times Square, near the theatres where she once starred. *Diana Keyt*

In 1926, one of Paramount Pictures' most promising contract players.

ESTHER RALSTON

The actress known as "The American Venus" was born in Bar Harbor, Maine, in 1902. At two years old her parents worked her into their act, which played vaudeville, the Chautauqua circuit, carnivals, burlesque, and repertory companies. They were billed as "The Ralston Family"—featuring Baby Esther, "America's Youngest Juliet."

By 1916 the Ralstons had arrived in Hollywood where Esther became a bit player in Hoot Gibson and Tom Mix westerns. In 1920 she got a tiny part in *The Kid,* which launched the career of Jackie Coogan. In 1922, Coogan made *Oliver Twist* with Lon Chaney, and Esther got a bigger role. She continued in westerns until Jesse Lasky and Walter Wanger gave her the chance to play the role of Mrs. Darling in *Peter Pan* (1925). She was young but the producers wanted a child's idea of a mother. It is still considered one of the finest silents ever made.

The American Venus (1925) gave her her title. That year she married George Webb, a director-actor. A great boost was *A Kiss for Cinderella* (1926), in which she played the fairy godmother. The same year she made the silent classic *Old Ironsides* with Charles Farrell. B. P. Schulberg cast Esther and the late Clara Bow as leads in *Children of Divorce* (1927).

Josef von Sternberg used her in *The Case of Lena Smith* (1928), under whom she emerged a dramatic star.

Richard Dix and Esther debuted together in talkies with *Wheel of Life* (1929). In 1931 she was Lawrence Tibbett's leading lady in *The Prodigal.* She played London's Palladium and toured the provinces for a year, and made *After the Fall* (1933) with the late Basil Rathbone and *Rome Express* (1933) opposite Conrad Veidt.

In 1933 Esther returned to Hollywood where she and Webb were divorced, and she signed with Metro-Goldwyn-Mayer. The lady was uncooperative with production head Louis B. Mayer who admired her and so she was loaned out for pictures hardly calculated to boast her career. She suffered through thirteen for Universal, did *Black Beauty* (1933), for Monogram, and was even subjected to a Ken Maynard western, *Wheels of Destiny* (1934) at Republic. Her only important film for M-G-M during the contract was the Joan Crawford starrer *Sadie McKee* (1934). That year she married Will Morgan, a singer.

In 1936 she appeared in *Reunion* with the Dionne quintuplets for Fox and returned to her old lot, Paramount, for *Hollywood Blvd.* with Bob Cummings. It included cameo performances by her contemporaries from silent days. Esther's other movies in the late thirties were either undistinguished or just plain bad. Examples are *Girl from Mandalay* (1936) with Conrad Nagel and *Shadows of the Orient* (1937) opposite Regis Toomey.

Esther's last picture of consequence was *Tin Pan Alley* (1940), an Alice Faye musical in which she played the great vaudevillian, Nora Bayes.

Her second marriage ended in 1938, and the following year she married Ted Lloyd, a newspaper man. In 1941 and 1942 Esther played the title role in the radio soap opera "Woman of Courage." She went into retirement through the ensuing forties to raise her children. From 1950 until 1952 she toured the straw hat circuit. Esther was divorced again in 1954 and has not remarried.

In 1956 she went to work at B. Altman's department store branch in Manhasset, Long Island. She left in 1961, as head of the Boy's Shop, for a running part in "Our Five Daughters" on NBC-TV, until 1962. There were TV appearances on the "Kraft Theatre" and "Texaco Playhouse" until 1965 when Esther dropped in to visit her old friend, actor's agent, Marge Kerr. She accepted a job and has been there ever since as vice-president of the Kerr Talent Agency.

She commutes daily from an apartment overlooking Lake Oakland in Queens, New York, to her Manhattan office. Her spare time is devoted to writing her autobiography.

"The American Venus" in her Manhattan office. *Diana Keyt*